THE MACARTHUR
NEW TESTAMENT
COMMENTARY

PHILIPPIANS

John MacArthur Jr.

MOODY PUBLISHERS/CHICAGO

Library of Congress Cataloging-in-Publication Data

MacArthur, John, 1939–
    Philippians / John MacArthur, Jr.
    p. cm. – (The MacArthur New Testament commentary)
    Includes bibliographical references and index.
    ISBN: 0-8024-5262-0
    ISBN-13: 978-0-8024-5262-7
    1. Bible. N.T. Philippians–Commentaries. I. Title.

BS2705.3 .M23 2001
227'.6077–dc21

2001030958

*To Chris Williams,
a choice friend and cherished colleague
whose devotion to Christ, love for the truth,
and faithful servant-leadership have been
invaluable assets to the ministry
of Grace to India for nearly two decades.*

Contents

Preface

It continues to be a rewarding, divine communion for me to preach expositionally through the New Testament. My goal is always to have deep fellowship with the Lord in the understanding of His Word and out of that experience to explain to His people what a passage means. In the words of Nehemiah 8:8, I strive "to give the sense" of it so they may truly hear God speak and, in so doing, may respond to Him.

Obviously, God's people need to understand Him, which demands knowing His Word of truth (2 Tim. 2:15) and allowing that Word to dwell in them richly (Col. 3:16). The dominant thrust of my ministry, therefore, is to help make God's living Word alive to His people. It is a refreshing adventure.

This New Testament commentary series reflects this objective of explaining and applying Scripture. Some commentaries are primarily linguistic, others are mostly theological, and some are mainly homiletical. This one is basically explanatory, or expository. It is not linguistically technical but deals with linguistics when that seems helpful to proper interpretation. It is not theologically expansive but focuses on the major doctrines in each text and how they relate to the whole of Scripture. It is not primarily homiletical, although each unit of thought is generally treated as one chapter, with a clear outline and logical flow of thought.

Most truths are illustrated and applied with other Scripture. After establishing the context of a passage, I have tried to follow closely the writer's development and reasoning.

My prayer is that each reader will fully understand what the Holy Spirit is saying through this part of His Word, so that His revelation may lodge in the mind of believers and bring greater obedience and faithfulness—to the glory of our great God.

Introduction

People today are consumed by the passionate pursuit of happiness. Self-help books, motivational speakers, and advice columnists claim to offer the key to happiness, but for many people the door remains locked. Unable to control their circumstances, they find themselves instead controlled by their circumstances. When their job, relationship, or house (or, in the case of Christians, church) fails to make them happy, they dump it and look for a new one. But on the merry-go-round of life, they can never quite seem to reach the brass ring. Having fruitlessly pursued happiness through pleasure and self-gratification, they arrive at the jaded view of life expressed by the Preacher in Ecclesiastes 1:2: "Vanity of vanities! All is vanity."

But if happiness, the fleeting feeling of exhilaration, is elusive, joy is not. Biblical joy, the settled conviction that God sovereignly controls the events of life for believers' good and His glory, is available to all who obey Him. In fact, God commands believers to rejoice (2:18; 3:1; 4:4; cf. 2 Cor. 13:11; 1 Thess. 5:16). That divine joy is the theme of Philippians; the Greek word for joy, in both its noun and verb forms, appears more than a dozen times in its four chapters (1:4, 18, 25; 2:2, 17, 18, 28, 29; 3:1; 4:1, 4, 10).

The circumstances of both the writer and the recipients of this brief epistle were not those that would be expected to produce joy and happiness. When the apostle Paul wrote this letter to his beloved Philippian congregation, he was a prisoner in Rome. Little in his tumultuous life since his dramatic conversion on the Damascus Road three decades earlier would have been expected to produce joy. He had faced fierce and unrelenting opposition, both from Gentiles and from his unbelieving Jewish countrymen (cf. 2 Cor. 11:23–30).

Immediately after his conversion, Paul's bold, fearless proclamation of the gospel aroused the ire of Damascus's Jewish population. They sought to kill him, and he was forced to flee the city by being lowered from the city wall at night in a basket (Acts 9:20–25). Later he was forced to flee from Iconium (Acts 14:5–6); was pelted with stones and left for dead at Lystra (Acts 14:19–20); was beaten and thrown into jail at Philippi (Acts 16:16–40); was forced to flee from Thessalonica after his preaching touched off a riot (Acts 17:5–9); went from there to Berea, from where he was also forced to flee (Acts 17:13–14); was mocked and ridiculed by Greek philosophers at Athens (Acts 17:16–34); was hauled before the Roman proconsul at Corinth (Acts 18:12–17); and faced both Jewish opposition (Acts 19:9; cf. 20:18–19) and rioting Gentiles at Ephesus (Acts 19:21–41; cf. 1 Cor. 15:32). As he was about to sail from Greece to Palestine, a Jewish plot against his life forced him to change his travel plans (Acts 20:3). On the way to Jerusalem, he met the Ephesian elders at Miletus and declared to them, "Bound in spirit, I am on my way to Jerusalem, not knowing what will happen to me there, except that the Holy Spirit solemnly testifies to me in every city, saying that bonds and afflictions await me" (Acts 20:22–23). When he got to Jerusalem, he was recognized in the temple by Jews from Asia Minor, savagely beaten by a frenzied mob, and saved from certain death when Roman soldiers arrived on the scene and arrested him (Acts 21:27–36). While Paul was in custody at Jerusalem, the Jews formed yet another plot against his life, prompting the Roman commander to send him under heavy guard to the governor at Caesarea (Acts 23:12–35). After his case dragged on without resolution for two years and two Roman governors, Paul exercised his right as a Roman citizen and appealed to Caesar (Acts 25:10–11). After an eventful trip, which included being shipwrecked in a violent storm, Paul arrived at Rome (Acts 27, 28). As he wrote Philippians, the apostle was in his fourth year of Roman custody, awaiting Emperor Nero's final decision in his case.

The Philippian church also had its share of problems. Its members were desperately poor, so much so that Paul was surprised at their contribution to the offering he was collecting for the poor in Jerusalem (2 Cor. 8:1–5). Like Paul, they were being persecuted for the cause of Christ (1:27–30). Worse, they were being attacked by false teachers (3:2, 18–19). On top of everything else, a feud between two prominent women in the congregation threatened to shatter the unity of the church (4:2–3; cf. 2:1–4, 14).

Yet despite the circumstances of both writer and recipients, joy permeates Philippians, so much so that it may be called "the epistle of joy." R. C. H. Lenski wrote, "Joy is the music that runs through this epistle, the sunshine that spreads over all of it. The whole epistle radiates joy and happiness" (*The Interpretation of St. Paul's Epistles to the Galatians, to the Ephesians, and to the Philippians* [Minneapolis: Augsburg, 1961], 691). Those who study its teaching and apply its principles will, like its human author, learn the secret of having joy, peace, and contentment in every circumstance (4:11–13).

THE CITY OF PHILIPPI

Philippi was an important city in eastern Macedonia (northeastern Greece). It was located on the fertile alluvial plain of the Strymon River, near the deep, swift-flowing stream known as the Gangites (cf. Acts 16:13). Philippi owed its importance in ancient times to its strategic location (it commanded the land route to Asia Minor). In Paul's day the important Roman road known as the Via Egnatia ran through Philippi. The city was also important because of the gold mines in the nearby mountains.

It was those gold mines that attracted the interest of Philip II of Macedon (the father of Alexander the Great). He annexed the region in 356 B.C. and fortified the small village of Krenides ("the little fountains"; so named because of the nearby springs), renaming it Philippi ("city of Philip") after himself. After the Romans conquered Macedonia in the second century B.C., Philippi was incorporated into the Roman province of that name. The city languished in relative obscurity for more than a century, until in 42 B.C. it became the site of one of the most crucial battles in Roman history. In that battle, known to history as the battle of Philippi, the forces of Antony and Octavian ("Caesar Augustus"; Luke 2:1) defeated the republican forces of Brutus and Cassius. The battle marked the end of the Roman republic and the beginning of the empire (the senate declared Octavian emperor in 29 B.C., after he defeated Antony and Cleopatra at the battle of Actium in 31 B.C.). Antony and Octavian settled many of their army veterans at Philippi, which was given the coveted status of a Roman colony (cf. Acts 16:12). Later, other Roman army veterans settled there.

As a colony, Philippi had the same legal status as cities in Italy. Citizens of Philippi were Roman citizens, were exempt from paying certain taxes, and were not subject to the authority of the provincial governor. The Philippians copied Roman architecture and style of dress, their coins bore Roman inscriptions, and Latin was the city's official language (although Greek was also spoken).

THE CHURCH AT PHILIPPI

The Philippian church was the first church Paul founded in Europe. The apostle came to Philippi on his second missionary journey, being directed there by the Holy Spirit in a most dramatic way:

> A vision appeared to Paul in the night: a man of Macedonia was standing and appealing to him, and saying, "Come over to Macedonia and help us." When he had seen the vision, immediately we sought to go into Macedonia, concluding that God had called us to preach the gospel to them. (Acts 16:9–10)

Though the initial converts were Jews or Jewish proselytes (Acts 16:13–15), Gentiles made up the majority of the congregation. That there was no synagogue in Philippi (or else the women Paul initially encountered would not have been meeting outside the city on the Sabbath) is evidence that the city's Jewish population was small. Two dramatic conversions, those of the wealthy proselyte Lydia (Acts 16:13–15) and the jailor (Acts 16:25–34), marked the church's birth. (For a description of the events surrounding the founding of the Philippian church, see chapter 18 of this volume.)

The Philippians had a deep affection for Paul, as he did for them. Though they were poor, they alone supported him financially at one stage of his ministry (4:15). Now, after many years, they had once again sent the apostle a generous gift in his time of need. (For a further discussion of the Philippians' financial support of Paul, see chapter 20 of this volume.) Half a century later, the Philippian church would show the same generosity to the church father Ignatius, who passed through their city on his way to martyrdom at Rome.

Paul penned this letter to his beloved Philippian congregation to thank them for their generous gift (4:10–19), explain why he was sending Epaphroditus back to them (2:25–30), inform them of his circumstances (1:12–26), and warn them about the danger of false teachers (3:2, 18–19).

AUTHOR

The divinely inspired text of Philippians introduces Paul as the author (1:1), thus making his authorship indisputable. In fact, except for a few radical nineteenth-century critics, the Pauline authorship of Philippians has never been questioned. Today most scholars, no matter what their theological persuasion, accept it as a genuine Pauline epistle. J. B. Lightfoot notes,

> Internal evidence will appear to most readers to place the genuineness of the Epistle to the Philippians beyond the reach of doubt. This evidence is of two kinds, positive and negative. On the one hand, the epistle completely reflects St. Paul's mind and character, even in their finest shades. On the other, it offers no motive which could have led to a forgery. Only as the natural outpouring of personal feeling, called forth by immediate circumstances, is it in any way conceivable. A forger would not have produced a work so aimless (for aimless in his case it must have been), and could not have produced one so inartificial. (*St. Paul's Epistle to the Philippians* [Reprint; Grand Rapids: Zondervan, 1953], 74)

DATE AND PLACE OF WRITING

Paul wrote Philippians, along with Colossians, Ephesians, and Philemon, from prison. Until the end of the eighteenth century, the church accepted that the four Prison Epistles were written during the apostle's imprisonment at Rome (Acts 28:14–31). In recent times, however, both Caesarea and Ephesus have been proposed as alternative locations.

The evidence that Paul wrote Philippians from Rome is impressive. The terms "praetorian guard" (1:13) and "Caesar's household" (4:22) are most naturally understood as references to the emperor's bodyguard and servants stationed in Rome. The details of Paul's imprisonment as recorded in Acts harmonize well with those in Philippians. Paul was guarded by soldiers (Acts 28:16; Phil. 1:13–14), allowed visitors (Acts 28:30; Phil. 4:18), and was free to preach the gospel (Acts 28:31; Phil. 1:12–14). That there was a large church in the city from which Paul wrote (cf. 1:12–14) also favors Rome. The church in the Imperial capital was undoubtedly much larger than that in either Ephesus or, especially, Caesarea.

Two primary objections have been raised to the traditional view that Paul wrote Philippians from Rome. First, some argue that while Paul intended to visit Spain after visiting Rome (Rom. 15:24, 28), the Prison Epistles record his plans to visit Philippi (2:24) and Colossae (Philem. 22) after his release. Therefore, they maintain, Philippians (and Colossians) must have been written before Paul reached Rome. While it is true that Paul had originally planned to visit Spain after visiting Rome, two facts caused him to change his plans. Paul had not anticipated arriving in Rome as a prisoner. He had spent four years in Roman custody, and during that time problems had arisen in the churches of Greece and Asia Minor. Paul therefore decided to revisit those churches before heading for Spain. Further, the fact that the Roman church was not united in support of him (cf. 1:14–17) caused the apostle to delay his visit to Spain (cf. Rom. 15:24).

Second, some believe that several trips between Philippi and the city from which Paul wrote are implied in Philippians. Because of the great distance between Rome and Philippi, they believe that those trips cannot have all taken place during Paul's Roman imprisonment. On the other hand, Ephesus was much closer to Philippi. (It should be noted that, if valid, that argument would be equally telling against a Caesarean origin of Philippians. Caesarea was not significantly closer to Philippi than was Rome.)

That argument, however, is not valid. Moises Silva notes that:

> It is quite possible to fit those three journeys [between Rome and Philippi] into a period of four to six months. But even if we allow a very generous two months for *each* of these journeys, far less than a year is necessary to account for them (and nothing in the data requires us to say that less than a year must have elapsed from Paul's arrival in Rome to his writing of Philippians). It is very difficult to understand why this argument against a Roman origin continues to be taken seriously. The matter should be dropped from any further consideration. If we do so, however, then the only clear argument against the traditional view [that Paul wrote Philippians from Rome] disappears. (*Philippians*, The Wycliffe Exegetical Commentary [Chicago: Moody, 1988], 7. Italics in original.)

The most convincing argument that Paul wrote Philippians from Rome lies in the decisive nature of the verdict the apostle expected. He would either be set free, as he confidently hoped (1:19, 24–26; 2:24), or executed (1:20–21, 23). Either way, the decision in his case would be final, and there would be no appeal. That fact appears to rule out both Caesarea and Ephesus, since as a Roman citizen Paul could (and did— Acts 25:11–12) exercise his right to appeal to the emperor (what one writer referred to as Paul's "trump card") from those cities.

The theories that Paul wrote Philippians from Caesarea or Ephesus face additional significant difficulties. Proponents of the Caesarean view note that the same Greek word translated "praetorian guard" in 1:13 is used in the Gospels and Acts to speak of the governor's palaces in Jerusalem (Matt. 27:27; Mark 15:16; John 18:28, 33; 19:9) and Caesarea (Acts 23:35). But the phrase "and to everyone else" (1:13) indicates that Paul was referring to the troops of the praetorian guard, not to a building. Paul's failure to mention Philip the Evangelist is puzzling if he wrote the

Prison Epistles from Caesarea, since he lived in that city and provided hospitality to Paul and his party (Acts 21:8). Further, Acts does not record a widespread preaching of the gospel in Caesarea such as that recorded in 1:12–18. Finally, Paul's expectation of a quick release (cf. 1:25; 2:24) does not fit the circumstances of his imprisonment in Caesarea. There the apostle's only hope of release was either to bribe Felix, or acquiesce to Festus's request that he return to Jerusalem for trial. Naturally, Paul refused either alternative and remained a prisoner in Caesarea until his appeal to the emperor.

The theory that Paul wrote Philippians (and the other Prison Epistles) from Ephesus, though a more popular alternative than Caesarea, also faces serious difficulties. The most obvious and serious one is that there is no record in Acts that Paul was ever in prison at Ephesus. That silence is particularly significant, since Luke devotes an entire chapter (Acts 19) to Paul's three-year ministry there. Further, Paul's declaration to the elders of the Ephesian church, "Night and day for a period of three years I did not cease to admonish each one with tears" (Acts 20:31), implies that his ministry in their city was continuous, not interrupted by a prolonged imprisonment. Another significant omission is Paul's failure to mention in the Prison Epistles the collection for the poor saints at Jerusalem—a collection he referred to in the epistles he wrote during the time of his stay in Ephesus (e.g., Romans, 1 and 2 Corinthians). Paul's failure to mention Gaius and Aristarchus to the Philippians is also strange if he wrote from Ephesus, since they were with him there (Acts 19:29). The church from which Paul wrote Philippians was not united in its support of him (1:14–17; cf. 2:20–21). That, however, was not true of the Ephesian church (cf. Acts 20:36–38). Nor is it likely that the Philippians would have felt the need to send a gift to Paul at Ephesus, where the apostle enjoyed the support both of the church and of close friends, such as Aquila and Prisca (cf. 1 Cor. 16:19; 1 Corinthians was written from Ephesus). Finally, while Luke was with Paul when he penned the Prison Epistles (Col. 4:14), he apparently was not with Paul at Ephesus (Acts 19 is not one of the "we passages" in Acts that indicate Luke's presence with Paul).

Since Rome fits the known facts of Paul's imprisonment, and Caesarea and Ephesus do not, there is no reason to reject the traditional view that Paul wrote Philippians near the end of his first Roman imprisonment (c. A.D. 61).

OUTLINE

I. Paul's Greeting (1:1–11)
II. Paul's Circumstances (1:12–26)
III. Paul's Exhortations (1:27–2:18)
   A. To Be Firm in Christ (1:27–30)
   B. To Be Humble Like Christ (2:1–11)
   C. To Be Lights for Christ (2:12–18)
IV. Paul's Companions (2:19–30)
   A. Timothy (2:19–24)
   B. Epaphroditus (2:25–30)
V. Paul's Warnings (3:1–4:1)
   A. Against Legalism (3:1–16)
   B. Against Lawlessness (3:17–4:1)
VI. Paul's Joy (4:2–9)
VII. Paul's Thankfulness (4:10–20)
VIII. Paul's Farewell (4:21–23)

The Epistle of Joy (Philippians 1:1–2)

1

Paul and Timothy, bond-servants of Christ Jesus, to all the saints in Christ Jesus who are in Philippi, including the overseers and deacons: Grace to you and peace from God our Father and the Lord Jesus Christ. (1:1–2)

We live in a generally sad world, a fallen world well acquainted with despair, depression, disappointment, dissatisfaction, and a longing for lasting happiness that often never comes to pass. Moments of pleasure and satisfaction are scattered through the general pain and sorrow of life. Many people have little hope that their situation in life will ever change much, if any, for the better. Hopelessness tends to increase with age. Long years of life often become long years of sorrow, unfulfillment, loss of loved ones and friends, and often physical limitations and pain. Such decreasing times of happiness tend to produce a morbid sadness and lessening satisfaction with life.

Most people define happiness as an attitude of satisfaction or delight based on positive circumstances largely beyond their control. Happiness, therefore, cannot be planned or programmed, much less guaranteed. It is experienced only if and when circumstances are favorable. It is therefore elusive and uncertain.

Spiritual joy, on the other hand, is not an attitude dependent on chance or circumstances. It is the deep and abiding confidence that, regardless of one's circumstances in life, all is well between the believer and the Lord. No matter what difficulty, pain, disappointment, failure, rejection, or other challenge one is facing, genuine joy remains because of that eternal well-being established by God's grace in salvation. Thus, Scripture makes it clear that the fullest, most lasting and satisfying joy is derived from a true relationship with God. It is not based on circumstances or chance, but is the gracious and permanent possession of every child of God. Therefore it is not surprising that joy is an important New Testament theme. The verb *rejoice* (*chairō*) appears ninety-six times in the New Testament (including those times when it is used as a greeting) and the noun *joy* (*chara*) another fifty-nine times. The two words appear thirteen times in Philippians.

A biblical theology of joy includes many features. First, joy is a gift from God. David declared, "You have put gladness in my heart, more than when their grain and new wine abound. In peace I will both lie down and sleep, for You alone, O Lord, make me to dwell in safety" (Ps. 4:7–8); "You will make known to me the path of life; in Your presence is fullness of joy; in Your right hand there are pleasures forever" (Ps. 16:11).

Second, God grants joy to those who believe the gospel. Announcing Christ's birth to the shepherds, the angel said, "Do not be afraid; for behold, I bring you good news of great joy which will be for all the people; for today in the city of David there has been born for you a Savior, who is Christ the Lord" (Luke 2:10–11). Jesus told His disciples, "These things I have spoken to you so that My joy may be in you, and that your joy may be made full" (John 15:11). Christ came to proclaim a gospel that would give true supernatural joy to those who receive Him as Savior and Lord.

Third, joy is produced by God the Holy Spirit. "For the kingdom of God is not eating and drinking," Paul said, "but righteousness and peace and joy in the Holy Spirit" (Rom 14:17). In his letter to the Galatian churches, the apostle wrote, "The fruit of the Spirit is love, joy, peace, patience, kindness, goodness, faithfulness, gentleness, self-control" (Gal. 5:22–23).

Fourth, joy is experienced most fully as believers receive and obey God's Word. The prophet Jeremiah exulted, "Your words were found and I ate them, and Your words became for me a joy and the delight of my heart; for I have been called by Your name, O Lord God of hosts" (Jer. 15:16). The apostle John wrote his first letter so that, among other things, his and his readers' "joy may be made complete" (1 John 1:4).

Fifth, believers' joy is deepened through trials. The full reality of joy is experienced when it is contrasted with sadness, sorrow, and difficulties. "You also became imitators of us and of the Lord," Paul wrote to the Thessalonians, "having received the word in much tribulation with the joy of the Holy Spirit" (1 Thess. 1:6). In his second letter to the believers at Corinth, Paul spoke of being "sorrowful yet always rejoicing" (2 Cor. 6:10). James counseled believers to "consider it all joy, my brethren, when you encounter various trials" (James 1:2), and Peter encouraged them with these words:

> Blessed be the God and Father of our Lord Jesus Christ, who according to His great mercy has caused us to be born again to a living hope through the resurrection of Jesus Christ from the dead, to obtain an inheritance which is imperishable and undefiled and will not fade away, reserved in heaven for you, who are protected by the power of God through faith for a salvation ready to be revealed in the last time. In this you greatly rejoice, even though now for a little while, if necessary, you have been distressed by various trials. (1 Peter 1:3–6)

Sixth, believers' joy is made complete when they set their hope on the glory of heaven. They are always to be "rejoicing in hope" (Rom. 12:12). Peter reminded them that, "though you have not seen Him, you love Him, and though you do not see Him now, but believe in Him, you greatly rejoice with joy inexpressible and full of glory" (1 Peter 1:8). Later in that letter he exhorted, "To the degree that you share the sufferings of Christ, keep on rejoicing, so that also at the revelation of His glory you may rejoice with exultation" (1 Peter 4:13). Jude concluded his brief letter with the beautiful benediction: "Now to Him who is able to keep you from stumbling, and to make you stand in the presence of His glory blameless with great joy, to the only God our Savior, through Jesus Christ our Lord, be glory, majesty, dominion and authority, before all time and now and forever. Amen" (Jude 24–25).

The love bond between Paul and the Philippian believers may have been stronger than the one he had with any other church. It was in large measure because of the joy that their love brought to him that the theme of Paul's letter to the Philippians is joy. The depth of their relationship with him encouraged the apostle during his imprisonment and added to his joy. He was concerned about their unity, their faithfulness, and many other important spiritual and practical matters. But his overriding concern was that their sorrow over his afflictions would be tempered by their joy over his faithfulness to the Lord and the great reward that awaited him in heaven. Paul wanted them not to be sad, but to share in the fullest measure his deep, abiding joy in Jesus Christ. It is a noteworthy testimony to the maturity of the Philippian believers that, although Paul warned and encouraged them, he made no mention of any theological or moral problem in the church at Philippi. That also brought the apostle joy.

In the first two verses the apostle described himself and Timothy as servants of Jesus Christ, the Philippian believers as saints in Jesus Christ, and offered his salutation to them in the name of their Lord.

THE SERVANTS

Paul and Timothy, bond-servants of Christ Jesus (1:1a)

Paul is the beloved apostle who wrote thirteen New Testament epistles and is arguably the most noble and privileged servant of Jesus Christ the world has ever known. Yet, he refered to himself and **Timothy** simply as **bond-servants of Christ Jesus.** He made no mention of his apostolic authority or his being chosen to record part of God's written Word. He viewed himself and every believer primarily as a slave of the Lord.

Perhaps the most concise and clear look at Paul anywhere in the New Testament comes from the apostle himself later in this letter. Speaking of his life in Judaism, he wrote,

> I myself might have confidence even in the flesh. [But] if anyone else has a mind to put confidence in the flesh, I far more: circumcised the eighth day, of the nation of Israel, of the tribe of Benjamin, a Hebrew of Hebrews; as to the Law, a Pharisee; as to zeal, a persecutor of the church; as to the righteousness which is in the Law, found blameless. But whatever things were gain to me, those things I have counted as loss for the sake of Christ. More than that, I count all things to be loss in view of the surpassing value of knowing Christ Jesus my Lord, for whom I have suffered the loss of all things, and count them but rubbish so that I may gain Christ, and may be found in Him, not having a righteousness of my own derived from the Law, but that which is through faith in Christ, the righteousness which comes from God on the basis of faith, that I may know Him and the power of His resurrection and the fellowship of His sufferings, being conformed to His death; in order that I may attain to the resurrection from the dead. (Phil. 3:4–11)

Paul's human credentials were remarkable. He was the epitome of Jewish manhood, an exemplary, traditional, zealous, and legalistic "Hebrew of Hebrews." In the eyes of his peers, he was blameless and righteous. But after his conversion he saw those things for what they were in God's eyes: mere rubbish. What he had considered to be positives before God he came to realize were actually destructive negatives. His former imagined righteousness was really unrighteousness, which he gladly forsook to gain the true righteousness that comes only "through faith in Christ, the righteousness which comes from God on the basis of faith" (3:9).

Timothy shared that righteousness, as a fellow bond-servant of **Christ Jesus.** He was Paul's son in the faith (1 Tim. 1:2), not only a protégé, but also a cherished companion, to whom the apostle would bequeath an extraordinary spiritual legacy and ministry. His two inspired letters to Timothy were written several years later, the first after the apostle had been released from his first imprisonment in Rome and the second during his second imprisonment there.

Bond-servants translates the plural of the oft-used Greek word *doulos,* which describes a person owned by someone else and thus subservient to and dependent on that person. Paul used it of himself at the beginning of three of his epistles (Rom. 1:1; Phil. 1:1; Titus 1:1), and in each case it precedes the mention of his apostleship. James (James 1:1), Peter (2 Peter 1:1), and Jude (Jude 1) use it in the same way.

When used in the New Testament of a believer's relationship to Jesus Christ, *doulos* describes willing, determined, and devoted service. It reflects the attitude of an Old Testament slave who refused the opportunity for freedom and voluntarily resubmitted himself to his master for life. The Mosaic Law provided that "if the slave plainly says, 'I love my master, my wife and my children; I will not go out as a free man,' then his master shall bring him to God, then he shall bring him to the door or the doorpost. And his master shall pierce his ear with an awl; and he shall serve him permanently" (Ex. 21:5–6). Speaking of all faithful believers, Paul declared, "Now we have been released from the Law, having died to that by which we were bound, so that we serve in newness of the Spirit and not in oldness of the letter" (Rom. 7:6). To the Corinthians he explained, "For he who was called in the Lord while a slave, is the Lord's freedman; likewise he who was called while free, is Christ's slave" (1 Cor. 7:22).

In that spirit **Paul** and **Timothy** did not think of being **bond-servants of Christ Jesus** in anything but positive terms. Nor did they think of themselves as **bond-servants** of the church, of Rome, or of any other person or institution, but exclusively of **Christ Jesus.** Paul reminded the elders from the Ephesian church of that single-minded devotion when he met them near Miletus: "I do not consider my life of any account as dear to myself, so that I may finish my course and the ministry which I received from the Lord Jesus, to testify solemnly of the gospel of the grace of God" (Acts 20:24). That devotion is required of every believer, but especially of those called to the ministry. Even if a pastor's or teacher's primary devotion is to the church, it will inevitably bring some measure of compromise, disappointment, and spiritual failure. But devotion to **Christ**

Jesus can never be disappointing or in vain. If his ministry is concerned with other believers' standards and opinions, a pastor will invariably stray from the gospel to some form of compromise. But devotion and obedience to the Lord and to His Word will just as invariably keep him on a godly and faithful course.

Paul's physical bonds were not really marks of his bondage to Rome but to his Lord. His imprisonment *by* Rome symbolized his bondage *to* Jesus Christ. "My imprisonment in the cause of Christ," he explained, "has become well known throughout the whole praetorian guard and to everyone else, and . . . most of the brethren, trusting in the Lord because of my imprisonment, have far more courage to speak the word of God without fear" (1:13–14). It was Jesus Christ who would assign all his duties and meet all his needs. He had the same spirit of devotion to Christ that David's servants had to him as king: "Then the king's servants said to the king, 'Behold, your servants are ready to do whatever my lord the king chooses'" (2 Sam. 15:15). Jesus declared unambiguously that "no one can serve two masters; for either he will hate the one and love the other, or he will be devoted to one and despise the other. You cannot serve God and wealth" (Matt. 6:24). And because the Lord is such a loving Master, His servants can testify with Paul, "And He has said to me, 'My grace is sufficient for you, for power is perfected in weakness.' Most gladly, therefore, I will rather boast about my weaknesses, so that the power of Christ may dwell in me" (2 Cor. 12:9).

THE SAINTS

to all the saints in Christ Jesus who are in Philippi, including the overseers and deacons: (1:1b)

Paul addresses his letter to **all the saints in Christ Jesus who are in Philippi.** Like *qodesh*, its Hebrew equivalent, *hagios* (**saints**) refers to someone who is set apart; specifically believers, who are set apart by God for Himself. Both words are often translated "holy."

Unfortunately, **saints** are often thought of as being a special, higher order of Christians who accomplished extraordinary good deeds and lived an exemplary life. In the Roman Catholic system, saints are revered people who are officially canonized after death because they have met certain demanding requirements. But Scripture makes it clear that all the redeemed, whether under the Old or New Covenant, are **saints,** set apart from sin to God.

When God commanded Ananias to lay his hands on the newly converted Saul (Paul) so that he would regain his sight, he answered,

"Lord, I have heard from many about this man, how much harm he did to Your saints at Jerusalem" (Acts 9:13). A few verses later Luke writes that "as Peter was traveling through all those regions, he came down also to the saints who lived at Lydda" (Acts 9:32). In both instances it is clear that **saints** refers to *all* believers in those cities (cf. Eph. 1:1; Col. 1:2). That Paul even referred to the worldly, immature believers at Corinth as saints indicates beyond dispute that the term has no relationship to spiritual maturity or character. To them he wrote, "To the church of God which is at Corinth, to those who have been sanctified in Christ Jesus, saints by calling, with all who in every place call on the name of our Lord Jesus Christ, their Lord and ours" (1 Cor. 1:2). Like all other believers, the Christians at Corinth were not saints because of their spiritual maturity (cf. 1 Cor. 3:1–3), but because they were "saints by calling," a reference to their call to salvation (cf. Rom. 8:29–30).

All believers are **saints,** not because they are themselves righteous, but because they are **in** their Lord, **Christ Jesus,** whose righteousness is imputed to them (Rom. 4:22–24). A Buddhist does not speak of himself as *in* Buddha, nor does a Muslim speak of himself as *in* Mohammed. A Christian Scientist is not *in* Mary Baker Eddy or a Mormon *in* Joseph Smith or Brigham Young. They may faithfully follow the teaching and example of those religious leaders, but they are not *in* them. Only Christians can claim to be *in* their Lord, because they have been made spiritually one with Him (cf. Rom. 6:1–11). "But God, being rich in mercy, because of His great love with which He loved us," Paul wrote, "even when we were dead in our transgressions, made us alive together with Christ (by grace you have been saved), and raised us up with Him, and seated us with Him in the heavenly places in Christ Jesus" (Eph. 2:4–6). To the Galatians he declared, "I have been crucified with Christ; and it is no longer I who live, but Christ lives in me" (Gal. 2:20). In Paul's letters, the phrase "in Christ Jesus" occurs fifty times, "in Christ" twenty-nine times, and "in the Lord" forty-five times. Being **in Christ Jesus** and therefore acceptable to God is the believer's supreme source of joy.

Overseers and deacons are called to lead the church. As is clear from Acts 20:17, 28 and Titus 1:5, 7, *overseer* is another term for *elder*, the most common New Testament name for the office (cf. Acts 11:30; 14:23; 15:2, 4, 6, 23; James 5:14). Elders are also referred to as pastors (or shepherds; Acts 20:28; 1 Peter 5:1–2), pastor-teachers (Eph. 4:11), and bishops (cf. Acts 20:28, marg.; 1 Tim. 3:2, marg.). Their high qualifications are set forth in 1 Timothy 3:1–7 and Titus 1:6–9. **Overseers,** or elders, are first mentioned in relation to famine relief money sent by the church at Antioch to the elders in Judea by the hands of Barnabas and Saul (Acts 11:30). They mediate the rule of Christ in local churches by preaching, teaching, setting godly examples, and giving Holy Spirit–guided leadership.

Although their role is primarily one of practical service rather than preaching and teaching, **deacons** are required to meet the same high moral and spiritual standards (1 Tim. 3:8–13) as elders. The distinction between the two offices is that elders are to be skilled teachers (1 Tim. 3:2; Titus 1:9).

THE SALUTATION

Grace to you and peace from God our Father and the Lord Jesus Christ. (1:2)

Paul used this common greeting in several of his letters to churches (Rom. 1:7; 1 Cor. 1:3; 2 Cor. 1:2; Eph. 1:2; Col. 1:2–3; 2 Thess. 1:2) as well as in one letter to an individual (Philem. 3). It is an expression of the apostle's deep love for fellow believers, even the immature ones in Corinth who caused him such grief. But he must have felt an especially deep sense of joy and gratitude for the saints in Philippi who, in stark contrast to those in Corinth, had brought him immeasurable satisfaction and comfort.

The saving, eternal **grace** that is granted to penitent, believing sinners is the supreme divine gift, and everlasting **peace** is its greatest blessing. The source of both is **God our Father and the Lord Jesus Christ.** This salutation expresses Paul's abiding love and concern for the faithful believers in Philippi and serves as an introduction to the many specific causes for rejoicing that he mentions throughout this tenderest of all his epistles.

The common New Testament salutary connection of **God our Father** with the **Lord Jesus Christ** repeatedly emphasizes the oneness of nature between the two (Rom. 1:7; 1 Cor. 1:3, 9; 2 Cor. 1:2–3; Gal. 1:1, 3; Eph. 1:1–2; Phil. 1:2; Col. 1:3; 1 Thess. 1:1, 3; 1 Tim. 1:1–2; 2 Tim. 1:2; Titus 1:4; Philem. 3; Heb. 1:1–3; James 1:1; 1 Peter 1:3; 2 Peter 1:1–2; 1 John 1:3; 2 John 3; Jude 1). **God** the **Father** shares His essential divine being with **the Lord Jesus Christ.** The emphasis on this equality establishes the deity of our Lord Jesus, which is the central truth of Christianity.

The Elements of Joy (Philippians 1:3–8)

2

I thank my God in all my remembrance of you, always offering prayer with joy in my every prayer for you all, in view of your participation in the gospel from the first day until now. For I am confident of this very thing, that He who began a good work in you will perfect it until the day of Christ Jesus. For it is only right for me to feel this way about you all, because I have you in my heart, since both in my imprisonment and in the defense and confirmation of the gospel, you all are partakers of grace with me. For God is my witness, how I long for you all with the affection of Christ Jesus. (1:3–8)

A popular test for depression rates people on a scale of one to ten. The higher the score, the more severe the depression. If the apostle Paul had taken such a test, he doubtless would have scored a zero, because his joy was complete and irrepressible. Like the writer of Psalms 42 and 43, he knew how to overcome depression, anxiety, and worry (cf. Pss. 42:5, 11; 43:5).

Yet Paul's circumstances at the time he wrote this letter were dire. He was imprisoned in Rome, possibly facing execution. As it turned out, he was released from this imprisonment, but he was not certain that would be the case when he wrote Philippians. He was under house arrest (Acts 28:23, 30), chained to a Roman soldier (Acts 28:16) to prevent any possibility of escape. Paul languished there, unable to do the work he loved, while others, taking advantage of his situation, preached the gospel out of contention and strife (1:15–17). Nevertheless, his heart overflowed with joy (1:18). If anything, those horrendous circumstances made Paul's joy all the greater, because he trusted the sovereign purpose of his Lord and turned even more to Him for strength and comfort.

True joy is an unwavering constant in a Spirit-filled life (cf. Rom. 14:17), not a transient emotional feeling that comes and goes depending on circumstances. Because Paul was constantly near to God, he was constantly joyful. He experienced the inexpressible peace (4:7) and contentment (4:11) provided by the Holy Spirit deep within his heart and soul because he had a conscience that was clear of offense against God (Acts 23:1; 24:16; 2 Cor. 1:12; 2 Tim. 1:3).

The Philippian church was not perfect. But in contrast to most of the other churches with which Paul was associated, they had no major moral or spiritual problems. He urged them, "Conduct yourselves in a manner worthy of the gospel of Christ, so that whether I come and see you or remain absent, I will hear of you that you are standing firm in one spirit, with one mind striving together for the faith of the gospel" (1:27). A few verses later he exhorted the Philippians, "Make my joy complete by being of the same mind, maintaining the same love, united in spirit, intent on one purpose. Do nothing from selfishness or empty conceit, but with humility of mind regard one another as more important than yourselves; do not merely look out for your own personal interests, but also for the interests of others" (2:2–4). Later he commanded them to "do all things without grumbling or disputing; so that you will prove yourselves to be blameless and innocent, children of God above reproach in the midst of a crooked and perverse generation, among whom you appear as lights in the world" (2:14–15). In chapter 4 he urged Euodia and Syntyche, who obviously had an unresolved point of contention, "to live in harmony in the Lord" (v. 2), and he encouraged the entire church to "be anxious for nothing, but in everything by prayer and supplication with thanksgiving let your requests be made known to God" (v. 6). But those admonitions are more a form of encouragement than a rebuke.

As Paul thought about this beloved congregation to whom he was writing, his joy overflowed. He was not thinking so much about his own circumstances as about their faithfulness (1:3–5), not so much about his own afflictions as about their love (2:1–2), not so much about his own physical suffering as about their spiritual steadfastness (2:12–16). He was thinking about their selfless generosity in sending him financial support (4:14–16). He was thinking about their "progress and joy in the faith" (1:25), about his "beloved brethren whom [he longed] to see, [his] joy and crown" (4:1). He could therefore say with utter sincerity, "I thank my God in all my remembrance of you" (1:3).

In 1:3–8 the apostle gives five specific elements of his Spirit-engendered joy as it related to other believers. He focuses on the joys of recollection (v. 3), of intercession (v. 4), of participation (v. 5), of anticipation (v. 6), and of affection (vv. 7–8).

THE JOY OF RECOLLECTION

I thank my God in all my remembrance of you, (1:3)

Thank is from *eucharisteō,* from which the English word "Eucharist," a name often used of the Lord's Supper, derives. In that ordinance believers give thanks to God in remembrance of Christ's substitutionary sacrifice on the cross. In this instance Paul gives thanks for his spiritual brothers and sisters in Philippi who, over the years, had brought him such abundant blessing and joy.

The phrase **my God** reflects Paul's deep intimacy and communion with the Lord, to whom he belonged and whom he served (Acts 27:23). His thankfulness for the Philippians was to **God,** emphasizing both that the Lord is the ultimate source of all joy and that it was the Philippians' relationship to Him through Christ that caused Paul to **thank . . . God.** Paul expressed similar thanksgivings for the believers in Corinth (1 Cor. 1:4), in Colossae (Col. 1:3), and in Thessalonica (1 Thess. 1:2; cf. 2:13), and for his beloved coworkers Timothy (2 Tim. 1:3) and Philemon (Philem. 4).

Paul's **remembrance** of the Philippians began with his second missionary journey, when the apostle first came to Philippi. He was specifically directed by the Holy Spirit to go to Macedonia (the province in which Philippi was located) rather than Bithynia, as he and Silas had intended (Acts 16:7–10). On the Sabbath they went outside the city to the riverside, where they expected to find Jewish worshipers. (Evidently there were not enough Jewish men in Philippi to form a synagogue.) The only ones present were a group of women at prayer. One of the women, Lydia, was "a worshiper of God," that is, a Gentile proselyte to Judaism. The Lord opened her heart to Christ. When she heard the gospel, she was baptized with her newly believing household, and she prevailed on Paul and those with him to be her guests (Acts 16:13–15). Lydia and her household were the first Christian converts in Europe and became the nucleus of that continent's first church. The generosity and hospitality they exhibited characterized that congregation for years to come.

Surely in Paul's remembrance was the young demon-possessed slave girl in Philippi who brought her owners considerable wealth from her fortune-telling. She dogged the apostle and his companions for many days and "kept crying out, saying, 'These men are bond-servants of the Most High God, who are proclaiming to you the way of salvation.'" Becoming "greatly annoyed, [Paul] turned and said to the spirit, 'I command you in the name of Jesus Christ to come out of her!' And it came out at that very moment" (Acts 16:16–18). Although Luke does not report it specifically, it seems probable that, like Lydia, she was born again and became a sister in Christ whom Paul now fondly remembered.

Paul also would have remembered the time he spent in jail in Philippi because of the slave girl's owners, who lost a great source of income and incited the townspeople against him and Silas (Acts 16:19–23). Not only did the Lord give Paul and Silas peace and joy despite their chains and literally put songs in their hearts (Acts 16:25), but He also used their imprisonment to bring the jailer and his household to salvation (Acts 16:26–34). On the way out of the city after being released from prison, Paul and Silas went to Lydia's house for a last time and were encouraged by the many believers there who came to see them off (Acts 16:40).

Paul must have often remembered that, after he left Macedonia, the Philippian church was the only one that helped him financially (Phil. 4:15–16). Those devoted believers continued their generosity by contributing toward the collection Paul made for the needy believers in Jerusalem (2 Cor. 8:1–5).

Having a genuine desire to remember and focus on the goodness, kindness, and successes of others does not involve denying their weaknesses and shortcomings but rather looking past them. The Holy Spirit prompts believers to appreciate others' love, generosity, and compassion and to forget the rest (cf. 4:8; 1 Cor. 13:4–7). On the other hand, a person who constantly focuses on the negatives, faults, shortcomings, and slights of others is a person not controlled by the Holy Spirit, and is perhaps an unbeliever. Bitterness, resentment, a critical spirit, holding grudges, and the like are works of the flesh, not of the Spirit.

Much of Paul's joy was based on the pleasant, loving recollections of believers who, like those in Philippi, were consistently faithful to the Lord, to their fellow believers, and to him.

THE JOY OF INTERCESSION

always offering prayer with joy in my every prayer for you all, (1:4)

Another indispensable element of joy for believers is interceding before God on behalf of others. Those who are obedient to the Holy Spirit will delight in the privilege of intercessory prayer. Faithful and sincere intercession is much more than an obligation; it is a joy. Faithful intercessors are more preoccupied with the needs and welfare of others than their own and ask God to pour out His divine blessing on them. An infallible test of godly joy is the degree to which a believer prays more earnestly for the benefit and blessing of others than for his own.

The noun *deēsis* (**prayer**), used twice in this verse, has the basic meaning of a request, entreaty, or supplication and, in the New Testament, is always addressed to God (cf. Luke 1:13; 5:33; Rom. 10:1; 2 Cor. 1:11; Heb. 5:7; James 5:16; 1 Peter 3:12).

As the apostle explains later in this chapter (vv. 12–21), he was at this time experiencing some of the most difficult and painful times of his ministry. Not only was he in prison, but, even more painful to him, he also was being maligned by fellow teachers and preachers who intended "to cause [him] distress in [his] imprisonment" (v. 17). Although he obviously was not unaware of or unconcerned about that unjust and hateful behavior, he was determined not to allow it to diminish his joy. Instead, Paul was grateful "that in every way, whether in pretense or in truth, Christ is proclaimed; and in this I rejoice. Yes, and I will rejoice" (v. 18).

Intercessory prayer sometimes involves disappointment and pain. Later in this letter he counseled the Philippians, "Join in following my example, and observe those who walk according to the pattern you have in us. For many walk, of whom I often told you, and now tell you even weeping, that they are enemies of the cross of Christ, whose end is destruction, whose god is their appetite, and whose glory is in their shame, who set their minds on earthly things" (3:17–19). Those false believers not only were uncharitable in the extreme but also were shamelessly worldly. They were "enemies of the cross of Christ." Their false teaching and immoral living seriously threatened the church, and that tragic state of affairs brought pain to the apostle. Paul reminded the church at Corinth that "out of much affliction and anguish of heart I wrote to you with many tears; not so that you would be made sorrowful, but that you might know the love which I have especially for you" (2 Cor. 2:4; cf. 11:29).

But Paul's prayers for the Philippians were offered with great appreciation, thankfulness, and joy. Neither the unbelieving false teachers, such as those just mentioned, nor squabbling believers, such as Euodia and Syntyche (4:2), could rob Paul of his joyful remembrance of this cherished congregation. After beseeching Clement and an unnamed elder at Philippi to help reconcile those two women, he exults, "Rejoice in the Lord always; again I will say, rejoice!" (4:3–4).

Like Paul, believers who possess God-given joy do not focus on themselves, even in the midst of pain or difficult circumstances. They are rather concerned about their fellow believers' pain, difficult circumstances, hardships, failures, and sorrows, and they earnestly intercede for them. They joyfully pray for God to bless their fellow believers in every way, above all for their spiritual welfare. Later in this letter Paul expresses this personal trait in an admonition: "Do not merely look out for your own personal interests, but also for the interests of others" (2:4).

It seems that throughout most of the history of the church only a minority of Christians have known the true, full joy that God gives to His obedient children. Lack of joy reveals itself in three ways: in negative thoughts and talk about others, in a lack of concern for their welfare, and in the failure to intercede on their behalf. Joyless believers are self-centered, selfish, proud, and often vengeful, and their self-centeredness inevitably manifests itself in prayerlessness.

THE JOY OF PARTICIPATION

in view of your participation in the gospel from the first day until now. (1:5)

A third element of God-given joy is **participation.** *Koinōnia* (**participation**) is commonly rendered "fellowship," or "communion," and has the root meaning of sharing something in common. It is used in several places of sharing possessions or money. Using the verb form, Paul declares that faithful believers should practice "contributing to the needs of the saints" (Rom. 12:13); and later in the letter he uses the noun form in speaking of "a contribution for the poor among the saints in Jerusalem" (Rom. 15:26; cf. 2 Cor. 8:4, where *koinōnia* is rendered "participation"; 9:13). In 1 Timothy 6:18 the adjectival form is rendered "ready to share," and in Hebrews 13:16 the noun is translated "sharing."

In the broadest sense, Paul rejoiced that the Philippians were saved and thus partners with him in the spread of the gospel. That **participation** included their generous financial support of him. Later in this letter he reminded them: "You yourselves also know, Philippians, that at the first preaching of the gospel, after I left Macedonia, no church shared with me in the matter of giving and receiving but you alone; for even in Thessalonica you sent a gift more than once for my needs" (4:15–16).

By far the most important thing all believers share is their spiritual oneness, their **participation in the gospel** of Jesus Christ. "God is faithful," Paul explained, "through whom you were called into fellowship with His Son, Jesus Christ our Lord" (1 Cor. 1:9). Fellowship includes cooperation in the preaching of the good news of salvation to those who have never heard it, so that the spiritual fellowship might be enlarged and bring still greater glory to God (cf. 2 Cor. 4:15). In this context the phrase **in the gospel** refers to the whole enterprise of gospel ministry, especially that of evangelism. So Paul here commends the Philippians for their faithful and enduring partnership with him in this supreme endeavor.

Paul's beautiful benediction in 2 Corinthians perhaps best summarizes the full depth and breadth of Christian *koinōnia*: "The grace of the Lord Jesus Christ, and the love of God, and the fellowship [*koinōnia*] of the Holy Spirit, be with you all" (2 Cor. 13:14). The justifying grace of the Son, the electing love of the Father, and the sanctifying fellowship of the Holy Spirit are inextricably coalesced in the partnership of the saints, a vast spiritual brotherhood that includes every person who has saving faith in Jesus Christ. Such fellowship was a great source of joy for Paul, as it is for all Christians who find strength, encouragement, support, comfort, and help through their fellowship with other believers.

In his commentary on Philippians, the noted commentator William Hendriksen lists eight aspects, or types, of Christian *koinōnia* (see *New Testament Commentary: Exposition of Philippians* [Grand Rapids: Baker, 1962], 51–53). His list is not meant to be comprehensive, and the eight aspects are not necessarily in order of importance. They are grace, faith, prayer and thanksgiving, love, service, contributing to the needs of others, separation from the world, and spiritual warfare. It is obvious that they overlap in varying degrees.

First and foremost is the fellowship of grace. This is not a natural, man-made fellowship but one sovereignly designed and effected by God through His Holy Spirit. "For by grace you have been saved through faith," Paul declared; "and that not of yourselves, it is the gift of God" (Eph. 2:8; cf. Acts 15:11; Rom. 4:5). All believers have been graciously chosen by God for salvation. Apart from His having chosen them, they could not have chosen Him. In John 6:44 Jesus declared, "No one can come to Me unless the Father who sent Me draws him; and I will raise him up on the last day." To the Romans Paul wrote, "For those whom [God] foreknew, He also predestined to become conformed to the image of His Son, so that He would be the firstborn among many brethren; and these whom He predestined, He also called; and these whom He called, He also justified; and these whom He justified, He also glorified" (Rom. 8:29–30; cf. John 15:16).

Those whom God chooses for salvation are made one with the Father, the Son, and the Holy Spirit as well as each other. Speaking of Himself, Jesus prayed to the Father, "Even as You gave Him [the Son] authority over all flesh, that to all whom You have given Him, He may give eternal life. This is eternal life, that they may know You, the only true God, and Jesus Christ whom You have sent" (John 17:2–3). Paul summarized that truth in these words: "The one who joins himself to the Lord is one spirit with Him" (1 Cor. 6:17).

Second is the fellowship of faith. On the human level, it is faith alone that brings sinners to salvation. Paul and Silas told the jailer in Philippi, "Believe in the Lord Jesus, and you will be saved, you and your household" (Acts 16:31; cf. Rom. 10:9–10). Yet, as noted above, even human faith has a divine origin: "For by grace you have been saved through faith; and that not of yourselves, it is the gift of God" (Eph. 2:8).

Third is the fellowship of prayer and thanksgiving. Nothing binds believers more closely together than worshiping God in corporate praise and thanksgiving. Christians are "always [to be] giving thanks for all things in the name of our Lord Jesus Christ to God, even the Father" (Eph. 5:20); and "whatever [they] do in word or deed, [they should] do all in the name of the Lord Jesus, giving thanks through Him to God the Father" (Col. 3:17). They are to "rejoice always; pray without ceasing; [and] in everything give thanks; for this is God's will for [them] in Christ Jesus" (1 Thess. 5:16–18).

Fourth is the fellowship of love, the supreme virtue that encompasses all other virtues. It is more important than speaking in tongues, prophecy, theological knowledge, faith, sacrificial generosity, and even martyrdom (1 Cor. 13:1–3). Paul went on to declare that "love is patient, love is kind and is not jealous; love does not brag and is not arrogant, does not act unbecomingly; it does not seek its own, is not provoked, does not take into account a wrong suffered, does not rejoice in unrighteousness, but rejoices with the truth; bears all things, believes all things, hopes all things, endures all things. Love never fails. . . . The greatest of these is love" (1 Cor. 13:4–8, 13). The apostle John taught that love is the definitive mark of Christian fellowship: "Beloved, let us love one another, for love is from God; and everyone who loves is born of God and knows God. The one who does not love does not know God, for God is love" (1 John 4:7–8).

Fifth is the fellowship of contributing to the needs of others. "While we have opportunity," Paul admonished, "let us do good to all people, and especially to those who are of the household of the faith" (Gal. 6:10). Even under the old covenant, believers were commanded: "Do not withhold good from those to whom it is due, when it is in your power to do it" (Prov. 3:27).

Sixth is the fellowship of promoting the gospel, already mentioned above. That is done through preaching, teaching, witnessing, and supporting those whom the Lord has specially called to those ministries. This fellowship is clearly a fulfillment of Jesus' Great Commission: "Make disciples of all the nations, baptizing them in the name of the Father and the Son and the Holy Spirit, teaching them to observe all that I commanded you" (Matt. 28:19–20).

Seventh is the fellowship of separation from the world. In His discourse in the Upper Room shortly before His arrest, Jesus told the remaining eleven disciples, "You are not of the world, but I chose you out of the world" (John 15:19). A negative but extremely important part of fellowship is keeping "oneself unstained by the world" (James 1:27), which has never been more difficult than in our own age. John exhorts believers, "Do not love the world nor the things in the world. [And] if anyone [does love] the world, the love of the Father is not in him. For all that is in the world, the lust of the flesh and the lust of the eyes and the boastful pride of life, is not from the Father, but is from the world" (1 John 2:15–16).

Eighth is the fellowship of spiritual warfare. In many ways this is an extension of the previous aspect. When a believer is truly separated from the world, he will come under attack from the world. "If you were of the world, the world would love its own," Jesus explained; "but because you are not of the world, but I chose you out of the world, because of this the world hates you. Remember the word that I said to you, 'A slave is not greater than his master.' If they persecuted Me, they will also persecute you" (John 15:19–20). In this great spiritual struggle "the weapons of our warfare are not of the flesh," because the conflict is not of the flesh, "but [they are] divinely powerful for the destruction of fortresses" (2 Cor. 10:4). In that warfare, believers are fellow soldiers (2 Tim. 2:3).

A Christian who willingly forsakes fellowship with other believers will inevitably be without genuine, Spirit-given joy. It is impossible to live faithfully or happily apart from fellow believers in Christ. But the believer who regularly is in the company of fellow saints, fulfilling the responsibilities that such fellowship requires and provides, will just as inevitably be filled with divine joy. To be in the company of those who are joint heirs with Christ, people who love, care for, understand, pray for and with each other, who minister and fight the good fight together, is to be assured of abundant and abiding joy.

That is the joy Paul expressed here in regard to the Philippian believers. They had faithfully served with him in their church, proclaimed the gospel with him, worshiped and prayed with him, and defended the faith with him. They had abundantly shared their material resources with him over and over again. They had tirelessly and selflessly been in partnership with him **from the first day until now,** over a period of several years.

THE JOY OF ANTICIPATION

For I am confident of this very thing, that He who began a good work in you will perfect it until the day of Christ Jesus. (1:6)

A fourth element of joy is anticipation. Nothing can encourage a Christian so much as the knowledge that, despite life's uncertainties and difficulties, and no matter how many spiritual defeats there may be long the way, one day he will be made perfect.

Confident translates *peithō,* which here means to be persuaded of and have confidence in. Paul's confidence was much more than human hope; it was the absolute confidence that comes from knowing and believing God's promise **that He [God] who began a good work in** him **will perfect it until the day of Christ Jesus.** Salvation is wholly God's work, and for that reason its completion is as certain as if it were already accomplished.

Began is from *enarchomai,* a compound verb meaning "to begin in." It is used only twice in the New Testament, both times in reference to salvation. Paul rebuked certain believers in the Galatian churches who believed that they could finish in their own power what God had divinely begun in their lives solely by the power of His Holy Spirit. "Are you so foolish?" he asked rhetorically. "Having begun by the Spirit, are you now being perfected by the flesh?" (Gal. 3:3). In the present text the apostle, in effect, responds to that same question, assuring the Philippians that their salvation is solely a gracious work of God. God requires faith for salvation, but faith is not a meritorious work. Salvation is by the power of God in response to faith; and, as already noted, faith itself is God's work, divinely initiated and divinely accomplished (Eph. 2:8–9). Although Lydia, the first convert in what would become the church at Philippi, believed the gospel of Christ, Luke made it clear that "the Lord opened her heart to respond to the things spoken by Paul" (Acts 16:14).

Later in the present epistle, Paul emphasized that "to you it has been granted for Christ's sake, not only to believe in Him, but also to suffer for His sake," and "it is God who is at work in you, both to will and to work for His good pleasure" (Phil. 1:29; 2:13). "As many as received Him [Christ]," John declared, "to them He gave the right to become children of God, even to those who believe in His name" (John 1:12). When "the apostles and the brethren who were throughout Judea heard that the Gentiles also had received the word of God" through the witness of Peter, "those who were circumcised took issue with him," believing that the gospel was only for Jews or Jewish converts. But after they heard Peter's report, "they quieted down and glorified God, saying, 'Well then, God has granted to the Gentiles also the repentance that leads to life'" (Acts

11:1–2, 18). "In the exercise of His will," James wrote, "He brought us forth by the word of truth, so that we would be a kind of first fruits among His creatures" (James 1:18).

As noted earlier, salvation is solely by God's grace. God "chose us in Him before the foundation of the world, that we would be holy and blameless before Him" (Eph. 1:4). God chose all believers before time, long before they could possibly choose Him; and apart from His choice of them, they could not choose Him (John 6:44). It has always been true, in every age and circumstance, that only "as many as had been appointed to eternal life [have] believed" (Acts 13:48). Paul clearly expressed that truth in Romans 5:8–10:

> God demonstrates His own love toward us, in that while we were yet sinners, Christ died for us. Much more then, having now been justified by His blood, we shall be saved from the wrath of God through Him. For if while we were enemies we were reconciled to God through the death of His Son, much more, having been reconciled, we shall be saved by His life.

Later in that epistle Paul gave a parallel to Philippians 1:6, noting that "those whom [God] foreknew, He also predestined to become conformed to the image of His Son, so that He would be the firstborn among many brethren; and these whom He predestined, He also called; and these whom He called, He also justified; and these whom He justified, He also glorified" (Rom. 8:29–30). All the chosen will be glorified. God will finish what He has begun.

Every aspect of salvation is by God's sovereign will and choice. Paul wrote to the Ephesians that:

> God, being rich in mercy, because of His great love with which He loved us, even when we were dead in our transgressions, made us alive together with Christ (by grace you have been saved), and raised us up with Him, and seated us with Him in the heavenly places in Christ Jesus, so that in the ages to come He might show the surpassing riches of His grace in kindness toward us in Christ Jesus. For by grace you have been saved through faith; and that not of yourselves, it is the gift of God. (Eph. 2:4–8; cf. Titus 3:4–6; James 1:18; 1 Peter 1:2–3)

It is the Lord who begins the work of salvation, and it is the Lord, through His Holy Spirit, who will **perfect it.** To the Galatians Paul wrote, "I have been crucified with Christ; and it is no longer I who live, but Christ lives in me; and the life which I now live in the flesh I live by faith in the Son of God, who loved me and gave Himself up for me" (Gal. 2:20).

Epiteleō (to **perfect**) is a compound, formed by the preposition *epi* and the verb *teleō* ("to complete") to give the intensified meaning of "fully completed." Paul was absolutely certain that God will fully complete His work of salvation in the Philippians. There is no possibility of failure or of partial fulfillment.

The eschatological expression **the day of Christ Jesus** does not refer to what both the Old and New Testaments prophesy as the final Day of the Lord, the time of God's judgment on the sinful world. The Day of the Lord is described by Paul in 1 Thessalonians:

> For you yourselves know full well that the day of the Lord will come just like a thief in the night. While they are saying, "Peace and safety!" then destruction will come upon them suddenly like labor pains upon a woman with child, and they will not escape. But you, brethren, are not in darkness, that the day would overtake you like a thief. (5:2–4; for more information on the Day of the Lord, see Isa. 13:6–22; Joel 1:15; 2:11; Acts 2:20; 2 Thess. 1:10, "that day"; 2 Peter 3:10, and *Revelation 1–11*, The MacArthur New Testament Commentary [Chicago: Moody, 1999], 199–201)

Also an eschatological expression, **the day of Christ Jesus,** on the other hand, clearly refers to the time when believers will be glorified, when their salvation will be completed and made perfect (1 Cor. 3:10–15; 2 Cor. 5:10). It is the same as "the day of Christ" that Paul mentions several times later in Philippians, the day for which Christians should be prepared by living sincerely and blamelessly (1:10) and by "holding fast the word of life" (2:16). In his first letter to the Corinthian church, the apostle called it "the day of our Lord Jesus Christ" (1 Cor. 1:8), and in his second letter to them he called it "the day of our Lord Jesus" (2 Cor. 1:14). In each instance, the personal names *Jesus* or *Christ* are given (rather than *Lord*), and in each instance the reference is to the time when believers will fully share the Lord's perfect righteousness, when "Christ is formed in [them]" (Gal. 4:19), and "[they] also will be revealed with Him in glory" (Col. 3:4).

Believers are "predestined to become conformed to the image of [God's] Son" (Rom. 8:29), because "just as [they] have borne the image of the earthy, [they] will also bear the image of the heavenly, . . . [and] in a moment, in the twinkling of an eye, . . . [they] will be changed. . . . For this perishable must put on the imperishable, and this mortal must put on immortality" (1 Cor. 15:49, 52–53). "We know that when [Christ] appears," John wrote, "we will be like Him, because we will see Him just as He is" (1 John 3:2). Peter wrote: "When the Chief Shepherd appears, [we] will receive the unfading crown of glory" (1 Peter 5:4). Although a believer living in unrepentant sin may be delivered temporarily to Satan for discipline, "his spirit [will] be saved in the day of the Lord Jesus" (1 Cor. 5:5). The day of Christ Jesus is the time of perfection and glorification, when the glorious manifestation of the children of God will finally come (Rom. 8:18–19, 23).

When God saves, He saves completely and eternally. In promissory covenant terms, to be justified is to be sanctified and glorified. There is no such thing as experiencing one of those aspects of salvation without the other two. Each is an integral and necessary part of the whole continuum of salvation. For God to begin salvation in a person's life is an irrevocable guarantee of His completing it. As William Hendriksen has observed, "God . . . is not like men. Men conduct experiments, but God carries out a plan. God never does anything by halves" (*Philippians*, 55).

The Lord said of David: "I will not break off My lovingkindness from him, nor deal falsely in My faithfulness" (Ps. 89:33; cf. v. 20). Jesus gives every believer the absolute promise that "all that the Father gives Me will come to Me, and the one who comes to Me I will certainly not cast out. . . . This is the will of Him who sent Me, that of all that He has given Me I lose nothing, but raise it up on the last day" (John 6:37, 39). Later He reiterated that promise, saying, "My sheep hear My voice, and I know them, and they follow Me; and I give eternal life to them, and they will never perish; and no one will snatch them out of My hand" (John 10:27–28). Paul declared, "I am convinced that neither death, nor life, nor angels, nor principalities, nor things present, nor things to come, nor powers, nor height, nor depth, nor any other created thing, will be able to separate us from the love of God, which is in Christ Jesus our Lord" (Rom. 8:38–39). The apostle wrote to Timothy that "the firm foundation of God stands, having this seal, 'The Lord knows those who are His'" (2 Tim. 2:19; cf. John 10:14). Peter exulted:

> Blessed be the God and Father of our Lord Jesus Christ, who according to His great mercy has caused us to be born again to a living hope through the resurrection of Jesus Christ from the dead, to obtain an inheritance which is imperishable and undefiled and will not fade away, reserved in heaven for you, who are protected by the power of God through faith for a salvation ready to be revealed in the last time. (1 Peter 1:3–5; cf. Jude 24)

It is easy for believers to become discouraged when they focus on their problems and imperfections (and those of other believers). Those sins should not be ignored or minimized; but neither should they be allowed to overshadow the marvelous reality of the future perfection of the church and of every individual believer, as God's Word guarantees so frequently and clearly. Remembering that glorious truth removes the debilitating pressure of doubt and fosters triumphant joy, gratitude, and anticipation. In so doing, it also frees God's people to live more abundantly and fruitfully.

The nineteenth-century commentator F. B. Meyer wrote,

> We go into the artist's studio and find there unfinished pictures covering large canvases, and suggesting great designs, but which have been left, either because the genius was not competent to complete the work, or because paralysis laid the hand low in death; but as we go into God's great workshop we find nothing that bears the mark of haste or insufficiency of power to finish, and we are sure that the work which His grace has begun, the arm of His strength will complete. (*The Epistle to the Philippians* [Grand Rapids: Baker, 1952], 28)

God has no unfinished works. The God who saves is the God who justifies, sanctifies, and glorifies. The God who begins is the God who completes. During His incarnation, the Lord gave this absolute and unambiguous assurance, which is a source of joy to all those who will ever trust in Him: "All that the Father gives Me will come to Me, and the one who comes to Me I will certainly not cast out" (John 6:37).

THE JOY OF AFFECTION

For it is only right for me to feel this way about you all, because I have you in my heart, since both in my imprisonment and in the defense and confirmation of the gospel, you all are partakers of grace with me. For God is my witness, how I long for you all with the affection of Christ Jesus. (1:7–8)

In these verses Paul's rejoicing reaches a crescendo as he presents a fifth element of joy—affection. There can be no greater or more exhilarating joy than that produced by deep, abiding, and genuine affection for others.

Dikaios (**right**) denotes more than mere appropriateness. It expresses moral and spiritual rightness; not merely that which is expected but that which is required. It was only **right** before men and before God for Paul **to feel this way** about the beloved saints in Philippi.

To feel translates a form of *phroneō*, which has the basic meaning of having a particular mental disposition or attitude. It refers to an act of intellect and will and is sometimes translated "to think," as it is in the King James Version rendering of this verse. Paul uses the verb numerous other times in this epistle: twice in 2:2 ("being of . . . mind," lit., "be . . . minded"); in 2:5 and 3:15 ("have . . . attitude"); in 3:19 ("set . . . minds") and 4:2 ("live in harmony," lit., "think the same"); and twice in 4:10 ("[have] concern," "were concerned"). In Romans, he uses a form of *phroneō* three times in admonishing believers "not to think more highly of [themselves] than [they] ought to think; but to think so as to have sound judgment, as God has allotted to each a measure of faith" (Rom. 12:3).

Obviously people love with their minds; love is first of all thought. But in the present passage Paul expands that concept by using the word **heart,** which includes the idea of feeling. The mind and heart are often synonymous in Scripture. Solomon warned, "Watch over your heart with all diligence, for from it flow the springs of life" (Prov. 4:23). The heart is used to trust and believe in God (Prov. 3:5; Jer. 29:13; Luke 24:25; Acts 8:37); to serve, obey, and follow Him (Deut. 11:13; 26:16; 1 Kings 2:4); and to worship and praise Him (Heb. 10:22). It is also a repository for God's Word (Ps. 119:11). Believers are commanded to have a clean heart (Ps. 51:10), a pure heart (Matt. 5:8), an obedient heart (Ps. 119:36), a worshiping heart (Ps. 57:7), a forgiving heart (Matt. 18:35), and a loving heart (Matt. 22:37; 2 Thess. 3:5).

Paul expressed his affection even for the immature, self-centered, and worldly believers at Corinth. "I do not speak to condemn you," he told them in his second letter, "for I have said before that you are in our hearts to die together and to live together" (2 Cor. 7:3). Paul's affection for his fellow believers, even those who grievously disappointed him, brought him much joy.

It was not hard for the apostle to cherish the beloved Philippian believers in his **heart.** Because of all they meant to him, he could hardly have thought of them in any other way. Thus, he reminds them that **both in my imprisonment and in the defense and confirmation of the gospel, you all are partakers of grace with me.** Both *apologia* (**defense**) and *bebaiōsis* (**confirmation**) are legal terms. *Apologia,* the source of the English words "apology" and "apologetics," refers to a speech given in defense. *Bebaiōsis* refers to the positive **confirmation** of the truth of the gospel. In the present text, these words allude either to the initial phase of the apostle's **imprisonment** and trial in Rome, during which he defended **the gospel,** or in a broader sense to his defense of the faith throughout his ministry. In either case, Paul affirmed that the Philippian church selflessly and sacrificially stood by him to give encouragement, to help alleviate his suffering, and to meet his needs in every way they could. They were his spiritual partners, **partakers of grace with** him, in the fullest sense.

Paul called on **God** as his **witness** to attest to his heartfelt longing **for** the Philippians **with the affection of Christ Jesus.** He wanted them to have no reservations about how fully and genuinely he loved them. Affection translates *splagchnon,* which literally refers to internal organs, specifically the bowels, or intestines. It is used in that physical sense only once in the New Testament, in reference to Judas's suicide (Acts 1:18). Elsewhere it is used figuratively to describe selfless, compassionate love. In Zacharias's prophecy it is rendered "tender mercy" (Luke 1:78); and in Colossians 3:12; Philemon 7, 12, 20; and 1 John 3:17, it is translated "heart(s)." In 2 Corinthians 6:12 and 7:15 and in Philippians 2:1, as in the present text, it is rendered "affection(s)." The Hebrew equivalent is used in a similar way—to describe feelings of sympathy (Isa. 16:11; 63:15; Jer. 31:20), of deep anguish or despair (Lam. 1:20; 2:11), and of marital love (Song 5:4).

All of the believers at Philippi, with no exceptions, were the objects of Paul's great **affection,** an affection so deep and pervasive as to reflect that of **Christ Jesus** Himself. It was enhanced and enriched by their warm and compassionate care for him that touched him so deeply. It was, in fact, a supernatural **affection,** instilled by the Lord both in his heart and theirs. It was no less than "the love of God [that had] been poured out within [their] hearts through the Holy Spirit" (Rom. 5:5). Paul wrote of this God-given love to the Thessalonians: "Now as to the love of the brethren, you have no need for anyone to write to you, for you yourselves are taught by God to love one another" (1 Thess. 4:9).

What robs believers of biblical joy? First, and by far the most important, is false salvation. The church has always included those whose faith is not genuine (cf. Matt. 13:24–30, 36–43; James 2:14–26). Because they do not possess the indwelling Holy Spirit, such false professors cannot possess biblical joy (Gal. 5:22). They may attend churches where God's Word is taught, and they may fellowship with genuine believers. Yet because they do not know the Lord, they cannot experience His joy. If they laugh, it is, sadly, "the laughter of the fool, [which] is futility" (Eccl. 7:6). For that reason Paul gives the somber warning: "Test yourselves to see if you are in the faith; examine yourselves! Or do you not recognize this about yourselves, that Jesus Christ is in you—unless indeed you fail the test?" (2 Cor. 13:5).

A second factor that hinders joy is the influence of Satan and his demons. "Be of sober spirit, be on the alert," Peter cautioned. "Your adversary, the devil, prowls around like a roaring lion, seeking someone to devour" (1 Peter 5:8). In many ways, including false teachers, the devil attempts to deceive believers. Although he cannot rob them of salvation, he can, and often does, rob them of joy (as does their sin; cf. Ps. 51:12).

A third factor that robs believers of joy is an inadequate understanding of God's sovereignty. For believers to fret and worry over their circumstances and to fear what the future may hold is tantamount to doubting God's sovereignty, as well as His power and love. God has promised that He will cause "all things to work together for good to those who love [Him], to those who are called according to His purpose" (Rom. 8:28). The incarnate Lord Jesus Christ promised, "I give eternal life to [My sheep], and they will never perish; and no one will snatch them out of My hand. My Father, who has given them to Me, is greater than all; and no one is able to snatch them out of the Father's hand" (John 10:28–29). In the Sermon on the Mount, Jesus commanded believers not to be anxious about anything (Matt. 6:25–34; cf. Phil. 4:6). And in perhaps the most beloved and cherished promise of all, He said, "Do not let your heart be troubled; believe in God, believe also in Me. In My Father's house are many dwelling places; if it were not so, I would have told you; for I go to prepare a place for you. If I go and prepare a place for you, I will come again and receive you to Myself, that where I am, there you may be also" (John 14:1–3). For believers, God's sovereignty is the overarching and all-encompassing reality that keeps everything in perspective. It is because of His divine sovereignty that, with utter confidence, believers can "cast [their] burden upon the Lord and [know that] He will sustain [them, because] He will never allow the righteous to be shaken" (Ps. 55:22).

When that reality is ignored or forgotten, joy will be lost. For example, when the prophet Habakkuk forgot that great truth, he cried out in despair,

> How long, O Lord, will I call for help, and You will not hear? I cry out to You, "Violence!" Yet You do not save. Why do You make me see iniquity, and cause me to look on wickedness? Yes, destruction and violence are before me; strife exists and contention arises. Therefore the law is ignored and justice is never upheld. For the wicked surround the righteous; therefore justice comes out perverted. (Hab. 1:2–4)

But by the time he reached the end of his message, his perspective had radically changed. Having come to his spiritual senses, he declared that, "though the fig tree should not blossom and there be no fruit on the vines, though the yield of the olive should fail and the fields produce no food, though the flock should be cut off from the fold and there be no cattle in the stalls, yet I will exult in the Lord, I will rejoice in the God of my salvation" (Hab. 3:17–18).

A fourth negative element that steals joy is prayerlessness. Believers who fail to pray inevitably lose sight of God's sovereignty and His love and care for us. Such believers either give up hope, as Habakkuk did for a while, or else seek help from other sources. There are times when it is appropriate to call on the leaders of the church for help (James 5:14–16). But that can never take the place of a believer's own prayers, as Paul makes clear later in this letter: "In everything by prayer and supplication with thanksgiving let your requests be made known to God"(4:6).

A fifth cause of joylessness is the emotional low that frequently follows a spiritual high. Elijah defeated and killed all the pagan prophets of Baal (1 Kings 18:38–40) on Mount Carmel. But when Queen Jezebel threatened his life, Elijah became "afraid and arose and ran for his life and came to Beersheba, which belongs to Judah, and . . . came and sat down under a juniper tree; and he requested for himself that he might die, and said, 'It is enough; now, O Lord, take my life, for I am not better than my fathers'"(1 Kings 19:3–4). Although neither their highs nor their lows have been that radical or dramatic, most believers have experienced similar kinds of spiritual success and letdown. Such times are surprising and bewildering, and can rob unwary believers of their joy.

A sixth way believers lose their joy is by focusing on circumstances. Despite the abundant blessings all believers have in the Lord, many become dissatisfied with their circumstances. They are unhappy with their physical or mental capacities, their appearance, the opportunities that come their way, or with the countless other things they do not have but think that they deserve. Jesus promised: "Peace I leave with you; My peace I give to you; not as the world gives do I give to you. Do not let your heart be troubled, nor let it be fearful" (John 14:27). Paul kept that promise constantly in mind, and his attitude toward ephemeral, non-eternal things was therefore unequivocal: "I have learned to be content in whatever circumstances I am. I know how to get along with humble means, and I also know how to live in prosperity; in any and every circumstance I have learned the secret of being filled and going hungry, both of having abundance and suffering need"(4:11–12).

A seventh negative element that robs believers of joy is ingratitude. Few things are more repugnant than ingratitude. Paul commanded that prayers and supplications to God be made with thanksgiving (4:6). In 1 Thessalonians he exhorted, "In everything give thanks; for this is God's will for you in Christ Jesus" (1 Thess. 5:18). Rebellious sinners are indicted and sentenced to divine judgment because of their ingratitude (Rom. 1:18–21).

An eighth cause of lack of joy is forgetfulness. Forgetting the Lord is not a mark of innocence but of faithlessness and sin. David reminded himself and all believers: "Bless the Lord, O my soul, and forget none of His benefits" (Ps. 103:2). The spiritual disharmony that causes division in churches is not incited by new converts but by those who have left their first love. The Lord warned the orthodox, hardworking, and persevering believers in Ephesus: "I have this against you, that you have left your first love. Therefore remember from where you have fallen, and repent and do the deeds you did at first; or else I am coming to you and will remove your lampstand out of its place—unless you repent" (Rev. 2:4–5).

A ninth factor in loss of joy is living by uncontrolled feelings, living by the flesh instead of by the Spirit. In his book *Spiritual Depression: Its Causes and Cure,* Dr. Martyn Lloyd-Jones writes,

> I suggest that the main trouble in this whole matter of spiritual depression is this, that we allow our self to talk to us instead of talking to our self. . . . Have you realized that most of your unhappiness in life is due to the fact that you are listening to yourself rather than talking to yourself? . . . The main art in the matter of spiritual living is to know how to handle yourself." ([Grand Rapids: Eerdmans, 1965], 20–21)

But proper talking to oneself does not include self-centeredness and morbid self-analysis, two of the worst plagues of much modern psychology. Contrary to what the world continually touts, self-centeredness is the surest source of dissatisfaction and discontentment. Neither does talking properly to one's self involve some sort of "positive confession" that supposedly creates reality. That is foolish. Talking to oneself about God, His Word, and His will is the issue.

A tenth and final reason for lack of joy is unwillingness to accept forgiveness. On the surface, that attitude can appear to reflect humility, but it is the furthest thing from that. It is, in fact, an insult to God's righteous character and the clear teaching of His Word. Our Lord made it plain that, "If [believers] forgive others for their transgressions, [their] heavenly Father will also forgive [them]. But if [they] do not forgive others, then [their] Father will not forgive [their] transgressions" (Matt. 6:14–15). David declared that, "as far as the east is from the west, so far has [the Lord] removed our transgressions from us" (Ps. 103:12), and John wrote that, "if we confess our sins, He is faithful and righteous to forgive us our sins and to cleanse us from all unrighteousness" (1 John 1:9; cf. 2:12). That basic truth alone is abundant reason for the believer never to be joyless.

From a somewhat reverse perspective, Scripture also teaches the amazing and humbling truth that faithful and obedient believers not only receive joy *from* God but also have the ability to give joy *to* God. It is beyond comprehension that our infinite, holy, and almighty God should rejoice in His children; but His Word teaches that He does.

God rejoices when unbelievers repent and turn from their sin to Him. Jesus said, "I tell you that . . . there will be more joy in heaven over one sinner who repents than over ninety-nine righteous persons who need no repentance" (Luke 15:7; cf. v. 10). "By faith Enoch was taken up so that he would not see death; and he was not found because God took him up; for he obtained the witness that before his being taken up he was pleasing to God" (Heb. 11:5).

God rejoices in the prayers and worship of His children and in their righteous behavior. "The sacrifice of the wicked is an abomination to the Lord, but the prayer of the upright is His delight. . . . The perverse in heart are an abomination to the Lord, but the blameless in their walk are His delight" (Prov. 15:8; 11:20). Before "the entire assembly" of Israel, David confessed: "Since I know, O my God, that You try the heart and delight in uprightness, I, in the integrity of my heart, have willingly offered all these things; so now with joy I have seen Your people, who are present here, make their offerings willingly to You" (1 Chron. 29:1, 17). Despite his many sins and failures, because David's heart was right, he brought joy to the Lord. In fact, God called him "a man after His own heart" (1 Sam. 13:14). In the parable of the talents, Christ promised that those who live faithfully for Him will one day share in His own divine joy: "His master said to him, 'Well done, good and faithful slave. You were faithful with a few things, I will put you in charge of many things; enter into the joy of your master'" (Matt. 25:21; cf. v. 23).

All of this leads to the inescapable conclusion that the fellowship of God's people should be a fellowship of joy. The non-Christian's joy must come from the outside; the Christian's comes from within. Despite the inevitable sorrows, disappointments, and pain of life, believers can always be joyful. Biblical joy is not based on circumstances, because it is the gift of the Holy Spirit (Gal. 5:22).

Essentials for Growth in Godliness (Philippians 1:9–11)

3

And this I pray, that your love may abound still more and more in real knowledge and all discernment, so that you may approve the things that are excellent, in order to be sincere and blameless until the day of Christ; having been filled with the fruit of righteousness which comes through Jesus Christ, to the glory and praise of God. (1:9–11)

Paul's passion for the spiritual development of the believers under his care was manifested not only in his preaching, teaching, and writing but also supremely in his prayer life. In Ephesians he assured his readers:

> [I] do not cease giving thanks for you, while making mention of you in my prayers; that the God of our Lord Jesus Christ, the Father of glory, may give to you a spirit of wisdom and of revelation in the knowledge of Him. I pray that the eyes of your heart may be enlightened, so that you will know what is the hope of His calling, what are the riches of the glory of His inheritance in the saints. (Eph. 1:16–18)

Later in that letter he added,

> For this reason I bow my knees before the Father, from whom every family in heaven and on earth derives its name, that He would grant you, according to the riches of His glory, to be strengthened with power through His Spirit in the inner man, so that Christ may dwell in your hearts through faith; and that you, being rooted and grounded in love, may be able to comprehend with all the saints what is the breadth and length and height and depth, and to know the love of Christ which surpasses knowledge, that you may be filled up to all the fullness of God. (Eph. 3:14–19)

His deep desire and prayer for the Colossians was that they "walk in a manner worthy of the Lord, to please Him in all respects, bearing fruit in every good work and increasing in the knowledge of God" (Col. 1:10). He affirmed his love for the Thessalonians with the assurance that "we give thanks to God always for all of you, making mention of you in our prayers" (1 Thess. 1:2). He remembered special individuals in the same way, assuring Timothy, "I constantly remember you in my prayers night and day" (2 Tim. 1:3), and Philemon, "I thank my God always, making mention of you in my prayers, . . . and I pray that the fellowship of your faith may become effective through the knowledge of every good thing which is in you for Christ's sake" (Philem. 4, 6).

In the present text, having greeted the Philippians (1:1–2) and mentioned his prayer on their behalf (1:3–8), Paul revealed the specific content of those prayers. As in all his recorded prayers, the apostle did not pray for physical needs or church growth. It was not that those things were unimportant to him, but that spiritual issues were of supreme importance. He performed miracles of physical healing (Acts 14:8–10; 19:11–12; 20:9–12) and advised Timothy to "no longer drink water exclusively, but use a little wine for the sake of your stomach and your frequent ailments" (1 Tim. 5:23). But the primary focus of his prayers was on the spiritual welfare of others.

There is no truer indicator of a Christian's level of spiritual maturity than his prayer life. Paul's prayer life reveals more of his true spirituality than all of his preaching, teaching, and miracles—marvelous and divinely blessed as those were. He was compelled to pray by the continual and powerful working of God's Spirit in his heart.

Clearly, prayer is a spiritual duty for Christians. Jesus taught "that at all times [believers] ought to pray and not to lose heart" (Luke 18:1). Paul exhorted believers to be "devoted to prayer" (Rom. 12:12) and to "be anxious for nothing, but in everything by prayer and supplication with thanksgiving let [their] requests be made known to God" (Phil. 4:6). Peter commanded believers to "be of sound judgment and sober spirit for the purpose of prayer" (1 Peter 4:7).

But prayer is much more than a duty; prayer is a compulsion for the spiritually mature Christian. Fervent prayer does not arise from a mere sense of duty but from a deep inner desire. It does not flow from external requirement but from internal passion. The deepest longings of the Spirit-filled heart for the honor of God and the blessing of men find their natural expression in prayer.

The measure of a person's spiritual maturity is not how well he or she conforms externally to the command to pray. The issue is how internally constrained that person is to pray by a strong love for God and others. The truest longings of the heart will come out in prayer. A selfish and superficial heart, focused primarily on personal problems, struggles, and interests, will produce selfish and superficial prayers. A heart focused on the glory of the Lord and His people will produce prayers focused on God's glory and others' needs. A strong sense of duty cannot compensate for a cold heart or produce fervent prayer. Early in the life of the church, the apostles set the standard when they instructed the congregation to appoint men to take care of the practical needs of the church. The apostles were to "devote [themselves] to prayer and to the ministry of the word"(Acts 6:4).

Paul was so committed to the Lord and to the souls of people that the Holy Spirit could easily generate within his heart a passion to pray. He prayed constantly, not because of a legalistic sense of duty but because of his genuine and deep love for the Lord and for people, especially the Lord's people. He prayed for the unsaved, including the pagan and despotic rulers under whom he and other Christians suffered such great injustice and affliction, and he commanded all believers to do likewise (1 Tim. 2:1–2; cf. Rom. 13:1–7; 1 Peter 2:13–17). He prayed with special fervor for his unsaved fellow Jews, for whom his "heart's desire and [his] prayer to God [was] for their salvation" (Rom. 10:1). That desire arose from such "great sorrow and unceasing grief in [his] heart"that he "could wish [himself] accursed, separated from Christ for the sake of [his] brethren, [his] kinsmen according to the flesh"(Rom. 9:2–3).

Paul prayed most often, however, for the church, for his spiritual kinsmen in Christ (Rom. 1:9; 2 Tim. 1:3). He exhorted other believers to pray fervently, just as he himself constantly made "petition for all the saints"(Eph. 6:18; cf. Col. 1:3; 1 Thess. 5:17). "To this end," he reminded the Thessalonians, "we pray for you always, that our God will count you worthy of your calling, and fulfill every desire for goodness and the work of faith with power, so that the name of our Lord Jesus will be glorified in you, and you in Him, according to the grace of our God and the Lord Jesus Christ" (2 Thess. 1:11–12).

The present text reveals five specific things for which Paul diligently prayed on behalf of the Philippians: their spiritual progress in love, excellence, integrity, good works, and in glorifying God. Those are the God-ordained spiritual essentials for which all Christians should pray on behalf of each other. Because of their indwelling sin and human frailty, believers cannot perfectly accomplish those spiritual objectives. But they are to be the unwavering goals of every child of God, especially those whom He has called into leadership in His church. "I have [not] already become perfect," the apostle himself confessed later in this letter, "but I press on so that I may lay hold of that for which also I was laid hold of by Christ Jesus" (3:12).

As in numerous other texts (cf. Rom. 5:3–4; 2 Peter 1:5–7), the things Paul mentions in Philippians 1:9–11 are sequential, each building on the foundation of the previous one. Abounding love produces spiritual excellence, which produces personal integrity, which produces genuine good works. Together they attain the supreme objective of God's praise and glory.

LOVE

And this I pray, that your love may abound still more and more in real knowledge and all discernment, (1:9)

Anyone who is in the least familiar with the New Testament knows that love—of God for men and of men for God and for each other—is at the very heart of biblical Christianity. The God of Scripture not only loves but *is* love (1 John 4:8, 16). "Love is from God; and everyone who loves is born of God and knows God. . . . and the one who abides in love abides in God, and God abides in him" (1 John 4:7, 16). God loves fallen humanity so much that "He gave His only begotten Son, that whoever believes in Him shall not perish, but have eternal life" (John 3:16). Love is an absolute and pervasive attribute of God's essential nature and a critical reality in the gospel of Jesus Christ.

No one understood the importance of love better than the apostle Paul. Because he loved the Philippian believers, he continually prayed for them. As with all those under his care, the apostle's constant concern for these saints was for their spiritual growth, for which growth in love was essential. He expressed that same concern for growth to the Galatians: "My children, with whom I am again in labor until Christ is formed in you" (Gal. 4:19). The responsibility of apostles, prophets, evangelists, and pastor-teachers is

> the equipping of the saints for the work of service, to the building up of the body of Christ; until we all attain to the unity of the faith, and of the knowledge of the Son of God, to a mature man, to the measure of the stature which belongs to the fullness of Christ. . . . [And] speaking the truth in love, we are to grow up in all aspects into Him who is the head, even Christ" (Eph. 4:12–13, 15).

The Greek word *agapē* (**love**) is used so uniquely in the New Testament that ancient Greek literature, even the Septuagint (the Greek translation of the Old Testament), sheds little light on its meaning in the New Testament. In both Testaments, however, **love** is the virtue that surpasses all others; indeed, it is the prerequisite for all the others. When a Pharisee asked Jesus, "Teacher, which is the great commandment in the Law?" He replied by quoting Deuteronomy 6:5 and Leviticus 19:18. "'You shall love the Lord your God with all your heart, and with all your soul, and with all your mind.' This is the great and foremost commandment. The second is like it, 'You shall love your neighbor as yourself.' On these two commandments depend the whole Law and the Prophets" (Matt. 22:36–40).

Paul also speaks of love in the opening sections of several other letters. Writing to the churches at Ephesus, Colossae, and Thessalonica, he commends believers for their love for each other and for fellow believers everywhere (Eph. 1:15; Col. 1:4; 1 Thess. 1:3; 2 Thess. 1:3). Later in Colossians he speaks of love as "the perfect bond of unity" (3:14). In 1 Corinthians, he elevates love above hope and even faith (1 Cor. 13:13). A few verses earlier he declares that love actually encompasses the other two, because love "believes all things [and] hopes all things" (v. 7). In fact, apart from genuine godly love, every other virtue and activity, no matter how seemingly biblical and sincere, amounts to nothing (vv. 1–3).

In the present verse, Paul mentions or implies at least five distinct but interrelated characteristics of Christian *agapē* **love.** This love is divine, de facto, decisive, dynamic, and discerning.

First, as the statement **And this I pray** implies, the **love** Paul wrote about is divine in its nature and in its origin. Paul petitioned God to provide the Philippians with more of the love that comes only from Him. He clearly agreed with his fellow apostle John that "love is from God; and everyone who loves is born of God and knows God. The one who does not love does not know God, for God is love. . . . In this is love, not that we loved God, but that He loved us and sent His Son to be the propitiation for our sins. . . . We love, because He first loved us" (1 John 4:7–8, 10, 19).

Godly **love** is produced only by the working of the Holy Spirit in the hearts of those who belong to Him. "The love of God has been poured out within our hearts through the Holy Spirit who was given to us" (Rom. 5:5). It is the first and foremost of the fruit of the Spirit (Gal. 5:22–23). Believers are taught by God Himself to love. "Now as to the love of the brethren," Paul explained, "you have no need for anyone to write to you, for you yourselves are taught by God to love one another; for indeed you do practice it toward all the brethren who are in all Macedonia. But we urge you, brethren, to excel still more" (1 Thess. 4:9–10).

Like God's general love for mankind (John 3:16–17) and His electing love for believers (John 17:23; 1 John 4:16), biblical **love** is a choice. It is based solely on the intent of the one who loves, not on any merit of those who receive it. The only exception, of course, is the believer's **love** for God, who is uniquely and supremely deserving.

Illustrating biblical **love** in the Sermon on the Mount Jesus declared,

> You have heard that it was said, 'You shall love your neighbor and hate your enemy.' But I say to you, love your enemies and pray for those who persecute you, so that you may be sons of your Father who is in heaven; for He causes His sun to rise on the evil and the good, and sends rain on the righteous and the unrighteous. For if you love those who love you, what reward do you have? Do not even the tax collectors do the same? (Matt. 5:43–46)

It is therefore clear that *agapē* **love** is not based on emotional or sentimental, much less physical, attraction. That is not to say that Christian love is without feeling or sentiment. It is inevitable that believers' love for others, even those who do not love in return, will produce an emotional attachment (cf. Rom. 9:1–4; 10:1). Paul's love for fellow believers, especially those like the Philippians, who loved and cared for him so much, was profoundly emotional. But that emotional attraction was not the basis of his love for them. On a volitional level, he also loved the immature, bickering, and ungrateful believers in Corinth.

Second, this **love** is what might be called de facto. The Philippians were already showing love for Paul and each other. That is why the apostle could say he wanted their **love** to **abound still more.** Scripture reveals that all genuine Christians possess godly love, because the Holy Spirit places it in their hearts (cf. Rom. 5:5; Gal. 5:22; 1 Thess. 4:9–10; 1 John 4:7–8).

Love of fellow Christians is a sure mark of saving faith. "By this all men will know that you are My disciples," Jesus said, "if you have love for one another" (John 13:35). Expanding on that truth, John later wrote: "We know that we have passed out of death into life, because we love the brethren. He who does not love abides in death. . . . If someone says, 'I love God,' and hates his brother, he is a liar; for the one who does not love his brother whom he has seen, cannot love God whom he has not seen" (1 John 3:14; 4:20).

Third, genuine **love** is decisive. As mentioned above, it is a love not based on feelings, but is rather a conscious, intentional choice to show kindness and generosity. In obedience to the Lord's command, believers willingly choose to express the love He has placed within them. They do so whether others are lovable or not, and whether they respond or not. Believers unselfishly love others because that is the way

God loves and because that is how He commands them to love. By obeying the Lord's command to "love one another, even as I have loved you" (John 13:34), believers become "imitators of God, as beloved children" (Eph. 5:1).

Jesus gave that command in the Upper Room, not long after He had washed the disciples' feet, a menial and unpleasant task normally performed only by servants. The Lord went on to explain:

> You call Me Teacher and Lord; and you are right, for so I am. If I then, the Lord and the Teacher, washed your feet, you also ought to wash one another's feet. For I gave you an example that you also should do as I did to you. Truly, truly, I say to you, a slave is not greater than his master, nor is one who is sent greater than the one who sent him. (John 13:13–16)

Jesus also illustrated this volitional, decisive, and sacrificial **love** in the parable of the Good Samaritan (Luke 10:30–35). The Samaritan helped the stranger who was beaten and robbed because the man needed help, not for his own self-satisfaction, self-fulfillment, or feeling of enhanced self-worth. To love our neighbor as ourselves is to do all we can to meet our neighbor's needs in the same way and to the same extent that we would want our own needs to be met under similar circumstances. It is to apply the Golden Rule: "In everything, therefore, treat people the same way you want them to treat you, for this is the Law and the Prophets" (Matt. 7:12).

Again Jesus is the supreme example of sacrificial love. In John 15:12–13 He declared: "This is My commandment, that you love one another, just as I have loved you. Greater love has no one than this, that one lay down his life for his friends." "Therefore be imitators of God, as beloved children," Paul wrote; "and walk in love, just as Christ also loved you and gave Himself up for us, an offering and a sacrifice to God as a fragrant aroma" (Eph. 5:1–2). Husbands are specifically commanded to "love [their] wives, just as Christ also loved the church and gave Himself up for her" (v. 25).

Paul gives perhaps the richest summary of godly love later in Philippians:

> Therefore if there is any encouragement in Christ, if there is any consolation of love, if there is any fellowship of the Spirit, if any affection and compassion, make my joy complete by being of the same mind, maintaining the same love, united in spirit, intent on one purpose. Do nothing from selfishness or empty conceit, but with humility of mind regard one another as more important than yourselves; do not merely look out for your own personal interests, but also for the interests of others. Have this attitude in yourselves which was also in Christ Jesus,

who, although He existed in the form of God, did not regard equality with God a thing to be grasped, but emptied Himself, taking the form of a bond-servant, and being made in the likeness of men. Being found in appearance as a man, He humbled Himself by becoming obedient to the point of death, even death on a cross. (2:1–8)

That kind of willful, humble, self-giving love is much needed in the church today, which is all too often influenced by the world's corrupted concept of love. People care little about beneficent, selfless love (not to mention godly love); the world's concept of love is one that plays on self-interest, even when promoting causes that are meant to help others. Tragically, even in the church people are sometimes asked to give to the Lord's work because doing so will make them feel good about themselves.

Fourth, godly **love** is dynamic. It has the capability to **abound. Love** is not mere emotion or feeling, and as it grows it always finds increasing expression in a righteous character and humble service. **Abound** is from *perisseuō*, which has the basic idea of overflowing in great abundance. In this verse, the present tense indicates a continual progress. Love is to grow and **abound** throughout the life of a believer. Jesus used the verb in the parable of the sower, explaining that "to you it has been granted to know the mysteries of the kingdom of heaven, but to them it has not been granted. For whoever has, to him more shall be given, and he will have an abundance; but whoever does not have, even what he has shall be taken away from him" (Matt. 13:11–12).

Because of its divine nature, this dynamic **love** energizes the fulfilling of divine law. Jesus declared that fulfilling the two supreme commandments to love God and men is the foundation of the whole Law and the Prophets (Matt. 22:37–40). In similar words, Paul said, "He who loves his neighbor has fulfilled the law. For this, 'You shall not commit adultery, you shall not murder, you shall not steal, you shall not covet,' and if there is any other commandment, it is summed up in this saying, 'You shall love your neighbor as yourself.' Love does no wrong to a neighbor; therefore love is the fulfillment of the law" (Rom. 13:8–10).

The second law of thermodynamics states that all matter and energy in the universe are in a constant state of entropy, a process of continual degradation and deterioration. That law of physics has a counterpart in the Christian life. There is a residual and destructive principle of spiritual entropy that pressures God's people to slip backwards. To avoid doing so, believers must diligently study and obey His Word, come before Him in prayer, and trust in His continuing grace and power to make them grow and **abound** in love.

Paul described his own struggle with that residual principle in Romans 7:21–25:

I find then the principle that evil is present in me, the one who wants to do good. For I joyfully concur with the law of God in the inner man, but I see a different law in the members of my body, waging war against the law of my mind and making me a prisoner of the law of sin which is in my members. Wretched man that I am! Who will set me free from the body of this death? Thanks be to God through Jesus Christ our Lord! So then, on the one hand I myself with my mind am serving the law of God, but on the other, with my flesh the law of sin.

In Ephesians he called this continuing propensity to sin "the old self, which is being corrupted in accordance with the lusts of deceit" (Eph. 4:22; cf. Col. 3:9). For that reason the apostle reminded the church at Corinth that only "God is able to make all grace abound to you, so that always having all sufficiency in everything, you may have an abundance for every good deed" (2 Cor. 9:8). It is also for that reason that he prayed for the Thessalonians that "the Lord [may] cause you to increase and abound in love for one another, and for all people, just as we also do for you" (1 Thess. 3:12; cf. 1 John 3:11).

The dynamic of godly love also abounds **in real knowledge,** namely, the true and infallible knowledge expressed in God's Word. Any love that is not grounded and growing in the truth and standards of Scripture falls short of genuine biblical love. **Real knowledge** is much more than mere factual information about God's Word, or even the acknowledgment of it as true and infallible. **Real knowledge** produces holiness through sincere devotion and obedience to the infallible Scriptures. It was because the faithful believers in Rome lived righteously that Paul could say to them: "And concerning you, my brethren, I myself also am convinced that you yourselves are full of goodness, filled with all knowledge and able also to admonish one another" (Rom. 15:14). Virtue is inseparably linked to the **real** (true) **knowledge** of God's truth. "For the fruit of the Light consists in all goodness and righteousness and truth [knowledge]" (Eph. 5:9). Likewise, Peter declares: "Since you have in obedience to the truth purified your souls for a sincere love of the brethren, fervently love one another from the heart" (1 Peter 1:22). "Fervently" is from *ektenōs,* which carries the basic idea of stretching, straining, or going to the limit, and figuratively speaks of great sincerity, earnestness, and fervor. Obedience to God's Word, the only source of **real knowledge,** purifies the soul and enables one to love to the limit.

Biblical love involves obedience to the Word. "If you love Me," Jesus said, "you will keep My commandments. . . . He who has My commandments and keeps them is the one who loves Me. . . . If anyone loves Me, he will keep My word; and My Father will love him, and We will come to him and make Our abode with him. . . . If you keep My commandments, you will abide in My love; just as I have kept My Father's commandments and abide in His love" (John 14:15, 21, 23; 15:10; cf. 1 John 3:24).

No impulse or feeling that leads one to disobey Scripture can be approved and blessed by God. Such "love" not only does not reflect godly love but also is the antithesis and enemy of it. For example, people who try to justify an immoral affair by claiming the Lord led them to fall in love with the other person repudiate God's Word. Scripture clearly condemns all sexual immorality without exception, including that of romantic attraction.

Fifth, godly love is discerning. It not only abounds in the life of one who has a true and accurate knowledge of God's Word but also does so in **all discernment.** *Aisthēsis* (**discernment**) is the source of the English word "aesthetic." But the meaning of *aisthēsis* is almost the opposite of "aesthetic," which largely has to do with personal taste and preference. Paul calls believers to put aside personal tastes and preferences and to focus rather on achieving mature insight and understanding. *Aisthēsis* appears only here in the New Testament and refers to a high level of biblical, theological, moral, and spiritual perception. It also implies the right application of that knowledge. In other words, **discernment** is the understanding and appreciation of the **real knowledge** of God's revelation that produces holy living. Unlike the way that worldly love is often characterized, biblical love is far from blind. On the contrary, it is wise and judicious. It understands "the mind of Christ" (1 Cor. 2:16), has knowledge, and makes wise assessments, which provide clear directives for holy living. It is a biblically knowledgeable and discriminating love that is under the control of a Spirit-controlled mind and heart. It is the kind of love that can fulfill Paul's admonition to the Thessalonians: "Examine everything carefully; hold fast to that which is good; abstain from every form of evil" (1 Thess. 5:21–22).

EXCELLENCE

so that you may approve the things that are excellent, (1:10a)

Having laid down the priority of love in verse 9, Paul continues his discussion of the elements of spiritual growth by looking at the second essential, excellence. The phrase **so that** indicates that the first essential is the foundation of the second. The progression is from love, which incorporates knowledge of God's truth and spiritual discernment, to excellence, that is, to thinking and living biblically. When a believer is dominated and controlled by the love of God, there will be a corresponding desire to live according to His will as fully and faithfully as possible. That desire is based in part on a sense of duty. Scripture commands believers "to be perfect, as [their] heavenly Father is perfect" (Matt. 5:48). Therefore believers can never completely fulfill their duty to God or to others. After telling a story about a slave obeying his human master, Jesus concluded by saying, "So you too, when you do all the things which are commanded you, say, 'We are unworthy slaves; we have done only that which we ought to have done'" (Luke 17:10). His point was that, if duty to a human master can never be exceeded, how much less can believers' duty to God?

But having a genuine, deep love for God—and, even more so, knowing and experiencing His love for them—raises believers' motive for obeying Him far above that of merely fulfilling a duty. Obedience motivated by love for God not only becomes believers' supreme objective but also their supreme pleasure and satisfaction.

Approve is from *dokimazō,* a commonly used New Testament verb that is variously rendered "allow, examine, prove," and even "discern." In classical Greek it was used of assaying metals to determine purity and of testing coins both for the purity of their metals and for their genuineness. In Luke 12:56 the word is translated "analyze" and is used in reference to predicting the weather: "You hypocrites!" Jesus said to a multitude who had come out to hear Him. "You know how to analyze the appearance of the earth and the sky, but why do you not analyze this present time?" A short while later, in telling a parable of the kingdom while dining with a group of leading Pharisees, He spoke of a man who excused himself from attending a dinner given by a wealthy man because he had "bought five yoke of oxen, and [was] going to try them out" (Luke 14:19). **Approve** means much more than simple acknowledgment or agreement that something is right or true. Paul's appeal is for believers to study, investigate, and determine the best possible ways to obey and please the Lord, and then to live accordingly.

As noted above, *dokimazō* (**approve**) can mean "to discern," which continues the call to discernment at the end of verse 9. The *New International Version* reading, "able to discern what is best" is helpful. To **approve the things that are excellent** is to assess, determine, and carefully identify whatever is the best, the most important, the most crucial. It is much like Paul's later injunction: "Finally, brethren, whatever is true, whatever is honorable, whatever is right, whatever is pure, whatever is lovely, whatever is of good repute, if there is any excellence and if anything worthy of praise, dwell on these things" (4:8). The **excellent** things are all the truths, attitudes, thoughts, words, and deeds that are expressions of God's will for the believer. They are the elements of sanctified, holy thinking and living.

Paul is not speaking of distinguishing good from evil, which only requires a basic knowledge of God's Word. Even the devil and his demons know what is good and evil, right and wrong, true and false. They know very well, for example, that there is only one God (James 2:19); and, early in His ministry, they knew (and even confessed) that Jesus was the Son of God (Luke 4:41; cf. vv. 3, 9). The idea here is rather the desire and ability to rightly discover **the things that are excellent,** so that believers can live their lives at the highest level of spiritual devotion and obedience. That ability separates the fully committed believer from the less committed, the mature from the immature, the strong in faith from the weak, and the effective servant of the Lord from the ineffective. Christians who live at the noblest level of devotion to God and His will are single-minded. They are highly focused and do not become preoccupied by the countless distractions that inevitably come their way.

Tragically, many Christians are easily led from one thing to another, bouncing from one commitment or interest to another. They wander about, continually reacting to whatever circumstance comes their way or to whatever idea comes into their minds. Consequently, like young children, they are "tossed here and there by waves and carried about by every wind of doctrine, by the trickery of men, by craftiness in deceitful scheming" (Eph. 4:14). Even when they attempt things that are good and biblically correct, their lack of discernment and persistence prevents the work from being truly effective. Worse than that, their immaturity prevents them from finding and pursuing the things that are most important, most vital, and most necessary to the kingdom, **the things that are excellent.** Throughout the history of the church, from Paul's day to the present, discerning Christians have been in short supply. Even the loving and faithful Philippians needed constant encouragement to pursue the most **excellent** spiritual objectives. Even those who are devoted to the pursuit of excellence are in constant danger of losing it by allowing their passion for the Lord to grow cold, as did the church at Ephesus (Rev. 2:4).

Approving **the things that are excellent** involves the mind; it is built on the "real knowledge and all discernment" (v. 9) produced in the mind by the diligent acquisition of the truths of Scripture. When Paul wrote, "We have the mind of Christ" (1 Cor. 2:16), he was referring to divine revelation, to Scripture, where the mind of Christ is revealed. Believers possess the Bible, but most Christians do not know the deep things of God, and do not think with the mind of Christ, which is to have the divine perspective on everything.

The discerning Christian cannot be a victim of his emotions and personal impulses if he is to successfully pursue and achieve spiritual excellence. Paul admonished the believers in Rome, "Do not be conformed to this world, but be transformed by the renewing of your mind, so that you may prove what the will of God is, that which is good and acceptable and perfect" (Rom. 12:2). Paul's call to renew the mind signifies that growing in grace is a continual process. Because Paul had achieved such excellence, he could justifiably put himself forward as a model: "The things you have learned and received and heard and seen in me, practice these things, and the God of peace will be with you" (Phil. 4:9).

Paul reminded the Colossians, "We proclaim Him [Christ], admonishing every man and teaching every man with all wisdom, so that we may present every man complete in Christ" (Col. 1:28). He exhorted the Ephesians to "walk as children of Light (for the fruit of the Light consists in all goodness and righteousness and truth), trying to learn what is pleasing to the Lord" (Eph. 5:8–10), and those in Thessalonica to "examine everything carefully; hold fast to that which is good" (1 Thess. 5:21). John had the same objective in mind when he wrote, "Beloved, do not believe every spirit, but test the spirits to see whether they are from God, because many false prophets have gone out into the world. By this you know the Spirit of God: every spirit that confesses that Jesus Christ has come in the flesh is from God" (1 John 4:1–2). Also echoing that cardinal objective, Peter admonished believers to "grow in the grace and knowledge of our Lord and Savior Jesus Christ" (2 Peter 3:18). The Lord commended the church at Ephesus for putting "to the test those who call themselves apostles, and they are not, and you found them to be false" (Rev. 2:2).

When John Wesley went away to Oxford, his godly mother, Susanna, wisely wrote in one of her many letters to him: "Whatever weakens your reason, impairs the tenderness of your conscience, obscures your sense of God, or takes off the delight for spiritual things, whatever increases the authority of your body over your mind, that thing is sin."

Christian character at its highest level comes from a divinely implanted and ever-growing love. That both leads to, and is directed by, a rich understanding of and faithful obedience to the divine truth revealed in Scripture.

INTEGRITY

in order to be sincere and blameless until the day of Christ; (1:10b)

A third essential for growth in godliness is personal and relational integrity. Like the phrase "so that" at the beginning of verse 10, the phrase **in order to be** signifies a continued progression. Spiritual integrity builds on spiritual excellence just as spiritual excellence builds on godly love. To have such integrity is to **be sincere and blameless until the day of Christ.**

The adjective *eilikrinēs* (**sincere**) has two possible meanings.

One possible root of that adjective conveys the idea of sifting, as of grain passing through a sieve to remove impurities. If that is the correct etymology, the meaning here is that of being separated *to* what is true and *from* what is false, *to* what is right and *from* what is wrong. But derivation from the other root seems more appropriate, because it carries the idea of testing something by sunlight. That is more consistent with Paul's previous emphasis on approving. That meaning also is consistent with the Latin word from which the English **sincere** is derived. In ancient Rome fine pottery was relatively thin and fragile and often developed cracks while being fired. Unscrupulous shops would fill the cracks with a hard, dark wax, which would be concealed when the object was painted or glazed but would melt when the pottery was filled with something hot. In ordinary light, the deception was usually undetectable, but when held up to the sunlight it was clearly exposed, because the wax appeared darker. Reputable dealers would often stamp their products *sine cera* ("without wax") as a guarantee of high quality.

Just as such pottery was held up to the sunlight to reveal cracks or other defects, the obedient, faithful believer makes sure to expose his life to the sunlight of Scripture. As the writer of Hebrews declared, "The word of God is living and active and sharper than any two-edged sword, and piercing as far as the division of soul and spirit, of both joints and marrow, and able to judge the thoughts and intentions of the heart" (Heb. 4:12). Unfortunately, many people try to cover their faults in various ways in order to appear less spiritually flawed than they really are. They use such things as regular church attendance, generous giving, activity in church functions, and spiritual talk to give the appearance of spiritual integrity. But when they are severely tempted or persecuted for their faith, the cracks show.

Because children are fallen sinners (Ps. 51:5), their parents are not wholly responsible for their behavior, even when they are small. But parents' spiritual and moral integrity, or lack of it, always has a profound influence on their children. Sometimes children in the most godly homes rebel against the Lord. More often than not, however, an errant child rebels because of the hypocrisy of his parents, knowing that the faith they profess—regardless of how genuine and sincere it may appear to others in the church and community—is not manifested in their private lives. Although that does not excuse the sins of such children, it does make their parents share in the guilt.

Except for unbelief, Jesus condemned no sin more than hypocrisy, in particular that of the outwardly religious, but self-righteous, scribes and Pharisees (cf. Matt. 7:5; 15:7; Luke 12:56; 13:15). Paul also hated insincerity and deception, admonishing, "Let love be without hypocrisy. Abhor what is evil; cling to what is good" (Rom. 12:9). The apostle could honestly testify to his own integrity, claiming that "we are not like many, peddling the word of God, but as from sincerity, but as from God, we speak in Christ in the sight of God" (2 Cor. 2:17).

Eilikrinēs also carries the ideas of cohesiveness, oneness, and unity. In a **sincere** Christian life, everything fits together and works together. Nothing in it is unrelated to the foundation of saving faith and holy living. The practical, everyday aspects of life are in complete harmony with such obviously spiritual disciplines as Bible reading, prayer, worship, theology, morality, and doing good works. Living the **sincere** life, the life of integrity, is like baking bread. It is not enough merely to pour all the right ingredients together in a pan, stick it in the oven, and hope to produce bread. All the ingredients must first be properly mixed, so that every ingredient touches every other ingredient to form a common, cohesive, single whole.

Spiritual integrity also involves relationships with others. In 2 Corinthians, Paul affirmed that "in holiness and godly sincerity, not in fleshly wisdom but in the grace of God, we have conducted ourselves in the world, and especially toward you" (2 Cor. 1:12; cf. Acts 24:16). He had previously counseled believers there to "give no offense either to Jews or to Greeks or to the church of God" (1 Cor. 10:32), and would entreat those in Rome "not [to] judge one another anymore, but rather determine this—not to put an obstacle or a stumbling block in a brother's way" (Rom. 14:13). The mature Christian determines not only to avoid sin in his own life but also to make sure that he says or does nothing that might cause another believer to stumble. Anything that harms even one of God's children causes harm to the church, which is the body of Christ. An offense against a fellow believer is therefore an offense against the Lord. In one of His most severe warnings, Jesus said, "Whoever causes one of these little ones who believe in Me to stumble, it would be better for him to have a heavy millstone hung around his neck, and to be drowned in the depth of the sea" (Matt. 18:6).

To have integrity is also to stand against the world. James made it clear that "pure and undefiled religion in the sight of our God and Father is this: to visit orphans and widows in their distress, and to keep oneself unstained by the world" (James 1:27). John warned, "Do not love the world nor the things in the world. If anyone loves the world, the love of the Father is not in him" (1 John 2:15). And Paul pleaded: "Do not be conformed to this world, but be transformed by the renewing of your mind, so that you may prove what the will of God is, that which is good and acceptable and perfect" (Rom. 12:2).

Blameless (*aproskopos*) expresses the extent and goal of integrity. It means "without stumbling, or offense," and has both the idea of not falling into sinful conduct and of not causing others to fall into iniquity. To be **blameless** is to move forward in one's life without moral failure.

This is not a call to the perfection in holiness that is true only of God and of saints in eternal glory, since Paul exhorted the Corinthians to: "Give no offense [*aproskopos*] either to Jews or to Greeks or to the church of God" (1 Cor. 10:32). It calls believers to do all they can to give glory to God and to live honorably before Him and others. Believers are to live lives of integrity as did Paul (cf. Acts 23:1; 24:16; 2 Cor. 1:12; 2 Tim. 1:3).

Falling into sin usually happens in stages. First, a believer merely tolerates something he knows is sinful, perhaps criticizing it but taking no strong stand against it. Next, he accommodates it, a little at a time, each time becoming less concerned about its wickedness, until it ceases to become an issue. Next, he attempts to legitimize it, by making excuses for it and defending it. Finally, and inevitably, he begins to participate in it, embracing it as part of his normal lifestyle. Worldly values and standards become so mixed with biblical ones that the difference is no longer noticed or cared about. In his famous *An Essay on Man*, Alexander Pope beautifully, but soberly, expressed that tragic pattern:

> Vice is a monster of so frightful mien,
> As to be hated needs but to be seen;
> Yet seen too oft, familiar with her face,
> We first endure, then pity, then embrace.

Satan seldom attacks believers head-on. Beginning with his first evil work in the Garden of Eden, he has used subtlety and deception to lead God's people astray (Gen. 3:1; Rev. 12:9). "He was a murderer from the beginning," Jesus said, "and does not stand in the truth because there is no truth in him. Whenever he speaks a lie, he speaks from his own nature, for he is a liar and the father of lies" (John 8:44). Because of that, believers who pursue excellence not only must know God's Word but also continually grow in understanding and application of it through the Holy Spirit. Every idea, every concept, every practice must be held up to Scripture's divine light, by which they are to be judged.

Godly love, excellence, and integrity are not optional. They are obligatory and permanent—**until the day of Christ,** when He returns to take His people to Himself (v. 6). It is that future time when "we must all appear before the judgment seat of Christ, so that each one may be recompensed for his deeds in the body, according to what he has done, whether good or bad" (2 Cor. 5:10), and where "each man's work will become evident; for the day will show it because it is to be revealed with fire, and the fire itself will test the quality of each man's work" (1 Cor. 3:13). "Therefore do not go on passing judgment before the time," Paul warned, "but wait until the Lord comes who will both bring to light the things hidden in the darkness and disclose the motives of men's hearts;

and then each man's praise will come to him from God" (1 Cor. 4:5). The truth will be revealed about us on that day.

GOOD WORKS

having been filled with the fruit of righteousness which comes through Jesus Christ, (1:11*a*)

The fourth essential for growth in godliness is good works, which Paul here refers to as **the fruit of righteousness.** The progression continues. Godly love produces spiritual excellence, which produces integrity, which produces good works.

Having been filled translates a perfect passive participle in the Greek text, referring to something that happened in the past and has continuing results. In other words, when believers stand before the Lord at the judgment seat, they already will have been **filled with the fruit of righteousness.** That refers to a divinely completed state, or condition, of **righteousness** that is based on the love, excellence, and integrity Paul has just explained.

The fruit of righteousness is an Old Testament idea, which the writer of Proverbs speaks of as "a tree of life" (Prov. 11:30). The prophet Amos accused his people of turning "justice into poison and the fruit of righteousness into wormwood" (Amos 6:12). In the New Testament, James refered to the concept in regard to the good works that are produced by God's righteousness in a believer's life. "The seed whose fruit is righteousness," he explained, "is sown in peace by those who make peace" (James 3:18).

The spiritual fruit that the Lord produces in believers includes winning the unsaved to Christ. In Romans 1:13 Paul said, "I do not want you to be unaware, brethren, that often I have planned to come to you (and have been prevented so far) so that I may obtain some fruit among you also, even as among the rest of the Gentiles." He emphasized the same truth in Colossians, explaining that "the word of truth, the gospel which has come to you, just as in all the world also . . . is constantly bearing fruit and increasing" (Col. 1:5–6).

Spiritual fruit also includes good works, which is what Paul has in mind in the present text. Such good works always begin with godly attitudes, some of which Paul enumerates in his letter to the churches of Galatia: "The fruit of the Spirit is love, joy, peace, patience, kindness, goodness, faithfulness, gentleness, self-control" (Gal. 5:22–23). These divinely bestowed attitudes are designed to produce divinely empowered good works. Paul spoke of the fruit of good works when he told the believers in Corinth that "He who supplies seed to the sower and bread for food will supply and multiply your seed for sowing and increase the harvest [fruit] of your righteousness" (2 Cor. 9:10; cf. Eph. 5:9). As with every other righteous thing the believer possesses, **the fruit of righteousness . . . comes through Jesus Christ.** It cannot be humanly generated.

It is God's purpose to produce such good works in all believers because "we are His workmanship, created in Christ Jesus for good works, which God prepared beforehand so that we would walk in them" (Eph. 2:10). Jesus made that truth especially clear in the Upper Room Discourse: "Abide in Me, and I in you. As the branch cannot bear fruit of itself unless it abides in the vine, so neither can you unless you abide in Me. I am the vine, you are the branches; he who abides in Me and I in him, he bears much fruit, for apart from Me you can do nothing" (John 15:4–5).

THE GLORY OF GOD

to the glory and praise of God. (1:11*b*)

The fifth essential for growth in godliness that Paul mentions is by far the most important: **the glory and praise of God.**

Jesus said, "My Father is glorified by this, that you bear much fruit, and so prove to be My disciples" (John 15:8). God makes believers fruitful for the sake of His **glory.** Paul therefore commanded: "Whether, then, you eat or drink or whatever you do, do all to the glory of God" (1 Cor. 10:31), and in another letter explains that "we have obtained an inheritance, . . . to the end that we who were the first to hope in Christ would be to the praise of His glory. In Him, you also . . . were sealed in Him with the Holy Spirit of promise, . . . to the praise of His glory" (Eph. 1:11–14). In the middle of that letter, as if overwhelmed by the wondrous truths he had just spoken of, he exulted: "Now to Him who is able to do far more abundantly beyond all that we ask or think, according to the power that works within us, to Him be the glory in the church and in Christ Jesus to all generations forever and ever. Amen" (Eph. 3:20–21).

The supreme objective and result of the life of godly love, excellence, integrity, and good works is to manifest **the glory and praise of God.** His **glory** is the sum of all His perfection and the honor for being who He is and doing what He has done, and His **praise** is the affirmation of that glory by those who recognize it.

The Joy of Ministry— Part 1: In Spite of Trouble and Detractors (Philippians 1:12–18)

4

Now I want you to know, brethren, that my circumstances have turned out for the greater progress of the gospel, so that my imprisonment in the cause of Christ has become well known throughout the whole praetorian guard and to everyone else, and that most of the brethren, trusting in the Lord because of my imprisonment, have far more courage to speak the word of God without fear. Some, to be sure, are preaching Christ even from envy and strife, but some also from good will; the latter do it out of love, knowing that I am appointed for the defense of the gospel; the former proclaim Christ out of selfish ambition rather than from pure motives, thinking to cause me distress in my imprisonment. What then? Only that in every way, whether in pretense or in truth, Christ is proclaimed; and in this I rejoice. Yes, and I will rejoice, (1:12–18)

One of the surest measures of a Christian's spiritual maturity is what it takes to rob him of his Spirit-bestowed joy. Paul's maturity is evident in the present text as he makes it clear that difficult, unpleasant, painful, even life-threatening circumstances did not rob him of joy but rather caused it to increase.

Although it is a gift from God to every believer and administered by the Holy Spirit (Gal. 5:22), joy is not always constant and full (cf. 1 John 1:4). The only certain cause for loss of joy in a believer's life is sin, which corrupts his fellowship with the Lord, who is the source of joy. Such sinful attitudes as dissatisfaction, bitterness, sullenness, doubt, fear, and negativism cause joy to be forfeited. Consequently, the only way to restore lost joy is to repent and return to proper worship of and obedience to God.

Anything other than sin—no matter how difficult, painful, or disappointing—need not take away the believer's joy. Yet even minor things can do so if believers react sinfully to them. A change for the worse in health, job, finances, personal relationships, or other important areas of life can easily cause believers to question the Lord, His sovereign wisdom, and His gracious provision. When that happens, joy is one of the first casualties. Believers are especially vulnerable when such things happen suddenly, taking them off guard. Their response is often one of anger, doubt, distrust, fear, self-pity, ingratitude, or complaining. In such cases, events that are not sinful in themselves lead to sinful responses that steal joy.

God's Word makes it clear that trouble in this life is certain to come (cf. Job 5:7; 14:1; Eccl. 2:23; John 16:33). Believers are not exempt from the common problems and difficulties all people face. They also face persecution for their faith from the hostile world system. "Remember the word that I said to you," Jesus said, "A slave is not greater than his master." If they persecuted Me, they will also persecute you" (John 15:20). A short while later He added: "In the world you have tribulation, but take courage; I have overcome the world" (John 16:33). To scattered Jewish Christians in the early church who were suffering great persecution, James wrote, "Consider it all joy, my brethren, when you encounter various trials, knowing that the testing of your faith produces endurance. And let endurance have its perfect result, that you may be perfect and complete, lacking in nothing" (James 1:2–4). But God can use even the most difficult trials for our good and for His glory.

No New Testament writer understood that truth better than Paul did. He was a larger-than-life model of a man of God whose joy never faltered. He resisted anything that threatened to come between him and his intimate fellowship with and trust in the Lord. Paul certainly experienced sorrow and tears, suffered grief and disappointment, and was troubled by sinful, weak, and contentious believers. Yet, there never seems to have been a time in his life as a believer when circumstances diminished his joy. In fact, it seems as if the worst affliction merely tightened his grip on salvation's joy (Phil. 4:4, 10–13).

By the time he wrote Philippians, Paul had experienced serious hardships of every sort. When he wrote this epistle, he was a prisoner in

Rome. He had long desired to preach in that great city, having only a few years earlier written to the church there:

> For God, whom I serve in my spirit in the preaching of the gospel of His Son, is my witness as to how unceasingly I make mention of you, always in my prayers making request, if perhaps now at last by the will of God I may succeed in coming to you. . . . I do not want you to be unaware, brethren, that often I have planned to come to you (and have been prevented so far) so that I may obtain some fruit among you also, even as among the rest of the Gentiles." (Rom. 1:9–10, 13; cf. v. 15)

The apostle was expressing more than a personal desire to minister in a new and challenging place. He was convinced of the importance of bringing the gospel to that citadel of paganism and using Rome as a springboard for further ministry (even to Spain, Rom. 15:24). It seems doubtful he had in mind ministering in Rome as a prisoner. Nor did he likely envision getting there only after enduring a tempestuous storm that resulted in a disastrous shipwreck (cf. Acts 21:33–28:31). But however he got there or whatever the circumstances after he arrived, Paul intensely wanted to preach the gospel there "by the will of God" (Rom. 1:10).

Although he was not writing this epistle from a dungeon but a private residence (Acts 28:16, 30), Paul was chained night and day to a Roman soldier. He had no privacy when he ate, when he slept, when he wrote, when he prayed, or when he preached, taught, or visited with friends (vv. 17–31). Yet for a period of two years this very lack of privacy made it impossible for the Roman soldiers guarding him to avoid hearing the gospel and witnessing Paul's remarkable Christlikeness. As the next verses suggest, this apparently led some of them to salvation (Phil. 1:13–14; cf. 4:22). Paul rejoiced because of the ministry to which the Lord had called him and because of the spiritual fruit that ministry produced, even while he was in chains.

Verses 12–26 of chapter one reveal four elements of Paul's joy in ministry. He was joyful in spite of trouble, as long as Christ's cause progressed (vv. 12–14); in spite of detractors, as long as Christ's name was proclaimed (vv. 15–18); in spite of death, as long as the Lord was glorified (vv. 19–21); and in spite of being in the flesh, as long as the church was benefited (vv. 22–26).

IN SPITE OF TROUBLE—AS LONG AS CHRIST'S CAUSE PROGRESSED

Now I want you to know, brethren, that my circumstances have turned out for the greater progress of the gospel, so that my

imprisonment in the cause of Christ has become well known throughout the whole praetorian guard and to everyone else, and that most of the brethren, trusting in the Lord because of my imprisonment, have far more courage to speak the word of God without fear. (1:12–14)

Now I want you to know translates a common Greek expression often found in ancient letters. Similar expressions—such as "I want you to get this" or "I want you to understand this"—are used today to call attention to an important point, especially one that might easily be missed, misunderstood, or hard to accept. Conversely, Paul often declared that he did not want his readers to be uninformed (cf. Rom. 1:13; 11:25; 1 Cor. 10:1; 12:1; 2 Cor. 1:8; 1 Thess. 4:13). In the present verse he wanted his beloved **brethren** to understand that he meant exactly what he said. Despite his circumstances, Paul was not bitter or discouraged but had great reason to rejoice.

My circumstances translates *ta kata eme*, which literally means "the things pertaining or relating to me." It is rendered "my circumstances" in Ephesians 6:21. In Colossians 4:7 it is translated "my affairs." Paul's **circumstances,** he explains, dire as they seem to be from a human perspective, **have turned out for the greater progress of the gospel.** He did not ignore or make light of his **imprisonment** (cf. 1:7, 14, 17; Col. 4:3, 18; Philem. 9, 13), but it was incidental to his willing, joyous, and immeasurably privileged status as a bondservant of Jesus Christ (1:1). *Mallon* (**greater**) is better translated "rather" (KJV), "actually" (NKJV), or "really" (NIV). Instead of hindering and restricting his ministry, Paul's difficult circumstances had done the very opposite (cf. 2 Cor. 12:9–10).

It was the **progress of the gospel** for which Paul lived so passionately. To the Ephesian elders he declared, "I do not consider my life of any account as dear to myself, so that I may finish my course and the ministry which I received from the Lord Jesus, to testify solemnly of the gospel of the grace of God" (Acts 20:24). Everything else in Paul's life had importance only to the degree that it affected **the progress of the gospel.**

Paul not only considered himself under obligation to the Lord, but also "both to Greeks and to barbarians, both to the wise and to the foolish.... For I am not ashamed of the gospel, for it is the power of God for salvation to everyone who believes, to the Jew first and also to the Greek" (Rom. 1:14, 16). So strong was that obligation that Paul declared himself to be "under compulsion; for woe is me," he said, "if I do not preach the gospel" (1 Cor. 9:16). "I do all things for the sake of the gospel," he explained a few verses later (v. 23). His ministry and his earthly life were inseparable. His earthly life would not be completed until his ministry was completed, and when his ministry was completed, his earthly life would have no further purpose (cf. Phil. 1:21–26; 2 Tim. 4:6–8).

Prokopē (**progress**) describes not merely moving ahead but doing so against obstacles. The related verb was used of an explorer or of an army advance team hacking a path through dense trees and under-brush, moving ahead slowly and with considerable effort. Resistance is therefore inherent to that sort of progress, and no one knew better than Paul how inevitable the resistance of Satan (1 Thess. 2:18) and the world (1 John 2:15–16) is to the **progress of the gospel.** Resistance by pagan Rome had placed him in his present two-year imprisonment, and resis-tance by unbelieving Jewish leaders had imprisoned him in Caesarea for two years before that (Acts 24:27). He explained to the Corinthians that, although "a wide door for effective service has opened to me, . . . there are many adversaries" (1 Cor. 16:9). To the Thessalonians he wrote: "After we had already suffered and been mistreated in Philippi, as you know, we had the boldness in our God to speak to you the gospel of God amid much opposition" (1 Thess. 2:2). He encouraged Timothy,

> Remember Jesus Christ, risen from the dead, descendant of David, according to my gospel, for which I suffer hardship even to imprison-ment as a criminal; but the word of God is not imprisoned. For this rea-son I endure all things for the sake of those who are chosen, so that they also may obtain the salvation which is in Christ Jesus and with it eternal glory" (2 Tim. 2:8–10).

Far from lamenting, resenting, or complaining about his hardships, Paul acknowledged them as an unavoidable element of ministry. In his own eyes, however, they were but a small cost that he was more than willing to pay, because God used those trials as a means for furthering **the progress of the gospel.**

John Bunyan's preaching was so popular and powerful, and so unacceptable to leaders in the seventeenth-century Church of England, that he was jailed in order to silence him. Refusing to be silent, he began to preach in the jail courtyard. He not only had a large audience of pris-oners, but also hundreds of the citizens of Bedford and the surrounding area would come to the prison daily and stand outside to hear him expound Scripture. He was silenced verbally by being placed deep inside the jail and forbidden to preach at all. Yet in that silence, he spoke loudest of all and to more people than he could have imagined. It was during that time that he wrote *The Pilgrim's Progress,* the great Christian classic that has ministered the gospel to tens of millions throughout the world. For several centuries, it was the most widely read and translated book in the world after the Bible. Bunyan's opponents were able to stop his preaching for a few years, but they were not able to stop his ministry. Instead, they provided opportunity for it to be extended from deep within a jail in the small town of Bedford to the ends of the earth.

Paul could say to his persecutors what Joseph said to his brothers after they sold him into slavery: "It was not you who sent me here, but God; and He has made me a father to Pharaoh and lord of all his household and ruler over all the land of Egypt.... As for you, you meant evil against me, but God meant it for good" (Gen. 45:8; 50:20). Countless numbers of God's saints have been able to echo that truth. Job could have expressed it to his "comforters," Esther to Haman, Jeremiah to the false prophets and rulers in Judah, and the apostle John to those who exiled him to Patmos. As always, the Lord can turn efforts to thwart His kingdom into means for advancing it.

God's supreme act of using men's and Satan's evil schemes to accomplish His purposes was, of course, His Son's work of redemption. By His death and resurrection, Jesus Christ conquered sin and death, defeated Satan, and provided redemption for all in every age who turn to Him in genuine saving faith.

Paul next focused on two important achievements of his ministry, first on the progress of the gospel outside the church (v. 13) and then on its progress within the church (v. 14). First, he rejoiced **that** his **imprisonment in the cause of Christ has become well known throughout the whole praetorian guard and to everyone else.** **Imprisonment** is from *desmon,* which literally refers to a bond, such as that made with a chain or rope. By extension, the term came to be used of any forced restriction or confinement, in particular that of a prisoner. Speaking to a group of Jewish leaders in Rome during the time he wrote Philippians, Paul mentioned "wearing this chain for the sake of the hope of Israel" (Acts 28:20), and in Ephesians he spoke of being "an ambassador in chains" (Eph. 6:20). Paul's "chains" (from *halusis*) were somewhat longer than a modern handcuff, about eighteen inches long. One end was attached to the prisoner's wrist, the other to the guard's. The chain was not removed from the prisoner as long as he was in custody, making both escape and privacy impossible. Although the apostle was allowed to live in private quarters (Acts 28:30), he was chained in that manner to a series of soldiers for a period of two years. Over those years, it is possible that several dozen different soldiers were assigned to guard Paul, each one becoming his captive audience. If they were not already aware of it, those soldiers soon came to realize that this amazing man was not imprisoned for committing a crime but for preaching the gospel. His faithfulness **in the cause of Christ** soon became **well known throughout the whole praetorian guard and to everyone else.** The faithful believers in the church at Rome had no doubt long prayed that the Lord would open a way to witness to the elite and influential **praetorian guard.** In His sovereign wisdom, He answered that prayer by making members of that **guard** captive to Paul for two years.

Praitōrion (**praetorian guard**) originally referred to an army commander's tent, then to the residence of high-ranking military officers, and still later to that of any wealthy or influential person. In the Gospels it is used of the Roman governor's residence in Jerusalem (cf. Matt. 27:27; Mark 15:16; John 18:28, 33; 19:9). In Acts 23:35 the governor's palace in Caesarea is called Herod's Praetorium.

Some commentators therefore take the reference in Philippians 1:13 to represent the barracks of the **praetorian guard.** But the following phrase (**and to everyone else**) indicates Paul was speaking of persons, not a place. The **praetorian guard** was originally composed of some ten thousand handpicked soldiers. It had been established by Caesar Augustus, who was emperor at the time of Jesus' birth (Luke 2:1). These men were dispersed strategically throughout the city of Rome to keep the general peace and especially to protect the emperor. Later emperors greatly increased their numbers, and Tiberius built them a conspicuous fortified camp to make sure they had a high-profile presence in Rome. Members of the **praetorian guard** served for twelve (later sixteen) years, after which they were granted the highest honors and privileges, including very generous severance pay. Eventually they became so powerful that they were considered "king-makers," who not only protected but also chose the emperors.

The results of Paul's stay in Rome were predictable. In addition to hearing his preaching and teaching, the soldiers also experienced firsthand his graciousness, his remarkable patience and perseverance in great affliction, his wisdom, his deep convictions, his genuineness, his humility, and his genuine love and concern for them. They were aware of the false accusations made against him in Caesarea and the personal risk he had taken by appealing to Caesar. Both his message and his character had a profound impact on those elite, hardened, and influential soldiers. How many of the **praetorian guard** became Christians is unknown, but those who did became evangelists. It was doubtless through those men that members of Caesar's own household were converted (4:22).

The news about Paul spread throughout the city of Rome (**to everyone else**), and for two years many visited him "in his own rented quarters, [where he] was welcoming all who came to him, preaching the kingdom of God and teaching concerning the Lord Jesus Christ with all openness, unhindered" (Acts 28:30–31). What to most people, including many Christians, would appear to have been an unmitigated disaster was an unequaled opportunity for **the progress of the gospel.**

F. B. Meyer comments:

> At times the hired room would be thronged with people, to whom the
> Apostle spoke words of life; and after they withdrew the sentry would
> sit beside him, filled with many questionings as to the meaning of the
> words which this strange prisoner spoke. At other times, when all had
> gone, and especially at night, when the moonlight shone on the distant
> slopes of Soracte, soldier and Apostle would be left to talk, and in those
> dark, lonely hours the Apostle would tell soldier after soldier the story
> of his own proud career in early life, of his opposition to Christ, and his
> ultimate conversion, and would make it clear that he was there as a
> prisoner, not for any crime, not because he had raised rebellion or
> revolt, but because he believed that Him whom the Roman soldiers
> had crucified, under Pilate, was the Son of God and the Saviour of men.
> As these tidings spread, and the soldiers talked them over with one
> another, the whole guard would become influenced in sympathy with
> the meek and gentle Apostle, who always showed himself so kindly to
> the men as they shared, however involuntarily, his imprisonment.
>
> How absolutely consistent the Apostle must have been! If there had been
> the least divergence, day or night, from the high standard which he
> upheld, his soldier-companion would have caught it, and passed it on to
> others. The fact that so many became earnest Christians, and that the
> Word of Jesus was known far and wide throughout the praetorian guard,
> indicates how absolutely consistent the Apostle's life was. (*The Epistle to
> the Philippians* [Grand Rapids: Baker, 1952], 36–37)

Paul's faithful perseverance not only was winning converts outside the church but also was strengthening and encouraging believers
within the church. The apostle's courage and faithfulness during his confinement caused **most** of his fellow **brethren,** both in Rome and
beyond, to be more **trusting in the Lord because of** his **imprisonment** and to **have far more courage to speak the word of God without fear.** His influence was pervasive and far-reaching. It was not merely
some believers, but **most of the brethren,** who were encouraged by his
imprisonment. Although influential and disruptive, those who criticized and slandered Paul (1:15, 17) were in the minority.

The implication is that, before his **imprisonment,** believers
were afraid, or at least reluctant, to openly share their faith. Hostility to
this new sect of Judaism, as it was commonly considered throughout the
empire, was growing. Not only were Jewish leaders intensifying their
opposition and persecution, but pagans also began to see Christianity as
a threat both to their religion and to their livelihood (Acts 19:23–41).

Paul's example gave his **brethren . . . far more courage to
speak the word of God without fear.** As they saw how God protected

him and blessed his ministry, despite persecution and imprisonment, their **courage** was renewed and their boldness and zeal intensified. His strength became their strength, as his example touched them. Through the Holy Spirit, the impact of that one faithful life revolutionized and energized the entire church. The apostle's fellow saints discovered that, like the cowardice they once experienced, **courage** is contagious.

Freedom to proclaim the gospel is understandably cherished today by Christians in the so-called free world. But many, if not most, of the great expansions of the faith and spiritual revivals within the church have come during times of opposition and persecution. Christianity was long outlawed in communist China and even today in much of that nation public expression of Christianity is still severely restricted. Yet by many responsible estimates, there are millions of Bible-believing Christians in that great country. By contrast, in most of the "free" Western world the influence, if not the size, of the evangelical church has been continually eroding.

Paul's circumstances were beyond most people's ability to comprehend. Yet he was a model of joy, contentment, and peace. Those inner qualities obviously were not based on his physical comfort, his possessions, his freedom, his self-satisfaction, or his reputation and prestige. They were based entirely on his trust in his gracious and sovereign Lord and his delight in the furtherance of the gospel.

IN SPITE OF DETRACTORS—
AS LONG AS CHRIST'S NAME WAS PROCLAIMED

Some, to be sure, are preaching Christ even from envy and strife, but some also from good will; the latter do it out of love, knowing that I am appointed for the defense of the gospel; the former proclaim Christ out of selfish ambition rather than from pure motives, thinking to cause me distress in my imprisonment. What then? Only that in every way, whether in pretense or in truth, Christ is proclaimed; and in this I rejoice. Yes, and I will rejoice, (1:15–18)

Like the Lord during His earthly ministry, Paul had more than his share of detractors, most of them from the Jewish and pagan religious establishments. The church soon came to have detractors within its own ranks who maligned their leaders, more often than not those who were the most godly and effective.

One of the most discouraging experiences for a servant of God is that of being falsely accused by fellow believers, especially coworkers in the church. To be maligned by an unbeliever is expected; to be maligned by another believer is unexpected. The pain runs very deep when one's ministry is slandered, misrepresented, and unjustly criticized by fellow preachers and teachers of the gospel. That is precisely the situation Paul faced in Rome, where **some** of the church leaders, in opposition to him, were **preaching Christ even from envy and strife.**

In the church at Corinth there were anti-Paul as well as pro-Paul factions in the congregation. "Now I mean this," he explained, "that each one of you is saying, 'I am of Paul,' and 'I of Apollos,' and 'I of Cephas,' and 'I of Christ'" (1 Cor. 1:12). Those who favored Apollos and Peter (Cephas, 1 Cor. 3:22) doubtless had reservations about Paul, as those who favored him probably had about the other two. The "Christ" faction apparently considered themselves the spiritual elite and the others as inferior.

Paul's detractors, who were **preaching Christ even from envy and strife,** were not heretics like the Judaizers, but were theologically orthodox. They preached and taught the true gospel of Jesus Christ. They were not heralding "a different gospel," as were some in Corinth and Galatia (2 Cor. 11:4; Gal. 1:6). Nor were they "false apostles, deceitful workers, disguising themselves as apostles of Christ" (2 Cor. 11:13) or part of "the false circumcision" mentioned later in the present letter (Phil. 3:2).

To be sure indicates a type of parenthesis, a brief departure from Paul's main theme of joy. "I realize full well," he was saying in essence, "that everything is not as it should be in the church. I am not naive about the motives of a few pastors and evangelists. I know they **are preaching Christ even from envy and strife.**" The problem was not in those preachers' theology but in their motives, not in what they preached but in why they preached it, namely, **from envy and strife.**

Phthonos (**envy**) is the desire to deprive others of what is rightfully theirs, to wish that they did not have it or had it to a lesser degree. It was "because of envy" that the Jewish multitude (Matt. 27:18) and the chief priests (Mark 15:10) handed Jesus over to Pilate for crucifixion. Among the many evil characteristics of "the ungodliness and unrighteousness of men who suppress the truth in unrighteousness" (Rom. 1:18) is **envy**—listed beside greed, murder, strife, deceit, malice, gossip, and other serious sins (Rom. 1:29; 13:13; 1 Cor. 1:11; 3:3; 2 Cor. 12:20; Gal. 5:19–21; 1 Tim. 6:4; Titus 3:9). Paul reminded Titus that "we also once were foolish ourselves, disobedient, deceived, enslaved to various lusts and pleasures, spending our life in malice and envy, hateful, hating one another" (Titus 3:3). But believers possess a new nature (2 Cor. 5:17) and are commanded by the Spirit's power to put "aside all malice and all deceit and hypocrisy and envy and all slander" (1 Peter 2:1). It goes without saying that Christians frequently fail to be obedient to the Word and submissive to the Spirit.

Envy, wishing others did not have what they have, is closely related to jealousy, which is wishing to have what someone else possesses. From the context, it seems likely that Paul's detractors were both envious and jealous of the apostle. They envied Paul's giftedness, his blessings, his intellect, his effectiveness in ministry, and, perhaps especially, his being highly respected and beloved in the church. They may even have envied his personal encounters with the resurrected and exalted Lord Jesus Christ (cf. Acts 9:1–6; 18:9–11; 22:17–18; 23:11). Consequently, like all those motivated by **envy** and jealousy, they considered the apostle to be a threat to their own prominence and influence in the church.

Strife is from *eris,* which refers to contention, especially with a spirit of enmity. As it is used here, it is frequently associated with **envy** and jealousy, as well as with other sinful passions, such as greed and malice. Envy leads to competition, hostility, and conflict.

Paul's purpose in confronting this issue was not to gain sympathy for himself, much less to retaliate against his detractors. He was rather pointing out that faithfulness in ministry includes right motives as well as right doctrine. There have always been those whose service in the church is to a large measure motivated by a desire to exceed others. That makes them resent those who are respected and whose ministries are fruitful. Such people inevitably breed **envy and strife** and thereby do great harm to Christ's church.

Exactly what was being said about Paul to hurt him and wreck his reputation is not revealed. But because the charges were false, the particulars are not important. The apostle's purpose was not to be defensive but simply to give a correct account of the situation. As in Corinth (cf. 1 Cor. 1:11–17), it is probable that several factions were involved, each claiming special allegiances, insight, and authority. When false teachers gained a hearing in Corinth, they ruthlessly attacked Paul, who wrote 2 Corinthians to answer those attacks (cf. 2 Cor. 10:10; 11:6). Like Job's friends, some of the envious preachers in Rome may have claimed that Paul's imprisonment was the Lord's punishment for some secret sin (cf. John 9:1–2). Others may have believed Paul was in prison because he lacked the victorious faith that would have gained his release. In their view, he obviously failed to fully tap into the Holy Spirit's power. The fact that they were free and he was in prison was proof to them that his spiritual power and usefulness were inferior to theirs. Otherwise, why did God not miraculously free Paul as He had at Philippi (Acts 16:25–26)?

Still others may have presumptuously thought that the Lord kept Paul in prison because of his supposed inadequate and misleading preaching of God's Word. With access to the apostle limited, people had more opportunity to listen to his opponents, who claimed a deeper and more complete understanding of the faith. Like some Christians today, they perhaps felt Paul was old-fashioned and that a fresher, more relevant approach was needed to reach the sophisticated people of Rome. Others may have argued that if Paul had been completely uncompromising and true to the faith he would have been martyred long beforehand. Therefore he must have made a deal with the Romans to protect his life and to secure favorable treatment. Such speculations provide some reasonable idea of what was being said about Paul.

But some also, Paul goes on to say with obvious gratification, preach the gospel **from good will.** Like envy and strife, **good will** (*eudokia*) pertains to motive, in this case the positive motive of desiring what is best for others. Those believers in Rome not only did not criticize Paul but also enthusiastically supported him and appreciated his work. Their motives were unselfishly pure. They were sympathetic and grateful to the apostle for his faithfulness in proclaiming the gospel and for his loving ministry to them.

Unlike the detractors, **the latter** (those with **good will**) preached Christ **out of love.** Only a few years earlier, in his first letter to the bickering and factious church in Corinth, he wrote,

> If I speak with the tongues of men and of angels, but do not have love, I have become a noisy gong or a clanging cymbal. If I have the gift of prophecy, and know all mysteries and all knowledge; and if I have all faith, so as to remove mountains, but do not have love, I am nothing. And if I give all my possessions to feed the poor, and if I surrender my body to be burned, but do not have love, it profits me nothing. . . . Now faith, hope, love, abide these three; but the greatest of these is love. (1 Cor. 13:1–3, 13)

Apart from the spirit and motive of love, nothing done in the Lord's name—no preaching, teaching, or service, no matter how orthodox or impressive—is truly acceptable to Him. It amounts to nothing.

In context, it seems that the **love** Paul speaks of here is primarily personal **love** for him. Those believers motivated by **good will** doubtless loved the Lord and each other, but the emphasis here is on their **love** for the apostle. They deeply cared about him and were concerned for his personal welfare as well as for the impact of his ministry. They knew he was not in prison because of any secret sin or shortcoming. They knew he was not there because of unfaithfulness but because of loyalty to the Lord, not because his work was a failure but because it was a powerful success, not because he was out of God's will but because he was in the very center of it. Those believers knew Paul was divinely **appointed for the defense of the gospel** (cf. Phil. 1:7) and were grateful for his faithful obedience to that call—an obedience that had brought them rich spiritual blessing.

Keimai (**appointed**), which has the root meaning of lying down or reclining, came to be used of an official appointment and sometimes of destiny. In the military it was used of a special assignment, such as guard duty or defense of a strategic position. When blessing the infant Jesus, Simeon "said to Mary His mother, 'Behold, this Child is appointed for the fall and rise of many in Israel, and for a sign to be opposed'" (Luke 2:34). Using the term in a more figurative way, Paul reminded the Thessalonians that they should not "be disturbed by [their] afflictions; for [they themselves knew] that we have been destined [*keimetha*] for this" (1 Thess. 3:3).

Paul was divinely **appointed for the defense of the gospel.** Jesus declared at the apostle's conversion that Paul was "to bear [His] name before the Gentiles and kings and the sons of Israel" (Acts 9:15; cf. 13:2; Gal. 1:15–16; Eph. 3:6–7). His imprisonment in Rome was neither an accident of fate nor primarily the decision of men, not even of Paul's decision to appeal to Caesar (Acts 25:11). Above all else, it was an integral part of his divine assignment to defend **the gospel.** In this case, he was destined to be in that incarceration by God's will, so he could preach **the gospel** in Rome.

In verse 17, Paul refers again to his detractors, **the former** group of believers (v. 15a), who **proclaim Christ out of selfish ambition rather than from pure motives.** As noted above, it was not their doctrine that was at fault; they did **proclaim Christ.** But they were not preaching **Christ** for His glory and honor but for their own, to fulfill their **selfish ambition.**

Eritheia (**selfish ambition**) did not originally have a bad connotation but merely referred to working for hire. Eventually, however, it acquired the meaning of looking out solely for one's own interests, regardless of the consequences to others. It was used of career professionals who ruthlessly tried to climb to the top of their fields in any way they could, and of politicians who sought office at any expense.

Paul's selfishly ambitious detractors obviously did not preach **from pure motives.** Not only were they self-seeking, but even worse, they also sought to do disservice to Paul, **thinking to cause [him] distress in [his] imprisonment.** They unjustly criticized and accused him for the malicious purpose of aggravating and intensifying his **distress.** They exhibited unbelievable cruelty born of jealousy, using Paul's imprisonment to discredit him and to promote themselves.

But Paul's primary distress was not due to his affliction, whether caused by Rome or his fellow believers. He knew that the hypocrisy and evil motives of his detractors were doing great harm to the cause of Christ, and that is what caused him the deepest grief. As already noted, he could not have helped being hurt personally. But he was not looking for sympathy or seeking to defend himself. He knew that other faithful leaders in the church faced criticism and opposition, both from the world and from fellow believers. His reaction to his present situation in Rome would set the example for other faithful servants of the Lord. They would then be able to face their own afflictions with the same peace of mind, spirit of forgiveness, and trust in the triumph of God's truth that he exhibited.

Paul was fully aware that immature believers are prone to "strife, jealousy, angry tempers, disputes, slanders, gossip, arrogance, disturbances" (2 Cor. 12:20). He warned Timothy to be on guard against anyone in the churches who "has a morbid interest in controversial questions and disputes about words, out of which arise envy, strife, abusive language, evil suspicions" (1 Tim. 6:4).

More important, though, he saw the larger picture. Because those envious men were actually preaching the true gospel, people were being saved. **"What then?"** he therefore asked rhetorically, answering: **Only that in every way, whether in pretense or in truth, Christ is proclaimed; and in this I rejoice. Yes, and I will rejoice.** In other words, if the cause of **Christ** was being served, even **in pretense** by those envious detractors, he was glad. Although the detractors' motive was not primarily to exalt **Christ** or to win souls but to exalt themselves at Paul's expense, he was not bitter. He knew that, although He did not honor those men who preached the truth out of **pretense,** the sovereign God nevertheless honored their message when **Christ [was] proclaimed.** That reality greatly pleased Paul.

God's Word is always powerful, no matter what the motives of the one who proclaims it. The last thing the prophet Jonah wanted to happen was for Nineveh to repent at his preaching; but the message he gave from God produced repentance in spite of his ill intentions (cf. Jonah 4:1–9). Even a preacher or teacher who is envious, jealous, and selfish can be used by God when his message is true to the Word. God always honors His Word, and His Word always bears fruit. "My word . . . which goes forth from My mouth . . . will not return to Me empty, without accomplishing what I desire, and without succeeding in the matter for which I sent it" (Isa. 55:11). As the nineteenth-century Scottish minister John Eadie wisely commented, "The virtue lies in the gospel, not in the gospeller; in the exposition, and not in the expounder" (*A Commentary on the Greek Text of the Epistle of Paul to the Philippians* [reprint; Grand Rapids: Baker, 1979], 40).

In truth refers back to those who were preaching "from good will; . . . out of love, . . . [and] from pure motives" (Phil. 1:15–17). **Truth** here refers not to the accuracy of what they said, but rather to the truthfulness and integrity of their hearts. In marked contrast to the detractors, they were not hypocrites preaching the pure gospel from impure motives.

Katangellō (**proclaimed**) refers to announcing or declaring something with authority. Whether the gospel was **proclaimed** by jealous, hurtful preachers, or by those who were faithfully and humbly preaching the gospel with pure motives, it was accurately **proclaimed,** it bore fruit, and Paul could only **rejoice.** He reinforced his earnestness by adding, **Yes, and I will rejoice.** His joy, his gracious attitude, and his grasp of the greater issue of gospel truth were not transitory, but were resolutely permanent (cf. Ps. 4:7–8; Rom. 12:12; 2 Cor. 6:10).

Absolutely nothing could steal Paul's God-given joy. He was expendable; the gospel was not. His own privacy and freedom were incidental, and he cared nothing for personal recognition or credit. Neither the painful chains of Rome nor the even more painful criticism of fellow Christians could keep him from rejoicing, because **Christ** was being **proclaimed** and His church was growing and maturing. The apostle's view of his life and ministry are perhaps best expressed in 2 Corinthians:

> And working together with Him, we also urge you not to receive the grace of God in vain—for He says, "At the acceptable time I listened to you, and on the day of salvation I helped you." Behold, now is "the acceptable time," behold, now is "the day of salvation"—giving no cause for offense in anything, so that the ministry will not be discredited, but in everything commending ourselves as servants of God, in much endurance, in afflictions, in hardships, in distresses, in beatings, in imprisonments, in tumults, in labors, in sleeplessness, in hunger, in purity, in knowledge, in patience, in kindness, in the Holy Spirit, in genuine love, in the word of truth, in the power of God; by the weapons of righteousness for the right hand and the left, by glory and dishonor, by evil report and good report; regarded as deceivers and yet true; as unknown yet well-known, as dying yet behold, we live; as punished yet not put to death, as sorrowful yet always rejoicing, as poor yet making many rich, as having nothing yet possessing all things. (2 Cor. 6:1–10)

Paul's example of selfless humility shows that the worse circumstances are, the greater joy can be. When the seemingly secure things in life begin to collapse, when suffering and sorrow increase, believers should be drawn into ever-deeper fellowship with the Lord. It is then that they will most fully experience the enduring joy the apostle knew so well. This joy is far greater and more satisfying than any fleeting circumstantial happiness. And this unmixed joy comes not because of circumstances but in spite of them and through them.

The Joy of Ministry— Part 2: In Spite of Death and the Flesh (Philippians 1:19–26)

5

for I know that this will turn out for my deliverance through your prayers and the provision of the Spirit of Jesus Christ, according to my earnest expectation and hope, that I will not be put to shame in anything, but that with all boldness, Christ will even now, as always, be exalted in my body, whether by life or by death. For to me, to live is Christ and to die is gain. But if I am to live on in the flesh, this will mean fruitful labor for me; and I do not know which to choose. But I am hard-pressed from both directions, having the desire to depart and be with Christ, for that is very much better; yet to remain on in the flesh is more necessary for your sake. Convinced of this, I know that I will remain and continue with you all for your progress and joy in the faith, so that your proud confidence in me may abound in Christ Jesus through my coming to you again. (1:19–26)

Despite the trials, sorrow, and suffering Paul experienced (cf. 2 Cor. 11:23–33), his ministry was nevertheless a joyful experience for him. In this section of Philippians, he discusses four issues that might seemingly have robbed him of joy: trouble, detractors, death, and the flesh. The first two issues (trouble [Paul's imprisonment] and detractors

[those preachers who sought to elevate themselves at Paul's expense])
were discussed in chapter 4 of this volume. The apostle now reveals that
both the threat of impending death and the sorrows of living on in the
flesh were also incapable of robbing him of his joy.

IN SPITE OF DEATH—
AS LONG AS THE LORD WAS GLORIFIED

**For I know that this will turn out for my deliverance through your
prayers and the provision of the Spirit of Jesus Christ, according
to my earnest expectation and hope, that I will not be put to
shame in anything, but that with all boldness, Christ will even
now, as always, be exalted in my body, whether by life or by
death. For to me, to live is Christ and to die is gain.** (1:19–21)

In the last analysis, it did not really matter to Paul that he was
imprisoned, maligned, and facing possible execution as long as the saving gospel of Christ was being preached. He was fully confident that,
despite his negative circumstances, the Lord's cause would triumph.
Therefore, he could face death without fear. In verses 19–21 he mentions
five realities on which that confidence was based: the precepts of the
Lord (v. 19*a*); the prayers of the saints (v. 19*b*); the provision of the Spirit
(v. 19*c*); the promise of Christ (v. 20*a*); and the plan of God (vv. 20*b*–21).

CONFIDENCE IN THE PRECEPTS OF THE LORD

For I know that this will turn out for my deliverance (1:19*a*)

Oida (**know**) means to know something with certainty. Paul was
convinced that his present suffering at the hands of both unbelievers
and believers would **turn out for [his] deliverance.** He quotes directly
from the Septuagint (the Greek translation of the Old Testament), citing
Job's reply to Zophar: "This also will be my salvation" (Job 13:16). Job
correctly understood that his terrible suffering was not God's punishment
for sin. Like Job, Paul fully believed that God would one day deliver him,
both from his physical afflictions and from the false accusations of those
who wrongly insisted that all of his suffering was the result of iniquity.

A few years earlier Paul had assured the believers in Rome that
"God causes all things to work together for good to those who love God,
to those who are called according to His purpose" (Rom. 8:28); now he
applied that marvelous truth to his own life. He knew his conscience was

clear (cf. Acts 23:1; 24:16; 2 Cor. 1:12; 1 Tim. 1:5; 3:9; 2 Tim. 1:3); he knew he was not being divinely chastened; and he was fully convinced that God would cause his present suffering to "work together for good."

Deliverance is from *sōtēria,* which is commonly rendered "salvation." Some commentators therefore believe Paul was referring to his **deliverance** from sin and death through faith in Jesus Christ. The idea then would be that he was confident in his eternal security. Others take this **deliverance** to refer to his vindication before Caesar and his consequent release from prison and **deliverance** from execution. The primary **deliverance** of which he was speaking could not have been from execution, however, because in verse 20 he qualifies his expectation with the words "whether by life or by death."

In any case, Paul knew that his present circumstances were temporary. One way or another, "by life or by death," he would be delivered from them. Verses 21–25 indicate his confident anticipation that he would live. His salvation would be perfected when he was ushered into his Lord's presence (v. 23). Again, like Job, he could declare, "As for me, I know that my Redeemer lives, and at the last He will take His stand on the earth. Even after my skin is destroyed, yet from my flesh I shall see God" (Job 19:25–26).

CONFIDENCE IN THE PRAYERS OF THE SAINTS

through your prayers (1:19b)

Paul believed in the limitless sovereignty of God and had perfect confidence that God's Word would be fulfilled and His purpose carried out. He also knew that God's sovereign plan incorporates the **prayers** of His people. He especially appreciated the **prayers** of the beloved congregation in Philippi and expressed to them his deepest convictions and personal longings.

The apostle knew that "the effective prayer of a righteous man can accomplish much" (James 5:16), and he therefore not only diligently prayed himself but also continually encouraged other believers to pray diligently. Facing difficult circumstances a few years earlier, he had appealed to the church in Corinth to pray for him:

> For just as the sufferings of Christ are ours in abundance, so also our comfort is abundant through Christ. . . . For we do not want you to be unaware, brethren, of our affliction which came to us in Asia, that we were burdened excessively, beyond our strength, so that we despaired even of life; indeed, we had the sentence of death within ourselves so that we would not trust in ourselves, but in God who raises the dead;

who delivered us from so great a peril of death, and will deliver us, He on whom we have set our hope. And He will yet deliver us, you also joining in helping us through your prayers, so that thanks may be given by many persons on our behalf for the favor bestowed on us through the prayers of many. (2 Cor. 1:5, 8–11)

Before Paul visited the church at Rome, he had implored those believers: "Now I urge you, brethren, by our Lord Jesus Christ and by the love of the Spirit, to strive together with me in your prayers to God for me" (Rom. 15:30). During the same imprisonment in which he wrote Philippians he admonished the Ephesians: "With all prayer and petition pray at all times in the Spirit, and with this in view, be on the alert with all perseverance and petition for all the saints, and pray on my behalf, that utterance may be given to me in the opening of my mouth, to make known with boldness the mystery of the gospel" (Eph. 6:18–19). To the Thessalonians he pleaded, "Brethren, pray for us" (1 Thess. 5:25); and later, "Brethren, pray for us that the word of the Lord will spread rapidly and be glorified, just as it did also with you" (2 Thess. 3:1).

Nothing is more encouraging to those in ministry than to know that fellow believers are holding them up before the Lord in prayer.

CONFIDENCE IN THE PROVISION OF THE SPIRIT

and the provision of the Spirit of Jesus Christ, (1:19c)

The Word of God, the prayers of the saints, and the power of the Holy **Spirit** always work together for the benefit of the servants of God. Jesus promised, "I will ask the Father, and He will give you another Helper, that He may be with you forever; that is the Spirit of truth, whom the world cannot receive, because it does not see Him or know Him, but you know Him because He abides with you and will be in you" (John 14:16–17; cf. 15:26; Mark 13:11; Luke 12:12; Rom. 8:9). But it seems Paul was speaking here not so much about Christ's provision of the **Spirit** to believers at salvation as of the Spirit's **provision** of divine power and protection after salvation.

Epichorēgia (**provision**) describes a full, bountiful, and sufficient supply of what is needed. The Holy **Spirit** is the believer's sufficient resource for everything he needs. He provides guidance when believers do not know what to say. "Do not worry about how or what you are to say," Jesus promised; "for it will be given you in that hour what you are to say. For it is not you who speak, but it is the Spirit of your Father who speaks in you" (Matt. 10:19–20). The **Spirit** helps believers to pray. When they are weak and "do not know how to pray as [they] should, . . . the Spirit Himself intercedes for [them] with groanings too deep for words" (Rom 8:26). The **Spirit** is the source of power. "You will receive power when the Holy Spirit has come upon you," Jesus promised just before His ascension; "and you shall be My witnesses both in Jerusalem, and in all Judea and Samaria, and even to the remotest part of the earth" (Acts 1:8). To the Ephesians Paul wrote that the Lord "is able to do far more abundantly beyond all that we ask or think, according to the power that works within us" (Eph. 3:20). Later in Philippians he said, "My God will supply all your needs according to His riches in glory in Christ Jesus" (Phil. 4:19). **The Spirit** produces in the believer's life an abundant harvest of spiritual fruit: "love, joy, peace, patience, kindness, goodness, faithfulness, gentleness, self-control" (Gal. 5:22–23).

CONFIDENCE IN THE PROMISE OF CHRIST

according to my earnest expectation and hope, that I will not be put to shame in anything, but that with all boldness, Christ will even now, as always, be exalted in my body, (1:20*a*)

The implicit idea is that Paul's **earnest expectation and hope** were grounded in the Lord's promise, not in the apostle's wishful thinking. *Apokaradokia* (**earnest expectation**) is a compound word that literally refers to stretching the neck. It often was used figuratively of an eager longing or expectancy, a connotation reinforced by the synonym **hope.** Paul was certain that, in the eyes of God, he would never truly be **put to shame,** whether before Caesar, the world, or the church. Ultimately, he would be vindicated. He expressed similar confidence to the Corinthians, saying, "Even if I boast somewhat further about our authority, which the Lord gave for building you up and not for destroying you, I will not be put to shame" (2 Cor. 10:8).

Paul expressed his supreme joy when he wrote that **Christ will even now, as always, be exalted in my body.** Knowing that the believer's body is "a temple of the Holy Spirit" (1 Cor. 6:19), he had presented his body as "a living and holy sacrifice, acceptable to God, which [was his] spiritual service of worship" (Rom. 12:1). He carried about in his own body "the dying of Jesus, so that the life of Jesus also [would] be manifested in [his] body" (2 Cor. 4:10). **Always,** including the tough situations, Paul would continue to be an instrument for exalting his Lord through faithful, holy obedience. He rejoiced greatly that, because of his faithfulness, he could testify that the churches of Judea (and throughout the empire) "were glorifying God because of me" (Gal. 1:24).

CONFIDENCE IN THE PLAN OF GOD

whether by life or by death. For to me, to live is Christ and to die is gain. (1:20*b*–21)

Paul was not certain what God's plan was for him, **whether** he would continue to serve and exalt Him through his **life** and ministry or through the final exaltation of **death.** Either way, the Lord's will would be done; His plan would be fully accomplished.

To the elders from Ephesus, who met him on the beach near Miletus, Paul declared unequivocally, "I do not consider my life of any account as dear to myself, so that I may finish my course and the ministry which I received from the Lord Jesus, to testify solemnly of the gospel of the grace of God" (Acts 20:24). A short while later he said to the believers in Caesarea who were distressed by Agabus's prophecy of Paul's impending arrest: "What are you doing, weeping and breaking my heart? For I am ready not only to be bound, but even to die at Jerusalem for the name of the Lord Jesus" (Acts 21:13). He reminded the believers in Rome that "not one of us lives for himself, and not one dies for himself; for if we live, we live for the Lord, or if we die, we die for the Lord; therefore whether we live or die, we are the Lord's. For to this end Christ died and lived again, that He might be Lord both of the dead and of the living" (Rom. 14:7–9). Whether he lived or died, the apostle could say now as he would to Timothy a few years later: "I am already being poured out as a drink offering, and the time of my departure has come. I have fought the good fight, I have finished the course, I have kept the faith" (2 Tim. 4:6–7). Either way, he would be victorious and Christ would be exalted.

The Greek phrase rendered **to live is Christ and to die is gain** contains no verb. It literally reads "to live Christ, to die gain." Paul knew that living **is Christ,** because he would continue to serve Him while he lived. He also knew that dying would be gain because then he would be in God's presence, able to worship and serve Him in holy perfection (cf. v. 23). Paul fully understood that wealth, power, influence, possessions, prestige, social standing, good health, business or professional success, and all other such things are transitory. Many acknowledge that truth, but not many live as if it is true. Few can say with Paul's utter sincerity **to me, to live is Christ and to die is gain.**

The apostle's very being was wrapped up in his Lord and Savior, Jesus **Christ.** He trusted, loved, served, witnessed for, and in every way was devoted to and dependent on Him. His only hope, his only purpose, his only reason **to live** was **Christ.** He traveled for **Christ,** preached for **Christ,** and was persecuted and imprisoned for **Christ.** Ultimately, he would **die** for **Christ.** But even death, by God's marvelous grace, was ultimately for Paul's eternal **gain.**

IN SPITE OF BEING IN THE FLESH—
AS LONG AS THE CHURCH WAS BENEFITED

But if I am to live on in the flesh, this will mean fruitful labor for me; and I do not know which to choose. But I am hard-pressed from both directions, having the desire to depart and be with Christ, for that is very much better; yet to remain on in the flesh is more necessary for your sake. Convinced of this, I know that I will remain and continue with you all for your progress and joy in the faith, so that your proud confidence in me may abound in Christ Jesus through my coming to you again. (1:22–26)

Adoniram Judson was the first overseas missionary sent out from America. In the early nineteenth century, he and his first wife went to India and, a short while later, to Burma, where he labored for nearly four decades. After fourteen years, he had a handful of converts and had managed to write a Burmese grammar. During that time he suffered a horrible imprisonment for a year and a half and lost his wife and children to disease. Like Paul, he longed to be with the Lord, but, also like the apostle, he considered his work for Christ to be infinitely more important than his personal longings. He therefore prayed that God would allow him to live long enough to translate the entire Bible into Burmese and to establish a church there of at least one hundred believers. The Lord granted that request and also allowed him to compile Burmese-English and English-Burmese dictionaries, which became invaluable to the Christian workers, both foreign and Burmese, who followed him. He wrote, "If I had not felt certain that every trial was ordered by infinite love and mercy, I could not have survived my accumulated sufferings."

Part of spiritual greatness is to know Christ intimately and to long to be with Him. But spiritual greatness also includes being totally committed to the advancement of the kingdom and serving Christ on earth. Every believer lives in such tension. Paul clearly did not escape that dilemma, which he expressed so beautifully and poignantly in verses 22–26. He longed to be with the Lord, but if it was God's will for him **to live on in the flesh,** he rejoiced. He knew that would **mean fruitful labor for** him to the glory of God. **The flesh** does not refer here to the seat of sinfulness, as in other passages (cf. Rom. 6:19; 7:5, 18; 8:5; 2 Cor. 7:1; 10:2; Gal. 3:3), but to physical life (cf. Rom. 1:3; 9:3; 1 Cor. 6:16; 2 Cor. 10:3; Gal. 2:20; 1 Peter 4:1–2).

Fruitful labor is the work of the Lord, which the Holy Spirit always blesses. When "the word of truth, the gospel" is faithfully proclaimed it will be "constantly bearing fruit and increasing" (Col. 1:5–6; cf. Phil. 1:15–18). Paul is not, of course, speaking of good works by which men vainly hope to redeem themselves. All human works are powerless to save and actually vitiate the gracious, redeeming work of Christ (Rom. 3:20–22, 28; 4:1–5; Gal. 2:16–21; Eph. 2:7–9). He is rather speaking of the Spirit-empowered **fruitful labor** for which we are "created in Christ Jesus, [the] good works which God prepared beforehand so that we would walk in them" (Eph. 2:10). It is the fruit of "God who is at work in you, both to will and to work for His good pleasure" (Phil. 2:13). Spiritual fruit encompasses the Spirit-directed and Spirit-empowered motives and behavior built on the foundation of Jesus Christ (1 Cor. 3:11). It can be divided into several categories. Attitudinal fruit includes the "fruit of the Spirit" (Gal. 5:22–23); action fruit consists of righteous deeds (cf. Phil. 1:11); fruit also includes converts (cf. Rom. 1:13).

Paul was in a quandary about his life and death, confessing, **I do not know which to choose.** *Gnōrizō* (**know**) is used twenty-seven times in the New Testament, over half of those times by Paul. It is used of revealing something that was previously unknown, whether by the Lord to men (as in Luke 2:15; John 15:15; Rom. 9:22–23) or by men to other men (as in Acts 7:13; 2 Cor. 8:1; Eph. 6:19, 21). Paul's point seems to be that he had **not** yet decided **which to choose** because the Lord had not yet made it known to him **which to choose.** Because he was not sure of the Lord's will in the matter, he was not sure of his own.

It was not that Paul opposed the Lord's will or wanted to be in heaven if God wanted him to continue his ministry on earth. He wanted to do both, and the two desires were equally strong and proper. It is like the dilemma of a wife whose husband has been working far from home for many months and asks her to visit him for a while. Though she loves him deeply and longs to be with him, she also loves her children and wants to stay near them.

Consequently, Paul said **I am hard-pressed from both directions.** *Sunechō* (**hard-pressed**) literally means "to hold together." It was often used of being hemmed in from both sides, as when walking through a narrow gorge. Luke used the word to describe the multitude in Galilee who were "pressing in on" Jesus (Luke 8:45) and of the Lord's warning, "For the days will come upon you when your enemies will throw up a barricade against you, and surround you and hem you in on every side" (Luke 19:43).

On the one hand, Paul explained that he had the **desire to depart and be with Christ. To depart** is from *analuō*, which means "to unloose," like a boat's being untied from its moorings when it is ready to set sail. The word was sometimes used of a prisoner's being freed from his bonds, of an animal's being freed of its burden, or of a military detachment's breaking camp. Paul alluded to the latter figure in 2 Corinthians 5:1: "We know that if the earthly tent which is our house is torn down, we have a building from God, a house not made with hands, eternal in the heavens." For Christians, death is simply breaking their temporary earthly camp and moving on to their eternal heavenly home. The related noun *analusis* was often used as a euphemism for death, which Paul had in mind in the present text. In his second letter to Timothy a few years later, he told his beloved son in the faith, "For I am already being poured out as a drink offering, and the time of my departure [*analusis*] has come" (2 Tim. 4:6).

Philippians 1:23 refutes the false doctrine of soul sleep, the teaching that the dead exist in a state of unconsciousness until their resurrection. When believers die, they immediately **depart** to **be with Christ,** like the penitent thief on the cross, to whom Jesus said, "Truly I say to you, today you shall be with Me in Paradise" (Luke 23:43; cf. 2 Cor. 5:8). Moses and Elijah's appearance at the Transfiguration (Matt. 17:3) and the fully conscious martyred Tribulation believers (Rev. 6:9–11) also refute soul sleep. The New Testament uses sleep as a metaphor for death. Stephen "called on the Lord and said, 'Lord Jesus, receive my spirit!' Then falling on his knees, he cried out with a loud voice, 'Lord, do not hold this sin against them!' Having said this, he fell asleep" (Acts 7:59–60; cf. John 11:11–14; 1 Cor. 11:30; 15:20, 51; 1 Thess. 4:13–15; 5:10).

The believer's supreme hope is to **be with Christ** throughout all eternity, and **to depart** to be with Him begins that blissful experience. **Very much better** translates a double comparative in Greek, expressing the highest superlative. Therefore, as far as believers' personal satisfaction and joy are concerned, going to heaven is obviously **very much better** than staying on earth.

Like Paul, all believers should "prefer rather to be absent from the body and to be at home with the Lord" (2 Cor. 5:8). Then they will be freed from the pain, sorrow, and suffering of this present life and ushered into the Lord's glorious presence. There they will experience the marvelous freedom of eternal righteousness and glory and

> serve Him day and night in His temple; and He who sits on the throne will spread His tabernacle over them. They will hunger no longer, nor thirst anymore; nor will the sun beat down on them, nor any heat; for the Lamb in the center of the throne will be their shepherd, and will guide them to springs of the water of life; and God will wipe every tear from their eyes. (Rev. 7:15–17)

Believers will no longer need to walk by faith, but by sight (cf. 2 Cor. 5:7). They will no longer see God through "a mirror dimly, but . . . face to face," no longer know "in part, but . . . fully just as [they] also have been fully known" (1 Cor. 13:12; cf. 1 Cor. 8:3). Because they "are children of God, . . . [they] will [then] be like Him, because [they] will see Him just as He is" (1 John 3:2). Job's confidence will be theirs: "Even after my skin is destroyed, yet from my flesh I shall see God; whom I myself shall behold, and whom my eyes will see and not another" (Job 19:26-27; cf. Pss. 16:10-11; 17:15; 49:15).

Paul's longing for heaven was not his only concern, however. To the Corinthians he wrote, "Therefore we also have as our ambition, whether at home [in heaven with Christ] or absent [continuing to serve Him on earth], to be pleasing to Him" (2 Cor. 5:9). Thus he could say to the Philippians, **To remain on in the flesh is more necessary for your sake.** As long as the Lord had work for him to do on earth, that is where Paul wanted to be. The apostle applied to himself the admonition he had given to the believers in Corinth: "My beloved brethren, be steadfast, immovable, always abounding in the work of the Lord, knowing that your toil is not in vain in the Lord" (1 Cor. 15:58). Although there was great "daily pressure on [him] of concern for all the churches" (2 Cor. 11:28), he did not consider that responsibility a burden to be alleviated but a joyful opportunity to serve the Lord through serving them.

Later in this epistle, Paul admonished the Philippians: "Do nothing from selfishness or empty conceit, but with humility of mind regard one another as more important than yourselves; do not merely look out for your own personal interests, but also for the interests of others" (2:3-4). They were to

> have this attitude in [themselves] which was also in Christ Jesus, who, although He existed in the form of God, did not regard equality with God a thing to be grasped, but emptied Himself, taking the form of a bond-servant, and being made in the likeness of men. Being found in appearance as a man, He humbled Himself by becoming obedient to the point of death, even death on a cross. (vv. 5-8)

Their following Christ's example would also make Paul's "joy complete by [their] being of the same mind, maintaining the same love, united in spirit, intent on one purpose" (v. 2). It was because he considered the Philippian believers to be better than himself that he could say to them, **To remain on in the flesh is more necessary for your sake.** Paul would gladly postpone his heavenly blessings for the sake of continuing to serve earthly saints.

Convinced of this need to finish his earthly work, Paul gave his readers the assurance, **I know that I will remain and continue with you all for your progress and joy in the faith, so that your proud confidence in me may abound in Christ Jesus through my coming to you again.** The apostle knew that the Philippians still needed him. It was not that he considered himself indispensable, but rather that he was **convinced** that his ministry to them was not yet complete. Because he had just expressed uncertainty about whether he would live or die (1:22–24), it seems that his being **convinced** reflects his personal conviction rather than a revelation from God. Had God told him he would not die until he had finished his work in the Philippian church, his living or dying would not have been an issue for discussion.

Paul was **convinced** that the church still needed his instruction and leadership. Despite their maturity, love, and gentleness of spirit, the Philippians needed to exemplify more of their Lord's humility (2:1–8). They needed to be on guard against false teachers (3:2), to observe and follow Paul's example, and to oppose the "enemies of the cross of Christ" (3:17–18). At least two members in the congregation needed to learn "to live in harmony in the Lord" (4:2–3). Some, perhaps many, were troubled by anxiety and needed to "be anxious for nothing, but in everything by prayer and supplication with thanksgiving let [their] requests be made known to God" (4:6). In addition to those things, they needed to keep their focus continually on "whatever is true, whatever is honorable, whatever is right, whatever is pure, whatever is lovely, whatever is of good repute" (4:8).

Paul hoped to **remain and continue with** the Philippians to promote both their **progress and [their] joy in the faith.** Earlier he had spoken of the general "progress of the gospel" (1:12). Using the same word (*prokopē*), he speaks here of the particular **progress** of the Philippian believers, first in their **joy** and then in **the faith.** As noted under the discussion of 1:12, *prokopē* has the idea of advancing against obstacles, of facing continual resistance. When Paul and Barnabas "returned to Lystra and to Iconium and to Antioch, strengthening the souls of the disciples, encouraging them to continue in the faith," they warned that "through many tribulations we must enter the kingdom of God" (Acts 14:21–22). Although **progress . . . in the faith** does not come without a price, it is always accompanied by **progress** in **joy.**

So that translates *hina*, which, when used with a subjunctive verb, introduces a purpose clause. Paul's continuing to serve the Philippian church would be for the purpose of causing their **proud confidence in** him to **abound in Christ Jesus through** his **coming to** them **again.** In the Greek text, the phrase **in Christ Jesus** precedes the phrase **in me,** and that is the order Paul must have had in mind, the idea being: "in order that your proud confidence may abound in Christ Jesus, as He is seen in me." In chapter 3 of Philippians he makes it clear that, despite his impeccable religious credentials (vv. 4–6),

> whatever things were gain to me, those things I have counted as loss for the sake of Christ. More than that, I count all things to be loss in view of the surpassing value of knowing Christ Jesus my Lord, for whom I have suffered the loss of all things, and count them but rubbish so that I may gain Christ, and may be found in Him, not having a righteousness of my own derived from the Law, but that which is through faith in Christ, the righteousness which comes from God on the basis of faith. (vv. 7–9)

He then goes on to confess: "Not that I have already obtained it or have already become perfect, but I press on so that I may lay hold of that for which also I was laid hold of by Christ Jesus. Brethren, I do not regard myself as having laid hold of it yet" (vv. 12–13).

Paul had cautioned the Corinthians, "Let no one boast in men. For all things belong to you, whether Paul or Apollos or Cephas or the world or life or death or things present or things to come; all things belong to you, and you belong to Christ; and Christ belongs to God" (1 Cor. 3:21–23). Thus, it was **Christ Jesus** working in him that would cause the Philippian believers' **proud confidence** to **abound.**

No circumstances, however severe, could steal Paul's joy. Nothing could diminish his enthusiasm for the ministry. Nothing could keep him from "always abounding in the work of the Lord, [because he knew] that [his] toil [was] not in vain in the Lord" (1 Cor. 15:58).

Conduct Worthy of the Church (Philippians 1:27–30)

6

Only conduct yourselves in a manner worthy of the gospel of Christ, so that whether I come and see you or remain absent, I will hear of you that you are standing firm in one spirit, with one mind striving together for the faith of the gospel; in no way alarmed by your opponents—which is a sign of destruction for them, but of salvation for you, and that too, from God. For to you it has been granted for Christ's sake, not only to believe in Him, but also to suffer for His sake, experiencing the same conflict which you saw in me, and now hear to be in me. (1:27–30)

Paul had a special love, respect, and appreciation for the church at Philippi. It was one of the most mature of the churches described in the New Testament. Nevertheless, its members had a few problems, some of them potentially serious. Like every church in every age, they needed to be on guard against false teachers (3:2) and repudiate those in the congregation who were "enemies of the cross of Christ" (3:17–18). The apostle knew that it does not take long even for a faithful church to slip into indifference and eventually into moral and doctrinal error.

In 1:27–30 Paul turns from the autobiographical emphasis of the first part of the letter to focus on the Philippian congregation. He calls on the Philippians to maintain their spiritual commitment, to continue to behave in a way that is consistent with the power of the gospel. He calls them to look carefully into their own hearts to determine if they have spiritual integrity. That appeal applies, of course, to every follower of Jesus Christ in every place and time.

Because he believed it was necessary for their spiritual well-being, Paul was confident that the Lord would allow him to "remain and continue with [them] for [their] progress and joy in the faith, so that [their] proud confidence in [him] may abound in Christ Jesus through [his] coming to [them] again" (1:25–26). But regardless of what happened to him, he implored, **Only conduct yourselves in a manner worthy of the gospel of Christ, . . . whether I come and see you or remain absent.** What truly mattered was their consistent, holy conduct. *Monon* (only) is placed at the beginning of the sentence in the Greek text for emphasis. Above all, Paul wanted their lives to reflect worthily on the **gospel of Christ.** It is a truth the apostle reiterates implicitly throughout the letter and explicitly in the next chapter, admonishing them: "Prove yourselves to be blameless and innocent, children of God above reproach in the midst of a crooked and perverse generation, among whom you appear as lights in the world, holding fast the word of life, so that in the day of Christ I will have reason to glory because I did not run in vain nor toil in vain" (2:15–16).

Politeuomai (conduct) is the main verb in verses 27–30, which in the Greek is a single sentence. It comes from the root word *polis* (city), which in earlier times usually referred to the city-states to which inhabitants gave their primary allegiance. The verb carries the basic meaning of being a citizen. But, by implication, it means being a *good* citizen, one whose **conduct** brings honor to the political body to whom one belongs.

Philippi had the distinction of being a Roman colony (Acts 16:12), a highly privileged status that gave its inhabitants many of the rights enjoyed by citizens of Rome itself. Such colonies considered themselves "little Romes" and took great pride in that association. They gave unqualified allegiance to Rome and to the emperor, adopted Roman dress and Roman names, and spoke Latin, the official language of Rome.

Roman society, like Greek society before it, was highly community-conscious. The individual was subordinate to the state, and a person's skills, talents, energy, and endeavors were devoted first of all to the interests of society at large. It was not a coerced subjection, as in modern totalitarian states, but was based on a willing sense of interdependence in which citizens took great pride. A responsible citizen was careful not to do anything that would bring disrepute on his *polis.* And he tried always to be considered an honorable citizen, so that he would never be removed from the list of citizens.

Paul may have had that sense of dedication in mind in using the term *politeuomai* (to **conduct**). If the citizens of Philippi were so devoted to the honor of their human kingdom, how much more should believers be devoted to the kingdom of **Christ** (cf. Col. 1:12–13)? Therefore, Paul charged them to **conduct** themselves **in a manner worthy of the gospel of Christ,** to live as faithful citizens of heaven (cf. 3:20). The church, though imperfect and temporal, is the earthly manifestation of that perfect and eternal kingdom of heaven in this present age (cf. Col. 1:13). Heavenly **conduct** is characterized by being "blameless and innocent, children of God above reproach in the midst of a crooked and perverse generation, among whom you appear as lights in the world" (2:15).

To live **in a manner worthy of the gospel of Christ** is to live a life consistent with God's revealed Word. That includes living a life that corresponds to the divine truth Christians profess to believe, preach, teach, and defend. In other words, it means living with integrity in every facet of life. This mandate is expressed elsewhere in the New Testament as walking "in a manner worthy of the calling with which you have been called" (Eph. 4:1), "in a manner worthy of the Lord, to please Him in all respects, bearing fruit in every good work and increasing in the knowledge of God" (Col. 1:10), and "in a manner worthy of the God who calls you into His own kingdom and glory" (1 Thess. 2:12; cf. 4:1). It means "showing all good faith so that [believers] will adorn the doctrine of God [their] Savior in every respect" (Titus 2:10), demonstrating "holy conduct and godliness," and being "diligent to be found by Him in peace, spotless and blameless" (2 Peter 3:11, 14).

The church's greatest testimony before the world is spiritual integrity. When Christians live below the standards of biblical morality and reverence for their Lord, they compromise the full biblical truth concerning the character, plan, and will of God. By so doing, they seriously weaken the credibility of the gospel and lessen their impact on the world. God's people have always been at enmity with the world, because the world is at enmity with God (Rom. 1:28; 5:10; Eph. 2:3; Col. 1:21). But the world can hardly be expected to embrace a faith whose proponents so little emulate its standards of holiness and fail to manifest the transforming power of Christ.

When the unsaved look at the church and do not see holiness, purity, and virtue, there appears to be no reason to believe the gospel it proclaims. When pastors commit gross sins and are later restored to positions of leadership in the church; when church members lie, steal, cheat, gossip, and quarrel; and when congregations seem to care little about such sin and hypocrisy in their midst, the world is understandably repulsed by their claims to love and serve God. And the name of Christ is sullied and dishonored.

The gospel is the good news of salvation through Jesus **Christ.** It is the truth that "Christ died for our sins according to the Scriptures, and that He was buried, and that He was raised on the third day according to the Scriptures" (1 Cor. 15:3–4). It is the message Paul describes as "the power of God for salvation to everyone who believes, to the Jew first and also to the Greek" (Rom. 1:16). The point here is that those who belong to **Christ** through saving faith in His **gospel** should demonstrate that power by their changed lives (cf. 2 Cor. 5:17).

Paul had just expressed his joyous expectation of visiting Philippi again (1:25–26); but that was not his primary concern. He understood that, like the church in Ephesus, the Philippians inevitably would be threatened by "savage wolves" and that, even from within their own congregation, false teachers would "arise, speaking perverse things, to draw away the disciples after them" (Acts 20:29–30). He understood that, despite the general spiritual maturity of the congregation, some of its members would prove their lack of saving faith by deserting Christ for a different gospel. Others, who had been saved by the power of the Holy Spirit, would fall into the legalistic trap of trusting in their own fleshly achievements for their sanctification (Gal. 1:6; 3:3). Whether or not Paul visited his beloved church at Philippi, their accountability was not to him but to **Christ.** Neither he nor anyone else was the source of their spiritual strength. His appeal therefore was **that whether** he was to **come and see** them **or remain absent,** they were to trust the Lord and live worthy of Him.

In the remainder of this passage, the apostle gives four characteristics of believers who live worthy of Christ: standing firm in Him (v. 27b); sharing with one another because of Him (v. 27c); striving together in obedience to Him (vv. 27d–28); and suffering for Him (vv. 29–30).

STANDING

I will hear of you that you are standing firm (1:27b)

Standing firm translates the single Greek verb *stēkō*, which refers to steadfastly holding one's ground regardless of danger or opposition (v. 28 supports the emphasis on strength in the midst of opposition). The word was used of a soldier who defended his position at all costs, even to the point of sacrificing his life. Figuratively, it refers to holding fast to a belief, conviction, or principle without compromise, regardless of personal cost. Being firmly fixed in matters of biblical truth and holy living is included in this injunction.

Standing firm is both positive and negative. It is to stand for

God and against Satan, to stand for truth and against falsehood, to stand for righteousness and against sin. Using an imperative form of the same verb, Paul makes a similar exhortation later in the letter: "Therefore, my beloved brethren whom I long to see, my joy and crown, in this way stand firm in the Lord, my beloved" (4:1). In Romans, he uses the word to describe the Lord's enabling His people to stand for Him (Rom. 14:4). In other letters he admonishes believers to "be on the alert, stand firm in the faith, act like men, be strong" (1 Cor. 16:13; cf. 1 Thess. 3:8; 2 Thess. 2:15), to "keep standing firm" in the freedom of grace and not to "be subject again to a yoke of slavery" (Gal. 5:1). In Ephesians he twice uses a related verb in calling on believers to "put on the full armor of God ... to stand firm against the schemes of the devil" and to "be able to resist in the evil day, and having done everything, to stand firm" (Eph. 6:11, 13). Only the armor of God can enable believers to stand firm, because they do not struggle "against flesh and blood, but against the rulers, against the powers, against the world forces of this darkness, against the spiritual forces of wickedness in the heavenly places" (Eph. 6:12).

Paul was not afraid of ridicule, hardship, suffering, or death. His convictions were firm and unwavering, so that he did not compromise divine truth. On such matters he was unshakeable. His one fear was that he would be disqualified from the ministry. No matter how sound his doctrine remained, Paul understood that the danger of disqualification stemmed in large measure from the misuse of his body. He therefore declared his determination to "discipline [his] body and make it [his] slave" (1 Cor. 9:27). The primary, if not the sole, misuse of the body he had in mind was sexual immorality. In the most sobering possible terms he said:

> Do you not know that your bodies are members of Christ? Shall I then take away the members of Christ and make them members of a prostitute? May it never be! Or do you not know that the one who joins himself to a prostitute is one body with her? For He says, "The two shall become one flesh." But the one who joins himself to the Lord is one spirit with Him. Flee immorality. Every other sin that a man commits is outside the body, but the immoral man sins against his own body. Or do you not know that your body is a temple of the Holy Spirit who is in you, whom you have from God, and that you are not your own? For you have been bought with a price: therefore glorify God in your body. (1 Cor 6:15–20)

New Testament requirements for church leadership are high, because leaders are to set the standard for how all believers are to live. In his first letter to Timothy, Paul wrote: "Deacons likewise must be men of dignity, not double-tongued, or addicted to much wine or fond of sordid gain, but holding to the mystery of the faith with a clear conscience. These men must also first be tested; then let them serve as deacons if they are beyond reproach. . . . Deacons must be husbands of only one wife, and good managers of their children and their own households" (1 Tim. 3:8–10,12).

The qualifications for elders are explicit. An elder

> must be above reproach, the husband of one wife, temperate, prudent, respectable, hospitable, able to teach, not addicted to wine or pugnacious, but gentle, peaceable, free from the love of money. He must be one who manages his own household well, keeping his children under control with all dignity (but if a man does not know how to manage his own household, how will he take care of the church of God?), and not a new convert, so that he will not become conceited and fall into the condemnation incurred by the devil. And he must have a good reputation with those outside the church, so that he will not fall into reproach and the snare of the devil. (1 Tim. 3:2–7; cf. Titus 1:5–9)

It is significant that in those passages setting forth the requirements for church leaders, Paul mentions three times that those leaders must be above reproach (1 Tim. 3:2; 10; Titus 1:6). And their standing firm in the truth and holiness sets the example for all the church to follow (cf. Heb. 13:7).

SHARING

in one spirit, with one mind (1:27*c*)

Along with standing firm in the faith, there also must be unity within the church, a mutual sharing of convictions and responsibilities **in one spirit, with one mind.**

Many interpreters have argued that the phrase should read **in one Spirit,** referring to the Holy Spirit. Paul is obviously speaking of the Holy Spirit when he says that "by one Spirit we were all baptized into one body, . . . and we were all made to drink of one Spirit" (1 Cor. 12:13). The same is true when he notes that through Christ "we both have our access in one Spirit to the Father," commanding believers to be "diligent to preserve the unity of the Spirit in the bond of peace" because "there is one body and one Spirit, . . . one Lord, one faith, one baptism, one God and Father of all who is over all and through all and in all" (Eph. 2:18; 4:3–6). But the context of the present passage, which focuses on believers' attitudes, seems to indicate that he is speaking of the believer's human **spirit.**

Psuchē (**mind**) is most often translated "soul." Here **mind** seems more appropriate, because, as just noted, Paul is speaking of personal attitudes and perspectives. **One spirit, with one mind** refers to the experience of unity, harmony, and interdependence. From its inception the church was of **one spirit, with one mind.** Within a few days after Pentecost,

> all those who had believed were together and had all things in common; and they began selling their property and possessions and were sharing them with all, as anyone might have need. Day by day continuing with one mind in the temple, and breaking bread from house to house, they were taking their meals together with gladness and sincerity of heart. (Acts 2:44–46; cf. 4:32)

Early in this letter Paul commends the Philippians for their "participation in the gospel from the first day until now" (1:5), and he later admonishes: "If there is any encouragement in Christ, if there is any consolation of love, if there is any fellowship of the Spirit, if any affection and compassion, make my joy complete by being of the same mind, maintaining the same love, united in spirit, intent on one purpose" (2:1–2). Still later, he urges "Euodia and . . . Syntyche to live in harmony in the Lord" (4:2), at the same time expressing great appreciation for those two women because they had "shared [his] struggle in the cause of the gospel" (v. 3).

Unity in His church was one of Jesus' great passions. At the Last Supper He told His disciples, "A new commandment I give to you, that you love one another, even as I have loved you, that you also love one another. By this all men will know that you are My disciples, if you have love for one another" (John 13:34–35). A short while later, in His High Priestly Prayer, He prayed that all who would believe in Him "may all be one; even as You, Father, are in Me and I in You, that they also may be in Us, so that the world may believe that You sent Me. The glory which You have given Me I have given to them, that they may be one, just as We are one" (17:21–22). That amazing request was answered in the spiritual unity that actually does exist in the body of Christ. Believers share the eternal life imparted by God in the new birth, so that they are one with the Lord and with each other (cf. 1 Cor. 10:16–17).

Paul desired to see the practical outworking of that true spiritual oneness in loving care and ministry. The functioning unity of the church was also one of Paul's great passions. He reminded the believers in Rome that, "just as we have many members in one body and all the members do not have the same function, so we, who are many, are one body in Christ, and individually members one of another. . . . Be of the same mind toward one another; do not be haughty in mind, but associate with the lowly" (Rom. 12:4–5, 16). He implored the factious church at Corinth: "I exhort you, brethren, by the name of our Lord Jesus Christ, that you all agree and that there be no divisions among you, but that you be made complete in the same mind and in the same judgment" (1 Cor. 1:10).

Church strife does not always involve such flagrant sins as adultery, stealing, lying, or defamation. It is often generated by such "lesser" sins as holding grudges over minor issues, unjust criticism, bitterness, dissatisfaction, and distrust. Sometimes disharmony arises that cannot even be clearly identified or attributed to any individual, incident, or issue. The enemy of the church succeeds when God's people turn their "freedom into an opportunity for the flesh," forgetting to "through love serve one another," and instead begin to "bite and devour one another," sometimes to the point even of being "consumed by one another" (Gal. 5:13, 15). The only solution is to "walk by the Spirit, and [thereby] not carry out the desire of the flesh" (v. 16). It requires taking special effort to "be kind to one another, tender-hearted, forgiving each other, just as God in Christ also has forgiven you" (Eph. 4:32).

Paul continually had to deal with divisions in the church between Jews and Gentiles, slaves and free, and men and women. In response to those issues, he declared that in Christ "there is neither Jew nor Greek, there is neither slave nor free man, there is neither male nor female; for you are all one in Christ Jesus" (Gal. 3:28). Again, speaking of Jews and Gentiles, he reminded the Ephesians: "Now in Christ Jesus you who formerly were far off have been brought near by the blood of Christ. For He Himself is our peace, who made both groups into one and broke down the barrier of the dividing wall" (Eph. 2:13–14; cf. vv. 18–22). "The one who joins himself to the Lord is one spirit with Him" (1 Cor. 6:17; 2 Cor. 12:18), and therefore should be of one spirit and mind with everyone else who belongs to Him.

Paul gives the key to true unity in the church when he writes, "[Be] of the same mind, maintaining the same love, united in spirit, intent on one purpose. Do nothing from selfishness or empty conceit, but with humility of mind regard one another as more important than yourselves; do not merely look out for your own personal interests, but also for the interests of others" (Phil. 2:2–4). In other words, he goes on to say, "Have this attitude in yourselves which was also in Christ Jesus" (v. 5).

STRIVING

striving together for the faith of the gospel; in no way alarmed by your opponents—which is a sign of destruction for them, but of salvation for you, and that too, from God. (1:27d–28)

A third characteristic of worthy conduct involves believers **striving together.** *Sunathleō* (**striving together**) is a compound Greek word, composed of the preposition *sun* (with) and the noun *athleō,* which means to compete in a contest, especially in a sport such as wrestling. It is the term from which the English words *athlete* and *athletics* are derived. Writing to Timothy, Paul used the verb twice in its literal sense as a spiritual analogy, declaring that "if anyone competes as an athlete, he does not win the prize unless he competes according to the rules" (2 Tim. 2:5).

In the present passage, **striving together** obviously is the idea Paul has in mind, rather than the opposite one of striving or competing against, as the word could also be rendered. He is emphasizing the attitude not of taking advantage of another for one's own benefit, but rather of sacrificing one's own welfare to promote the welfare of others. The idea of contending against is implied, but only in the sense that the church must also be **striving together** against sin and the common enemy, Satan and his demon hosts.

Paul stresses here the positive relationship of believers with each other. More than one athletic team with many outstanding players has failed to win a championship because most of those players concentrated on their own success rather than the team's. A less talented team can often win against one that is more talented because the weaker team works efficiently together to achieve a common objective. A player with outstanding talent may be temporarily sidelined or even put off the team, because, impressive as his individual efforts might be, he does his team more harm than good. **Striving together** in the church means playing as a team to advance the truth of God.

Genuine unity of any sort must have a purpose. Trying to achieve unity for unity's sake is an exercise in futility, because it must have the motivation and focus of a common cause and objective. The church's only true unity is grounded in **the faith of the gospel,** which refers to the Christian faith. In other places, Paul calls it "the gospel of Christ" (Gal. 1:7) and "the glorious gospel of the blessed God," with which he and Timothy, as well as all other believers, have been entrusted (1 Tim. 1:11; 6:20; cf. Rom. 1:1; 2 Tim. 1:14; cf. 4:7). Jude refers to it as "the faith which was once for all handed down to the saints" (Jude 3).

As already noted, striving together not only advances **the faith of the gospel** but also halts the advance of whatever opposes it. The church has always faced a hostile world. Some hostility is obvious and direct, such as that from atheists, humanistic philosophers, and other religions. Much of the hostility, however, is indirect and subtle, which often is more dangerous. False teaching has found its way into churches that were once biblical and evangelical. Proponents of false gospels, whatever the form, "distort . . . the Scriptures, to their own destruction" (2 Peter 3:16), as well as to the destruction of those they deceive.

At no time in the history of the church has there been greater need for discernment than in our own day. The church desperately needs to heed the Lord's warning, "Beware of the false prophets, who come to you in sheep's clothing, but inwardly are ravenous wolves" (Matt. 7:15; cf. Acts 20:28–30; Jude 4)."Sheep's clothing" is any ungodly idea, principle, or practice that is couched in Christian terminology. Such demon doctrines, apart from thorough examination, seem to be biblical. Like Timothy, believers must constantly and carefully "guard what has been entrusted to [them], avoiding worldly and empty chatter and the opposing arguments of what is falsely called 'knowledge'" (1 Tim. 6:20; cf. 2 Tim. 1:14).

The positive goal of striving together is proclaiming **the faith of the gospel.** At Pentecost, Peter declared, "Repent, and each of you be baptized in the name of Jesus Christ for the forgiveness of your sins; and you will receive the gift of the Holy Spirit" (Acts 2:38). Not long afterward he testified before the Jewish leaders in that city:

> Let it be known to all of you and to all the people of Israel, that by the name of Jesus Christ the Nazarene, whom you crucified, whom God raised from the dead. . . . He is the stone which was rejected by you, the builders, but which became the chief corner stone. And there is salvation in no one else; for there is no other name under heaven that has been given among men by which we must be saved. (Acts 4:10–12)

From the outset of the apostolic preaching of the gospel, its absolute and unambiguous claims have been ridiculed. To the unbelieving world, such claims are the great scandal of the gospel. But those unique and exclusive truths are the gospel's very heart and substance. Jesus declared, "I am the way, and the truth, and the life; no one comes to the Father but through Me" (John 14:6), and that affirmation is reiterated throughout the New Testament.

Tragically, evangelism today seeks to remove the offense of preaching on sin and repentance, holiness and humility, in an effort to make the message more acceptable to fallen, depraved human nature. A growing number of churches intentionally play down the biblical elements of salvation and the demands of true discipleship. In so doing, the true gospel is trivialized or reduced to an impotent level, and packaged in those reductionist counterfeits are various forms of amusement and entertainment.

In the attempt to make the gospel appealing and acceptable, many churches minister in ways that effectively, though unintentionally, vitiate the very Word of God they proclaim. It is encouraging that biblically grounded, carefully reasoned, and theologically sound expository preaching is making a comeback. But, by and large, most evangelical worship services, Sunday school classes (including adult), youth meetings, and other activities are designed primarily to emotionally gratify those who attend. God-focused, reverent, and thoughtful worship, coupled with serious instruction, exhortation, and correction from the Word, is rare.

Much as Christians praise great preachers and theologians of the past such as George Whitefield, Jonathan Edwards, or Charles Spurgeon, most church members today would not be content to listen to any of those men for more than a few minutes, much less a few hours (the length of some of their sermons!). They would claim that those men were wonderful instruments of the Lord for their own days, but terribly out of touch with where people are today.

Paul encouraged the Philippian believers to be **in no way alarmed by your opponents. Alarmed** is from *pturō,* a verb used only here in the New Testament. It did not necessarily mean abject fright, as the King James Version's rendering "terrified" would suggest. But it did refer to serious, fearful concern. It was used of a startled horse who bolted, often because of something perfectly harmless, and threw his rider. Christians in Paul's day, including those in Philippi, often had good human reason to be terrified of possible beatings, imprisonment, and even execution by **opponents** of the gospel. Others faced somewhat less serious **opponents:** family members, friends, and neighbors who ridiculed and disowned them. But however serious their conflict might be, they were not to be **alarmed,** because the very fact that they were being attacked because of the gospel was proof that their opponents were headed for **destruction. But** it was also **a sign** of believers' eternal **salvation.** Both signs are **from God,** the first to mark out His enemies, the second to mark out His children. Similarly, Paul encouraged the faithful Thessalonians, saying, "We ourselves speak proudly of you among the churches of God for your perseverance and faith in the midst of all your persecutions and afflictions which you endure," and then he explained that "this is a plain indication of God's righteous judgment" (2 Thess. 1:4–5; cf. vv. 6–8).

Sign is from *endeixis,* which refers to proving, or giving evidence, that something is true. In other words, by their very hostility to believers and to the gospel, the **opponents** of the gospel give twofold evidence that testifies against them and for believers.

First, the **sign** shows that the enemies of God and His people are under His severe judgment. Paul describes that judgment as **destruction,** a reference to eternal punishment, not annihilation. It is that everlasting suffering in hell described in 2 Thessalonians:

Therefore, we ourselves speak proudly of you among the churches of God for your perseverance and faith in the midst of all your persecutions and afflictions which you endure. This is a plain indication of God's righteous judgment so that you will be considered worthy of the kingdom of God, for which indeed you are suffering. For after all it is only just for God to repay with affliction those who afflict you, and to give relief to you who are afflicted and to us as well when the Lord Jesus will be revealed from heaven with His mighty angels in flaming fire, dealing out retribution to those who do not know God and to those who do not obey the gospel of our Lord Jesus. (1:4–8)

The Lord Jesus Christ referred to this destruction in hell as everlasting fire and torment (Matt. 25:30, 41). As Psalm 73 makes clear, the wicked who seem to prosper and escape pain and suffering are, in fact, in a pitiful state and headed for destruction.

The second thing this **sign** gives evidence of is the **salvation** of those who suffer hostility from the **opponents** of the gospel. Persecution for the sake of Christ proves believers belong to Him. Thus persecution that tends to be discouraging to believers should be a source of confidence and joy because it shows they are saved. Paul was honored to "bear on [his] body the brand-marks of Jesus" (Gal. 6:17; cf. Col. 1:24), that is, to have been afflicted by those who hated Christ.

As the church struggles to fulfill its divine mission, it must never be intimidated, either by unbelieving opponents in the world or by critics from within its own ranks. Both its opponents' **destruction** and its **salvation** are divinely secured, because the outcomes are **from God.**

In reverse order, Jesus spoke of the same dual truth in John 3:16–21. In this powerful and unambiguous declaration, the Lord asserts the eternal damnation of unbelievers as well as the assurance of eternal life for believers. The warning of damnation is implied in the phrases "shall not perish" (v. 16c) and "might be saved" (v. 17c) and then given specifically:

> He who does not believe has been judged already, because he has not believed in the name of the only begotten Son of God. This is the judgment, that the Light has come into the world, and men loved the darkness rather than the Light, for their deeds were evil. For everyone who does evil hates the Light, and does not come to the Light for fear that his deeds will be exposed. (vv. 18b–20)

SUFFERING

For to you it has been granted for Christ's sake, not only to believe in Him, but also to suffer for His sake, experiencing the

same conflict which you saw in me, and now hear to be in me.
(1:29–30)

The fourth mark of conduct "worthy of the gospel of Christ" is believers' suffering because of their faith in Him. As with the previous mark, the provision here is twofold. **For Christ's sake,** God provides His children with both faith and suffering.

Has been granted is from *charizō,* which is from the same root as the noun *charis* (grace) and literally means "to give, render, or grant graciously." In His sovereign grace, God not only gave believers the marvelous gift of faith to believe in Him, but also the privilege to suffer for His sake. Such suffering provides the reward of future glory (Rom. 8:17; 1 Peter 4:12–16).

The first thing believers have **been granted for Christ's sake** is saving faith to **believe in Him.** Through that faith comes the salvation Paul has just mentioned (v. 28). In Ephesians, he explains in more detail that

> God, being rich in mercy, because of His great love with which He loved us, even when we were dead in our transgressions, made us alive together with Christ (by grace you have been saved), and raised us up with Him, and seated us with Him in the heavenly places in Christ Jesus, so that in the ages to come He might show the surpassing riches of His grace in kindness toward us in Christ Jesus. For by grace you have been saved through faith; and that not of yourselves, it is the gift of God. (Eph. 2:4–8)

All that is in salvation, including the grace and the faith, is a gift from God. As John proclaims in the introduction to his gospel, "As many as received Him, to them He gave the right to become children of God, even to those who believe in His name" (John 1:12). Later in that gospel, Jesus told the Samaritan woman, "If you knew the gift of God, and who it is who says to you, 'Give Me a drink,' you would have asked Him, and He would have given you living water" (4:10).

The second gift that God grants to His children **for Christ's sake** is not as appealing as the first. Nevertheless, it is also an integral part of divine grace. Paul reminded Timothy, "Indeed, all who desire to live godly in Christ Jesus will be persecuted" (2 Tim. 3:12). During His earthly ministry, Jesus made clear to those who truly sought to follow Him,

> You will be hated by all because of My name, but it is the one who has endured to the end who will be saved. . . . A disciple is not above his teacher, nor a slave above his master. It is enough for the disciple that he become like his teacher, and the slave like his master. If they have called the head of the house Beelzebul, how much more will they

malign the members of his household! (Matt. 10:22, 24–25; cf. John 16:2–3)

"If anyone wishes to come after Me," He declared, "he must deny himself, and take up his cross and follow Me" (Mark 8:34).

Yet not long after that He said,

> Truly I say to you, there is no one who has left house or brothers or sisters or mother or father or children or farms, for My sake and for the gospel's sake, but that he will receive a hundred times as much now in the present age, houses and brothers and sisters and mothers and children and farms, along with persecutions; and in the age to come, eternal life. (Mark 10:29–30)

On another occasion, after He commanded, "Take My yoke upon you and learn from Me," He immediately added the divine assurance: "for I am gentle and humble in heart, and you will find rest for your souls. For My yoke is easy and My burden is light" (Matt. 11:29–30).

That is the point here: **To suffer for** Christ's sake not only is a command but also a privilege. Paul never forgot the Lord's prediction through Ananias that he would be "a chosen instrument of Mine, to bear My name before the Gentiles and kings and the sons of Israel," and that "he must suffer for My name's sake" (Acts 9:15–16). Later in Philippians, he makes it clear that, in light of the immense, eternal riches believers receive in Christ, nothing on this earth that they forsake for Him can truly be a sacrifice. Paul affirms that

> whatever things were gain to me, those things I have counted as loss for the sake of Christ. More than that, I count all things to be loss in view of the surpassing value of knowing Christ Jesus my Lord, for whom I have suffered the loss of all things, and count them but rubbish so that I may gain Christ, and may be found in Him, not having a righteousness of my own derived from the Law, but that which is through faith in Christ, the righteousness which comes from God on the basis of faith. (3:7–9)

Among the immeasurable blessings he had received through faith in Christ were not only that of knowing "Him and the power of His resurrection," but also sharing in "the fellowship of His sufferings, being conformed to His death" (v. 10). Suffering for Christ's **sake** is not a burden but rather a high honor He graciously bestows on His faithful saints.

Believers are, in fact, to "exult in [their] tribulations, knowing that tribulation brings about perseverance; and perseverance, proven character; and proven character, hope; and hope does not disappoint, because the love of God has been poured out within our hearts through the Holy Spirit who was given to us" (Rom. 5:3–5; cf. James 1:2–4). Reminding believers of their heavenly inheritance, Peter echoes Paul's admonition:

> In this you greatly rejoice, even though now for a little while, if necessary, you have been distressed by various trials, so that the proof of your faith, being more precious than gold which is perishable, even though tested by fire, may be found to result in praise and glory and honor at the revelation of Jesus Christ; and though you have not seen Him, you love Him, and though you do not see Him now, but believe in Him, you greatly rejoice with joy inexpressible and full of glory. (1 Peter 1:6–8; cf. 4:13; 5:10; Acts 5:41)

When they suffer for the Lord's sake, Paul goes on to tell his readers, they are **experiencing the same conflict which you saw in me, and now hear to be in me. The conflict which you saw in me** refers to the hostile opposition and persecution he and Silas faced when they were imprisoned in Philippi (Acts 16:16–40). **And now hear to be in me** refers, of course, to the apostle's present imprisonment in Rome, which he has already mentioned (vv. 12–18).

It is the mandate of the church to stand, to share, to strive, and to suffer for the sake of the Lord Jesus Christ. It is for this "that we have been destined" (1 Thess. 3:3).

The Formula
for Spiritual Unity
(Philippians 2:1–4)

7

Therefore if there is any encouragement in Christ, if there is any consolation of love, if there is any fellowship of the Spirit, if any affection and compassion, make my joy complete by being of the same mind, maintaining the same love, united in spirit, intent on one purpose. Do nothing from selfishness or empty conceit, but with humility of mind regard one another as more important than yourselves; do not merely look out for your own personal interests, but also for the interests of others. (2:1–4)

Perhaps the greatest danger facing the church is an attack on its source of authority, namely, the Word of God. Spiritual apathy and a general coldness and indifference to biblical truth and God's standards of righteousness also pose serious risks. Such indifference is usually denied, often with an aura of self-deceptive sincerity, but it attacks the spirituality of the church. Equally to be feared is whatever attacks the unity of the church. All of these can disrupt, weaken, and destroy a church by causing discord, disharmony, conflict, and division. When Paul closed his last letter to the Corinthians, he expressed his fear of sins that destroy unity: "For I am afraid that perhaps when I come I may find you to be not what I wish and may be found by you to be not what you wish;

that perhaps there will be strife, jealousy, angry tempers, disputes, slanders, gossip, arrogance, disturbances" (2 Cor. 12:20). He also feared sins that destroyed the purity of the church: "I am afraid that when I come again my God may humiliate me before you, and I may mourn over many of those who have sinned in the past and not repented of the impurity, immorality and sensuality which they have practiced" (v. 21).

Apparently the Philippian church faced the danger of discord and division from the personal conflict between Euodia and Syntyche (4:2). Disunity is a potential danger for every church, a danger Paul addressed to some extent in every one of his letters to churches. To the church at Rome he wrote, "Now may the God who gives perseverance and encouragement grant you to be of the same mind with one another according to Christ Jesus, so that with one accord you may with one voice glorify the God and Father of our Lord Jesus Christ. Therefore, accept one another, just as Christ also accepted us to the glory of God" (Rom. 15:5–7; cf. 12:5, 16). To the Corinthians he wrote, "Now I exhort you, brethren, by the name of our Lord Jesus Christ, that you all agree and that there be no divisions among you, but that you be made complete in the same mind and in the same judgment" (1 Cor. 1:10), and "Brethren, rejoice, be made complete, be comforted, be like-minded, live in peace; and the God of love and peace will be with you" (2 Cor. 13:11). He warned the Galatians, "Let us not become boastful, challenging one another, envying one another" (Gal. 5:26; cf. 6:2–3). He implored the believers in Ephesus,

> Walk in a manner worthy of the calling with which you have been called, with all humility and gentleness, with patience, showing tolerance for one another in love, being diligent to preserve the unity of the Spirit in the bond of peace. There is one body and one Spirit, just as also you were called in one hope of your calling; one Lord, one faith, one baptism, one God and Father of all who is over all and through all and in all. (Eph. 4:1–6)

True spiritual unity is grounded in the unfathomable unity of the Trinity itself.

To the Colossians Paul wrote,

> Put on a heart of compassion, kindness, humility, gentleness and patience; bearing with one another, and forgiving each other, whoever has a complaint against anyone; just as the Lord forgave you, so also should you. Beyond all these things put on love, which is the perfect bond of unity. Let the peace of Christ rule in your hearts, to which indeed you were called in one body; and be thankful. (Col. 3:12–15)

He commended the Thessalonians, saying, "Now as to the love of the brethren, you have no need for anyone to write to you, for you yourselves are taught by God to love one another; ... But we urge you, brethren, to excel still more" (1 Thess. 4:9–10; cf. 2 Thess. 1:3).

The foundation for believers' oneness is the unity God granted in answer to Jesus' prayer that His people "may all be one; even as You, Father, are in Me and I in You, that they also may be in Us, so that the world may believe that You sent Me" (John 17:21). That prayer was answered when the Holy Spirit came at Pentecost and afterward to indwell all believers, bringing to them the eternal life in which all believers are partakers (cf. 1 Cor. 6:17, 19; 12:12–14). That essential unity of all believers in the body of Christ should be lived out in practice.

Disunity among His people deeply grieves the Lord. It should be every pastor's, church leader's, and church member's prayer that men will not tear asunder what God has divinely joined together in the body of Christ. Because fracturing Christ's church is one of Satan's major objectives, the challenge to preserve the unity of the spirit is constant. A divided, factious, and bickering church is spiritually weak. It therefore offers little threat to the devil's work and has little power for advancing the gospel of Christ. Endeavoring to maintain, or to restore, the spiritual unity of a congregation is easily the most pressing, difficult, and constant challenge for its leaders.

Although sound doctrine, moral purity, and passionate commitment to the Lord and to His work are essential to a church's effective ministry, they alone cannot guarantee protection from discord. William Barclay perceptively observed that

> the one danger which threatened the Philippian church was that of disunity. There is a sense in which that is the danger of every healthy church. It is when people are really in earnest, when their beliefs really matter to them, that they are apt to get up against each other. The greater their enthusiasm, the greater the danger that they may collide. It is against that danger Paul wished to safeguard his friends. (*The Letters to the Philippians, Colossians, and Thessalonians.* Rev. ed., [Louisville, Ky.: Westminster, 1975], 31)

Paul's concern here is not about doctrines, ideas, or practices that are clearly unbiblical. It is about interpretations, standards, interests, preferences, and the like that are largely matters of personal choice. Such issues should never be allowed to foment controversy within the body of Christ. To insist on one's own way in such things is sinful, because it senselessly divides believers. It reflects a prideful desire to promote one's personal views, style, or agenda. Believers must never, of course, compromise doctrines or principles that are clearly biblical. But to humbly defer to one another on secondary issues is a mark of spiritual strength, not weakness (cf. Rom. 14:1–15:7). It is a mark of maturity and love that God highly honors, because it promotes and preserves harmony in His church.

This unity that the Word so highly exalts is inward, not outward; it is internally desired, not externally compelled. It is spiritual, not ecclesiastical; more heartfelt than creedal. It is not grounded in sentimentalism but in careful, thoughtful, and determined obedience to God's will. It is the Spirit-motivated and Spirit-empowered bonding of the hearts, minds, and souls of God's children to each other. And preserving unity in the church is not an option (cf. Eph. 4:3).

As an analogy, consider a bag filled with marbles. There are many marbles of various colors, sizes, and composition packed closely together. But they are bound together exclusively by the container. If the bag is opened or ripped, the marbles spill out in all directions, because there is nothing internal that binds them to each other. In contrast, consider a magnet placed into a pile of iron shavings. By their nature, the shavings respond to the power of the magnet and are drawn together. If some outside force causes them to be pulled apart, the attractive force remains and they will reunite as soon as the separating cause is removed. In the same way, faithful Christians who are separated by circumstances beyond their control will maintain their mutual attraction through the "magnetic" power of the Spirit working within them. Like a close human family that is tragically divided by war or natural disaster, they will continually seek to be reunited as the spiritual family they are. That divinely empowered internal unity of spirit is essential to the church's joy and effectiveness.

That unity was manifested in the infant church following Pentecost. The thousands of new believers (most of them previously strangers and some perhaps even former enemies) "were continually devoting themselves to the apostles' teaching and to fellowship. . . . And all those who had believed were together and had all things in common. . . . Day by day continuing with one mind in the temple, and breaking bread from house to house, they were taking their meals together with gladness and sincerity of heart" (Acts 2:42, 44, 46).

Although their oneness in Christ is permanent, the human frailty that believers are still subject to makes their unity fragile. It is for that reason that Paul counseled the Ephesians to be "diligent to preserve the unity of the Spirit in the bond of peace" (Eph. 4:3). "Diligent" is from *spoudazō*, which describes making a persistent effort. Spiritual unity must be constantly cultivated and preserved with selfless devotion and energy. As already noted, it is easily the greatest challenge of spiritual oversight and leadership in a church.

The church at Philippi was for the most part theologically sound, devoted, moral, loving, zealous, courageous, prayerful, and generous. Yet it faced the danger of discord that often is generated by only a few people. Such troublemakers can stir up the contention and strife that fractures an entire congregation. And because disunity is so tragically debilitating, Paul gently but firmly pleads with believers to be constantly and diligently on guard against it. He had just expressed to the Philippians his hope to "hear of [them] that [they] are standing firm in one spirit, with one mind striving together for the faith of the gospel" (1:27).

In 2:1–4 Paul gives what is perhaps the most concise and practical teaching about unity in the New Testament. In these four powerful verses, he outlines a formula for spiritual unity that includes three necessary elements on which that unity must be built: the right motives (vv. 1–2a), the right marks (v. 2b), and the right means (vv. 3–4). Through them, he clarifies *why* believers should be of one mind and spirit, *what* is meant by one mind and spirit, and *how* they can truly become of one mind and spirit.

THE RIGHT MOTIVES FOR SPIRITUAL UNITY

Therefore if there is any encouragement in Christ, if there is any consolation of love, if there is any fellowship of the Spirit, if any affection and compassion, make my joy complete (2:1–2a)

The updated (1995) edition of the *New American Standard Bible* used here reverses the order of the previous rendering of "If therefore." The new order more clearly connects **therefore** to what Paul has just said, which many scholars believe was his intent. The meaning, then, is that what he is about to say is grounded, at least in part, on what he has just said. The point is that, "Because we have the divine injunction to be of one mind and spirit (1:27), we must **therefore** ..."

There are four "ifs" in verse 1. The Greek particle *ei* (**if**) is always conditional when used with an indicative verb. In Paul's writings, however, the related verb often is only implied and needs to be supplied in the translation, as it is here (**there is**). *Ei* here introduces a first-class conditional clause, which expresses the idea, "If this condition is true, and it is, then . . ." Consequently, the word may better be rendered "because," "since," or "so" in order to give a more complete idea of its meaning.

In the present context, **therefore** and **if** refer to two closely related conditions. As already noted, **therefore** looks *back* to the principle that, because they have the divine injunction to be of one mind and spirit (1:27), believers must ... **If** looks *forward* to the divinely bestowed realities of **encouragement in Christ, ... consolation of love, ... fellowship of the Spirit, ... [and] affection and compassion.** Both principles should motivate believers to desire and actively seek the unity of mind, love, spirit, and purpose mentioned in the following verse (2:2). Paul is not speaking of theological abstractions but of personal relationships between Christians. To reinforce his point, he repeats the *ei* (**if**) before each of the four marvelous realities. The first two relate primarily to Christ, the first one explicitly and the second implicitly. The second two relate primarily to the Holy Spirit, again the first one explicitly and the second implicitly.

The first reality that motivates unity is **encouragement in Christ.** *Paraklēsis* (**encouragement**) has the root meaning of coming alongside someone to give assistance by offering comfort, counsel, or exhortation. It is precisely the kind of assistance exemplified by the Good Samaritan, who, after doing everything he could for the robbed and beaten stranger, "took out two denarii and gave them to the innkeeper and said, 'Take care of him; and whatever more you spend, when I return I will repay you'" (Luke 10:35; cf. vv. 30–34).

Using a closely related word, Jesus referred to the Holy Spirit as "another Helper [*paraklēton*]," whom He would ask the Father to send to all who would believe in Him, so "that He may be with [them] forever" (John 14:16). The most important and powerful **encouragement in Christ** comes directly from the indwelling Spirit. Paul's admonition here is that, in light of that **encouragement**, the Philippians should "conduct [themselves] in a manner worthy of the gospel of Christ" (1:27) by endeavoring to be of one mind and spirit with each other. This profound spiritual principle demands pursuing unity as a grateful response to the believer's union with Christ. Paul asks, in effect, "Shouldn't the divine influence of Christ in your life compel you to preserve the unity that is so precious to Him?"

The second reality that motivates unity is the **consolation of love.** *Paramuthion* (**consolation**) has the literal meaning of speaking closely with someone, and with the added idea of giving comfort and solace. Its basic meaning is close to that of *paraklēsis* (**encouragement**); both words involve a close relationship marked by genuine concern, helpfulness, and **love.** The consoling **love** is that which the Lord grants to unworthy sinners in the grace of salvation. He continuously bestows that **love** on believers (Rom. 5:5), who in turn show **love** for fellow believers. That demonstrates gratitude for God's **love** for them. Paul told the Corinthians that it was Christ's **love** for him that made him to be so devoted to the Lord and the truth as to appear insane (2 Cor. 5:13–14).

The third reality that motivates unity is the **fellowship of the Spirit**. *Koinōnia* (**fellowship**) describes partnership and mutual sharing. This fellowship is intimate because every believer is a temple of the Holy **Spirit** (1 Cor. 6:19). He is the seal and guarantor of believers' eternal inheritance (Eph. 1:13–14; 4:30; 2 Cor. 1:22), the source of spiritual power (Acts 1:8; cf. Rom. 15:19), spiritual gifts (1 Cor. 12:4–11; Rom. 12:6–8), and spiritual fruit (Gal. 5:22–23). The **Spirit** "helps [us in] our weakness," and because "we do not know how to pray as we should, . . . the Spirit Himself intercedes for us with groanings too deep for words" (Rom. 8:26). Believers are to be continually filled with the Spirit (Eph. 5:18). To inhibit or be indifferent to spiritual unity is to both grieve the **Spirit** (Eph. 4:30) and quench His work (1 Thess. 5:19). The new believers after Pentecost give the most vivid illustration in the New Testament of Spirit-led unity (Acts 2:41–47). Paul closes 2 Corinthians with the beautiful benediction, "The grace of the Lord Jesus Christ, and the love of God, and the fellowship of the Holy Spirit, be with you all" (2 Cor. 13:14). Earlier he had reminded the same congregation that "by one Spirit we were all baptized into one body, whether Jews or Greeks, whether slaves or free, and we were all made to drink of one Spirit" (1 Cor. 12:13). The proper response of believers should be a compelling motivation to be "diligent to preserve the unity of the Spirit" by always pursuing peace (Eph. 4:3).

The fourth reality that motivates unity is that of **affection and compassion**. Those qualities characterize Christ, who tenderly comforts and encourages the weak and oppressed (cf. Isa. 42:3; Matt. 12:18–20). Such graces are also blessings of the Spirit of Christ. **Affection** is from *splanchna*, which refers literally to the bowels, or viscera, but was commonly used metaphorically of the emotions. Paul commended the church in Corinth for their gracious treatment of Titus and assured them that "his affection abounds all the more toward you, as he remembers the obedience of you all, how you received him with fear and trembling" (2 Cor. 7:13, 15). The word sometimes was used in connection with deep, personal longing, especially for those who are dearly loved. Near the beginning of the present letter, the apostle specifically used the word in that way, assuring the Philippians: "I long for you all with the affection of Christ Jesus" (1:8). **Compassion** is from *oiktirmos*, which Paul uses twice of the compassion ("mercies") of God. He pleads with believers, "by the mercies of God, to present your bodies a living and holy sacrifice, acceptable to God, which is your spiritual service of worship" (Rom. 12:1), and he speaks of God as "the Father of mercies" (2 Cor. 1:3). "As those who have been chosen of God, holy and beloved," believers should reflect His own compassion by putting "on a heart of compassion, kindness, humility, gentleness and patience" (Col. 3:12).

There is an implied negative side to all four of these positive admonitions, namely, that failing to seek and preserve spiritual unity weakens Christ's church. Even more significantly, such failure to pursue unity is a sin. It is the ultimate act of ingratitude to God. It is to be willing and eager to receive every blessing that the Lord offers, but unwilling to offer Him anything in return. Like every other sin, that indifference is a violation of God's revealed Word. It also despises the glorious truth that the "Lord Jesus Christ Himself and God our Father . . . has loved us and given us eternal comfort and good hope by grace" (2 Thess. 2:16).

The apostle bases his plea primarily on the grace and goodness of the Lord, as evidenced in the four realities just mentioned. But at the beginning of verse 2 he adds a personal desire: **make my joy complete.** To so reward a faithful servant of the Lord is a legitimate goal for believers to have. The New Testament makes it clear that churches are to love, honor, respect, and appreciate their human leaders. Paul admonished the Thessalonians, "We request of you, brethren, that you appreciate those who diligently labor among you, and have charge over you in the Lord and give you instruction, and that you esteem them very highly in love because of their work" (1 Thess. 5:12–13). The writer of Hebrews commands: "Obey your leaders and submit to them, for they keep watch over your souls as those who will give an account. Let them do this with joy and not with grief, for this would be unprofitable for you" (Heb. 13:17). To love, honor, and appreciate pastors and other church leaders is perfectly consonant with loving, honoring, and being grateful to the Lord. Because both are divinely commanded, the former is one way of expressing the latter.

THE RIGHT MARKS OF SPIRITUAL UNITY

by being of the same mind, maintaining the same love, united in spirit, intent on one purpose. (2:2b)

The spiritual blessings Paul has enumerated demand a proper response. In this single verse Paul gives four essential marks of spiritual unity.

The first is **being of the same mind.** That phrase translates *to auto phronēte,* which literally means "to think the same thing," or "to be like-minded." Thinking right is essential to the spiritual unity that is a major theme of Philippians—of the twenty-six occurrences of the verb *phroneō* in the New Testament, ten are found in this letter.

Paul is not talking here about doctrine or moral standards. In this context, **being of the same mind** means to actively strive to achieve common understanding and genuine agreement. A few verses later, the apostle declares that the only way to have such harmony is to "have this attitude in yourselves which was also in Christ Jesus" (2:5). Through God's Word and the indwelling Holy Spirit, believers can know the very "mind of Christ" (1 Cor. 2:16). After declaring his determination to "press on so that I may lay hold of that for which also I was laid hold of by Christ Jesus . . . [and to] press on toward the goal for the prize of the upward call of God in Christ Jesus" (3:12, 14), he admonishes the Philippian believers to have that same attitude (Phil. 3:15). Those who have a contrary attitude prove that they have "set their minds on earthly things" (3:19). Paul later gives practical advice for **being of the same mind:** "Finally, brethren, whatever is true, whatever is honorable, whatever is right, whatever is pure, whatever is lovely, whatever is of good repute, if there is any excellence and if anything worthy of praise, dwell on these things" (4:8).

In Romans Paul gives added insights regarding **being of the same mind.** The first is that believers must "not walk according to the flesh but according to the Spirit. For those who are according to the flesh set their minds on the things of the flesh, but those who are according to the Spirit, the things of the Spirit" (Rom. 8:4–5). As Paul reminded the Colossian believers, conflict in the church always comes from believers' setting their minds "on the things that are on earth" rather than "on the things above" (Col. 3:2). Paul further notes in Romans that a believer is "not to think more highly of himself than he ought to think," which is a subjective and erroneous opinion, "but to think so as to have sound judgment, as God has allotted to each a measure of faith" (Rom. 12:3). Obeying the commands to have a mind set on the things of the Spirit and to think with sound judgment results in "the God who gives perseverance and encouragement" granting believers the ability "to be of the same mind with one another according to Christ Jesus" (15:5). Paul could therefore confidently admonish even the immature, divided church at Corinth to "rejoice, be made complete, be comforted, be like-minded, live in peace; and the God of love and peace will be with you" (2 Cor. 13:11).

A second mark of spiritual unity is **maintaining the same love,** which flows out of and augments "being of the same mind." To have the **same love** is to love others equally. On a purely emotional level, having equal love for others is impossible, because people are not equally attractive. *Agapē* (**love**), however, is the love of will, not of preference or attraction. It is based on an intentional, conscious choice to seek the welfare of its object. It is because *agapē* (**love**) is based on the will that it can be commanded.

To have **the same love** is to "be devoted to one another in brotherly love; [giving] preference to one another in honor," and includes the desire to serve others by such things as "contributing to the needs of the saints, [and] practicing hospitality" (Rom. 12:10, 13). As Paul goes on to say in that passage, *agapē* love embraces unbelievers—even those who persecute are to be blessed rather than cursed (v. 14). But in the present text, Paul is focusing on **the same** special and mutual **love** that believers are to have for each other, the love he speaks of in another letter as "the love of each one of you toward one another [that] grows ever greater" (2 Thess. 1:3).

In his first letter, John makes it unequivocally clear that love for other believers characterizes a genuine Christian: "We know that we have passed out of death into life," he says, "because we love the brethren. He who does not love abides in death" (1 John 3:14). In other words, a lack of at least some measure of genuine *agapē* (**love**) for other Christians exposes a lack of salvation. Genuine love is not merely sentimental affection but sacrificial services. "Whoever has the world's goods, and sees his brother in need and closes his heart against him, how does the love of God abide in him?" John asks rhetorically (v. 17). Believers are not to love merely "with word or with tongue, but in deed and truth" (v. 18), which may even require "lay[ing] down our lives for the brethren," just as Christ "laid down His life for us" (v. 16).

Minds governed by selfless humility (Phil. 2:3) produce lives that overflow with genuine, practical **love** for fellow believers. On the other hand, sinful, self-centered thinking inhibits love and unity. Dissension and lack of unity in the church inevitably stem from lack of **love.**

A third mark of spiritual unity is being **united in spirit,** which is inextricably related to having the same mind and maintaining the same love. *Sumpsuchos* (**united**) literally means "one-souled" and is used only here in the New Testament. It has the same emphasis as the "one spirit" spoken of in 1:27. To be **united in spirit** is to live in selfless harmony with fellow believers. By definition, it excludes personal ambition, selfishness, hatred, envy, jealously, and the countless other evils that are the fruit of self-love.

Like every other Christian virtue, unity of **spirit** must be grounded in the objective truth of God's Word. But it also has a subjective aspect. Such unity involves a deep and passionate concern for God, His Word, His work, His gospel, and His people. No two Christians—no matter what their level of spiritual maturity and knowledge of Scripture— will understand everything exactly alike. But if they are controlled by humility and love, they will be genuinely **united in spirit.** They will not allow inconsequential differences to divide them or to hinder their service for the Lord.

A fourth mark of spiritual unity is being **intent on one purpose,** which is the natural companion of the preceding three. **Intent on one**

purpose translates a participial form of *phroneō,* which Paul used earlier in this verse ("being of the . . . mind") and uses again in verse 5 ("have . . . attitude"). The phrase *to en phronountes* (**intent on one purpose**) literally means "thinking one thing" and is therefore virtually synonymous with having "the same mind."

In this one verse the apostle presents a full circle of unity—from one mind, to one love, to one spirit, to one purpose, which, as just noted, basically refers again to the mind. These four principles are complementary, overlapping, and inseparable. The same basic idea is expressed in four ways, each with a somewhat different but important emphasis.

In Colossians, Paul beautifully summarizes these marks of spiritual unity:

> So, as those who have been chosen of God, holy and beloved, put on a heart of compassion, kindness, humility, gentleness and patience; bearing with one another, and forgiving each other, whoever has a complaint against anyone; just as the Lord forgave you, so also should you. Beyond all these things put on love, which is the perfect bond of unity. Let the peace of Christ rule in your hearts, to which indeed you were called in one body; and be thankful. Let the word of Christ richly dwell within you, with all wisdom teaching and admonishing one another with psalms and hymns and spiritual songs, singing with thankfulness in your hearts to God. (3:12–16)

THE RIGHT MEANS FOR SPIRITUAL UNITY

Do nothing from selfishness or empty conceit, but with humility of mind regard one another as more important than yourselves; do not merely look out for your own personal interests, but also for the interests of others. (2:3–4)

In presenting these five means, Paul answers the question of how genuine spiritual unity is achieved. After what he has just said in verses 1–2, these means require little explanation or comment. Like the four marks of spiritual unity, these five means are interrelated and inseparable. Three are negative and two are positive.

It is not surprising that rejecting **selfishness** is listed first, since it is the root of every other sin. It was by placing his will above God's that Satan fell (cf. Isa. 14:12–17), and it was by placing their own wills above God's that Adam and Eve first brought sin into the world (Gen. 3). Self-will has been at the heart of every subsequent sin. There is no verb (**do**) in the Greek text, but the grammatical form (*mēden kat eritheia,* lit., "nothing by way of selfishness") expresses a negative command. That prohibition goes far beyond mere action; **selfishness** is also to be totally excluded from the innermost thoughts of the heart.

Paul used *eritheia* (**selfishness**) earlier in this letter, where it was rendered "selfish ambition" (1:17). As noted in the discussion of that text, the term did not originally have a negative connotation and merely referred to a day laborer. But it came to be used metaphorically, and almost exclusively, of a person who persistently seeks personal advantage and gain, regardless of the effect on others. It often was used of the unfair pursuit and self-serving preservation of political office. By New Testament times, it had come to mean unbridled, selfish ambition in any field of endeavor. For obvious reasons, *eritheia* was often associated with personal and party rivalry, quarreling, infighting, and strife (as the King James Version renders it here). It usually carried the idea of building oneself up by tearing someone else down, as in gambling, where one person's gain is derived from others' losses. The word accurately describes someone who strives to advance himself by using flattery, deceit, false accusation, contentiousness, and any other tactic that seems advantageous. It is hardly surprising, then, that Paul lists *eritheia* ("disputes") as one of the works of the flesh (Gal. 5:20).

Selfishness is a consuming and destructive sin. The first and inevitable casualty is the person who manifests it, even if no one else is harmed. Because this sin, like every other, begins in a sinful heart, anyone can commit it—regardless of whether there is an opportunity for it to be outwardly expressed. Even when not outwardly manifested, **selfishness** breeds anger, resentment, and jealousy. No church, even the most doctrinally sound and spiritually mature, is immune from the threat of this sin, and nothing can more quickly divide and weaken a church. Selfish ambition is often clothed in pious rhetoric by those who are convinced of their own superior abilities in promoting the cause of Christ.

Judging from the New Testament record, no church had a greater problem with this sin than the one in Corinth. Paul implored them: "I exhort you, brethren, by the name of our Lord Jesus Christ, that you all agree and that there be no divisions among you, but that you be made complete in the same mind and in the same judgment. For I have been informed concerning you, my brethren, by Chloe's people, that there are quarrels among you" (1 Cor. 1:10–11). Various factions in the church followed Apollos, Peter, or Paul. One group, probably the most self-righteous, claimed to follow only "Christ." But "has Christ been divided?" the apostle asked with astonishment. "Paul was not crucified for you, was he? Or were you baptized in the name of Paul?" (vv. 12–13; cf. 3:4–6). In a strong rebuke, he later told them,

I, brethren, could not speak to you as to spiritual men, but as to men of flesh, as to infants in Christ. I gave you milk to drink, not solid food; for you were not yet able to receive it. Indeed, even now you are not yet able, for you are still fleshly. For since there is jealousy and strife among you, are you not fleshly, and are you not walking like mere men? (3:1–3)

The objects of personal loyalty in the Corinthian church (Apollos, Peter, and Paul) were faithful leaders who were entirely worthy of the congregation's respect and admiration. Two of them were leading apostles. But the real loyalty of those factious Corinthians, even that of the "Christ" faction, was to themselves. The factions sought not so much to honor those favored leaders as to create exclusive cliques for their own personal elevation. Each of the groups was self-serving. Promoting the cause of Christ and the unity of His church were far from their primary purposes. Rather than serving Christ and others in His name, they were serving themselves while using His name. Selfish ambition is produced by and is a clear mark of the "deeds of the flesh" (Gal. 5:19–20). It poisons even work done on behalf of clearly biblical causes. Hypocritically presuming to serve God while actually serving self marked the scribes and Pharisees (cf. Matt. 15:1–9).

Discord and division are inevitable when people focus on their agendas to the exclusion of others in the church. Often such a narrow focus arises out of genuine passion for an important ministry. But disregard of fellow believers, no matter how unintentional, is a mark of loveless, sinful indifference that produces jealousy, contention, strife, and the other enemies of spiritual unity. Wherever "jealousy and selfish ambition exist," whatever the cause, "there is disorder and every evil thing" (James 3:16).

A second means for promoting spiritual unity is forsaking **empty conceit**. **Empty conceit** translates the compound Greek word *kenodoxia*, which appears only here in the New Testament. It is formed by the adjective *kenos* ("empty") and the noun *doxa* ("glory"), hence the King James Version rendering "vainglory." It refers to a highly exaggerated self-view, which is nothing but **empty conceit**. Whereas selfish ambition pursues personal goals, **empty conceit** seeks personal glory and acclaim. The former pertains to personal accomplishments; the latter to an overinflated self-image. Understandably, a person with such **conceit** considers himself always to be right and expects others to agree with him. The only unity he seeks or values is centered on himself.

Empty conceit is arrogant pride, being "wise in your own estimation" (Rom. 11:25). The ancient Greeks did not admire humility, thinking it was a mark of weakness. But even they recognized that a person's view of himself could become so exaggerated as to be presumptuous and contemptible. Their term for such exalted pride, a word still used in English and many other modern languages, was *hubris*. In his long list of sins that characterize unbelieving, rebellious mankind, Paul uses a word derived from *hubris*, which is rendered "insolent" (Rom. 1:30). In his letter to the Galatian churches, he warned, "For if anyone thinks he is something when he is nothing, he deceives himself" (Gal. 6:3). Because **empty conceit** is, by nature, self-deceptive, believers must be on constant guard against it. It is an implacable enemy of spiritual unity.

The third means of promoting spiritual unity Paul mentions here is positive: **humility of mind.** It is the very opposite of selfish ambition and empty conceit and is the corrective for them. **Humility of mind** is the bedrock of Christian character and of spiritual unity. It is not incidental that the first and foundational Beatitude refers to being "poor in spirit" (Matt. 5:3), which is synonymous with **humility of mind.**

Humility of mind translates the Greek word *tapeinophrosunē*, which literally means "lowliness of mind." In Acts 20:19 and Ephesians 4:2 it is rendered "humility." In secular Greek literature, the adjective *tapeinos* ("lowly") was used exclusively in a derisive way, most commonly of a slave. It described what was considered base, common, unfit, and having little value. Thus, it is not surprising that the noun *tapeinophrosunē* has not been found in any extra-biblical Greek literature before the second century. It seems, therefore, to have originated in the New Testament, where, along with its synonyms, it always has a positive connotation. **Humility of mind** is the opposite of pride, the sin that has always separated fallen men from God, making them, in effect, their own gods.

Humility is also a dominant virtue in the Old Testament. "When pride comes, then comes dishonor," warns Solomon, "but with the humble is wisdom" (Prov. 11:2). Later he declares, "It is better to be humble in spirit with the lowly than to divide the spoil with the proud" (16:19). Zechariah describes the coming messianic King as "just and endowed with salvation, humble, and mounted on a donkey, even on a colt, the foal of a donkey" (Zech. 9:9), a prophecy Matthew specifically applies to Jesus' triumphal, yet humble, entry into Jerusalem on Palm Sunday (Matt. 21:5).

Moses was "very humble, more than any man who was on the face of the earth" (Num. 12:3). David said, "For though the Lord is exalted, yet He regards the lowly, but the haughty He knows from afar" (Ps. 138:6). In another psalm, he wrote, "The humble will inherit the land" (Ps. 37:11), a passage Jesus quoted in the Beatitudes: "Blessed are the gentle [meek], for they shall inherit the earth" (Matt. 5:5). Jesus described Himself as "gentle and humble in heart" (11:29). Without pride or hypocrisy, Paul could testify honestly of himself to the elders from Ephesus, "You yourselves know, from the first day that I set foot in Asia, how I was with you the whole time, serving the Lord with all humility" (Acts 20:18–19). Three times in two verses in his first letter Peter calls for humility: "All of you, clothe yourselves with humility toward one another, for God is opposed to the proud, but gives grace to the humble. Therefore humble yourselves under the mighty hand of God, that He may exalt you at the proper time" (1 Peter 5:5–6).

Genuine humility involves believers' not thinking too highly of themselves and requires that they **regard one another as more important than** themselves. **Regard** is from a verb that means more than just having an opinion. It refers to a carefully thought-out conclusion based on the truth. It does not mean to pretend that others are more important, but to believe that others actually are **more important.**

More important translates a participial form of *huperechō,* which incorporates the Greek word from which the English word *hyper* is taken. It intensifies and elevates what is in view, so that it means "to excel, surpass, or be superior to." In Romans, Paul uses the word in speaking of the "governing [lit. 'supreme'] authorities" to which "every person is to be in subjection" (Rom. 13:1). Similarly, Peter uses the word in commanding believers to "submit [themselves] . . . to a king as the one in authority [lit., 'as being supreme']" (1 Peter 2:13). Later in the present letter, Paul uses the word to describe "the surpassing [supreme, unexcelled] value of knowing Christ Jesus my Lord" (Phil. 3:8), and to proclaim that "the peace of God, which surpasses [far exceeds, is superior to] all comprehension, will guard your hearts and your minds in Christ Jesus" (4:7).

It is clear that Paul has in mind a view of others that is not natural to man and is extremely difficult even for believers to achieve. Perhaps the best way to approach that seemingly unrealistic and impossible challenge is for believers to consider their own sins. Believers know far more about their own hearts than about the heart of anyone else. Recognizing the sinfulness of their hearts should exclude any boastful self-exaltation. If Paul viewed himself as "the least of the apostles, and not fit to be called an apostle" (1 Cor. 15:9), "the very least of all saints" (Eph. 3:8), and even the foremost of sinners (1 Tim. 1:15), how could any believers honestly think of themselves in any higher way?

A fourth means for promoting spiritual unity is the negative admonition, **do not merely look out for your own personal interests.** *Skopeō* (**look out for**) means to observe something. But, as in this context, it often carried the additional ideas of giving close attention and special consideration. By including **merely** (as well as **also** in the following phrase), the apostle excludes the unbiblical idea that asceticism reflects a deeper level of spirituality and earns special divine approval. On the contrary, it is a subtle and deceptive manifestation of legalistic pride.

Paul carefully disciplined his body to make it his slave, to avoid becoming its slave and thereby disqualifying himself for ministry (1 Cor. 9:27). He experienced "labor and hardship, through many sleepless nights, in hunger and thirst, often without food, in cold and exposure" (2 Cor. 11:27). But he never purposely starved himself or caused any self-inflicted harm to his body. During His earthly ministry, Jesus neither practiced nor approved of ascetic self-denial. He ate and slept regularly, took care of His body, and expected His followers to do the same. It should be noted that biblical fasting (Matt. 6:16–17; 9:14–15) is not to be equated with harsh, self-destructive asceticism.

Christians who do not take reasonable care of their bodies cannot live or minister effectively. Nor are they required to forsake all **personal interests** in other regards. Paul's point here relates primarily, though certainly not exclusively, to **personal interests** in serving the Lord. As already noted, many quarrels and divisions in churches concern programs or policies that may be equally biblical and important. Problems arise when people seek to promote their own ministry priorities at the expense of others. Some may consider youth ministry more important than adult ministry. Others may view personal evangelism as a higher priority than group Bible study. The possibilities for conflicts are almost endless. But division in the church is destructive. In every instance, the best **interests** of the Lord and other believers are sacrificed.

Honest discussion that seeks a biblical understanding of doctrinal and moral issues is perfectly legitimate and of great importance. But even the most serious debate over those critical matters should be carried on in a spirit of humility and mutual respect. Problems arise when defense of God's Word becomes clouded by self-defense.

It is an immeasurable tragedy that modern culture (including much of the church) has, largely through the influence of secular psychology, rejected the divinely commanded principles of humility and selflessness. When the supreme virtue is self-love and the supreme purpose in life is self-fulfillment, mutual respect is replaced by disrespect, mutual service by apathy and indifference, and mutual love by enmity and hatred.

The fifth and final means Paul mentions here for promoting spiritual unity is that of looking out **also for the interests of others.** It is the positive side of the preceding principle of not merely looking out for one's own personal interests. Like the others, this principle is related primarily to relationships between believers, especially those working together in ministry. It is broad and general, not mentioning any particular **interests** or suggesting who is included by **others.**

Like the other principles mentioned here, looking out **for the interests of others** is indispensable for spiritual unity. Also like them, it

requires deliberate and persistent effort to apply sincerely and uncondi-
tionally. And although the meaning is obvious and easy to understand, it
is difficult to apply. It is the practical outcome of the exceedingly difficult
command to regard others as more important than ourselves.

Among other things, looking out **for the interests of others** requires believers to "rejoice with those who rejoice, and weep with those
who weep" (Rom. 12:15), to continually "pursue the things which make
for peace and the building up of one another," to not "eat meat or . . .
drink wine, or . . . do anything by which [a] brother stumbles" (14:19, 21),
and to "bear the weaknesses of those without strength and not just please
ourselves" (15:1). It is to "bear one another's burdens, and thereby fulfill
the law of Christ" (Gal. 6:2).

The Model for Spiritual Unity (Philippians 2:5–8)

8

Have this attitude in yourselves which was also in Christ Jesus, who, although He existed in the form of God, did not regard equality with God a thing to be grasped, but emptied Himself, taking the form of a bond-servant, and being made in the likeness of men. Being found in appearance as a man, He humbled Himself by becoming obedient to the point of death, even death on a cross. (2:5–8)

In his book *Miracles,* C. S. Lewis offers some helpful insights for understanding the unfathomable reality of Christ's incarnation:

> In the Christian story God descends to re-ascend. He comes down; down from the heights of absolute being into time and space, down into humanity. . . . But He goes down to come up again and bring the whole ruined world up with Him. One has the picture of a strong man stooping lower and lower to get himself underneath some great complicated burden. He must stoop in order to lift, he must almost disappear under the load before he incredibly straightens his back and marches off with the whole mass swaying on his shoulders. Or one may think of a diver, first reducing himself to nakedness, then glancing in mid-air, then gone with a splash, vanished, rushing down through green

and warm water into black and cold water, down through increasing pressure into the deathlike region of ooze and slime and old decay; then up again, back to colour and light, his lungs almost bursting, till suddenly he breaks surface again, holding in his hand the dripping, precious thing that he went down to recover. He and it are both coloured now that they have come up into the light: down below, where it lay colourless in the dark, he lost his colour too.

In this descent and re-ascent everyone will recognise a familiar pattern: a thing written all over the world. It is the pattern of all vegetable life. It must belittle itself into something hard, small and deathlike, it must fall into the ground: thence the new life re-ascends. It is the pattern of all animal generation too. There is descent from the full and perfect organisms into the spermatozoon and ovum, and in the dark womb ... the slow ascent to the perfect embryo, to the living, conscious baby, and finally to the adult. So it is also in our moral and emotional life. The first innocent and spontaneous desires have to submit to the deathlike process of control or total denial: but from that there is a re-ascent to fully formed character in which the strength of the original material all operates but in a new way. Death and Re-birth—go down to go up—it is a key principle. Through this bottleneck, this belittlement, the highroad nearly always lies.

The doctrine of the Incarnation, if accepted, puts this principle even more emphatically at the centre. The pattern is there in Nature because it was first there in God. All the instances of it which I have mentioned turn out to be but transpositions of the Divine theme into a minor key. I am not now referring simply to the Crucifixion and Resurrection of Christ. The total pattern, of which they are only the turning point, is the real Death and Re-birth: for certainly no seed ever fell from so fair a tree into so dark and cold a soil as would furnish more than a faint analogy to this huge descent and re-ascension in which God dredged the salt and oozy bottom of Creation. (New York: Macmillan, 1947, 115–17)

The Incarnation is the central miracle of Christianity, the most grand and wonderful of all the things that God has ever done. That miracle of miracles is the theme of Philippians 2:5–8. Some scholars believe this passage was originally a hymn, sung by early Christians to commemorate and celebrate the incarnation of the Son of God. It has been called a Christological gem, a theological diamond that perhaps sparkles brighter than any other in Scripture. In a simple, brief, yet extraordinarily profound way, it describes the condescension of the second Person of the Trinity to be born, to live, and to die in human form to provide redemption for fallen mankind.

Yet as profound and unfathomable as this passage is theologically, it is also ethical. As the introductory words (**Have this attitude in**

yourselves which was also in Christ Jesus) make clear, it is primarily designed to motivate Christians to live like their Lord and Savior. Paul was not merely describing the Incarnation to reveal its theological truths, magnificent as those are. He presents the supreme, unparalleled example of humility to serve as the most powerful motive to believers' humility. The Incarnation calls believers to follow Jesus' incomparable example of humble self-denial, self-giving, self-sacrifice, and selfless love as He lived out the Incarnation in obedient submission to His Father's will (cf. Luke 2:49; John 3:16–17; 5:30; 12:49; 15:10).

Verse 5 is a transition from exhortation to illustration, and the phrase **this attitude** looks both backward and forward. It looks backward to the principle just given, "Do nothing from selfishness or empty conceit, but with humility of mind regard one another as more important than yourselves; do not merely look out for your own personal interests, but also for the interests of others" (vv. 3–4). It looks forward to the illustration of that principle in Jesus' perfect fulfillment of it as described in verses 6–8.

The goal of believers having **this attitude** is spiritual unity in the church by their being "of the same mind, maintaining the same love, united in spirit, intent on one purpose" (v. 2). Unity in the church can come only from an **attitude** of genuine humility, of believers truly regarding others as more important than themselves—the **attitude** that was supremely manifested in **Christ Jesus** during His incarnation. The apostle John makes it clear that "the one who says he abides in [Christ] ought himself to walk in the same manner as He walked" (1 John 2:6). Jesus commanded: "Take My yoke upon you and learn from Me, for I am gentle and humble in heart, and you will find rest for your souls" (Matt. 11:29).

Addressing the ethical impact of this passage, Paul Rees writes:

"Don't forget," cries Paul, "that in all this wide universe and in all the dim reaches of history there has never been such a demonstration of self-effacing humility as when the Son of God in sheer grace descended to this errant planet! Remember that never—never in a million aeons—would He have done it if He were the kind of Deity who looks 'only to his own interests' and closes His eyes to the 'interests of others'! You must remember, my brethren, that through your union with Him, in living, redemptive experience, this principle and passion by which He was moved must become the principle and passion by which you are moved." (*The Adequate Man: Paul in Philippians* [Westwood, N.J.: Revell, 1954], 43)

In yourselves is not directed at the individual believer's personal virtue, but targets the whole church, which is so susceptible to the division and strife produced by pride and self-exaltation. The whole church must manifest the humility of the Lord and head of the church. One of the most revealing instances of that humility was His washing the disciples' feet during the Last Supper. The menial task of washing dirty feet was reserved for the lowest servants. Jesus had just been acknowledged as the prophesied Deliverer and Messiah, the "King of Israel," at His triumphal entry into Jerusalem a few days earlier (John 12:12–15). He was well aware "that the Father had given all things into His hands, and that He had come forth from God and was going back to God" (13:3). Yet in gentle humility He "got up from supper, and laid aside His garments; and taking a towel, He girded Himself. Then He poured water into the basin, and began to wash the disciples' feet and to wipe them with the towel with which He was girded" (vv. 4–5). This act was especially poignant because the disciples, insensitive to Jesus' coming suffering, were engaged in wrangling with each other over which of them would be the "greatest" in the Messiah's kingdom (cf. Luke 22:24).

Afterward the Lord asked, "Do you know what I have done to you?" Knowing full well that they did not understand the significance of what He had just done, He did not wait for an answer but continued to explain:

> You call Me Teacher and Lord; and you are right, for so I am. If I then, the Lord and the Teacher, washed your feet, you also ought to wash one another's feet. For I gave you an example that you also should do as I did to you. Truly, truly, I say to you, a slave is not greater than his master, nor is one who is sent greater than the one who sent him. If you know these things, you are blessed if you do them. (John 13:12–17)

That demonstration of humility so clearly exemplifies the **attitude . . . which was also in Christ Jesus** that it may well be the very one the apostle had in mind when he wrote this passage. It also exemplifies his admonition to the church in Rome that "we who are strong ought to bear the weaknesses of those without strength and not just please ourselves. Each of us is to please his neighbor for his good, to his edification. For even Christ did not please Himself" (Rom. 15:1–3). Accentuating again the inseparable relationship between humility and spiritual unity, he added, "Now may the God who gives perseverance and encouragement grant you to be of the same mind with one another according to Christ Jesus, so that with one accord you may with one voice glorify the God and Father of our Lord Jesus Christ. Therefore, accept one another, just as Christ also accepted us to the glory of God" (vv. 5–7).

Because Paul consistently followed that principle, he could remind the Corinthians, "I also please all men in all things, not seeking my own profit but the profit of the many," and then admonish them to "be imitators of me, just as I also am of Christ" (1 Cor. 10:33–11:1; cf. 2 Cor. 8:7–9). Similarly, he reminded the Thessalonians that "our gospel did not come to you in word only, but also in power and in the Holy Spirit and with full conviction; just as you know what kind of men we proved to be among you for your sake," offering the encouraging commendation that "you also became imitators of us and of the Lord, . . . so that you became an example to all the believers in Macedonia and in Achaia" (1 Thess. 1:5–7).

The way of humility is not the way of the world. It is especially not the choice of its honored leaders, who are expected to take the very best of everything for themselves. They are accorded the highest places of honor and respect, and they are expected to be served rather than to serve. Jesus described the scribes and Pharisees as men who

> tie up heavy burdens and lay them on men's shoulders, but they them-selves are unwilling to move them with so much as a finger. But they do all their deeds to be noticed by men; for they broaden their phy-lacteries and lengthen the tassels of their garments. They love the place of honor at banquets and the chief seats in the synagogues, and respectful greetings in the market places, and being called Rabbi by men. (Matt. 23:4–7; cf. 20:25–28 for a similar Gentile attitude)

Most Jews of Jesus' day, including the Twelve for most of His min-istry, expected the Messiah to come as a conquering, reigning, and highly honored deliverer. Like those Jews, if Christians were somehow by them-selves to imagine a plan for the incarnation of God's Son, they doubtless would expect Him to be born into a prominent family and attend the finest schools. He would be surrounded by the brightest minds and most capable helpers and live in regal splendor, with countless assistants to do His bidding and satisfy His every need and want. He would have con-stant protection from physical danger and from destructive criticism. And He would deserve it all.

But that was not God's way. His only begotten Son was born into the humblest of families in the humblest of places. In the eyes of those around Him, including His own family and friends, He lived an unexcep-tional life. The twelve men He chose to be His apostles were, with the possible exception of Matthew, common men with little education, skills, or position. He submitted to every humiliation and indignity from His enemies and refused to defend Himself. The highest of all became the lowest of all.

Obviously, believers cannot follow the example of Christ's deity, incarnation, moral and spiritual perfection, miracles, or redemptive work. But they are commanded to follow His example of humility as expressed in His incarnation. In marked contrast to the glory-loving scribes and Pharisees, Jesus commanded His followers not to

> be called Rabbi; for One is your Teacher, and you are all brothers. Do not call anyone on earth your father; for One is your Father, He who is in heaven. Do not be called leaders; for One is your Leader, that is, Christ. But the greatest among you shall be your servant. Whoever exalts himself shall be humbled; and whoever humbles himself shall be exalted. (Matt. 23:8–12)

As he expounded Jesus' ethically flawless example of humility, Paul also chronicled theologically the descent of the Son of God from heaven to earth, describing the exalted position that He left, then presenting a series of downward steps from that glory and honor to ever-increasing indignity. These parallel categories will be dealt with together in regard to each of the descending stages mentioned in this passage.

THE EXALTED POSITION JESUS LEFT

although He existed in the form of God, (2:6*a*)

Jesus' humiliating step downward was from the exalted position seen in the truth that **He existed in the form of God.** Both before, during, and after His incarnation, He was, by His very nature, fully and eternally **God. Existed** translates a present active participle of the compound verb *huparchō,* which is formed from *hupo* ("under") and *archē* ("beginning") and denotes the continuance of a previous state or existence. It stresses the essence of a person's nature, that which is absolutely unalterable, inalienable, and unchangeable. William Barclay comments that the verb refers to "that part of a [person] which, in any circumstances, remains the same" (*The Letters to the Philippians, Colossians, and Thessalonians.* Rev. ed. [Louisville, Ky.: Westminster, 1975], 35).

Jesus Christ eternally and immutably **existed,** and will forever continue to exist, **in the form of God.** *Morphē* (**form**) refers to the outward manifestation of an inner reality. The idea is that, before the Incarnation, from all eternity past, Jesus preexisted in the divine **form of God,** equal with **God** the Father in every way. By His very nature and innate being, Jesus Christ is, always has been, and will forever be fully divine.

The Greek word *schēma* is also often translated "form," but the meaning is quite different from that of *morphē.* As Barclay points out,

> *Morphē* is the essential form which never alters; *schēma* is the outward form which changes from time to time and from circumstance to

circumstance. For instance, the essential *morphē* of any human being is humanity and this never changes; but his *schēma* is continually changing. A baby, a child, a boy, a youth, a man of middle age, an old man always have the *morphē* of humanity, but the outward *schēma* changes all the time. (*Philippians*, 35–36)

To the Colossians, Paul expressed the truth of Christ's deity in these words:"He [Jesus Christ] is the image of the invisible God, the first-born of all creation" (Col. 1:15). Speaking of Christ, John opened his gospel with the declaration:"In the beginning was the Word, and the Word was with God, and the Word was God. He was in the beginning with God. . . . And the Word became flesh, and dwelt among us, and we saw His glory, glory as of the only begotten from the Father, full of grace and truth" (John 1:1–2, 14). Jesus said of Himself,"Truly, truly, I say to you, before Abraham was born, I am" (John 8:58), and later prayed,"Now, Father, glorify Me together with Yourself, with the glory which I had with You before the world was. . . . Father, I desire that they also, whom You have given Me, be with Me where I am, so that they may see My glory which You have given Me, for You loved Me before the foundation of the world" (17:5, 24). The writer of Hebrews reminds us that God "in these last days has spoken to us in His Son, whom He appointed heir of all things, through whom also He made the world. And He is the radiance of His glory and the exact representation of His nature, and upholds all things by the word of His power" (Heb. 1:2–3).

In light of the profound reality of Jesus' full and uncompromised deity, His incarnation was the most profound possible humiliation. For Him to change in any way or to any degree, even temporarily by the divine decree of His Father, required descent. By definition, to forsake perfection requires taking on some form of imperfection. Yet without forsaking or in any way diminishing His perfect deity or His absolute holiness, in a way that is far beyond human comprehension, the Creator took on the form of the created. The Infinite became finite, the Sinless took sin upon Himself. The very heart of the gospel of redemption is that the Father "made Him who knew no sin to be sin on our behalf, so that we might become the righteousness of God in Him" (2 Cor. 5:21). Although that infinitely marvelous and cardinal gospel truth is impossible to understand, it is necessary to believe.

The example for those who have saving faith in Christ is clear. Because of their relationship to Christ, they have special standing and privilege before God. Through Christ, they are God's children. "As many as received Him, to them He gave the right to become children of God, even to those who believe in His name" (John 1:12); and because they are His children,"when He appears, [they] will be like Him, because [they] will

see Him just as He is" (1 John 3:2). Although they will always be His servants, He deigns to call them His friends: "I have called you friends, for all
things that I have heard from My Father I have made known to you" (John
15:15). Believers are indwelt by Jesus Christ (Eph. 3:17) and by the Holy
Spirit (John 14:17; Rom. 8:9, 11; 2 Tim. 1:14). While on earth, they are the
living temples of God (1 Cor. 6:19) and "ambassadors for Christ" (2 Cor.
5:20). They have been divinely "blessed . . . with every spiritual blessing in
the heavenly places in Christ," chosen "in Him before the foundation of
the world," predestined "to adoption as sons through Jesus Christ to Himself" (Eph. 1:3–5). They are "predestined to become conformed to the
image of His Son" (Rom. 8:29), "called according to His purpose, . . . justified," and one day will be glorified (8:28, 30). They are "living stones, . . .
being built up as a spiritual house for a holy priesthood, to offer up spiritual sacrifices acceptable to God through Jesus Christ . . . a chosen race, a
royal priesthood, a holy nation, a people for God's own possession" (1
Peter 2:5, 9; cf. Rev. 1:6; 5:10; 20:6).

But Christians are God's children solely by adoption (Rom. 8:15;
Gal. 4:5; Eph. 1:5), not by inherent right. Every marvelous blessing and
privilege they have is entirely because of divine grace, theirs because of
their union with God's only true eternal Son, Jesus Christ. Therefore, if
God's eternal Son humbled Himself in such an incomparably sacrificial
way, how much more should God's adopted children be determined to
live humbly and sacrificially?

It is tragic that, in self-centered disregard both of their Lord's
teaching and example, some Christians take pride in their position as
children of God. As "children of the King," they believe that they deserve
to live like royalty, although the King of kings, the Lord Jesus Christ, often
had "nowhere to lay His head" (Matt. 8:20; cf. John 7:53–8:1) and commands His followers to "take My yoke upon you and learn from Me, for I
am gentle and humble in heart" (Matt. 11:29). It is not by accident that
the first Beatitude reads: "Blessed are the poor in spirit, for theirs is the
kingdom of heaven" (Matt. 5:3).

STEP ONE

did not regard equality with God a thing to be grasped, (2:6b)

From His exalted position as God, Christ's first step downward
was not to **regard equality with God a thing to be grasped.**
Although He continued to fully exist as God, during His incarnation He
refused to hold on to His divine rights and prerogatives. **Equality with
God** is synonymous with the preceding phrase "form of God." In repeat-

ing the declaration of Christ's true nature and essence, Paul emphasizes its absolute and incontestable reality. It is interesting that *isos* (**equality**) is in a plural form (*isa,* "equalities"), suggesting that Paul may have been referring to every aspect of Jesus' deity. The term refers to exact equivalence. An isosceles triangle has two equal sides. Isomers are chemicals that differ in certain properties and structure but are identical in atomic weight. In becoming a man, Jesus did not in any way forfeit or diminish His absolute **equality with God.**

During His earthly ministry, Jesus never denied or minimized His deity. He was unambiguous in acknowledging His divine sonship and oneness with the Father (John 5:17–18; 10:30, 38; 14:9; 17:1, 21–22; 20:28), His "authority over all flesh" and power to "give eternal life" (John 17:2), and His divine "glory which [He] had with [the Father] before the world was" (John 17:5; cf. v. 24). Yet He never used His power or authority for personal advantage, because such prerogatives of His divinity were not **a thing to be grasped.** That was the choice that set the Incarnation into motion. He willingly suffered the worst possible humiliation rather than demand the honor, privilege, and glory that were rightly His. Nor did He use the powers of His undiminished sovereign deity to oppose the purpose of His Father because the price was too high.

To be grasped translates the Greek noun *harpagmos,* which refers to something that is seized or carried off by force. It was also sometimes used of a prize or award. Because Jesus already possessed **equality with God,** the meaning of **to be grasped** is not taking hold of but of holding on to, or clinging to. He had all the rights and privileges of God, which He could never lose. Yet He refused to selfishly cling to His favored position as the divine Son of **God** nor view it as a prized possession to be used for Himself. At any time He could have appealed to His Father and at once received "more than twelve legions of angels" to come to His defense (Matt. 26:53). But that would have thwarted His Father's plan, with which He fully concurred, and He would not do it. Although He was doubtless terribly hungry after fasting for forty days in the wilderness, He refused to turn stones into bread in order to feed Himself (Matt. 4:3–4). Yet He graciously multiplied the loaves and fish so the hungry multitudes might be fed (Mark 6:38–44; 8:1–9).

It is that attitude of selfless giving of oneself and one's possessions, power, and privileges that should characterize all who belong to Christ. They should be willing to loosen their grip on the blessings they have, which they have solely because of Him. Christians are set apart from the world as children of God and joint heirs with Jesus Christ. Yet they must not clutch those privileges and blessings. Instead, like their Lord, they must hold them loosely and be willing to sacrifice them all for the benefit of others.

STEP TWO

but emptied Himself, (2:7a)

In the next step downward, Jesus continued to not cling to His divine prerogatives. Instead, He **emptied Himself.** The Greek conjunction *alla* (**but**) means "not this but that," indicating a clear contrast of ideas. Although He was absolutely "full" of deity, as it were, He **emptied Himself** of all of its prerogatives. **Emptied** is from *kenoō*, which means to empty completely. It is translated "nullified" in Romans 4:14 and "made void" in 1 Corinthians 1:17. Jesus Christ **emptied Himself** completely of every vestige of advantage and privilege, refusing to assert any divine right on His own behalf. He who created and owned everything forsook everything.

It must always be kept in mind that Jesus **emptied Himself** only of certain aspects of His prerogatives of deity, not of His deity itself. He was never anything, and never will be anything, but fully and eternally God, as Paul was careful to state in the previous verse. All four gospels make it clear that He did not forsake His divine power to perform miracles, to forgive sins, or to know the minds and hearts of people. Had He stopped being God (an impossibility), He could not have died for the sins of the world. He would have perished on the cross and remained in the grave, with no power to conquer sin or death. As R. C. H. Lenski comments, "Even in the midst of his death, he had to be the mighty God in order by his death to conquer death" (*The Interpretation of St. Paul's Epistles to the Galatians, to the Ephesians, and to the Philippians* [Minneapolis: Augsburg, 1961], 782). Another scholar, Bishop Handley C. G. Moule, writes,

> Whatever is meant by the "made Himself void" [emptied Himself], *eauton ekenōsen*, which describes His Incarnation here, one thing it could never possibly mean—a *"kenōsis"* which could hurt or distort His absolute fitness to guide and bless us whom He came to save. That [emptying] placed Him indeed on the creaturely level in regard of the reality of human experience of growth, and human capacity for suffering. But never for one moment did it, could it, make Him other than the absolute and infallible Master and Guide of His redeemed. (*Philippian Studies* [London: Pickering & Inglis, n.d.], 99)

The Son of God **emptied Himself** of five divine rights. First, He temporarily divested Himself of His divine glory. Shortly before His arrest, Jesus lifted "up His eyes to heaven" and implored: "Father, the hour has come; glorify Your Son, that the Son may glorify You. . . . Now, Father, glorify Me together with Yourself, with the glory which I had with You before the world was" (John 17:1, 5; cf. v. 24). The Son of God forsook the worship of the saints and angels in heaven and submitted to misunderstanding, denials, unbelief, false accusations, and every sort of reviling and persecution by sinful men. He gave up all the shining brilliance of heaven to suffer an agonizing and ignominious death on the cross.

It was not that He forfeited His divine glory but rather that it was veiled, hidden in His humanity (John 7:5, 24; cf. 2 Cor. 4:4–6) from men's view. Glimpses of it were seen in His many miracles, in His gracious words, in the humble attitude that Paul here calls His followers to emulate, and certainly in His ultimate sacrifice for sin on the cross. It was briefly and partially manifested to Peter, James, and John on the Mount of Transfiguration (Luke 9:31–32; cf. 2 Peter 1:16–18). But it was not witnessed again until His resurrection and ascension, and then only by those who belonged to Him.

Second, Jesus **emptied Himself** of independent divine authority. The operation of the Trinity is, of course, a great mystery. Within the Godhead there is perfect harmony and agreement in every possible way and to every possible degree. Jesus unambiguously stated His full equality with the Father when He declared, "I and the Father are one" (John 10:30; cf. 17:11, 21). Yet He just as clearly declared during His incarnation that "I can do nothing on My own initiative. As I hear, I judge; and My judgment is just, because I do not seek My own will, but the will of Him who sent Me" (John 5:30), and "I have come down from heaven, not to do My own will, but the will of Him who sent Me" (John 6:38). While teaching in the temple, Jesus said, "You both know Me and know where I am from; and I have not come of Myself, but He who sent Me is true, whom you do not know. I know Him, because I am from Him, and He sent Me" (John 7:28–29). In the Garden of Gethsemane on the night of His betrayal and arrest, He pleaded three times: "My Father, if it is possible, let this cup pass from Me"; yet He followed each request with the submissive, "yet not as I will, but as You will" (Matt. 26:39–44). The writer of Hebrews notes that, "although He was a Son, He learned obedience from the things which He suffered" (Heb. 5:8).

Third, Jesus **emptied Himself** of the voluntary exercise of some of His divine attributes, though not the essence of His deity. He did not stop being omniscient, omnipresent, omnipotent, or immutable; He chose not to exercise the full limit of those attributes during His earthly life and ministry. He did, however, exercise some of them selectively and partially. Without having met him, Jesus knew omnisciently that Nathanael was "an Israelite indeed, in whom there is no deceit, . . . because He did not need anyone to testify concerning man, for He Himself knew what was in man" (John 1:47; 2:25). Through His omnipresence, He knew where Nathanael was even before He saw him (1:48). Yet He confessed that, as to the exact time of His return, "of that day and hour no one knows, not even the angels of heaven, nor the Son, but the Father alone" (Matt. 24:36).

Fourth, Jesus **emptied Himself** of His eternal riches. "For your sake He became poor," Paul explains, "so that you through His poverty might become rich" (2 Cor. 8:9). Although many commentators have interpreted His "poverty" as a reference to His earthly economic condition, it has nothing to do with that. The point is not that Christ gave up earth's riches, but that He gave up heaven's riches. As already noted, He forsook the adoration, worship, and service of angels and the redeemed in heaven, because "the Son of Man did not come to be served, but to serve, and to give His life a ransom for many" (Matt. 20:28).

Fifth, He **emptied Himself** temporarily of His unique, intimate, and face-to-face relationship with His heavenly Father—even to the point of being forsaken by Him. To fulfill the divine plan of redemption, the Father "made Him who knew no sin to be sin on our behalf, so that we might become the righteousness of God in Him" (2 Cor. 5:21). That was the Father's will, which Jesus came to fulfill and prayed would be done. Yet even the brief separation from His Father caused by His sin-bearing caused Him to cry "out with a loud voice, saying, 'Eli, Eli, lama sabachthani?' that is, 'My God, My God, why have You forsaken me?'" (Matt. 27:46). It was the unbelievably horrible prospect of being alienated from His Father and bearing sin that had caused Him earlier to sweat drops of blood in great agony, being "deeply grieved, to the point of death" (Luke 22:44; Matt. 26:38).

Christians obviously cannot empty themselves to the degree that the Lord **emptied Himself,** because He started so high and Christians start so low. Believers have infinitely less to empty themselves of. Even what they have is given to them by His grace. Believers are obligated to follow their Lord's example by emptying themselves of everything that would hinder their obedience and service to Him.

Just as Jesus did not cease to be God when He emptied Himself, neither do Christians cease to be His children when they empty themselves as He did (cf. Eph. 5:1–2). Just as Jesus' self-giving obedience made Him pleasing to the Father (Matt. 3:17), so does believers' self-giving obedience make them pleasing to Him (25:21, 23). The humble believer is aware of his rights and privileges as a child of God but refuses to cling to them. He empties himself of all claims to any earthly benefits that those rights and privileges might seem to merit.

STEP THREE

taking the form of a bond-servant, (2:7b)

In the next statement of His descent, as He further emptied Himself, Jesus forsook the full rights of lordship by **taking the form of a bond-servant,** a slave. Although He had the inherent *morphē* (**form**) of God (v. 6), He willingly took upon Himself **the form** (*morphē*), the very essence and nature, **of a bond-servant.** Just as certainly and fully as He "existed in the form [*morphē*] of God," He now existed in **the form of a bond-servant.** He did not merely put on a slave's garment, so to speak; He actually became a slave in the fullest sense.

A *doulos* (**bond-servant**) owned nothing, not even the clothes on his back. Everything he had, including his life, belonged to his master. Jesus did own His own clothes, but He owned no land or house, no gold or jewels. He owned no business, no boat, and no horse. He had to borrow a donkey when He rode into Jerusalem on Palm Sunday, borrow a room for the Last Supper, and even was buried in a borrowed tomb. He refused any property, any advantages, any special service to Himself. Relative to His glory, the King of Kings and Lord of Lords willingly became the **Bond-servant** of bond-servants. The one who "was in the beginning with God" and through whom "all things came into being" (John 1:2–3) claimed as His own nothing that He had created. Among other things, a **bond-servant** was required to carry other people's burdens. As the supreme **Bond-servant,** Jesus carried the burden that no other man could carry, the sin-burden for all who would believe. As Isaiah revealed, "The Lord has caused the iniquity of us all to fall on Him" (Isa. 53:6).

Jesus came to do His Father's will and to serve the needs of His people in His Father's name. He completely waived His rights as the Son of God and became **a bond-servant,** also claiming no rights as the Son of Man. As He Himself testified while heading toward Jerusalem for the last time: "The Son of Man did not come to be served, but to serve, and to give His life a ransom for many" (Matt. 20:28). A few days later, during the Last Supper, He asked the disciples rhetorically, "Who is greater, the one who reclines at the table or the one who serves? Is it not the one who reclines at the table? But I am among you as the one who serves" (Luke 22:27).

Through His provision of salvation, Jesus served others more completely than any other servant or slave who has ever lived. But He was also an example of servanthood for His disciples to follow. He reminded them that "a disciple is not above his teacher, nor a slave above his master" (Matt. 10:24) and that, "If I then, the Lord and the Teacher, washed your feet, you also ought to wash one another's feet. For I gave you an example that you also should do as I did to you. Truly, truly, I say to you, a slave is not greater than his master, nor is one who is sent greater than the one who sent him. If you know these things, you are blessed if you do them" (John 13:14–17). He declared that "the greatest among you shall be your servant" (Matt. 23:11). Yet after they have faithfully done "all the things which are commanded," Christians are to take no credit for themselves but rather confess with genuine humility: "We are unworthy slaves; we have done only that which we ought to have done"(Luke 17:10).

STEP FOUR

and being made in the likeness of men. (2:7c)

Continuing His move downward, Jesus was **made in the likeness of men.** God **made** Him thus by His miraculous conception and virgin birth (Luke 1:30–35). *Homoiōma* (**likeness**) refers to that which is made to be like something else, not just in appearance (cf. v. 7) but in reality. Jesus was not a clone, a disguised alien, or merely some reasonable facsimile of a man. He became exactly like all other human beings, having all the attributes of humanity, a genuine man among **men.** He was so obviously like other human beings that even His family and disciples would not have known of His deity had not the angels (Matt. 1:20–21; Luke 1:26–35; 2:9–11), God the Father (Matt. 3:17; 17:5), and Jesus Himself (John 8:58; 14:1–4; 16:13–15; 17:1–26) revealed it to them. And despite His countless miracles, His enemies rejected the idea of His deity out of hand. In their eyes, He not only was merely human but the lowest kind of human, a blasphemer (John 5:18; 10:33).

It is important to understand that Jesus did not become the second, or last, Adam (1 Cor. 15:45), in the sense of being like pre-Fall mankind. Rather, in the Incarnation, He took upon Himself all the frailties, limitations, problems, and suffering that were the heritage of the Fall, enduring all its terrible earthly consequences.

Without a human father, Jesus was "born of a woman" (Gal. 4:4) in a "fleshly body" (Col. 1:22) and, as any human child, He needed the attention and care of loving parents (Luke 2:40–51). Except in degree, He grew and developed like other children, "increasing in wisdom and stature, and in favor with God and men" (v. 52). He became hungry and thirsty, suffered pain, and felt sadness. Like other men, He became tired and weak and needed sleep. "Since the children share in flesh and blood, He Himself likewise also partook of the same" (Heb. 2:14); and although He was completely without personal sin, He nevertheless was "tempted in all things as we are" (Heb. 4:15; cf. Matt. 4:1–11). As the writer explained earlier, it was because "He Himself was tempted in that which He has suffered, [that] He is able to come to the aid of those who are tempted" (Heb. 2:18).

Because Jesus was "in the likeness of sinful flesh" (Rom. 8:3), He was subject to physical death. In fact, it was only through His death that He could fulfill His divine purpose of redemption. Again as the writer of Hebrews explains, Jesus "had to be made like His brethren in all things, so that He might become a merciful and faithful high priest in things pertaining to God, to make propitiation for the sins of the people" (2:17). He came to die.

Although Jesus forgave sins (Matt. 9:2, 6; Luke 7:47) and acknowledged the propriety of His being worshiped as the Son of God (Matt. 28:17; John 9:38), He did not ask for or accept any special privilege or honor as a man. In the greatest conceivable humility, He lived and acted not merely as a man among men, but as a Servant of servants. He took His place among the common people (cf. 1 Cor. 1:26–29).

STEP FIVE

Being found in appearance as a man, (2:8*a*)

The descent continued with Jesus **being found in appearance as a man,** advancing the truth that He was "made in the likeness of men." Having been made a true human being by divine power through the virgin conception, Christ was **found,** or recognized, **as a man** by those who saw and observed Him during His incarnation. *Schēma* (**appearance**) is the source of the English word "scheme." Unlike *morphē* ("form," vv. 6–7) and *homoiōma* ("likeness," v. 7), which refer to essence and basic nature, *schēma* refers to outward shape or form; not to actuality but to **appearance.** Jesus suffered, and still suffers, the added humiliation of being considered a mere **man.** Paul used the word in speaking of "the form (*schēma*) of this world [which] is passing away" (1 Cor. 7:31). Both Paul and Peter used a compound negative form (*suschēmatizō*) in warning believers to "not be conformed to this world" (Rom. 12:2) and to "not be conformed to the former lusts which were yours in your ignorance" (1 Peter 1:14).

As Isaiah had predicted some seven hundred years earlier, the Messiah "was despised and forsaken of men, a man of sorrows and acquainted with grief; and like one from whom men hide their face He was despised, and we did not esteem Him" (Isa. 53:3). And as John wrote, "He was in the world, and the world was made through Him, and the world did not know Him. He came to His own, and those who were His own did not receive Him" (John 1:10–11). They said, "Is not this Jesus, the son of Joseph, whose father and mother we know? How does He now say, 'I have come down out of heaven'?" (John 6:42). Sadly, "not even His brothers were believing in Him" (John 7:5). Some of the religious but unbelieving Jews declared: "We know where this man is from; but whenever the Christ may come, no one knows where He is from" (John 7:27), and "For a good work we do not stone You, but for blasphemy; and because You, being a man, make Yourself out to be God" (John 10:33). Still others accused Him of having a demon (John 7:20; 8:48).

STEP SIX

He humbled Himself (2:8*b*)

Continuing this profound description of Christ's descent, Paul says that Jesus **humbled Himself.** The emphasis here moves from Jesus' nature and form to that of His personal attitude. He was not merely humiliated by the nature and circumstances of His incarnation. **Humbled Himself** translates *tapeinoō*, which has the idea of lying low. Jesus lowered **Himself** not only relative to God, but also to other men.

The most dramatic and poignant time of Jesus' self-abasement was during His arrest, trial, and crucifixion. He was mocked, falsely accused, spat upon, beaten with fists, scourged, and had part of His beard painfully plucked out. Yet He was never defensive, never bitter, never demanding, never accusing. He refused to assert His rights as God or even as a human being.

Seeing the ethical implications of this humbling, Paul Rees perceptively wrote:

> Look at Him—this amazing Jesus! He is helping Joseph make a yoke in that little carpenter's shop at Nazareth. This is the One who, apart from His self-emptying, could far more easily make a solar system or a galaxy of systems.
>
> Look at Him again! Dressed like a slave, with towel and basin for His menial equipment, He is bathing the feet of some friends of His who, but for their quarrelsomeness, should have been washing *His* feet. . . .
>
> " 'He humbled himself!' "Don't forget this," cries Paul to these dear friends of his at Philippi. "Don't forget this when the slightest impulse arises to become self-assertive and self-seeking, and so to break the bond of your fellowship with one another!" (*The Adequate Man: Paul in Philippians* [Westwood, N.J.: Revell, 1954], 45–46)

STEP SEVEN

by becoming obedient to the point of death, (2:8*c*)

In His stepping downward, Jesus was willing to suffer humiliation and degradation even to **becoming obedient to the point of death.** His **obedience** and its impact on redemption is the theme of Romans 5:12–19, where the key thought is "through the obedience of the One the many will be made righteous" (v. 19). Ralph Martin insightfully observes that

> His obedience is a sure token of His deity and authority, for . . . only a divine being can accept death as *obedience;* for ordinary men it is a necessity. He alone as the obedient Son of His Father could choose death as His destiny; and He did so because of His love, a love which was directed both to His Father's redeeming purpose and equally to the world into which He came. "I come to do thy will" (Heb. 10:7f.) was the motto-text of His entire life. (*The Epistle of Paul to the Philippians.* Tyndale New Testament Commentaries [Grand Rapids: Eerdmans, 1975], 102. Italics in original.)

One would think that somewhere short of that ultimate sacrifice He would have said, "It is enough!" But His perfect submission took Him all the way to **death,** because that was the Father's will. Even in agony, as He implored God in the garden, "My Father, if it is possible, let this cup pass from Me," He acknowledged that avoiding crucifixion was not possible within His Father's will as He continued to pray, "yet not as I will, but as You will" (Matt. 26:39). Commitment to God's will was His will.

Speaking of that heart-wrenching time, the writer of Hebrews says of the Lord: "In the days of His flesh, He offered up both prayers and supplications with loud crying and tears to the One able to save Him from death, and He was heard because of His piety." Yet, as he goes on to explain, "although He was a Son, He learned obedience from the things which He suffered. And having been made perfect, He became to all those who obey Him the source of eternal salvation" (Heb. 5:7–9; cf. 10:7).

Long before His arrest Jesus had declared, "For this reason the Father loves Me, because I lay down My life so that I may take it again" (John 10:17). Peter vehemently objected to Jesus' clear prediction of His impending and necessary **death** and was strongly rebuked: "Peter took Him aside and began to rebuke Him, saying, 'God forbid it, Lord! This shall never happen to You.' But He turned and said to Peter, 'Get behind Me, Satan! You are a stumbling block to Me; for you are not setting your mind on God's interests, but man's'" (Matt. 16:22–23). Because Jesus' mind was set entirely on God's interests, not man's or His own, He willingly and gladly became **obedient to the point of death.** "While we were still helpless, at the right time Christ died for the ungodly" (Rom. 5:6).

The Father did not force **death** upon the Son. It was the Father's will, but it was the Son's will always to perfectly obey the Father. He had a free choice. Had He not had a choice, He could not have been **obedient.** "No one has taken [My life] away from Me," He said, "but I lay it down on My own initiative. I have authority to lay it down, and I have authority to take it up again. This commandment I received from My Father" (John 10:18). He was commanded by the Father, but not compelled. As love incarnate, He became the perfect example of the truth He Himself had declared: "Greater love has no one than this, that one lay down his life for his friends" (John 15:13).

STEP EIGHT

even death on a cross. (2:8*d*)

In the final feature of His descent and degradation, Jesus submitted **even [to] death on a cross.** There were many ways by which He could have been killed. He could have been beheaded, such as John the Baptist was, or stoned or hanged. But He was destined not for just any kind of death but for **death on a cross.**

Crucifixion is perhaps the most cruel, excruciatingly painful, and shameful form of execution ever conceived. It was originally devised by the ancient Persians or Phoenicians and later perfected by the Romans. It was reserved for slaves, the lowest of criminals, and enemies of the state. No Roman citizen could be crucified, no matter how egregious his crime. In his book *The Life of Christ,* Frederick Farrar describes crucifixion as follows:

> A death by crucifixion seems to include all that pain and death can have of the horrible and ghastly—dizziness, cramp, thirst, starvation, sleeplessness, traumatic fever, shame, publicity of shame, long continuance of torment, horror of anticipation, mortification of intended wounds—all intensified just up to the point at which they can be endured at all, but all stopping just short of the point which would give to the sufferer the relief of unconsciousness.... The unnatural position made every movement painful; the lacerated veins and crushed tendons throbbed with incessant anguish. (Vol. 2 [New York: E. P. Dutton, 1877], 403–4)

The Jews considered crucifixion to be a form of hanging, and those who were hung to be cursed by God. The law demanded that a man's "corpse shall not hang all night on the tree, but you shall surely bury him on the same day (for he who is hanged is accursed of God), so that you do not defile your land which the Lord your God gives you as an inheritance" (Deut. 21:23). For that reason, the idea of a crucified Messiah was an insurmountable stumbling block to unbelieving Jews (1 Cor. 1:23). Like Peter, they could not even conceive of the Messiah being put to death, much less being put to death by an ignominious, horrifying, humiliating, and accursed **death on a cross.** The curse of Deuteronomy 21:23 meant being outside God's covenant, banned from His people and His blessing. But Jesus bore the curse for believers to bring them to God and to glory.

But in God's perfect plan, the crucifixion of His Son not only was acceptable but mandatory. "Christ redeemed us from the curse of the Law," Paul explains, "having become a curse for us—for it is written, 'Cursed is everyone who hangs on a tree'" (Gal. 3:13). As Peter declares, "He Himself bore our sins in His body on the cross, so that we might die to sin and live to righteousness; for by His wounds you were healed" (1 Peter 2:24). In God's infinite wisdom, **death on a cross** was the only way of redemption for fallen, sinful, and condemned mankind. Crucifixion was bloody, as were the Old Testament sacrifices that prefigured it. Priests in the service of the temple were butchers, blood-splattered in their duty. The Lamb of God would also die a bloody death.

After reflecting on the divine plan of salvation for the first eleven chapters of Romans, Paul declared in awe and wonder: "Oh, the depth of the riches both of the wisdom and knowledge of God! How unsearchable are His judgments and unfathomable His ways!" (Rom. 11:33).

The Exaltation of Christ (Philippians 2:9–11)

9

For this reason also, God highly exalted Him, and bestowed on Him the name which is above every name, so that at the name of Jesus every knee will bow, of those who are in heaven and on earth and under the earth, and that every tongue will confess that Jesus Christ is Lord, to the glory of God the Father. (2:9–11)

When a Muslim with whom he was speaking slighted Christ, the nineteenth-century missionary Henry Martyn declared that he could not endure existence if Jesus were to be always dishonored (Constance E. Padwick, *Henry Martyn* [Chicago: Moody 1980], 225–26). His attitude is reminiscent of David's, when he declared that "the reproaches of those who reproach You have fallen on me" (Ps. 69:9). When the Lord is reviled and dishonored, those who love Him feel the pain of that reviling and dishonor.

Nothing else in history could possibly match the scorn and defamation that fallen, sinful, rebellious men inflicted upon the Son of God during His incarnation (2:6–8). But in the next three verses, which comprise the second half of this hymn of celebration, the apostle briefly depicts the magnificent and unequaled exaltation that the Father then bestowed on the Son. No passage of Scripture more beautifully portrays the depth of condescension and the height of exaltation experienced by Jesus Christ than does Philippians 2:5–11. The gospel message is not complete apart from these monumental realities.

It was because of "the joy set before Him" that Christ "endured the cross, despising the shame, and has sat down at the right hand of the throne of God" (Heb. 12:2). As Peter explains, the dominant theme of the Old Testament prophets was the suffering of the Messiah and His subsequent glory. They sought intensely "to know what person or time the Spirit of Christ [Messiah] within them was indicating as He predicted the sufferings of Christ and the glories to follow" (1 Peter 1:11).

In 2:1–4, Paul establishes that the practical result of believers following the Lord's example of humility is unity in the church.

> If there is any encouragement in Christ, if there is any consolation of love, if there is any fellowship of the Spirit, if any affection and compassion, make my joy complete by being of the same mind, maintaining the same love, united in spirit, intent on one purpose. Do nothing from selfishness or empty conceit, but with humility of mind regard one another as more important than yourselves; do not merely look out for your own personal interests, but also for the interests of others.

Humility is the key to the unity in the church for which the apostle is so strongly appealing. It is the key for believers to be truly one in Jesus Christ as He is one with the Father (John 17:21).

In this day of overweening pride, self-love, and self-promotion, even among many professing Christians, it is important to understand that "whoever exalts himself shall be humbled" (Matt. 23:12). The self-righteous Pharisee who prayed, "God, I thank You that I am not like other people: swindlers, unjust, adulterers, or even like this tax collector. I fast twice a week; I pay tithes of all that I get," was merely "praying . . . to himself," not to God (Luke 18:11–12). Because he exalted himself, God would humble him (v. 14). Just as surely as God "gives grace to the humble," He "is opposed to the proud" (1 Peter 5:5).

But for those who follow the Lord's example of humility, who "have this attitude in [themselves] which was also in Christ Jesus" (Phil. 2:5), there is promise of great reward. Like their Master, they will be exalted by their heavenly Father. As Jesus promised: "Whoever exalts himself shall be humbled; and whoever humbles himself shall be exalted" (Matt. 23:12; cf. Luke 14:11; 18:14). Echoing that principle, James said, "Humble yourselves in the presence of the Lord, and He will exalt you" (James 4:10); and Peter wrote: "Humble yourselves under the mighty hand of God, that He may exalt you at the proper time" (1 Peter 5:6). Philippians 2:5–11 is not simply a picture of the humiliation and exaltation of the

Son of God. It is also a profound illustration of a divine principle that brings immeasurable blessing to God's obedient and humble servants. By God's matchless grace, just as they are humbled with Christ, they also will be glorified with Him. "The glory which You have given Me," Jesus said, "I have given to them, that they may be one, just as We are one" (John 17:22).

The central truth of this hymn, as in this epistle and the entire New Testament, is the exalted sovereign lordship of Christ. Paul begins Philippians by proclaiming himself and Timothy to be "bond-servants of . . . the Lord Jesus Christ" (1:1–2), and he ends the passage by declaring that one day "every tongue will confess that Jesus Christ is Lord" (2:11). That cardinal truth of the gospel will be further developed later in this chapter.

The exaltation of Jesus Christ is nowhere more beautifully portrayed than in the first chapter of Hebrews.

> In these last days [God] has spoken to us in His Son, whom He appointed heir of all things, through whom also He made the world. And He is the radiance of His glory and the exact representation of His nature, and upholds all things by the word of His power. When He had made purification of sins, He sat down at the right hand of the Majesty on high. . . . And when He again brings the firstborn into the world, He says, 'And let all the angels of God worship Him.' . . . But of the Son He says, 'Your throne, O God, is forever and ever, and the righteous scepter is the scepter of His kingdom.'" (Heb. 1:2–3, 6, 8; cf. v. 13)

In the last days, only the exalted Son of God, Jesus Christ, will be worthy to take the scroll from His Father's right hand and open it (Rev. 5:1–7). This scroll, which might be called the title deed to the universe, delineates Christ's rightful inheritance of all creation, which He made and over which He will rule throughout all eternity (cf. Rev. 11:15). No wonder Paul exulted, "For from Him and through Him and to Him are all things. To Him be the glory forever. Amen" (Rom. 11:36).

The humble, incarnate Savior has been exalted as the almighty and sovereign Lord. Because of that, believers have the assurance that their redemption is certain and that their place in heaven is secured forever. He is also to be obeyed as divine Lord, and honored and worshiped throughout all time and eternity.

In the second half of this hymn, Paul presents four aspects of the Father's exaltation of the Son: the source (2:9a), the title (2:9b), the response (2:10–11a), and the purpose (2:11b).

THE SOURCE OF CHRIST'S EXALTATION

For this reason also, God highly exalted Him, (2:9*a*)

For this reason refers back to Jesus' humiliation described in verses 6–8. His exaltation was "the joy set before Him" for which He willingly endured the cross, despised the shame, suffered the hostility of sinners, and was seated "at the right hand of the throne of God" (Heb. 12:2–3). The way to exaltation is always through humiliation. If that principle was true for the Son of God, how much more is it true for His followers?

Highly exalted translates the compound verb *huperupsoō,* composed of *huper* (over) and *hupsoō* (to lift, or raise up). **God** lifted up His beloved Son in the most magnificent way possible. It involved four steps upward: His resurrection, His ascension, His coronation, and His intercession.

First, Jesus was resurrected from the dead. When the women came to the tomb where Jesus had been buried, the angel said to them, "Do not be amazed; you are looking for Jesus the Nazarene, who has been crucified. He has risen; He is not here; behold, here is the place where they laid Him" (Mark 16:6). Peter explained to his hearers at Pentecost that "this Jesus God raised up again, to which we are all witnesses" (Acts 2:32; cf. Rom. 1:4). Later, after being released from prison in Jerusalem, Peter and the other apostles with him testified before the Sanhedrin: "The God of our fathers raised up Jesus, whom you had put to death by hanging Him on a cross" (Acts 5:30; cf. 13:33–39). Many years later, Paul wrote that God the Father "raised [Jesus] from the dead and seated Him at His right hand in the heavenly places" (Eph. 1:20).

The second aspect of the Father's exaltation of Jesus was His ascension. When the Lord appeared to Mary Magdelene after His resurrection He "said to her, 'Stop clinging to Me, for I have not yet ascended to the Father; but go to My brethren and say to them, "I ascend to My Father and your Father, and My God and your God"'" (John 20:17). Later, after He had given last instructions to the eleven on the Mount of Olives, "He was lifted up while they were looking on, and a cloud received Him out of their sight" (Acts 1:9; cf. John 14:2; 16:7; Heb. 4:14). As Paul explained to Timothy, Jesus was "taken up in glory" (1 Tim. 3:16).

The third aspect of Jesus' exaltation was His coronation. When giving the Great Commission, Jesus proclaimed, "All authority has been given to Me in heaven and on earth" (Matt. 28:18). Having ascended, Jesus "is at the right hand of God, having gone into heaven" (1 Peter 3:22). Peter and the others testified to the Sanhedrin that "[Jesus] is the one whom God exalted to His right hand as a Prince and a Savior, to grant repentance to Israel, and forgiveness of sins" (Acts 5:31). As Stephen was about to die, "being full of the Holy Spirit, he gazed intently into heaven and saw the glory of God, and Jesus standing at the right hand of God; and he said, 'Behold, I see the heavens opened up and the Son of Man standing at the right hand of God'" (Acts 7:55–56; cf. Heb. 2:9; 10:12).

From heaven, the Lord Jesus Christ forever reigns "far above all rule and authority and power and dominion, and every name that is named, not only in this age but also in the one to come," because the Father "put all things in subjection under His feet" (Eph. 1:21–22; cf. 4:10; Pss. 2:8; 89:27; 1 Peter 3:22; Jude 25). Because of His authority and power, Jesus will forever "be Lord both of the dead and of the living," because it was "to this end Christ died and lived again" (Rom. 14:9). As the "myriads of myriads" of worshipers around the heavenly throne will one day declare: "Worthy is the Lamb that was slain to receive power and riches and wisdom and might and honor and glory and blessing. . . . The kingdom of the world has become the kingdom of our Lord and of His Christ; and He will reign forever and ever" (Rev. 5:11–12; 11:15). The end will come "when He hands over the kingdom to the God and Father, when He has abolished all rule and all authority and power" (1 Cor. 15:24).

The fourth and final aspect of Jesus' exaltation is His honored position of High Priest, from which He continually intercedes for believers. Christ, who died and was raised for us and "who is at the right hand of God . . . also intercedes for us" (Rom. 8:34; cf. v. 26). As believers' great High Priest, "He is able also to save forever those who draw near to God through Him, since He always lives to make intercession for them. For it was fitting," the writer of Hebrews goes on to say, "for us to have such a high priest, holy, innocent, undefiled, separated from sinners and exalted above the heavens" (Heb. 7:25–26; cf. 4:14; 5:1–6; 6:20; 7:21; 8:1–6; 9:24).

For the most part, Jesus' exaltation involved the restoration of what He had eternally possessed before His incarnation. In His High Priestly Prayer, He implored: "Now, Father, glorify Me together with Yourself, with the glory which I had with You before the world was" (John 17:5). Yet from the passages just cited, as well as from many others, it seems clear that in some ways Jesus received even more in His exaltation than He had surrendered in His incarnation. He was not, of course, any more divine or perfect. It was not possible for Him to be further elevated in any way as far as His essential nature and being are concerned. But because of His perfect redemptive work, the Father bestowed on the Son even more rights, privileges, honors, and responsibilities than He had before. The exaltation was therefore more than merely a reversal of the Incarnation. It was the Father's giving the Son honor and tribute He could receive only after His redemptive sacrifice, which He made in obedience to the Father's will.

Included in Jesus' authority and power is that of being the final

Judge. "For not even the Father judges anyone," Jesus explained, "but He has given all judgment to the Son, so that all will honor the Son even as they honor the Father" (John 5:22–23). Peter declared to the newly converted Cornelius and his household that God "ordered us to preach to the people, and solemnly to testify that this is the One who has been appointed by God as Judge of the living and the dead" (Acts 10:42; cf. Rom. 2:16; 2 Tim. 4:1). Every human being that has ever lived will stand before Jesus Christ the Judge:

> For not even the Father judges anyone, but He has given all judgment to the Son. . . . Truly, truly, I say to you, an hour is coming and now is, when the dead will hear the voice of the Son of God, and those who hear will live. For just as the Father has life in Himself, even so He gave to the Son also to have life in Himself; and He gave Him authority to execute judgment, because He is the Son of Man. Do not marvel at this; for an hour is coming, in which all who are in the tombs will hear His voice, and will come forth; those who did the good deeds to a resurrection of life, those who committed the evil deeds to a resurrection of judgment. (John 5:22, 25–29)

Every believer will "appear before the judgment seat of Christ, so that each one may be recompensed for his deeds in the body, according to what he has done, whether good or bad" (2 Cor. 5:10).

In a way completely incomprehensible to the human mind, Jesus Christ not only became the God-man in the incarnation but also will forever continue to be that. As High Priest, He continually intercedes for all those He saves. Because a priest must represent both God and men, He could not have been believers' High Priest apart from His deigning to become a man. If He had never been touched with the feelings of their infirmities, including being tempted in every way as they are, He could not have fully identified with them and thereby been able to encourage, strengthen, and encourage them in their temptations (Heb. 2:18; 4:15; 9:28; 1 Peter 2:24).

William Hendriksen cogently describes Jesus' coronation in the following comment:

> He who stood condemned in relation to the divine law (because of the sin of the world which rested on him) has exchanged this penal for the righteous relation to the law. He who was poor has become rich. He who was rejected has been accepted (Rev. 12:5, 10). He who learned obedience has entered upon the actual administration of the power and authority committed to him.
>
> As *king*, having by his death, resurrection, and ascension achieved and displayed his triumph over his enemies, he now holds in his hands the reins of the universe, and rules all things in the interest of his

church (Eph. 1:22, 23). As *prophet* he through his Spirit leads his own in all the truth. And as *priest* (High-priest according to the order of Melchizedek) he, on the basis of his accomplished atonement, *not only intercedes but actually lives forever to make intercession* for those who draw near to God through him (Heb. 7:25). (*New Testament Commentary: Exposition of Philippians* [Grand Rapids: Baker, 1962], 114. Italics in original.)

THE TITLE OF CHRIST'S EXALTATION

and bestowed on Him the name which is above every name, (2:9*b*)

Bestowed is from *charizomai*, which conveys the idea of giving freely and generously. The Father conferred upon the Son **the name which is above every name** with the most divinely perfect love. Jesus so completely satisfied the Father in fulfilling the work of His incarnation, in providing redemption for the elect, that He generously granted Him this exalted title. "Having become as much better than the angels," the writer of Hebrews explains, "He has inherited a more excellent name than they" (Heb. 1:4).

This **name** was given Him to emphasize His rank above all other beings. It reflects not only His divine essence and nature but also the new and unique privileges mentioned above that the Father gave Him in response to His redemptive work. This **name** is incomparable, the superlative of superlatives.

Paul does not reveal the supreme name, **the name which is above every name,** until verse 11, where he declares that "every tongue will confess that Jesus Christ is *Lord*" (emphasis added). Lord is the title of majesty, authority, honor, and sovereignty. One day that exalted name will be expanded to "King of kings and Lord of lords" (Rev. 19:16). Obviously Lord, used in the sense of ultimate sovereign authority and command, ranks over all other names. Whoever is Lord is over everyone else —and that is precisely the point in so titling the Savior—has absolute supremacy and the right to be obeyed as divine Master.

In the marvelous grace of God, believers not only will be fellow heirs with Jesus Christ but also will share His names. Through the apostle John, God promises: "He who overcomes," that is, every true believer (1 John 5:4–5), "I will make him a pillar in the temple of My God, and he will not go out from it anymore; and I will write on him the name of My God, and the name of the city of My God, the new Jerusalem, which comes down out of heaven from My God, and My new name" (Rev. 3:12; cf. 2:17). When they are glorified, all believers will be stamped with the name of God the Father ("My God"), with the name of heaven ("the city of My God, the New Jerusalem"), and with Christ's supreme title of Lord ("My new name"). Those names will mark them out, brand them, as it were, as belonging to God and identifying with Him in the fullest and most intimate way.

THE RESPONSE TO CHRIST'S EXALTATION

so that at the name of Jesus every knee will bow, of those who are in heaven and on earth and under the earth, and that every tongue will confess that Jesus Christ is Lord, (2:10–11a)

When the Greek word *hina* (**so that**) is used with a subjunctive verb (such as *kampsē,* **will bow;** and *exomologēsētai,* **will confess**) it introduces a purpose clause. Paul is therefore saying:"Jesus is given the name which is above every name for the purpose that, or with the result that, **every knee will bow, of those who are in heaven and on earth and under the earth, and that every tongue will confess** the supreme name of **Jesus Christ,** which is **Lord.**" It is critical to understand that this response will not be to the name **Jesus.** A form of Joshua (meaning "Jehovah, or Yahweh saves"), Jesus was a common name in New Testament times. It obviously could not be the unique, much less supreme, name intended by God as a title of exaltation. It is rather **at the name of Jesus,** that is, at another name (**Lord**) given to **Jesus Christ** in His exaltation by the Father, that **every knee will bow** and **every tongue will confess.**

There had long been indications of what His supreme name would be. *Kurios* ("lord") was a common term of respect in New Testament times, similar to the English word *sir* but carrying a much higher degree of respect (cf. Matt. 10:24–25; 18:27–34; Luke 12:42–47). During His earthly ministry, Jesus was sometimes respectfully addressed in this way. It seems probable that some of those who called Him "lord" did not, at least when they first encountered Him, consider Him to be more than a great teacher (cf. John 8:11; 9:35–38). Even the Twelve's understanding of His true identity was gradual and often tentative. And, as Jesus Himself made clear, even calling Him Lord as an acknowledgment of His deity is not necessarily evidence of a saving relationship with Him.

> Not everyone who says to Me, "Lord, Lord," will enter the kingdom of heaven, but he who does the will of My Father who is in heaven will enter. Many will say to Me on that day, "Lord, Lord, did we not prophesy in Your name, and in Your name cast out demons, and in Your name perform many miracles?" And then I will declare to them, "I never knew you; depart from Me, you who practice lawlessness." (Matt. 7:21–23)

Because the Jews considered God's name too holy to utter, they substituted the title Lord in place of His personal, covenant name, *Yahweh* (or *Jehovah*), whenever it would have been spoken. (Most modern English translations of the Old Testament therefore render the Hebrew *YHWH* [*Yahweh*] as LORD.) Consequently, God was called both *adonai* ("Lord"), a title of divine authority, and *YHWH* ("LORD"), referring to His covenant name, which has the basic meaning of "I am" (cf. Ex. 3:13–15). When Scripture was read, only a knowledge of the Hebrew text would enable a listener to know which term was involved. In preaching, teaching, or ordinary conversation, a listener could judge only by context.

In the present text, **Lord** obviously refers to Jesus' deity and sovereign, exalted authority in the highest sense. It represents the divine title and name as well as all the divine rights, honors, and prerogatives. Ultimately, whether by choice or by force, every creature, human and angelic, will submit to **Jesus Christ** as the divine and exalted **Lord.**

In the first act of homage, **every knee will bow,** just as Isaiah had prophesied some seven hundred years earlier. Through him the Lord declared, "Turn to Me and be saved, all the ends of the earth; for I am God, and there is no other. I have sworn by Myself, the word has gone forth from My mouth in righteousness and will not turn back, that to Me every knee will bow" (Isa. 45:22–23). **Jesus Christ** is that divine Savior and **Lord,** to whom **every knee will bow.**

Those who will submit to the supreme authority of **Jesus Christ** will comprise three groups. First will be **those who are in heaven,** which will include the holy angels and the saints, the redeemed believers of all ages. That heavenly group, of course, has long been worshiping **Jesus Christ** as **Lord** (cf. Heb. 1:6; 12:23; Rev. 4:8–11; 5:8–14).

The second group will be those who are **on earth,** both redeemed and unredeemed. The redeemed will continue their worship of Him that began when they were saved. "When He comes to be glorified in His saints on that day," He will "be marveled at among all who have believed" (2 Thess. 1:10). At that same time, however, though unwillingly and in terror, the unredeemed will also be forced to bow their knees before Him. He will "[deal] out retribution to those who do not know God and to those who do not obey the gospel of our Lord Jesus, [who then] will pay the penalty of eternal destruction, away from the presence of the Lord and from the glory of His power" (vv. 8–9).

The third group who will worship the exalted Lord will be those who are **under the earth,** the fallen angels and unredeemed dead who are awaiting final judgment and eternal punishment. Revelation 20:11–13, perhaps the most frightening passage in all of Scripture, depicts the ultimate fate of the unredeemed:

Then I saw a great white throne and Him who sat upon it, from whose presence earth and heaven fled away, and no place was found for them. And I saw the dead, the great and the small, standing before the throne, and books were opened; and another book was opened, which is the book of life; and the dead were judged from the things which were written in the books, according to their deeds. And the sea gave up the dead which were in it, and death and Hades gave up the dead which were in them; and they were judged, every one of them according to their deeds.

This third group will also include "the spirits now in prison," the demons already bound in the abyss to whom Jesus "went and made proclamation" between His death and resurrection, by which He triumphed over them (1 Peter 3:19; cf. Col. 2:14–15).

As Isaiah predicted (Isa. 45:23), in the second step of this universal worship of the exalted Son of God, **every tongue will confess that Jesus Christ is Lord.** *Glōssa* (**tongue**) is frequently used, as here, to represent a language. No matter what their language, every human and angelic being will declare Jesus' lordship. The holy angels, the redeemed saints in heaven and on earth, and all the enemies of God on earth and in hell, forever confined by His unbreakable power that holds them in eternal punishment, will bow their knees before His sovereign authority. Even the damned demons, including Satan, will have no choice but to agree with and **confess** the reality **that Jesus Christ is Lord.**

Exomologeō (**will confess**) is an intensive form of *homologeō* (to confess, agree with) and refers to an open, public declaration. At the time about which Paul is here speaking, however, such a confession will not lead to salvation, because that supreme blessing will already have been received or forever forfeited. Before death or the Lord's return, the promise is that "if you confess with your mouth Jesus as Lord, and believe in your heart that God raised Him from the dead, you will be saved" (Rom. 10:9). But as the apostle makes clear later in that same letter, in the day of judgment that confession will not change the spiritual status of those making it. Quoting Isaiah, he says, "For it is written, 'As I live, says the Lord, every knee shall bow to Me, and every tongue shall give praise to God'" (Rom. 14:11; cf. Isa. 45:23). On the lips of those who belong to God, this will be a willing, continuing, and loving declaration of allegiance and adoration. For those who have rejected Him, the confession will be unwilling but irresistible, a compelled acknowledgment of Jesus Christ as the sovereign **Lord** of the universe by those under His immutable judgment.

Jesus already possesses His full divine title and authority, but it is not yet the Father's time for that authority to be fully manifested. Jesus already sits at the Father's right hand on His heavenly throne, but not everything has yet been brought into subjection to Him (cf. 1 Cor. 15:27–28). While there is time, the Savior continues to call men and women to Himself in saving faith, to proclaim and receive Him willingly as Lord. Paul rejoiced that he had "found mercy, so that in me as the foremost [of sinners], Jesus Christ might demonstrate His perfect patience as an example for those who would believe in Him for eternal life" (1 Tim. 1:16).

At Jesus' birth, the angel announced to the shepherds that "today in the city of David there has been born for you a Savior, who is Christ the Lord" (Luke 2:11). Jesus told His disciples, "You call Me Teacher and Lord; and you are right, for so I am" (John 13:13), and after the Resurrection Thomas confessed Him as "My Lord and my God!" (20:28). At Pentecost Peter proclaimed, "Therefore let all the house of Israel know for certain that God has made Him both Lord and Christ—this Jesus whom you crucified" (Acts 2:36; cf. 10:36). Paul told the Romans: "If you confess with your mouth Jesus as Lord, and believe in your heart that God raised Him from the dead, you will be saved" (Rom. 10:9; cf. v. 12). Later in the same letter he said, "For to this end Christ died and lived again, that He might be Lord both of the dead and of the living" (14:9; cf. v. 11). He reminded the Corinthians that "there is but one God, the Father, from whom are all things and we exist for Him; and one Lord, Jesus Christ, by whom are all things, and we exist through Him" (1 Cor. 8:6; cf. 12:3; 15:57).

Contrary to much popular teaching and preaching, Scripture nowhere speaks of a person making Jesus Lord. Although many people who use that phrase are merely referring to believers' obedient submission to Jesus' sovereign authority, such expressions are seriously misleading and confusing. The problem is especially serious because some evangelicals maintain that confessing Jesus as Lord is not an integral part of saving faith. They wrongly view that as an optional, though desirable, step that believers should take sometime after they are saved. The notion is that it is possible to be saved by confessing Jesus as Savior but not as commanding, ruling Lord. But as just cited, it was God the Father who "has made Him both Lord and Christ" (Acts 2:36), and in order to be saved it is necessary for a person to "confess . . . Jesus as Lord, and believe in [his] heart that God raised Him from the dead" (Rom. 10:9), a truth repeated a few verses later: "Whoever will call on the name of the Lord will be saved" (v. 13). Acknowledging Jesus as Lord must include submission and obedience, because, by definition, the title of Lord assumes it.

The centrality to the gospel of the lordship of Jesus Christ is abundantly clear. In the New Testament, He is called Lord some 747 times. In the book of Acts, He is referred to as Savior only twice, but as Lord 92 times. The first known creed of the early church was "Jesus is Lord!" The lordship of Jesus Christ is the very essence of Christianity and the necessary confession of anyone who desires to be saved. Jesus frequently reiterated the necessity of obedience as an element of saving faith (Matt. 7:22–27; 19:21–22; Luke 14:25–33; John 8:31; 14:23–24; 15:14).

Jesus is Savior so that He may be Lord, and He will not save those for whom He cannot be Lord. As mentioned above, even verbally professing Him as Lord without allowing Him to be Lord is worthless. Early in His ministry He declared:

> Not everyone who says to Me, "Lord, Lord," will enter the kingdom of heaven, but he who does the will of My Father who is in heaven will enter. Many will say to Me on that day, "Lord, Lord, did we not prophesy in Your name, and in Your name cast out demons, and in Your name perform many miracles?" And then I will declare to them, "I never knew you; depart from Me, you who practice lawlessness." (Matt. 7:21–23; cf. Luke 6:46–49)

Jesus was not, of course, teaching works righteousness—that salvation comes through obedience—but that a profession of faith that produces no true obedience to His lordship is worthless.

The argument that the title *Lord* refers only to the fact of Jesus' deity is spurious in the extreme, robbing the term of its essential meaning. By definition, *Lord* denotes a master, a supreme authority, a sovereign ruler. Not only that, but the reality of deity itself inherently carries those same meanings. The notion of some critics of "lordship salvation," that confessing Jesus as Savior is an act of faith, whereas confessing Him as Lord is a form of works righteousness, is absurd. Both saving confessions are made possible only through the gracious provision and power of God (Eph. 2:8; 1 Cor. 12:3).

I have commented on this very essential and often maligned requirement of Jesus' lordship in my book *The Gospel According to Jesus:*

> When we come to Jesus for salvation, we come to the One who is Lord over all. Any message that omits this truth cannot be called the gospel. It is a defective message that presents a savior who is not Lord, a redeemer who does not demonstrate authority over sin, a weakened, sickly messiah who cannot command those he rescues.
>
> The gospel according to Jesus is nothing like that. It represents Jesus Christ as Lord and Savior and demands that those who would receive him take him for who he is. In the words of Puritan John Flavel, "The gospel offer of Christ includes all his offices, and gospel faith just so receives him; to submit to him as well as to be redeemed by him; to imitate him in the holiness of his life, as well as to reap the purchases and fruits of his death. It must be an entire receiving of the Lord Jesus Christ."

A. W. Tozer wrote in the same vein, "To urge men and women to believe in a divided Christ is bad teaching, for no one can receive half of Christ, or a third of Christ, or a quarter of the Person of Christ! We are not saved by believing in an office nor in a work."

He is Lord, and those who refuse him as Lord cannot use him as Savior. Everyone who receives him must surrender to his authority, for to say we receive Christ when in fact we reject his right to reign over us is utter absurdity. It is a futile attempt to hold onto sin with one hand and take Jesus with the other. What kind of salvation is it if we are left in bondage to sin? (Rev. ed. [Grand Rapids: Zondervan, 1994], 235–36)

R. A. Torrey, second president of Moody Bible Institute, dean of the Bible Institute of Los Angeles, and a prominent evangelist, advised those who witness for Christ: "Lead [an unbeliever] as directly as you can to accept Jesus Christ as a personal Saviour, and to surrender to Him as his Lord and Master" (*How to Work for Christ* [Old Tappan, N.J.: Revell, n.d.], 32). W. H. Griffith Thomas, a cofounder of Dallas Theological Seminary, wrote:

> Our relation to Christ is based on His death and resurrection and this means His Lordship. Indeed the Lordship of Christ over the lives of His people was the very purpose for which He died and rose again. We have to acknowledge Christ as our Lord. Sin is rebellion, and it is only as we surrender to Him as Lord that we receive our pardon from Him as our Savior. We have to admit Him to reign on the throne of the heart, and it is only when He is glorified in our hearts as King that the Holy Spirit enters and abides. (*St. Paul's Epistle to the Romans* [Grand Rapids: Eerdmans, n.d.], 371)

THE PURPOSE OF CHRIST'S EXALTATION

to the glory of God the Father. (2:11b)

Finally, as for everything in the saga of redemption, the purpose of Jesus' exaltation is **the glory of God the Father.** To proclaim the sovereign lordship of His Son is the greatest **glory** that can be given to **God the Father.** Christ's universal acknowledgment as Lord does not make **the Father** jealous. Instead, that is the supreme objective and fulfillment of the Father's divine will as He demonstrates His perfect love for the Son.

Herein, of course, is a great mystery, a mystery that confounds everyone who presumes to fully understand the Trinity. The three Persons are but one **God,** wholly united and indivisible. They never compete, disagree, or differ with one another in the slightest degree. Men therefore are not called to worship **God** through Jesus, but to worship Jesus *as*

God. Jesus explained that "The Son of Man [is] glorified, and God is glorified in Him; if God is glorified in Him, God will also glorify Him in Himself" (John 13:31–32; cf. 14:13; Rom. 9:5; 11:36; 16:27). It is the Father's and the Son's supreme pleasure to glorify each other. In His High Priestly Prayer, Jesus said, "Father, the hour has come; glorify Your Son, that the Son may glorify You. . . . I glorified You on the earth, having accomplished the work which You have given Me to do. Now, Father, glorify Me together with Yourself, with the glory which I had with You before the world was" (John 17:1, 4–5). Whoever honors the Son honors the Father, and whoever dishonors the Son dishonors the Father (John 5:23). Throughout all eternity, the Father will continue to say of the exalted Lord Jesus Christ: "This is My beloved Son, in whom I am well-pleased" (Matt. 3:17; cf. 17:5).

God at Work in You— Part 1: The Believer's Role in Sanctification (Philippians 2:12)

10

So then, my beloved, just as you have always obeyed, not as in my presence only, but now much more in my absence, work out your salvation with fear and trembling; (2:12)

From the earliest days of the church, the relationship between the power of God and the responsibility of believers in living the Christian life has been debated. Is the Christian life essentially a matter of passive trust or of active obedience? Is it all God's doing, all the believer's doing, or a combination of both? This is not an unusual question when dealing with spiritual truth; in fact, the same question arises about salvation itself. Is it all God's doing, or is there a requirement on man's part in response to the command to believe the gospel? Scripture makes it clear that it involves both God's sovereignty and human response. Paul reminded the Ephesians: "For by grace you have been saved through faith; and that not of yourselves, it is the gift of God; not as a result of works, so that no one may boast" (Eph. 2:8–9). In John 6:44 Jesus declared, "No one can come to Me unless the Father who sent Me draws him"; yet Acts 16:31 commands, "Believe in the Lord Jesus, and you will be saved." Salvation is not by human works, yet it is always through personal faith. Other doctrines also involve seeming paradoxes. For example, Jesus Christ is both fully God and fully man, and while Scripture was written by human authors, every word of it was inspired by God. The gospel is offered to the whole world, yet applied only to the elect. God eternally secures believers' salvation, yet they are commanded to persevere.

Christians who try to reconcile every doctrine in a humanly rational way are inevitably drawn to extremes. To achieve their goal of full understanding without mystery or apparent paradox, they emphasize one truth or aspect of God's Word at the expense of others, which, to the finite mind, seem to contradict it. In regard to sanctification, the view that emphasizes God's role while virtually eliminating the believer's involvement is often referred to as quietism. The opposite extreme is called pietism.

The quietist views believers as passive in sanctification. A common maxim is, "Let go and let God." Another is, "I can't; God can." Quietism tends to be mystical and subjective, focusing on personal feelings and experiences. A person who is utterly submitted to and dependent on God, they say, will be divinely protected from sin and led into faithful living. Trying to strive against sin or to discipline oneself to produce good works is considered to be not only futile but unspiritual and counterproductive.

A prominent exponent of this view of sanctification was the devout Quaker Hannah Whithall Smith, whose book *The Christian's Secret of a Happy Life* has been read by millions. In it she writes,

> What *can* be said about man's part in this great work but that he must continually surrender himself and continually trust? But when we come to God's side of the question, what is there that may not be said as to the manifold ways, in which He accomplishes the work entrusted to Him? It is here that the growing comes in. The lump of clay could never grow into a beautiful vessel if it stayed in the clay pit for thousands of years; but when it is put into the hands of a skilful potter it grows rapidly, under his fashioning, into the vessel he intends it to be. And in the same way the soul, abandoned to the working of the Heavenly Potter, is made into a vessel unto honor, sanctified, and meet for the Master's use. (Westwood, N.J.: Revell, 1952, 32. Italics in original.)

In response to the question about how a Christian can fall into sin, quietists maintain that such a person obviously misunderstands the matter of complete surrender and takes himself out of the hands of the Heavenly Potter. But one wonders how, if God were completely in control, a believer could ever take himself out of the divine Potter's hands. How could one not blame God for his defection from complete surrender?

Pietists, on the other hand, are typically aggressive in their pursuit of correct doctrine and moral purity. Historically, this movement originated in seventeenth-century Germany as a reaction to the dead orthodoxy of many Protestant churches. To their credit, most pietists place strong emphasis on Bible study, holy living, self-discipline, and practical Christianity. They emphasize such passages as "Let us cleanse ourselves from all defilement of flesh and spirit, perfecting holiness in the fear of God" (2 Cor. 7:1) and "Even so faith, if it has no works, is dead, being by itself" (James 2:17). Yet they often stress self-effort to the virtual exclusion of dependence on divine power. As would be expected, pietism frequently leads to legalism, moralism, self-righteousness, a judgmental spirit, pride, and hypocrisy.

In Philippians 2:12–13, Paul presents the appropriate resolution between the believer's part and God's part in sanctification. Yet he makes no effort to rationally harmonize the two. He is content with the incomprehensibility and simply states both truths, saying, in effect, that, on the one hand, sanctification is of believers (v. 12) and on the other hand, it is of God (v. 13).

The same dual emphasis is found throughout the New Testament and a consideration of the pertinent texts is helpful. Peter, in his second letter, reminds believers that God's

> divine power has granted to us everything pertaining to life and godliness, through the true knowledge of Him who called us by His own glory and excellence. For by these He has granted to us His precious and magnificent promises, so that by them you may become partakers of the divine nature, having escaped the corruption that is in the world by lust. (2 Peter 1:3–4)

Based on that divine provision, Peter then charges believers:

> Now for this very reason also, applying all diligence, in your faith supply moral excellence, and in your moral excellence, knowledge, and in your knowledge, self-control, and in your self-control, perseverance, and in your perseverance, godliness, and in your godliness, brotherly kindness, and in your brotherly kindness, love. For if these qualities are yours and are increasing, they render you neither useless nor unfruitful in the true knowledge of our Lord Jesus Christ. For he who lacks these qualities is blind or short-sighted, having forgotten his purification from his former sins. Therefore, brethren, be all the more diligent to make certain about His calling and choosing you; for as long as you practice these things, you will never stumble. (vv. 5–10)

Paul wrote to the Corinthians that "by the grace of God I am what I am, and His grace toward me did not prove vain"; and then went on to say, "but I labored even more than all of them, yet not I, but the grace of God with me" (1 Cor. 15:10). In that inspired statement, the apostle makes it clear that God's divine grace and power undergird the faithful and obedient effort of believers. His declaration that "I have been crucified with Christ; and it is no longer I who live, but Christ lives in me; and the life which I now live in the flesh I live by faith in the Son of God, who loved me and gave Himself up for me" (Gal. 2:20) is complemented by the corresponding declaration that "we proclaim Him, admonishing every man and teaching every man with all wisdom, so that we may present every man complete in Christ. For this purpose also I labor, striving according to His power, which mightily works within me" (Col. 1:28–29). James first admonished, "Submit therefore to God," and then, "Resist the devil and he will flee from you" (James 4:7). Believers' sanctification requires their diligent effort. Yet it is empowered by God, who, according to His sovereign power, works out His will for and in His children.

That divine-human synergy working in and through believers has always existed and is exemplified in the Old Testament. When Pharaoh's army threatened the people of Israel, Moses was so confident in the Lord that he cried out, "Do not fear! Stand by and see the salvation of the Lord which He will accomplish for you today; for the Egyptians whom you have seen today, you will never see them again forever. The Lord will fight for you while you keep silent" (Ex. 14:13–14). But the Israelites also had a part to play: "The Lord said to Moses, 'Why are you crying out to Me? Tell the sons of Israel to go forward. As for you, lift up your staff and stretch out your hand over the sea and divide it, and the sons of Israel shall go through the midst of the sea on dry land'" (vv. 15–16). It was not the Lord's will that His people merely keep silent and be passive but that they participate actively in accomplishing His purpose. His purpose *for* them was to be accomplished *through* them.

That principle can also be seen in Solomon's dedication of the temple. As the king stood before the assembly of Israel, he prayed,

> Blessed be the Lord, who has given rest to His people Israel, according to all that He promised; not one word has failed of all His good promise, which He promised through Moses His servant. May the Lord our God be with us, as He was with our fathers; may He not leave us or forsake us, that He may incline our hearts to Himself, to walk in all His ways and to keep His commandments and His statutes and His ordinances, which He commanded our fathers. And may these words of mine, with which I have made supplication before the Lord, be near to the Lord our God day and night, that He may maintain the cause of His servant and the cause of His people Israel, as each day requires, so that all the peoples of the earth may know that the Lord is God; there is no one else. Let your heart therefore be wholly devoted to the Lord our God, to walk in His statutes and to keep His commandments, as at this day. (1 Kings 8:56–61)

Solomon realized that God Himself provides the guidance and strength for His people to faithfully obey His commands and to serve and worship Him. Consequently, no believer has an excuse for disobedience or failure to serve the Lord. To trust *is* to obey.

As James explained many centuries later, "Even so faith, if it has no works, is dead, being by itself" (James 2:17). It is not, of course, that the Lord does not accomplish many things for His people apart from anything they do. But they are commanded to obey His will. To not do what one knows should be done is sin: "To one who knows the right thing to do and does not do it, to him it is sin" (James 4:17).

The point of all this recitation of Scripture is not to provide a clear grasp of the "spiritual pathology" of sanctification and end all mystery, but to make it clear that the apparent paradox is exactly what Scripture repeatedly teaches. So as he addresses the topic of sanctification, Paul focuses first on the believer's role in sanctification. Some misguided interpreters completely misread this exhortation, as if it said, "work *for* your salvation," "work *at* your salvation," or "work *up* your salvation." But both in the immediate context of this letter and the broader context of the New Testament, none of those interpretations is correct. Paul is not speaking of attaining salvation by human effort or goodness, but of living out the inner transformation that God has graciously granted.

In Romans Paul made it clear that

> apart from the Law the righteousness of God has been manifested, being witnessed by the Law and the Prophets, even the righteousness of God through faith in Jesus Christ for all those who believe; for there is no distinction; for all have sinned and fall short of the glory of God, being justified as a gift by His grace through the redemption which is in Christ Jesus. (Rom. 3:21–24)

To the Ephesians he wrote, "For by grace you have been saved through faith; and that not of yourselves, it is the gift of God; not as a result of works, so that no one may boast" (Eph. 2:8–9).

Faith alone has always been the way of salvation. It was "by faith [that] Abel offered to God a better sacrifice than Cain, through which he obtained the testimony that he was righteous, God testifying about his gifts, and through faith, though he is dead, he still speaks" (Heb. 11:4), and it was "by faith [that] Enoch was taken up so that he would not see death; and he was not found because God took him up; for he obtained the witness that before his being taken up he was pleasing to God" (v. 5). Noah was a righteous man (Gen. 6:9) by faith (Heb. 11:7). Abraham was saved by God's grace working through his personal faith: "Abraham believed God, and it was credited to him as righteousness. Now to the one who works, his wage is not credited as a favor, but as what is due. But to the one who does not work, but believes in Him who justifies the ungodly, his faith is credited as righteousness" (Rom. 4:3–5; cf. Heb. 11:8–10). The law given through Moses did not alter the way of salvation. It was only by faith that Moses himself, as well as all other Old Testament saints, were saved (Heb. 11:23–38). All of those believing men and women "gained approval through their faith" (v. 39), by which God granted them His righteousness on account of the death His Son would die.

As Paul emphasizes in verse 13 of Philippians 2, salvation is from God. But in verse 12 he focuses on the responsibility of believers to live lives that are consistent with the divine gift of salvation. Because "we live by the Spirit," that is, have the divine life of Christ within us, we should "also walk by the Spirit" (Gal. 5:25).

Everything in life requires energy. It takes energy to walk and to work. It takes energy to think and to meditate. It takes energy to obey and to worship God. The point of the present verse is that it takes spiritual energy to grow as a Christian, to live a life that is holy, fruitful, and pleasing to the Lord. The main verb in this verse, *katergazomai* (**work out**), specifically calls for the constant energy and effort necessary to finish a task. In 2:12, Paul's words suggest five truths that believers must understand to sustain such energy: their example; their being loved; their obedience; their personal responsibilities and resources; and the consequences of their sin.

UNDERSTAND YOUR EXAMPLE

So then, (2:12*a*)

The first element of believers' working out their sanctification is understanding Christ's example. **So then** translates the Greek particle *hōste,* which was used to draw a conclusion from a preceding statement. Here it refers back to the example of Jesus Christ, whose perfect model of humility, submission, and obedience was described in verses 5–8. In His incarnation, Jesus did not cling to His equality with God the Father, but emptied Himself of His divine rights and prerogatives. Taking the form of a humble bond-servant, He was obedient to His heavenly Father, even to the point of dying on the cross as a sacrifice for sin. It is also true that the self-emptying of the Son of God placed Him in the role of a servant to the will of the Father and the power of the Holy Spirit. One of the greatest realities of the Incarnation was the fact that what Jesus did He did in the Spirit's power (Luke 4:1, 14, 18; 5:17; Acts 10:38; cf. Matt. 12:18, 28–32). The essence of living the Christian life is being obedient like

Him: "The one who says he abides in [Christ] ought himself to walk in the same manner as He walked" (1 John 2:6).

UNDERSTAND THAT YOU ARE LOVED

my beloved, (2:12*b*)

Paul's next words suggest a second element of believers' working out their sanctification—understanding that they are greatly loved. **My beloved** was unmistakably a word of comfort and encouragement. The apostle knew that the Philippians would face many disappointments and failures as they sought to follow the Lord's example in living for Him. Paul's love for them reflected Christ's love for His church (cf. 1:8).

Paul was well aware of their weaknesses and shortcomings. He understood the dangers they faced from worldly false teachers, including both Jewish legalists and Gentile libertines. All of them were "enemies of the cross of Christ, whose end is destruction, whose god is their appetite, and whose glory is in their shame, who set their minds on earthly things" (Phil. 3:18–19). He knew of the conflict between Euodia and Syntyche, sisters in Christ whom he admonished "to live in harmony in the Lord" (4:2). It is likely that many believers in the church were inclined to be proud, hence the urgent call to follow Christ's example of humility (2:1–8). Just as the Lord did with him and does with all of His children, the apostle made allowance for their failures. They did not serve a hard, merciless deity, as did their pagan neighbors. They served a merciful, forgiving, gracious Lord who was always willing to restore them to fellowship with Himself.

Despite their imperfections, the Philippian believers were Paul's and the Lord's **beloved** brothers and sisters, for whom he longed "with the affection of Christ Jesus" (1:8). In 4:1 he twice speaks of them as his "beloved," and as his "joy and crown," whom he longed to see and entreated to "stand firm in the Lord." He understood that, like himself, they had not yet "become perfect," that they, too, were pressing on to "lay hold of that for which [they had been] laid hold of by Christ Jesus," not regarding themselves "as having laid hold of it yet; . . . forgetting what lies behind and reaching forward to what lies ahead," and were faithfully pressing "on toward the goal for the prize of the upward call of God in Christ Jesus" (3:12–14).

Paul's charge for them to work out their salvation was not an indifferent directive. It was rather an affectionate call to follow Christ's example in confidence of His love by practicing the things they had "learned and received and heard and seen" in Paul (4:9).

UNDERSTAND OBEDIENCE

just as you have always obeyed, (2:12c)

The third element of believers' working out their sanctification is understanding the need for obedience to the Lord. Paul encourages the Philippians to continue in faithful submission to God's will. **Obeyed** translates a form of *hupakouō*, a compound verb composed of the preposition *hupo* and the verb *akouō*, from which the English word *acoustics* derives. The compound verb has the basic meaning of placing oneself under what has been heard, and therefore of submitting and obeying. A believer obviously must listen to God's Word if he is to be obedient to it, so this is indirectly an appeal for believers to continue to study and obey Scripture (cf. Matt. 28:19–20).

Lydia obeyed the Word that she heard Paul preach. She was already a worshiper of God, and as she "was listening, . . . the Lord opened her heart to respond to the things spoken by Paul" (Acts 16:14). So, too, did the Philippian jailer, who may have been among those to whom the apostle was now writing. After Paul and Silas "spoke the word of the Lord to him together with all who were in his house, . . . he took them that very hour of the night and washed their wounds, and immediately he was baptized, he and all his household" (Acts 16:32–33). In much the same way, the Jews in Berea "received the word with great eagerness," because they were "examining the Scriptures daily to see whether these things were so" (Acts 17:11).

God's command to Peter, James, and John on the Mount of Transfiguration is His command to everyone: "This is My beloved Son, with whom I am well-pleased; listen to Him!" (Matt. 17:5). To preach the gospel is more than merely sharing one's faith and offering an invitation; it is to call sinners to obey God, "to bring about the obedience of faith . . . for His name's sake" (Rom. 1:5). To be saved is to "obey the gospel of our Lord Jesus" (2 Thess. 1:8; cf. Rom. 6:17; 1 Peter 1:2). Believers are to "be careful how [they] walk, not as unwise men but as wise" (Eph. 5:15). Paul wrote to Titus: "Concerning these things I want you to speak confidently, so that those who have believed God will be careful to engage in good deeds. These things are good and profitable for men" (Titus 3:8). The writer of Hebrews charges fellow believers: "Therefore let us be diligent to enter that rest, so that no one will fall, through following the same example of disobedience" (Heb. 4:11). Jesus' Great Commission includes the command to teach converts from "all the nations . . . to observe all that I commanded you" (Matt. 28:19–20). Obedience is essential to sanctification, which cannot take place without it.

UNDERSTAND PERSONAL RESPONSIBILITIES AND RESOURCES

not as in my presence only, but now much more in my absence, (2:12*d*)

The fourth aspect of believers' working out their sanctification is understanding their personal responsibilities and resources. Because believers are sinful, they are inclined to be self-justifying, blaming circumstances or other people for their problems and failures. Paul commends the Philippians for their faithful pattern of obedience to Christ while they were in his **presence.** But he goes on to say that they were just as obligated to obey during his **absence.**

The bond of affection between Paul and the church at Philippi was particularly deep and strong. Those believers had had the unbelievable privilege of being taught by Paul—perhaps the greatest teacher of God's Word the world has ever seen, except for the Lord Jesus Christ. Much of what he preached, taught, and wrote became Scripture, including thirteen New Testament books. It could hardly have been otherwise that many of the Philippian believers developed an exceptionally strong dependence on that noble servant of God.

But at the time of this writing, Paul was hundreds of miles away, incarcerated in Rome. The only means of contact were letters, such as the present one, and occasional reports from mutual friends. But as disappointing and challenging as the situation was, Paul reminds them that their spiritual responsibility was not to him but to the Lord. They were to obey the Lord in spite of Paul's **absence.**

The apostle repeats an admonition he made earlier: "Conduct yourselves in a manner worthy of the gospel of Christ, so that whether I come and see you or remain absent, I will hear of you that you are standing firm in one spirit, with one mind striving together for the faith of the gospel" (1:27). His point is that there is never a time when a true believer is not responsible to obey the Lord. Believers must never be primarily dependent on their pastor, teacher, Christian fellowship, or anyone else for their spiritual strength and growth. Their supreme example is the Lord Jesus Christ, and their true power comes from the Holy Spirit. Believers, gratefully, are never without Christ's example and never without the Spirit's power.

UNDERSTAND THE CONSEQUENCES OF SIN

work out your salvation with fear and trembling; (2:12*e*)

The fifth motive for believers' working out their sanctification is understanding the consequences of sin. Although God is loving, merciful, and forgiving, He nevertheless holds believers accountable for disobedience. Like John, Paul understood well that "if we say that we have no sin, we are deceiving ourselves and the truth is not in us. If we confess our sins, He is faithful and righteous to forgive us our sins and to cleanse us from all unrighteousness" (1 John 1:8–9). Knowing that he serves a holy and just God, the faithful believer will always live with **fear and trembling. Fear** translates *phobos,* which describes fright or terror (cf. Matt. 14:26; Luke 21:26; 1 Cor. 2:3) as well as reverential awe (cf. Acts 2:43; 9:31; 2 Cor. 5:11; 7:1). **Trembling** is from *tromos,* which refers to shaking and is the word from which the English word *tremor* derives. Both of those are proper reactions to the awareness of one's own spiritual weakness and the power of temptation. The Lord seeks such an attitude in His children, as His words in Isaiah 66:2 indicate: "To this one I will look, to him who is humble and contrite of spirit, and who trembles at My word."

An important Old Testament truth is "The fear of the Lord is the beginning of wisdom" (Ps. 111:10; cf. Prov. 1:7; 9:10). This is not a fear of being doomed to eternal torment, nor a hopeless dread of judgment that leads to despair. It is rather a reverential fear, a holy concern to give God the honor He deserves and avoid the chastening of His displeasure. Such fear protects against temptation and sin and gives motivation for obedient, righteous living.

Aware of his own personal weakness, Paul spoke of his "fear and . . . trembling" as he ministered to the church in Corinth (1 Cor. 2:3), and later of those believers who received Titus with the same kind of "fear and trembling" (2 Cor. 7:15). This kind of "fear and trembling" is closely related both to obedience to the Lord and to love and affection for Him and for fellow believers. It is for that reason that Solomon could declare: "How blessed [happy] is the man who fears always" (Prov. 28:14).

Such **fear** involves self-distrust, a sensitive conscience, and being on guard against temptation. It necessitates opposing pride, and being constantly aware of the deceitfulness of one's heart, as well as of the subtlety and strength of one's inner corruption. It is a dread that seeks to avoid anything that would offend and dishonor God.

Believers should have a serious dread of sin and yearning for what is right before God (cf. Rom. 7:14ff.). Aware of their weakness and the power of temptation, they should fear falling into sin and thereby grieving the Lord. Godly **fear** protects them from wrongfully influencing fellow believers, compromising their ministry and testimony to the unbelieving world, enduring the Lord's chastening, and from sacrificing joy.

To have such godly **fear and trembling** involves more than merely acknowledging one's sinfulness and spiritual weakness. It is the solemn, reverential **fear** that springs from deep adoration and love. It acknowledges that every sin is an offense against holy God and produces a sincere desire not to offend and grieve Him, but to obey, honor, please, and glorify Him in all things. Those who **fear** the Lord willingly accept the Lord's chastening, knowing that God "disciplines us for our good, so that we may share His holiness" (Heb. 12:10). This **fear and trembling** will cause believers to pray earnestly for God's help in avoiding sin, as the Lord taught them: "Do not lead us into temptation, but deliver [rescue] us from evil" (Matt. 6:13). That prayer again reflects the spiritual tension that exists between believers' duty and God's power.

Work out translates a present middle imperative of *katergazomai* and indicates a command that has a continuing emphasis. The idea is, "Keep on working out to completion, to ultimate fulfillment." *Heautōn*, here rendered **your**, actually has the more emphatic meaning of "your own." The command is for believers to make a continuing, sustained effort to **work out** to ultimate completion their **salvation**, which has been graciously granted to them by God through their faith in Jesus Christ.

The principle of working out **salvation** has two aspects. The first pertains to personal conduct, to faithful, obedient daily living. Such obedience obviously involves active commitment and personal effort, for which Scripture is replete with injunctions, both negative and positive. Sin in every form is to be renounced and put off and replaced by righteous thinking. Believers are to cleanse themselves "from all defilement of flesh and spirit, perfecting holiness in the fear of God" (2 Cor. 7:1), setting their minds "on the things above, not on the things that are on earth," because they have died to sin and their lives are now "hidden with Christ in God" (Col. 3:2–3). Just as they once "presented [their] members as slaves to impurity and to lawlessness, resulting in further lawlessness," they should "now present [their] members as slaves to righteousness, resulting in sanctification" (Rom. 6:19), walking "in a manner worthy of the calling with which [they] have been called" (Eph. 4:1).

The apostle exhorted the Corinthians to strenuous effort in living the Christian life:

> Do you not know that those who run in a race all run, but only one receives the prize? Run in such a way that you may win. Everyone who competes in the games exercises self-control in all things. They then do it to receive a perishable wreath, but we an imperishable. Therefore I run in such a way, as not without aim; I box in such a way, as not beating the air; but I discipline my body and make it my slave, so that, after I have preached to others, I myself will not be disqualified. (1 Cor. 9:24–27)

His words later in the present letter also demand aggressive Christian living:

> Not that I have already obtained it or have already become perfect, but I press on so that I may lay hold of that for which also I was laid hold of by Christ Jesus. Brethren, I do not regard myself as having laid hold of it yet; but one thing I do: forgetting what lies behind and reaching forward to what lies ahead, I press on toward the goal for the prize of the upward call of God in Christ Jesus. Let us therefore, as many as are perfect, have this attitude; and if in anything you have a different attitude, God will reveal that also to you; however, let us keep living by that same standard to which we have attained. (Phil. 3:12–16)

He exhorted Timothy: "Flee from these [evil] things, you man of God, and pursue righteousness, godliness, faith, love, perseverance and gentleness. Fight the good fight of faith; take hold of the eternal life to which you were called, and you made the good confession in the presence of many witnesses" (1 Tim. 6:11–12; cf. 4:15–16; Heb. 12:1–3). To the Colossians Paul wrote:

> So, those who have been chosen of God, holy and beloved, put on a heart of compassion, kindness, humility, gentleness and patience; bearing with one another, and forgiving each other, whoever has a complaint against anyone; just as the Lord forgave you, so also should you. And beyond all these things put on love, which is the perfect bond of unity. Let the peace of Christ rule in your hearts, to which indeed you were called in one body; and be thankful. Let the word of Christ richly dwell within you, with all wisdom teaching and admonishing one another with psalms and hymns and spiritual songs, singing with thankfulness in your hearts to God. Whatever you do in word or deed, do all in the name of the Lord Jesus, giving thanks through Him to God the Father. (Col. 3:12–17; cf. vv. 5–11)

If living the Christian life were merely a matter of passive yielding and surrender, of "letting go and letting God," then such admonitions not only would be superfluous but presumptuous. But those injunctions, and countless others like them throughout God's Word, presuppose believers' personal responsibility for obedience. They must choose to live righteously, to **work out** their **salvation** in daily living, while at the same time realizing that all the power for that obedience comes from God's Spirit.

The second aspect of working out one's **salvation** is perseverance, of faithful obedience to the end. Salvation has three time dimensions: past, present, and future. The past dimension is that of justification, when believers placed their faith in Jesus Christ as Savior and Lord and were redeemed. The present dimension is sanctification, the time between a believer's justification and his death or the Rapture. The future aspect is glorification, when salvation is completed and believers receive their glorified bodies. Believers therefore have been saved, are being saved, and will be saved. They are to pursue sanctification in this life to the time of glorification. In that glorious moment believers will see the Lord "face to face" and come to know fully even as they are fully known (1 Cor. 13:12). They "will be like Him, because [they] will see Him just as He is" (1 John 3:2). It was for that glorious moment that Paul so deeply longed. Looking forward to that time he exclaimed:

> More than that, I count all things to be loss in view of the surpassing value of knowing Christ Jesus my Lord, for whom I have suffered the loss of all things, and count them but rubbish so that I may gain Christ, and may be found in Him, not having a righteousness of my own derived from the Law, but that which is through faith in Christ, the righteousness which comes from God on the basis of faith, that I may know Him and the power of His resurrection and the fellowship of His sufferings, being conformed to His death; in order that I may attain to the resurrection from the dead. Not that I have already obtained it or have already become perfect, but I press on so that I may lay hold of that for which also I was laid hold of by Christ Jesus. Brethren, I do not regard myself as having laid hold of it yet; but one thing I do: forgetting what lies behind and reaching forward to what lies ahead, I press on toward the goal for the prize of the upward call of God in Christ Jesus. (Phil. 3:8–14)

Because the fulfillment of that hope was a divinely decreed certainty, Paul could say with complete confidence that "salvation is nearer to us than when we believed" (Rom. 13:11). Although it is not yet completed, the testimony of Scripture is that every believer's salvation is utterly secure.

In the Olivet Discourse, Jesus declared, "The one who endures to the end, he will be saved" (Matt. 24:13). Paul and Barnabas urged new believers in Pisidian Antioch "to continue in the grace of God" (Acts 13:43) and encouraged "them to continue in the faith" (14:22). In his letter to the church at Rome, Paul declared that God will give eternal life "to those who by perseverance in doing good seek for glory and honor and immortality" (Rom. 2:7; cf. 11:22). He promised the Colossians that Christ would present them before God the Father "blameless and beyond reproach—if indeed [they] continue in the faith firmly established and steadfast, and not moved away from the hope of the gospel that [they] have heard" (Col. 1:22–23). He admonished Timothy: "Pay close attention to yourself and to your teaching; persevere in these things, for as you do this you will ensure salvation both for yourself and for those who hear you" (1 Tim. 4:16). The writer of Hebrews notes, "We have become partakers of Christ, if we hold fast the beginning of our assurance firm until the end" (Heb. 3:14; cf. 8:9; 10:38–39; cf. James 1:22–25). In each of His letters to the seven churches in Asia, the Lord described believers as overcomers (Rev. 2:7, 11, 17, 26; 3:5, 12, 21).

Perseverance in the faith is the duty of every true believer, and yet not the power of their security. It is, however, the unmistakable and inevitable evidence of divine power operating in the soul (Col. 1:29).

Believers will persevere because God's power keeps their salvation secure. Jesus repeatedly emphasized that truth. To the multitudes at Capernaum, He declared emphatically that "all that the Father gives Me will come to Me, and the one who comes to Me I will certainly not cast out. This is the will of Him who sent Me, that of all that He has given Me I lose nothing, but raise it up on the last day" (John 6:37, 39). Later, in Jerusalem, He declared, "I give eternal life to them, and they will never perish; and no one will snatch them out of My hand. My Father, who has given them to Me, is greater than all; and no one is able to snatch them out of the Father's hand" (John 10:28–29; cf. 17:2, 12, 24; 18:9). Earlier in Philippians, Paul wrote that he was "confident of this very thing, that He who began a good work in you will perfect it until the day of Christ Jesus" (1:6). Peter gave believers a similar assurance, saying that they "are protected by the power of God through faith for a salvation ready to be revealed in the last time" (1 Peter 1:5).

From beginning to end, the entire divine work of salvation is under God's control. In a well-loved passage Paul wrote,

> We know that God causes all things to work together for good to those who love God, to those who are called according to His purpose. For those whom He foreknew, He also predestined to become conformed to the image of His Son, so that He would be the firstborn among many brethren; and these whom He predestined, He also called; and these whom He called, He also justified; and these whom He justified, He also glorified. (Rom. 8:28–30)

To the Ephesians he wrote, "For by grace you have been saved through faith; and that not of yourselves, it is the gift of God; not as a result of works, so that no one may boast. For we are His workmanship, created in Christ Jesus for good works, which God prepared beforehand so that we would walk in them" (Eph. 2:8–10).

So the call for believers to work out their salvation is found all through the New Testament. That is only fitting and proper, since it is a call for the necessary commitment on the believer's part that is a prerequisite for the joys, blessings, and usefulness of sanctification.

God at Work in You— Part 2: God's Role in Sanctification (Philippians 2:13)

11

for it is God who is at work in you, both to will and to work for His good pleasure. (2:13)

As the previous chapter stated, there are two equal and opposite errors into which Christians may fall concerning the doctrine of sanctification. On the one hand, quietists stress God's role in sanctification, to the virtual exclusion of any human effort. Pietists, in contrast, emphasize self-effort at the expense of reliance on God's power. In Philippians 2:12–13, the apostle Paul avoids both of those unbiblical extremes, and presents the true balanced view of sanctification.

Having presented the believer's responsibility in sanctification in 2:12, Paul in verse 13 focused on God's role in the believer's sanctification. While the believer is working "out," God is working "in." In fact, apart from the reality of verse 13, the fulfillment of verse 12 would be impossible.

Jesus stressed that truth in the Upper Room Discourse, given to His disciples on the night before His death: "Abide in Me, and I in you. As the branch cannot bear fruit of itself unless it abides in the vine, so neither can you unless you abide in Me. I am the vine, you are the branches; he who abides in Me and I in him, he bears much fruit, for apart from Me you can do nothing" (John 15:4–5).

In this verse, Paul indicates the divine work in sanctification by emphasizing five key features about **God:** His person, His power, His presence, His purpose, and His pleasure.

HIS PERSON

for it is God (2:13*a*)

The first truth about God's part in believers' sanctification is His personhood, which is made clear by the personal pronouns **who** and **His** and by the verbs **to will** and **to work.**

Most pagan deities are described as impersonal, remote, and indifferent. That is not surprising, because false gods are fabricated by men out of fear and superstition. Even those that have personal characteristics are not portrayed as desiring fellowship with their worshipers. Understandably, their worshipers have no desire to fellowship with them. Since these false gods are fronts for demons, what the demons do impersonating the deities is only evil and harmful. That guarantees that they are worshiped solely for the purpose of appeasement—negatively to assuage the deities' anger and thus to avoid problems, and positively to gain health, prosperity, power, and other benefits.

But the true and living God of Scripture is real and personal. The Bible does not try to prove that **God** is a person because it assumes that reality. In both testaments He is spoken of in anthropomorphic (humanlike) terms, such as having eyes and seeing, of having ears and hearing, of having feet and walking, of loving and hating, weeping and laughing, condemning and forgiving. He thinks, feels, acts, and speaks—all elements of personhood. As a person, He has a personal concern for mankind, and especially for His children. That personal concern is seen in His work in believers.

The God of Scripture has unimaginable love for fallen, sinful mankind, which has rebelled against Him, blasphemed Him, and vilified Him. He has such great love for them "that He gave His only begotten Son, that whoever believes in Him shall not perish, but have eternal life. For God did not send the Son into the world to judge the world, but that the world might be saved through Him" (John 3:16–17). It is not the Lord's will "for any to perish but for all to come to repentance" (2 Peter 3:9).

For those who belong to Him, the God of Scripture has even greater love and the closest of personal relationships. In the Old Testament (Isa. 63:16; 64:8), and especially in the New (cf. Matt. 5:16, 45, 48; 6:1, 9; 23:9), He is referred to as His people's Father. Adam and Eve, Moses, and many other Old Testament saints spoke with **God** directly. "The Lord used to speak to Moses face to face, just as a man speaks to his friend" (Ex. 33:11). The prophet Malachi wrote that

> those who feared the Lord spoke to one another, and the Lord gave attention and heard it, and a book of remembrance was written before Him for those who fear the Lord and who esteem His name. "They will be Mine," says the Lord of hosts, "on the day that I prepare My own possession, and I will spare them as a man spares his own son who serves him." (Mal. 3:16–17)

The omnipotent, omniscient, and omnipresent Creator and Sustainer of the universe loves His children with everlasting love and kindness. **God** protects them according to His everlasting covenant and promises, forgives and cleanses with everlasting grace through His Son, and calls, gifts, and empowers them by His Spirit for spiritual service with everlasting impact. He sanctifies and will glorify those whom He has justified, bringing them into His heavenly kingdom to live with Him for all eternity.

No wonder Paul exulted:

> Oh, the depth of the riches both of the wisdom and knowledge of God! How unsearchable are His judgments and unfathomable His ways! For who has known the mind of the Lord, or who became His counselor? Or who has first given to Him that it might be paid back to Him again? For from Him and through Him and to Him are all things. To Him be the glory forever. Amen." (Rom. 11:33–36)

HIS POWER

who is at work (2:13*b*)

The second essential truth emphasized here about God's part in believers' sanctification is His divine power. Above all else, it is God **who is at work** in the lives of His children. He calls them to obey, and then, through His sovereign power, empowers their obedience. He calls them to His service, and then empowers their service. He calls them to holiness, and then empowers them to pursue holiness.

Work is from the verb *energeō*, the source of the English word *energy*. God energizes His children to obey and serve Him; His power enables their sanctification. As noted in the previous chapter, believers can do nothing holy or righteous in their own power or resources. Just as no one can be justified by the work of the flesh (Rom. 3:20), so no one can be "perfected [sanctified] by the flesh" (Gal. 3:3). Paul confessed that "nothing good dwells in me, that is, in my flesh; for the willing is present in me, but the doing of the good is not" (Rom. 7:18). He confessed that "by the grace of God I am what I am, and His grace toward me did not prove vain; but I labored even more than all of them, yet not I, but the grace of God with me" (1 Cor. 15:10). He encouraged the Corinthians to "be steadfast, immovable, always abounding in the work of the Lord," because he could assure them "that [their] toil [was] not in vain in the Lord" (v. 58). Paul did not underestimate the importance of faithful obedience. But he knew that underlying all acceptable service is the gracious power of God. It is "not that we are adequate in ourselves to consider anything as coming from ourselves," he wrote, "but our adequacy is from God" (2 Cor. 3:5). He reminded the Ephesians that he "was made a minister, according to the gift of God's grace which was given to [him] according to the working of His power," and rejoiced, "Now to Him who is able to do far more abundantly beyond all that we ask or think, according to the power that works within us, to Him be the glory in the church and in Christ Jesus to all generations forever and ever. Amen" (Eph. 3:7, 20–21).

Before Jesus gave the Great Commission, "Make disciples of all the nations, baptizing them in the name of the Father and the Son and the Holy Spirit, teaching them to observe all that I commanded you; and lo, I am with you always, even to the end of the age," He reminded the disciples that "all authority [or power] has been given to Me in heaven and on earth" (Matt. 28:18–20). And before He gave the final call to "be My witnesses both in Jerusalem, and in all Judea and Samaria, and even to the remotest part of the earth," He promised the disciples, "You will receive power when the Holy Spirit has come upon you" (Acts 1:8).

It is important that believers minister to each other, because that is God's will (Gal. 5:13). It is also God's will that preachers and teachers minister to the church (Eph. 4:11–13). It is important that the holy angels minister to believers, because God sends out those "ministering spirits ... to render service for the sake of those who will inherit salvation" (Heb. 1:14). But above all else, God Himself is believers' supreme and indispensable resource and power. The wonder of all wonders is that **it is God who is at work in** them. Paul summed it up in Colossians 1:29 when he said, "I labor, striving according to His power, which mightily works within me."

It is for that reason that sanctification will continue throughout the believer's life (1:6). Those whom God justifies He invariably sanctifies. He will accomplish His will by saving and preserving those who come to Him (John 6:40, 44). David understood that great truth when he wrote, "The Lord is my shepherd" (Ps. 23:1). He knew that he would not lack anything he needed (v. 1), that God would protect him (v. 4) and guide him (v. 3). Above all, David had the divine assurance that he would live forever in God's presence (v. 6).

In perhaps the most magnificent passage declaring God's preservation of believers Paul wrote,

> What then shall we say to these things? If God is for us, who is against us? He who did not spare His own Son, but delivered Him over for us all, how will He not also with Him freely give us all things? Who will bring a charge against God's elect? God is the one who justifies; who is the one who condemns? Christ Jesus is He who died, yes, rather who was raised, who is at the right hand of God, who also intercedes for us. Who will separate us from the love of Christ? Will tribulation, or distress, or persecution, or famine, or nakedness, or peril, or sword? Just as it is written, "For Your sake we are being put to death all day long; we were considered as sheep to be slaughtered." But in all these things we overwhelmingly conquer through Him who loved us. For I am convinced that neither death, nor life, nor angels, nor principalities, nor things present, nor things to come, nor powers, nor height, nor depth, nor any other created thing, will be able to separate us from the love of God, which is in Christ Jesus our Lord. (Rom. 8:31–39)

The revival under King Hezekiah illustrates God at work in the lives of His people. That mighty spiritual work began with the restoration of the temple. Hezekiah charged the Levites, "Consecrate yourselves now, and consecrate the house of the Lord, the God of your fathers, and carry the uncleanness out from the holy place. . . . My sons, do not be negligent now, for the Lord has chosen you to stand before Him, to minister to Him, and to be His ministers and burn incense" (2 Chron. 29:5, 11). The next day, "King Hezekiah arose early and assembled the princes of the city and went up to the house of the Lord" (v. 20). Later, he called all the city together, and everyone "rejoiced over what God had prepared for the people" (v. 36). Continuing his pursuit of spiritual revival, "Hezekiah sent to all Israel and Judah and wrote letters also to Ephraim and Manasseh, that they should come to the house of the Lord at Jerusalem to celebrate the Passover to the Lord God of Israel" (30:1). A decree was circulated throughout the country, calling the people to the long-neglected Passover feast. The edict included both a warning and a promise:

> Do not stiffen your neck like your fathers, but yield to the Lord and enter His sanctuary which He has consecrated forever, and serve the Lord your God, that His burning anger may turn away from you. For if you return to the Lord, your brothers and your sons will find compassion before those who led them captive and will return to this land. For

the Lord your God is gracious and compassionate, and will not turn His face away from you if you return to Him" (vv. 8–9).

The people responded favorably because "the hand of God was also on Judah to give them one heart to do what the king and the princes commanded by the word of the Lord" (v. 12). God commanded His people to return to Him and then gave them the heart to do it, graciously energizing the fulfillment of His command.

His Presence

in you, (2:13c)

The third essential truth about God's part in believers' sanctification is His divine presence. The preposition **in** is often featured in Paul's writings as he records the beloved truth that Jesus Christ dwells in believers (cf. Rom. 8:9–10; Gal. 2:20; Col. 1:27). The Lord Himself spoke of His indwelling presence in John 17:22–23: "The glory which You have given Me I have given to them, that they may be one, just as We are one; I in them and You in Me, that they may be perfected in unity, so that the world may know that You sent Me, and loved them, even as You have loved Me."
David understood and gloried in the reality of the Lord's continual presence with him: "You scrutinize my path and my lying down, and are intimately acquainted with all my ways" (Ps. 139:3). As noted above, the Lord was his Shepherd, who never forsook or neglected him or failed to protect him and abundantly provide for his needs (Ps. 23). In ways that are far beyond human comprehension, God indwells His people, both as individuals and collectively in the church. Jesus promised the disciples and all future believers: "I will ask the Father, and He will give you another Helper, that He may be with you forever; that is the Spirit of truth, whom the world cannot receive, because it does not see Him or know Him, but you know Him because He abides with you and will be in you" (John 14:16–17; cf. Acts 1:8). Perhaps because of their immaturity and worldliness, Paul reminded the Corinthians of that truth at least three times. "Do you not know that you are a temple of God and that the Spirit of God dwells in you?" (1 Cor. 3:16), he asked rhetorically. Later he added, "Do you not know that your body is a temple of the Holy Spirit who is in you, whom you have from God, and that you are not your own?" (6:19). In his second epistle he wrote, "We are the temple of the living God; just as God said, 'I will dwell in them and walk among them; and I will be their God, and they shall be My people'" (2 Cor. 6:16; cf. Ex. 29:45; Heb. 13:5).

God works unceasingly for the welfare of His people (Rom. 8:28). His holiness, wisdom, power, love, presence, and mercy are infinite. Having begun their new life in Christ through the power of His Spirit, believers are perfected by that same divine power. Because some believers in the Galatian churches were seeking to live by their own wisdom and resources, Paul asked in dismay, "Are you so foolish? Having begun by the Spirit, are you now being perfected by the flesh?" (Gal. 3:3).

HIS PURPOSE

both to will and to work (2:13d)

The fourth essential truth emphasized here, which is at the heart of God's work in believers' sanctification, is His divine purpose. That purpose is revealed by what He energizes believers to do—**to will and to work.**

The phrase **both to will and to work** is best interpreted as referring not to God's **will** and **work** but to that of believers. The **will** to do what is right before God must precede any effective **work** that is done toward that end. A genuine desire to do God's will, as well as the power to obey it, originates with Him.

To will is from *thelō*, which refers to thoughtful, purposeful choice, not to mere whim or emotional desire. It is what the psalmist had in mind when he prayed, "Incline my heart to Your testimonies" (Ps. 119:36; cf. 110:3) and what Ezra spoke of when he reported that "the heads of fathers' households of Judah and Benjamin and the priests and the Levites arose, even everyone whose spirit God had stirred to go up and rebuild the house of the Lord which is in Jerusalem" (Ezra 1:5; cf. 7:27). Later Ezra gave thanks that God also inclined the heart of King Artaxerxes of Persia to permit the Jews "to adorn the house of the Lord which is in Jerusalem" (7:27). Proverbs declares that "the king's heart is like channels of water in the hand of the Lord; He turns it wherever He wishes" (Prov. 21:1).

God uses two means to move believers' wills. First is what might be called holy discontent, the humble recognition that one's life always falls short of God's standard of holiness. When Isaiah beheld "the Lord sitting on a throne, lofty and exalted, with the train of His robe filling the temple," he could only exclaim in reverential fear, "Woe is me, for I am ruined! Because I am a man of unclean lips, and I live among a people of unclean lips" (Isa. 6:1, 5). Like all righteous people, he was dissatisfied with his spiritual state—a dissatisfaction immeasurably intensified by that awesome experience. Although Paul could say, "I am conscious of nothing against myself," he was quick to add, "yet I am not by this acquitted" (1 Cor. 4:4). As carefully and honestly as he examined his life, he knew that his finite perception could not detect every sin or spiritual shortcoming. His holy discontent led him to lament in his letter to the church at Rome, "Wretched man that I am! Who will set me free from the body of this death?" (Rom. 7:24).

The second means God uses to move believers' wills is holy aspiration, the positive side of holy discontent. After He instills a genuine hatred of sin, He cultivates a genuine desire for righteousness. After He makes believers discontent with what they are, He gives them the aspiration to greater holiness. Above all, it is the desire to be like Christ, "to become conformed to the image of [God's] Son" (Rom. 8:29). In Philippians Paul brings together his own holy discontent and holy aspiration when he confesses:

> Not that I have already obtained it or have already become perfect, but I press on so that I may lay hold of that for which also I was laid hold of by Christ Jesus. Brethren, I do not regard myself as having laid hold of it yet; but one thing I do: forgetting what lies behind and reaching forward to what lies ahead, I press on toward the goal for the prize of the upward call of God in Christ Jesus. (3:12–14)

Holy resolve leads to holy living. A godly **will** produces godly **work.**

It cannot be overemphasized that only God can produce in believers the **will** or the **work** that He commands of them. **To work** is from *energeō,* which refers to being energized and active in a particular endeavor. James noted that "every good thing given and every perfect gift is from above, coming down from the Father of lights" (James 1:17). Understanding that truth, the writer of Hebrews wrote, "Now the God of peace, who brought up from the dead the great Shepherd of the sheep through the blood of the eternal covenant, even Jesus our Lord, equip you in every good thing to do His will, working in us that which is pleasing in His sight, through Jesus Christ" (Heb. 13:20–21).

Just as believers are not saved by good works but wholly by God's grace working through their faith (Eph. 2:8–9), so also they are sanctified by His grace working through their obedience. They are God's "workmanship, created in Christ Jesus for good works, which God prepared beforehand so that [they] would walk in them" (v. 10). Just as believers are sovereignly predestined to salvation, so also are they predestined to sanctification. Again, Romans 8 is helpful:

> For those whom He foreknew, He also predestined to become conformed to the image of His Son, so that He would be the firstborn among many brethren; and these whom He predestined, He also

called; and these whom He called, He also justified; and these whom
He justified, He also glorified. (Rom. 8:29–30)

HIS PLEASURE

for His good pleasure. (2:13*e*)

The fifth and final essential reality about God's part in believers'
sanctification is the overwhelming truth that God works in their sanctification **for His** own **good pleasure.** His will for believers is that they
think and do what pleases Him. Although that is accomplished primarily
by His own power, when His children seek His will and do His work, it
brings Him great **pleasure. Good pleasure** translates *eudokias,* which
expresses great enjoyment and satisfaction. Because God is infinitely
self-sufficient, one cannot but wonder how anything or anyone, especially a sinful human being, could add to His satisfaction. Yet that clearly is
what Paul is saying. Even when they were weak, vacillating, and fearful,
Jesus assured the disciples, "Do not be afraid, little flock, for your Father
has chosen gladly to give you the kingdom" (Luke 12:32). Giving a place
in His kingdom to His children brings God great pleasure.

Because believers' sanctification brings Him satisfaction, God
grants them the resources to pursue it. Paul wrote to the Ephesians that
"the God and Father of our Lord Jesus Christ . . . has blessed us with every
spiritual blessing in the heavenly places in Christ . . . [and has] made
known to us the mystery of His will, according to His kind intention
which He purposed in Him" (Eph. 1:3, 9). To the Thessalonians he added
that God will "fulfill every desire for goodness and the work of faith with
power" (2 Thess. 1:11).

Even when they rebel against Him, God still desires to bless His
people if they turn and obey. Isaiah addressed these encouraging words
to wayward Israel: "Seek the Lord while He may be found; call upon Him
while He is near. Let the wicked forsake his way and the unrighteous
man his thoughts; and let him return to the Lord, and He will have compassion on him, and to our God, for He will abundantly pardon" (Isa.
55:6–7). Through Hosea, the Lord said to His beloved people, "How can I
give you up, O Ephraim? How can I surrender you, O Israel?. . . My heart is
turned over within Me, all My compassions are kindled. I will not execute
My fierce anger; I will not destroy Ephraim again. For I am God and not
man, the Holy One in your midst, and I will not come in wrath" (Hos.
11:8–9).

Believers' supreme purpose is to obey, worship, and glorify God,
and their fulfilling that purpose brings **pleasure** to Him. That magnificent truth is one of the many unique realities of Christianity. The sover-

eign God of the universe takes personal pleasure in what He Himself inspires and empowers His redeemed children to be and to do.

Every Christian should understand that sanctification takes his most strenuous effort, but is nonetheless totally dependant on God's power. Like many other truths of Scripture, those seemingly irreconcilable realities are hard to understand. Having done all they can, believers are to give God all the credit. Just as the Lord instructed, after they have done "all the things which are commanded," they are to confess, "We are unworthy slaves; we have done only that which we ought to have done" (Luke 17:10).

Stop Complaining (Philippians 2:14–16)

12

Do all things without grumbling or disputing; so that you will prove yourselves to be blameless and innocent, children of God above reproach in the midst of a crooked and perverse generation, among whom you appear as lights in the world, holding fast the word of life, so that in the day of Christ I will have reason to glory because I did not run in vain nor toil in vain. (2:14–16)

Modern Western society is by far the most prosperous culture in the history of mankind. Except for the very poor, people have all they need and much of what they want; yet many are seldom satisfied. Consequently, ours is also arguably the most discontented society ever. As the economy has become increasingly richer, people appear more discontent and complain more with each passing generation. Adding to the discontent are the fantasy worlds of movies, television, and advertising. The media, to create dissatisfaction, continually assault with the intent the senses with alluring and often unrealistic images that have been described as "plastic perfection." Fueling that enchantment is the staunch conviction that personal happiness, though elusive and unattained, is the supreme objective of life.

I once heard a sociologist observe that the typical modern

young person lives in a state of sullen discontent, continually dissatisfied with things as they are. Part of the problem, he suggested, is small families, in which fewer children are able to demand more of their parents' attention and do not have to share anything with brothers and sisters. Combined with affluence and materialism, that situation tends to produce selfish, self-indulgent children who are never content with what they have. Instead of bending to the needs of the family, as is necessary in larger families, the family bends to them. Absent parents, gone to work, shop, and play, try quick fixes for their children's demands, usually giving them what they want to stop the conflict. Children in that situation have little desire to grow up, realizing that adult society will not cater to their every whim. They want to postpone the responsibilities of a job, marriage and family, and other such commitments as long as possible, because those things demand a considerable degree of conformity to others. When such children become adults and don't get what they want when they want it, discontentment increases, as do frustration, anger, anxiety, and complaining.

Discontentment also breeds impatience, another defining characteristic of our times. Among the seemingly endless causes of impatience, and often hostility, are long lines, interruptions, talkative people, rude people, high prices, traffic jams, inconsiderate drivers, and crying babies. The last two have actually become causes of serious crime. Inconsiderate drivers often produce road rage, which, with increasing frequency, results in gunfire and even murder. Crying babies have led to child abuse, which occasionally results in the murder of a helpless baby.

Mounting discontent through the years produces the trauma of a so-called "mid-life crisis." That phenomenon is the reality that there is less of life ahead than behind, and the dreams of bliss are dying.

The biblical commands to believers not to complain (cf. James 5:9; 1 Peter 4:9) are evidence that the church is not immune from discontent. The church today has more than its share of malcontents and complainers. People often leave a church because their children don't like it, or because they are dissatisfied with some minor aspect of leadership, organization, or policy. Churches that promote self-esteem and self-fulfillment fuel the fires of discontent and complaining. Churches devoted to entertainment and meeting felt needs also create expectations for superficial satisfaction that they continually have to try to meet.

Adam was the first complainer. Immediately after he disobeyed God, he blamed Eve for his sin, complaining to the Lord that "the woman whom You gave to be with me, she gave me from the tree, and I ate" (Gen. 3:12). Instead of blaming himself, he blamed God. Some years later, his firstborn, Cain, complained bitterly to God that his punishment for murdering his brother Abel was too severe (4:13–14). Moses complained to the Lord because He did not deliver Israel from Pharaoh quickly enough (Ex. 5:22–23). After God miraculously delivered them by drowning the pursuing Egyptians in the Red Sea, Moses and the people sang a glorious song of praise to the Lord (Ex. 15:1–18). But after going only three days into the wilderness, they complained again because the water at Marah was not fit to drink. The Lord graciously responded by making that water sweet and then leading them to an oasis at Elim, "where there were twelve springs of water and seventy date palms, and they camped there beside the waters" (vv. 23–27; cf. 17:1–7). Shortly after that, however, the people were grumbling again, this time about a supposed lack of food (16:2–8).

After Caleb, Joshua, and the other men returned from spying out the land of Canaan, Caleb "quieted the people before Moses and said, 'We should by all means go up and take possession of it, for we will surely overcome it'" (Num. 13:30). Except for Caleb and Joshua, however, the other spies were afraid and faithless, telling their fellow Israelites,

> "We are not able to go up against the people, for they are too strong for us." So they gave out to the sons of Israel a bad report of the land which they had spied out, saying, "The land through which we have gone, in spying it out, is a land that devours its inhabitants; and all the people whom we saw in it are men of great size. There also we saw the Nephilim (the sons of Anak are part of the Nephilim); and we became like grasshoppers in our own sight, and so we were in their sight." (vv. 31–33)

Because of those men's faithless complaining, "All the sons of Israel grumbled against Moses and Aaron; and the whole congregation said to them, 'Would that we had died in the land of Egypt! Or would that we had died in this wilderness!'" (14:2). They then grumbled against God, saying, "'Why is the Lord bringing us into this land, to fall by the sword? Our wives and our little ones will become plunder; would it not be better for us to return to Egypt?' So they said to one another, 'Let us appoint a leader and return to Egypt'" (vv. 3–4). Their complaining turned into outright rebellion as they determined to stone Caleb and Joshua, and perhaps Moses and Aaron as well (v. 10). They rejected God's plan, God's chosen leaders, and God Himself. In response,

> The Lord said to Moses, "How long will this people spurn Me? And how long will they not believe in Me, despite all the signs which I have performed in their midst? ... Surely all the men who have seen My glory and My signs which I performed in Egypt and in the wilderness, yet have put Me to the test these ten times and have not listened to My voice, shall by no means see the land which I swore to their fathers, nor

shall any of those who spurned Me see it.... Say to them, 'As I live,' says the Lord, 'just as you have spoken in My hearing, so I will surely do to you; your corpses will fall in this wilderness, even all your numbered men, according to your complete number from twenty years old and upward, who have grumbled against Me.... According to the number of days which you spied out the land, forty days, for every day you shall bear your guilt a year, even forty years, and you will know My opposition. I, the Lord, have spoken, surely this I will do to all this evil congregation who are gathered together against Me. In this wilderness they shall be destroyed, and there they will die.'" As for the men whom Moses sent to spy out the land and who returned and made all the congregation grumble against him by bringing out a bad report concerning the land, even those men who brought out the very bad report of the land died by a plague before the Lord. (vv. 11, 22–23, 28–29, 34–37)

Recalling that tragic time, Asaph lamented, "How often they rebelled against Him in the wilderness and grieved Him in the desert! Again and again they tempted God, and pained the Holy One of Israel" (Ps. 78:40–41). Another psalmist wrote, "They despised the pleasant land; they did not believe in His word, but grumbled in their tents; they did not listen to the voice of the Lord" (Ps. 106:24–25).

Referring to those same times, Paul warned the Corinthians: "Let us [not] try the Lord, as some of them did, and were destroyed by the serpents. Nor grumble, as some of them did, and were destroyed by the destroyer" (1 Cor. 10:9–10). In response to those who complain because God sovereignly "has mercy on whom He desires, and He hardens whom He desires" and who then presumptuously ask, "Why does He still find fault? For who resists His will?" Paul replied: "On the contrary, who are you, O man, who answers back to God? The thing molded will not say to the molder, 'Why did you make me like this,' will it? Or does not the potter have a right over the clay, to make from the same lump one vessel for honorable use and another for common use?" (Rom. 9:18–21; cf. Isa. 29:16; 45:9; Jer. 18:6). Jude warned of apostates who were "grumblers, finding fault, following after their own lusts; they speak arrogantly, flattering people for the sake of gaining an advantage" (Jude 16).

In reality, every complaint a believer makes is against the Lord and is one of the ugliest of sins. And complaining against other believers is especially serious, an affront to God, because those believers are His children. James therefore warned, "Do not complain, brethren, against one another, so that you yourselves may not be judged; behold, the Judge is standing right at the door" (James 5:9). Similarly, Peter admonished, "Be hospitable to one another without complaint. [Rather], as each one has received a special gift, employ it in serving one another as good stewards of the manifold grace of God" (1 Peter 4:9–10).

Believers' failure to willingly, even joyfully, submit to God's providential will is a deep-seated and serious sin. Discontentment and complaining are attitudes that can become so habitual that they are hardly noticed. But those twin sins demonstrate a lack of trust in His providential will, boundless grace, and infinite wisdom and love. Consequently, those sins are especially odious in His sight and merit His discipline. As Paul explained to the Corinthians, the numerous Old Testament accounts of God's severe dealing with Israel's complaints in the wilderness were given "as an example, and they were written for our instruction" (1 Cor. 10:11). Jeremiah asked, "Why should any living mortal, or any man, offer complaint in view of his sins?" (Lam. 3:39). If that is true of everyone, how much more does it apply to believers, whose sins have been graciously forgiven by the Lord?

To deal with the complainers in the Philippian congregation and beyond, Paul first commands them to stop complaining, then gives them reasons for obeying that command.

THE COMMAND TO STOP COMPLAINING

Do all things without grumbling or disputing; (2:14)

The phrase **all things** refers back to the previous two verses (2:12–13) and sets forth the attitude with which believers are to work out their salvation. Everything involved in that process should be done **without grumbling or disputing.** Negatively, the basic attitude for working out salvation is **without grumbling or disputing.** Positively, as the apostle emphasizes throughout this letter, it is an attitude of determination to "rejoice in the Lord always" (Phil. 4:4; see also, e.g., 1:4, 18, 25; 2:18; 4:1).

Grumbling is from *gongusmos,* an onomatopoetic word that sounds like the guttural, muttering sounds people often make when they are disgruntled. It is a negative response to something unpleasant, inconvenient, or disappointing, arising from the self-centered notion that it is undeserved. The related verb is used of the resentful laborers who "grumbled at the landowner" for being paid the same as those who had only worked one hour (Matt. 20:11). It also describes the Pharisees and scribes who "began grumbling at [Jesus'] disciples, saying, 'Why do you eat and drink with the tax collectors and sinners?'" (Luke 5:30). It is used in John 6:61 of certain professed disciples who were offended when Jesus said, "Truly, truly, I say to you, unless you eat the flesh of the Son of Man and drink His blood, you have no life in yourselves" (v. 53). Paul uses the term to describe the Israelites in the wilderness, who grumbled "and were destroyed by the destroyer" (1 Cor. 10:10).

Disputing is from *dialogismos*, which has the basic meaning of inner reasoning and is the term from which the English word *dialogue* derives. But it soon developed the more specific ideas of questioning, doubting, or **disputing** the truth of a matter. In Romans 14:1, the word is used of passing judgment on another believer's opinions and in 1 Timothy 2:8 it is rendered "dissension." Whereas **grumbling** is essentially emotional, **disputing** is essentially intellectual. A person who continues to murmur and grumble against God will eventually argue and dispute with Him.

Behind this sin is the reality that although they are citizens of heaven (Phil. 3:20), believers live in a fallen world and in unredeemed bodies (Rom. 7:18; 8:23). The Lord often leads believers through times of trial and testing (James 1:2–3) and warns that they can expect to be persecuted because of their faithfulness (Matt. 5:10–12; John 15:20). It is therefore inevitable that circumstances will not always be favorable or pleasant.

Paul had forsaken the many worldly advantages and privileges he had in his former life, counting them as less than nothing (Phil. 3:4–7). He counted it a great privilege, however, to be imprisoned for the cause of Christ, which circumstance "turned out for the greater progress of the gospel," because "most of the brethren, trusting in the Lord because of [his] imprisonment, [had] far more courage to speak the word of God without fear" (1:12, 14). The apostle longed to know Christ ever more intimately, to share in "the power of His resurrection and the fellowship of His sufferings," even to the point of being "conformed to His death" (3:10). All believers have "been granted for Christ's sake" the same marvelous privilege, "not only to believe in Him, but also to suffer for His sake" (1:29).

Every circumstance of life is to be accepted willingly and joyfully, without murmuring, complaint, or disappointment, much less resentment. There is no exception. There should never be either emotional **grumbling** or intellectual **disputing.** It is always sinful for believers to complain about anything the Lord calls them to do or about any circumstance which He sovereignly allows. Whether the task is difficult or easy, whether the situation involves a blessing or a trial, negative attitudes are forbidden. As he testifies later in this letter, Paul's own spiritual growth had led him to enjoy this attitude: "I have learned to be content in whatever circumstances I am. I know how to get along with humble means, and I also know how to live in prosperity; in any and every circumstance I have learned the secret of being filled and going hungry, both of having abundance and suffering need" (Phil. 4:11–12). His example shows that such righteous behavior is possible.

THE REASONS TO STOP COMPLAINING

so that you will prove yourselves to be blameless and innocent, children of God above reproach in the midst of a crooked and perverse generation, among whom you appear as lights in the world, holding fast the word of life, so that in the day of Christ I will have reason to glory because I did not run in vain nor toil in vain. (2:15–16)

Paul gives three reasons why believers should stop complaining: for their own sakes, for the sake of the unsaved, and for the sake of pastors.

FOR BELIEVERS' OWN SAKES

so that you will prove yourselves to be blameless and innocent, children of God above reproach (2:15*a*)

So that translates the Greek conjunction *hina,* which, when used with a subjunctive verb as it is here, indicates a purpose clause. Believers are to stop complaining **so that** they may become the kind of **children of God** He wants them to be; namely, **blameless and innocent.** Christians are **children of God** by faith (John 1:12; Gal. 3:26), by adoption (Rom. 8:15, 23; Gal. 4:5), and by spiritual birth (John 1:13; 3:3–6; 1 Peter 1:23). Because they are His **children,** they should "be imitators of God" (Eph. 5:1); every Christian is in the process of becoming more like Christ (2 Cor. 3:18). That process includes becoming more **blameless and innocent.** To forsake grumbling and complaining is an essential part of advancing that process.

Blameless is from *amemptos,* which has the root meaning of being without defect or blemish. The believer is to seek to be without moral or spiritual blemish. Zacharias and Elizabeth, the parents of John the Baptist, "were both righteous in the sight of God, walking blamelessly in all the commandments and requirements of the Lord" (Luke 1:6). To the Thessalonians, Paul expressed his deep desire that God would "establish [their] hearts without blame in holiness before our God and Father at the coming of our Lord Jesus with all His saints" (1 Thess. 3:13). Later in Philippians he speaks of himself as having been "found blameless" as far as "the righteousness which is in the Law" was concerned (Phil. 3:6). The writer of Hebrews comments that, "if that first covenant had been faultless [*amemptos*], there would have been no occasion sought for a second" (Heb. 8:7).

Innocent is from *akeraios,* which has the basic meaning of being unmixed or unadulterated. The term was used to describe pure wine that was unmixed with water and pure metal that was not alloyed. Metaphorically, *akeraios* was sometimes used of what was harmless or innocent. Jesus commanded His disciples to "be shrewd as serpents and innocent as doves" (Matt. 10:16). Similarly, Paul admonished the Romans "to be wise in what is good and innocent in what is evil" (Rom. 16:19). The believer's life is to be absolutely pure, unmixed with sin and evil. Concerned for the spiritual welfare of the immature Corinthians, Paul wrote: "I am jealous for you with a godly jealousy; for I betrothed you to one husband, so that to Christ I might present you as a pure virgin" (2 Cor. 11:2).

As **children of God,** Christians also are to be **above reproach.** *Amōmos* (**above reproach**) is closely related in meaning to *amemptos* (**blameless**); both words describe what is without blemish or imperfection. *Amōmos* is used numerous times in the Septuagint in regard to sacrificial animals. Moses prescribed that a Nazirite "shall present his offering to the Lord: one male lamb a year old without defect for a burnt offering and one ewe-lamb a year old without defect for a sin offering and one ram without defect for a peace offering," and that all "the sons of Israel [should] bring . . . an unblemished red heifer in which is no defect and on which a yoke has never been placed" (Num. 6:14; 19:2).

Metaphorically, *amōmos* was used of being without blame or guilt. The character of the **children of God** should be above any legitimate blame, criticism, or censure. Paul uses the word twice in Ephesians, admonishing believers to "be holy and blameless before [Christ] . . . that He might present to Himself the church in all her glory, having no spot or wrinkle or any such thing; but that she would be holy and blameless" (Eph. 1:4; 5:27; cf. Col. 1:22). The writer of Hebrews uses *amōmos* of the Lord Jesus Christ, saying, "How much more will the blood of Christ, who through the eternal Spirit offered Himself without blemish to God, cleanse your conscience from dead works to serve the living God?" (Heb. 9:14), as also does Peter, who speaks of Him as "a lamb unblemished and spotless" (1 Peter 1:19). Like every other spiritual virtue, being **above reproach** is impossible in a believer's own power. It is only the unblemished and spotless Christ Himself who "is able to keep [believers] from stumbling, and to make [them] stand in the presence of His glory blameless with great joy" (Jude 24). Believers are in position blameless in His perfect righteousness and need to pursue that holy standard in their practice.

Writing to Titus, Paul gives the supreme motive for pure, blameless living:

Adorn the doctrine of God our Savior in every respect. For the grace of God has appeared, bringing salvation to all men, instructing us to deny ungodliness and worldly desires and to live sensibly, righteously and godly in the present age, looking for the blessed hope and the appearing of the glory of our great God and Savior, Christ Jesus, who gave Himself for us to redeem us from every lawless deed, and to purify for Himself a people for His own possession, zealous for good deeds. (Titus 2:10–14)

After briefly describing the "day of the Lord [which] will come like a thief, in which the heavens will pass away with a roar and the elements will be destroyed with intense heat, and the earth and its works will be burned up," Peter asks rhetorically, "Since all these things are to be destroyed in this way, what sort of people ought you to be in holy conduct and godliness," and then makes the same point in the form of an admonition: "Therefore, beloved, since you look for these things, be diligent to be found by Him in peace, spotless and blameless" (2 Peter 3:10–11, 14).

FOR THE SAKE OF THE UNSAVED

in the midst of a crooked and perverse generation, among whom you appear as lights in the world, holding fast the word of life, (2:15b–16a)

The second reason for not complaining is the negative impact it has on the unsaved, those who belong to **a crooked and perverse generation**—a description of the whole unbelieving **world. Generation** refers to the populace in broad terms, **world** to the evil satanic system by which they conduct their lives. The whole phrase **crooked and perverse generation** is borrowed from Deuteronomy 32:5, where Moses describes unfaithful and rebellious Israel as a people who had become "a perverse and crooked generation." Paul applies that description of Israel to unsaved, corrupt humanity. **Crooked** is from *skolios,* referring to what is bent, curved, or twisted. The medical condition scoliosis involves an abnormal curvature and misalignment of the spine. The term was used metaphorically of anything that deviates from a standard or norm, and in Scripture, it is often used of things that are morally or spiritually corrupt. It is used in the Septuagint (the Greek translation of the Old Testament), where Solomon speaks of "those who leave the paths of uprightness to walk in the ways of darkness; who delight in doing evil and rejoice in the perversity of evil; whose paths are crooked (*skolios*), and who are devious in their ways" (Prov. 2:13–15; cf. 21:8; 28:18).

Perverse translates a participial form of the verb *diastrephō*, which has the same basic idea as *skolios* but in a more active and dynamic form. Jesus spoke of an "unbelieving and perverted [*diestrammenē*] generation" (Matt. 17:17). The multitude that stood before Pilate and demanded Jesus' crucifixion accused Him of "misleading [or perverting, *diastrephonta*] our nation and forbidding to pay taxes to Caesar, and saying that He Himself is Christ, a King" (Luke 23:2). On the island of Paphos, Paul excoriated the magician and false prophet Bar-Jesus (or Elymas), saying, "You who are full of all deceit and fraud, you son of the devil, you enemy of all righteousness, will you not cease to make crooked [*diastrephōn*] the straight ways of the Lord?" (Acts 13:10). Several years later he warned the elders from Ephesus that "from among your own selves men will arise, speaking perverse things, to draw away the disciples after them" (Acts 20:30).

The crookedness and perversity of the modern world are so obvious and pervasive that examples are hardly necessary. Most of modern culture has radically distorted and deviated from God's standards of truth and righteousness. As with the church of Paul's time, the church today does not exist near the **crooked and perverse** world but lives inescapably in its **midst.** Because of the expansive development of communications technology, Christians today are continually and vividly barraged with vile language, ideas, and practices to a degree that believers in earlier days never encountered.

It is from this **crooked and perverse generation** that people need to be saved. In his Pentecost sermon, Peter admonished his hearers "with many other words [as] he solemnly testified and kept on exhorting them, saying, 'Be saved from this perverse generation!'" (Acts 2:40). Jesus identified the scribes and Pharisees who demanded a sign to prove His authenticity as the Messiah as part of "an evil and adulterous generation" (Matt. 12:23, 39; cf. v. 45).

In His High Priestly Prayer, Jesus spoke of the world as hating those who are not part of it, namely, those who believe in Him (John 17:14, 16). Yet He asked His Father not "to take them out of the world, but to keep them from the evil one" (17:15). He prayed, "Sanctify them in the truth; Your word is truth. As You sent Me into the world, I also have sent them into the world . . . that they may be perfected in unity, so that the world may know that You sent Me, and loved them, even as You have loved Me" (John 17:17–18, 23). Living faithfully and purely is an absolute prerequisite for fulfilling the Lord's mandate to carry His divine message of salvation to a world lost in sin.

In the first part of verse 15, Paul speaks of Christian character, what believers are to be ("blameless and innocent, children of God above reproach"). Here he speaks about what believers are to say, the content of what they preach and teach **as lights in the world.** The way that believers live as children of God has a dramatic impact on how they influence the godless world around them. But just as right doctrine without right character is hypocritical and ineffective, so also is right living ineffective if believers are not proclaiming gospel truth. To effectively carry out the Great Commission of Matthew 28:19–20, Christians must **appear as lights in the world,** in other words,"shine as lights." In its literal sense, _phōstēr_ (**lights**) was most often used of the stars. Using the term metaphorically, Paul declares that Christians are to be moral and spiritual luminaries who radiate God's truth, **the word of life,** into an otherwise sinfully dark universe.

God's calling His people to be **lights** to an unbelieving **world** did not begin with the New Testament church. Daniel declared that "those who have insight will shine brightly like the brightness of the expanse of heaven, and those who lead the many to righteousness, like the stars forever and ever" (Dan. 12:3). Isaiah wrote that the Messiah was to be "a light of the nations so that [God's] salvation may reach to the end of the earth" (Isa. 49:6; cf. 42:6). In Romans, Paul addressed unbelieving Jews who

> bear the name "Jew" and rely upon the Law and boast in God, and know His will and approve the things that are essential, being instructed out of the Law, and are confident that [they themselves] are a guide to the blind, a light to those who are in darkness, a corrector of the foolish, a teacher of the immature, having in the Law the embodiment of knowledge and of the truth. (Rom. 2:17–20)

He then sternly warns, "You, therefore, who teach another, do you not teach yourself? . . . You who boast in the Law, through your breaking the Law, do you dishonor God? For 'The name of God is blasphemed among the Gentiles because of you,' just as it is written" (Rom. 2:21, 23–24; cf. Isa. 52:5).

In his Spirit-inspired prophecy, Zacharias spoke of Jesus as the coming "Sunrise from on high," who would "shine upon those who sit in darkness and the shadow of death, to guide our feet into the way of peace" (Luke 1:78–79). "In Him was life, and the life was the Light of men," John declared. "The Light shines in the darkness, and the darkness did not comprehend it" (John 1:4–5). In the Sermon on the Mount, the Lord Jesus Christ called believers "the light of the world" and charged them to let their "light shine before men in such a way that they may see [their] good works, and glorify [their] Father who is in heaven" (Matt. 5:14, 16). All Christians "were formerly darkness" but are now "light in the Lord" and should therefore "walk as children of Light" (Eph. 5:8), as "sons of light and sons of day" (1 Thess. 5:5).

Obedient Christians will have an extraordinary impact on the world around them. But not every one they come in contact with will receive the gospel light. "This is the judgment," Jesus said, "that the Light has come into the world, and men loved the darkness rather than the Light, for their deeds were evil" (John 3:19). The light of God's Word not only reveals truth but exposes evil. Yet just as the Lord promised, some will be convicted by the Holy Spirit, see a believer's "good works, and glorify [their] Father who is in heaven" (Matt. 5:16), that is, be saved.

F. B. Meyer wrote,

> It is almost terrible to live with these thoughts pressing on one's heart—that one can never speak a word, never transact a piece of business, that one's face is never seen lighted up with the radiance of God, or clouded and despondent, without it being harder or easier for other men to live a good life. Every one of us, every day, resembles Jeroboam, the son of Nebat, who made other men sin; or we are lifting other men into the light, and peace, and joy of God. No man liveth to himself, and no man dieth to himself; but the life of every one is telling upon an increasing number of mankind. What a solemn responsibility it is to live!" (*The Epistle to the Philippians* [Grand Rapids: Baker, 1952], 116)

The quality of a believer's life, whether faithful and obedient or unfaithful and disobedient, is the platform of his testimony. A grumbling, complaining Christian will not have a positive effect on others. For obvious reasons, unbelievers are not attracted to that kind of life.

Holding fast is from *epechō*, which is perhaps better rendered "holding forth," as in the King James Version. The terms Paul normally used for the idea of holding fast, or holding on to, were *echō* or *katechō* (cf. 1 Cor. 11:2; 15:2; 1 Thess. 5:21; 1 Tim. 1:19; 3:9; 2 Tim. 1:13). The context of the present text also makes clear that the point is not believers' remaining faithful to (i.e., holding onto) God's truth, but rather their sharing with others (holding out) the redeeming **word** that brings eternal **life.**

The word of life refers to Scripture and, more specifically, to the gospel. Jesus said, "It is the Spirit who gives life; the flesh profits nothing; the words that I have spoken to you are spirit and are life" (John 6:63). When many professing followers then turned away, Jesus asked "the twelve, 'You do not want to go away also, do you?'" Peter responded, "Lord, to whom shall we go? You have words of eternal life" (John 6:66–68). Many years later, the apostle John opened his first epistle by declaring, "What was from the beginning, what we have heard, what we have seen with our eyes, what we have looked at and touched with our hands, concerning the Word of Life—and the life was manifested, and we have seen and testify and proclaim to you the eternal life, which was with the Father and was manifested to us" (1 John 1:1–2). After the angel of the Lord released Peter and the other apostles from prison in Jerusalem, he instructed them to "stand and speak to the people in the temple the whole message of this Life" (Acts 5:20; cf. 13:26), the message Peter later called "the living and enduring word of God" (1 Peter 1:23).

FOR THE SAKE OF PASTORS

so that in the day of Christ I will have reason to glory because I did not run in vain nor toil in vain. (2:16*b*)

The third reason for not complaining is for the sake of the leaders in the church, who have given their lives in ministry. Paul's pastoral heart shines through in his deep desire that the Philippians would stop grumbling and complaining, **so that in the day of Christ** he **will have reason to glory.** He anticipated **the day of Christ,** when he could look back and rejoice in the faithfulness of those beloved brethren. The people he served would be a source of eternal joy.

It is important to note that **the day of Christ** is not synonymous with another similar term, the Day of the Lord, which focuses on the punishment of the unrepentant wicked. Paul reminded the Thessalonians, "You yourselves know full well that the day of the Lord will come just like a thief in the night. While they are saying, 'Peace and safety!' then destruction will come upon them suddenly like labor pains upon a woman with child, and they will not escape" (1 Thess. 5:2–3; cf. 2 Thess. 2:1–8). But **the day of Christ** will be solely for believers (cf. Phil. 1:6, 10). Although it will also be a time of judgment, in the sense that believers will "appear before the judgment seat of Christ," the focus will be only on rewards, not punishment, "so that each one may be recompensed for his deeds in the body, according to what he has done, whether good or bad" (2 Cor. 5:10; cf. 1 Cor. 3:8; cf. 3:13–14; 4:5).

In saying that he would **have reason to glory,** the apostle was not expressing sinful pride in his ministry or an obsession with his own importance to the kingdom or in eternal heaven. The verb *kauchaomai* (**to glory**) can have the meaning of sinful boasting, as it clearly does in James 4:16. But it can also describe rejoicing, as it does in the present text (the King James Version reads, "may rejoice"). In Romans 5:11, the term is rendered "exult." Paul was looking forward to receiving the joy that the Lord promises to every faithful believer. "These things I have spoken to you," Jesus said, "so that My joy may be in you, and that your joy may be made full" (John 15:11). Joy is a fruit of the Spirit, which, like love, peace, patience, kindness, and the others (Gal. 5:22–23), is to be sought and cherished. John wrote his letters in part that his "joy may be made complete" (1 John 1:4; cf. 3 John 4) and longed to be "face to face"with those to whom he wrote that their "joy [would] be made full" (2 John 12). David prayed, "Restore to me the joy of Your salvation" (Ps. 51:12), and another psalmist exulted, "Those who sow in tears shall reap with joyful shouting"(Ps. 126:5).

As already noted, in the present text Paul is speaking specifically of the **glory,** or joy, he would experience at **the day of Christ** (cf. 1:6, 10).The apostle was now in prison and, for all he knew at the time, might possibly die there (see 1:13–14, 20–21). As he expressed later in this letter, His beloved brethren in Philippi were even then his "joy and crown" in the Lord and he longed to see them again (Phil. 4:1). Whether that hope was fulfilled or not, he knew that he longed to have the reward of ultimate joy in heaven for his faithful ministry among them.

In His Upper Room Discourse, Jesus told the disciples, "You will grieve, but your grief will be turned into joy. . . . I will see you again, and your heart will rejoice, and no one will take your joy away from you" (John 16:20, 22). To desire and anticipate joy not only acknowledges Jesus' promise but follows His example: "[He] for the joy set before Him endured the cross, despising the shame, and has sat down at the right hand of the throne of God" (Heb. 12:2). To the Thessalonians, Paul wrote, "For who is our hope or joy or crown of exultation? Is it not even you, in the presence of our Lord Jesus at His coming?" (1 Thess. 2:19). In the closing benediction of his short letter, Jude wrote, "Now to Him who is able to keep you from stumbling, and to make you stand in the presence of His glory blameless with great joy, to the only God our Savior, through Jesus Christ our Lord, be glory, majesty, dominion and authority, before all time and now and forever. Amen" (Jude 24–25).

The best thing believers can do for their pastors is faithfully to live out the truths of God's Word that he has preached and taught, so that he can say with Paul, **I did not run in vain nor toil in vain.** Every pastor desires that the reward of his efforts will be full, that the people under his care love and obey the Lord without grumbling or complaining and with their lives and words effectively demonstrate the gospel to be true and believable. It is the church's responsibility and privilege to "appreciate those who diligently labor among [them], and have charge over [them] in the Lord and give [them] instruction" (1 Thess. 5:12). "Obey your leaders and submit to them," the writer of Hebrews admonishes, "for they keep watch over your souls as those who will give an account. Let them do this with joy and not with grief, for this would be unprofitable for you" (Heb. 13:17). The greatest joy of any servant of God is the godly living of his flock. "I have no greater joy than this," John said, "to hear of my children walking in the truth" (3 John 4).

Model
Spiritual Servants
(Philippians 2:17–30)

13

But even if I am being poured out as a drink offering upon the sacrifice and service of your faith, I rejoice and share my joy with you all. You too, I urge you, rejoice in the same way and share your joy with me.

But I hope in the Lord Jesus to send Timothy to you shortly, so that I also may be encouraged when I learn of your condition. For I have no one else of kindred spirit who will genuinely be concerned for your welfare. For they all seek after their own interests, not those of Christ Jesus. But you know of his proven worth, that he served with me in the furtherance of the gospel like a child serving his father. Therefore I hope to send him immediately, as soon as I see how things go with me; and I trust in the Lord that I myself also will be coming shortly. But I thought it necessary to send to you Epaphroditus, my brother and fellow worker and fellow soldier, who is also your messenger and minister to my need; because he was longing for you all and was distressed because you had heard that he was sick. For indeed he was sick to the point of death, but God had mercy on him, and not on him only but also on me, so that I would not have sorrow upon sorrow. Therefore I have sent him all the more eagerly so that

when you see him again you may rejoice and I may be less concerned about you. Receive him then in the Lord with all joy, and hold men like him in high regard; because he came close to death for the work of Christ, risking his life to complete what was deficient in your service to me. (2:17–30)

Anyone who has spent much time in the writings of the noble servants of God develops a certain understanding of their hearts and minds. Usually their most intriguing and admirable quality is a willingness to make great sacrifices.

The seventeenth-century Puritan Thomas Brooks wisely observed that "example is the most powerful rhetoric" (cited in I. D. E. Thomas, *A Puritan Golden Treasury* [Edinburgh: Banner of Truth, 1977], 96). Perhaps the single most important aspect of spiritual leadership is having a godly life to emulate. Personal example illustrates biblical principles in action, showing how they should be lived out. When believers carefully consider God's standards in light of their sins, shortcomings, weaknesses, and failures, those standards often seem impossible to achieve. Jesus is the believer's supreme example (1 John 2:6). But He was the sinless, perfect Son of God, and what was possible for Him can seem impossible for His followers. However, when believers see another Christian living out God's standards triumphantly, they are encouraged.

Philippians 2:17–30 presents three men whose lives are exceptional patterns for godly living. These three—Paul, Timothy, and Epaphroditus—were together in Rome at this time. Paul was a prisoner in his own rented quarters. Though chained to a soldier, he was free to carry on his work unhindered (Acts 28:16, 30–31). Timothy, the apostle's son in the faith (1 Tim. 1:2), had been with him for some time. Epaphroditus had been sent from the Philippian church to bring financial support for Paul and to minister to his needs. The men were knit together geographically, spiritually, and ministerially in a common cause. Each was passionately devoted to the Lord Jesus Christ, not consumed with his own interests. For the Lord's sake, each had risked his health, his freedom, and even his life.

Although all three exemplified the qualities Paul has previously stressed, each also reflected distinct personal and spiritual characteristics. Paul might therefore be described as the sacrificial rejoicer, Timothy as the single-minded sympathizer, and Epaphroditus as the loving gambler.

PAUL: THE SACRIFICIAL REJOICER

But even if I am being poured out as a drink offering upon the sacrifice and service of your faith, I rejoice and share my joy with

you all. You too, I urge you, rejoice in the same way and share your joy with me. (2:17–18)

Nothing characterized Paul's life and ministry more than love—for the Lord, His work, and His people. He also loved the unsaved, especially those among his fellow Jews, about whom he testified: "I could wish that I myself were accursed, separated from Christ for the sake of my brethren, my kinsmen according to the flesh" (Rom. 9:3). But he had a special love for believers, as exemplified by his testimony to those in Corinth: "For out of much affliction and anguish of heart I wrote to you with many tears; not so that you would be made sorrowful, but that you might know the love which I have especially for you" (2 Cor. 2:4).

That love compelled Paul to serve unreservedly and sacrificially. He feared that unless he gave his maximum effort, he would be disqualified and his reward diminished (1 Cor. 9:24–27). He was keenly aware that he had a special calling, giftedness, and empowerment for which the Lord would hold him accountable. He wrote of that accountability to the Corinthians: "Let a man regard us in this manner, as servants of Christ and stewards of the mysteries of God. In this case, moreover, it is required of stewards that one be found trustworthy" (1 Cor. 4:1–2). Because of that accountability, Paul exercised self-discipline: "I discipline my body and make it my slave, so that, after I have preached to others, I myself will not be disqualified" (1 Cor. 9:27). He was confident "that in the day of Christ [he would have] reason to glory because [he] did not run in vain nor toil in vain" (Phil. 2:16).

One cannot help wondering why Paul had such great confidence in his own example. Most believers would be reluctant to offer themselves as an example, believing it would be presumptuous and prideful. But the Holy Spirit empowered Paul to that confidence. Because Paul was Spirit led and obedient, he did not have the self-conscious sense of inadequacy that the majority of believers possess. Though he was humble and had a deep sense of his weakness (1 Tim. 1:15), he could still use himself as an example because his motives were pure and his life holy. With both sincerity and genuine humility he therefore could admonish the Corinthians, "Be imitators of me, just as I also am of Christ" (1 Cor. 11:1; cf. 4:16). Paul was a human example because he followed the divine example, the Lord Jesus Christ. As the writer of Hebrews admonishes, Paul fixed his "eyes on Jesus, the author and perfecter of faith" (Heb. 12:2).

Even if translates a first-class conditional clause, which refers to something that is known to be true. A more appropriate rendering therefore is "because **I am being poured out as a drink offering.**" That whole phrase translates the single Greek word *spendō*, which means "to be poured out as a libation" (cf. 2 Tim. 4:6). Paul's example was evident in the price he was paying in pouring out his life to God like an Old Testament drink offering.

Contrary to what some interpreters suggest, Paul was not here speaking of his eventual martyrdom. The present tense clearly indicates that he was speaking of his current experience as a prisoner in Rome. He saw his life, not his death, as his ultimate act of sacrifice to the Lord. He was a living sacrifice, not a dead one (Rom. 12:1). His comments elsewhere in this letter indicate that he did not anticipate imminent execution, although he clearly understood that that was a possibility. He had already said: "To remain on in the flesh is more necessary for your sake. Convinced of this, I know that I will remain and continue with you all for your progress and joy in the faith" (1:24–25). Later in the present chapter he wrote, "I trust in the Lord that I myself also will be coming shortly" (2:24).

Both Jews and Gentiles would have understood the implied imagery of a **drink offering,** or libation, a ritual that was familiar to many ancient people (cf. Lev. 23:18, 37; 2 Kings 16:10–16; Jer. 7:18; Hos. 9:4). After placing the sacrificial animal on the altar, the priests would take wine (or sometimes water or honey) and pour it either on the burning sacrifice or on the ground in front of the altar. That act symbolized the rising of the sacrifice into the nostrils of the deity to whom it was being offered.

Paul's **drink offering** was also made on behalf of his beloved brethren in Philippi, an offering made **upon the sacrifice and service of** their **faith.** He spoke as if their faithfulness was greater than his own, which he described as being poured out on their greater **sacrifice and service.** Here the apostle reflects the sincere humility that marks the spiritually noble believer and that was supremely exemplified by the Lord Himself in His incarnation (2:1–8).

Thusia (**sacrifice**) was used of actual sacrifices (Matt. 9:13; Acts 7:41; 1 Cor. 10:18; Heb. 5:1). It was also used figuratively, as it is here (cf. 4:18; Rom. 12:1; Heb. 13:15; 1 Peter 2:5). **Service** translates *leitourgia,* which was most commonly used of religious **service** and is the term from which the English word *liturgy* derives. In 2 Corinthians, Paul used it of financial offerings given for "supplying the needs of the saints" (2 Cor. 9:12). Like Peter, Paul saw all believers as being priests of Jesus Christ, "living stones, [who] are being built up as a spiritual house for a holy priesthood, to offer up spiritual sacrifices acceptable to God through Jesus Christ" (1 Peter 2:5).

The Philippians were partners with Paul in sacrificial service to God (1:25–30; 4:10–19), especially through the ministry of Epaphroditus (2:25–30). They were suffering severely for their faith in an extremely hostile pagan environment. The more the church grew, the more it was resented and persecuted. Therefore the apostle admonished them, "[Be] in no way alarmed by your opponents—which is a sign of destruction for them, but of salvation for you, and that too, from God" (Phil. 1:28). He went on to explain, "To you it has been granted for Christ's sake, not only to believe in Him, but also to suffer for His sake" (v. 29). Their persecution also reflected his own; they were "experiencing the same conflict which [they] saw in [him], and [heard] to be in [him]" (v. 30). Theirs was a common offering; Paul poured his drink offering onto the burning sacrifice of the Philippian church.

Therefore, he writes, **I rejoice and share my joy with you all.** The apostle has already mentioned several reasons for his joy. He rejoiced because of his love for them and their love for him (4:1, 10). Simply remembering his beloved brethren at Philippi was cause for rejoicing (1:3–4). Even his seemingly unfortunate circumstances in Rome had "turned out for the greater progress of the gospel, so that [his] imprisonment in the cause of Christ [had] become well known throughout the whole praetorian guard and to everyone else" (vv. 12–13). The way in which he graciously accepted that imprisonment encouraged the believers in Rome, Philippi, and elsewhere to "have far more courage to speak the word of God without fear" (v. 14). Even when the gospel was preached with pretense and out of selfish ambition and envy, Paul rejoiced (vv. 17–18).

Even apart from such blessings, sacrificial service to the Lord is in itself a privilege and a cause for rejoicing. Believers are to rejoice not in spite of their suffering for Christ but because of it (cf. Acts 5:41), knowing that "all who desire to live godly in Christ Jesus will be persecuted" (2 Tim. 3:12). Believers' greatest joy comes at the point of greatest sacrifice, because serving God is the supreme purpose of their existence. The apostle wrote earlier in Philippians: "[It is] my earnest expectation and hope, that I will not be put to shame in anything, but that with all boldness, Christ will even now, as always, be exalted in my body, whether by life or by death. For to me, to live is Christ and to die is gain" (1:20–21). A few years earlier he wrote, "Not one of us lives for himself, and not one dies for himself; for if we live, we live for the Lord, or if we die, we die for the Lord; therefore whether we live or die, we are the Lord's" (Rom. 14:7–8).

Unfortunately, many believers experience joy in much the same way as the world does. When circumstances are favorable, they are happy; but when circumstances are unfavorable, they are sad and sometimes resentful. The only things that bring them joy are those that promote their own interests and welfare. But when believers seek to do the Father's will and please Him, they view sacrifice for Him with joy. The reason many believers know little about Paul's kind of joy is that they know little about his kind of sacrifice.

It is difficult for self-centered, worldly believers to understand how missionaries can live for years under primitive, demanding, and often dangerous conditions yet still maintain their joy. Through it all they rejoice, because, like Paul and the Philippians, they offer their lives as a continual sacrifice to God. They have learned that the greater the sacrifice, the greater the joy. They have the same attitude as Peter and the other apostles who, after being flogged and ordered "not to speak in the name of Jesus, . . . went on their way from the presence of the Council, rejoicing that they had been considered worthy to suffer shame for His name" (Acts 5:40–41).

Selfless service for Christ is a sacrifice only in the sense of being an offering to God. It is never a sacrifice in the sense of being a loss. A believer can sacrifice nothing for the Lord that is not replaced with something infinitely more valuable and gratifying (cf. 2 Cor. 4:17). It is always an exchange of the lesser for the greater, leading Paul to write, "I count all things to be loss in view of the surpassing value of knowing Christ Jesus my Lord, for whom I have suffered the loss of all things, and count them but rubbish so that I may gain Christ" (Phil. 3:8). What he forsook was mere "rubbish"; what he gained was Christ and the immeasurable blessings of salvation and eternal life (vv. 9–11). This reality of justification extends into sanctification.

Paul not only is a model for selfless, sacrificial service but also for the joy that service produces. As he wrote to the Corinthians: "I am filled with comfort; I am overflowing with joy in all our affliction" (2 Cor. 7:4; cf. Eph. 3:13) and to the Colossians: "Now I rejoice in my sufferings for your sake, and in my flesh I do my share on behalf of His body, which is the church, in filling up what is lacking in Christ's afflictions" (Col. 1:24). He assured the Thessalonians that "for this reason, brethren, in all our distress and affliction we were comforted about you through your faith; for now we really live, if you stand firm in the Lord. For what thanks can we render to God for you in return for all the joy with which we rejoice before our God on your account" (1 Thess. 3:7–9). In the same way James admonished: "Consider it all joy, my brethren, when you encounter various trials, knowing that the testing of your faith produces endurance. And let endurance have its perfect result, so that you may be perfect and complete, lacking in nothing" (James 1:2–4). Likewise, Peter counseled his readers, "To the degree that you share the sufferings of Christ, keep on rejoicing, so that also at the revelation of His glory you may rejoice with exultation" (1 Peter 4:13).

Thus it was with integrity and sincerity that Paul could say, **I rejoice and share my joy with you all.** *Sunchairō* (**share . . . joy**) is a compound (and thus intensified) form of the preceding verb (*chairō*, **rejoice**) and describes a deep mutuality of purpose and feeling. It was used by Luke to describe the neighbors and relatives of Elizabeth who "were rejoicing with her" over the birth of John the Baptist (Luke 1:58). It was used by Jesus of the man who rejoiced over finding his lost sheep (Luke 15:6) and of the woman who, in the same way, rejoiced over finding her lost coin (15:9; cf. 1 Cor. 12:26; 13:6). Because Paul and the Philippians had sacrificed and served together, they were able to rejoice together. Using the same word (*sunchairō*) that he had just used of himself, he now admonishes them, **You too, I urge you, rejoice in the same way and share your joy with me.**

TIMOTHY: THE SINGLE-MINDED SYMPATHIZER

But I hope in the Lord Jesus to send Timothy to you shortly, so that I also may be encouraged when I learn of your condition. For I have no one else of kindred spirit who will genuinely be concerned for your welfare. For they all seek after their own interests, not those of Christ Jesus. But you know of his proven worth, that he served with me in the furtherance of the gospel like a child serving his father. Therefore I hope to send him immediately, as soon as I see how things go with me; and I trust in the Lord that I myself also will be coming shortly. (2:19–24)

The second model of a spiritual servant is Timothy, Paul's beloved son in the faith. Like Paul, his mentor and model, Timothy is a trustworthy example for other believers to emulate.

Because his imprisonment prevented Paul from going to Philippi, it was his **hope in the Lord Jesus** (that is to say, in the Lord's will) **to send Timothy** there **shortly, so that** he **also** might **be encouraged when** he learned **of** the Philippians' **condition.** The apostle's **hope** was not an idle wish but the deep longing of his heart. Because he never wanted to act independently of his Master's will, his **hope** and expectation was **in** line with the purpose of **the Lord Jesus.** Paul no doubt prayed earnestly for the Lord's direction and was determined to adjust or discard his own plans if necessary.

Timothy was a native of Lystra in the province of Galatia (part of modern Turkey). His mother, Eunice, was Jewish and his father was a Greek and probably a pagan. Paul led him to Christ (1 Cor. 4:17; 1 Tim. 1:2, 18; 2 Tim. 1:2), probably during the apostle's visit to Lystra on his first missionary journey (Acts 14:6–23). Both his mother and his grandmother, Lois, were believers (2 Tim. 1:5) and had instructed Timothy in the Old Testament (2 Tim. 3:15). That he was not circumcised as a child suggests that his father had educated him in Greek learning and culture. Along with his spiritual maturity, his combined Jewish and Greek heritage made him uniquely qualified to minister the gospel with Paul to the Gentile world. To make Timothy more acceptable to the Jews, especially to those in Galatia who knew of him, Paul circumcised him (Acts 16:3). By the time Paul wrote Philippians, Timothy had been his almost constant companion for about ten years.

With great affection, Paul spoke of him as "my true child in the faith" (1 Tim. 1:2), "my beloved son" (2 Tim. 1:2), "my beloved and faithful child in the Lord" (1 Cor. 4:17), "my fellow worker" (Rom. 16:21; 1 Thess. 3:2; cf. 1 Cor. 16:10), "our brother" (2 Cor. 1:1; 1 Thess. 3:2; cf. Heb. 13:23), and, in the present letter, as a fellow bond-servant of Christ Jesus (Phil. 1:1). Timothy was with Paul in Corinth (Acts 18:5), was sent into Macedonia (19:22), and accompanied the apostle on his return trip to Jerusalem (20:4). He was associated with Paul in the writing of Romans (Rom. 16:21), 2 Corinthians (2 Cor. 1:1), Philippians (Phil. 1:1), Colossians (Col. 1:1), both Thessalonian epistles (1 Thess. 1:1; 2 Thess. 1:1), and Philemon (Philem. 1). He served as Paul's troubleshooter in Corinth (1 Cor. 4:17), Thessalonica (1 Thess. 3:2), Ephesus (1 Tim. 1:3–4), and Philippi (Phil. 2:19).

Timothy was faithful and dependable in every way and clearly was qualified to be a model for the Philippians to emulate. They were well acquainted with him, since he doubtless was with Paul when the church there was founded (cf. Acts 16:3, 12–40). It is therefore hardly surprising that the apostle was eager **to send Timothy to** them **shortly.** Later in this chapter, Paul explains what he means by **shortly,** saying, "I hope to send him immediately, as soon as I see how things go with me" (v. 23). Some interpreters believe Paul wanted to learn whether he would remain in prison, be released, or be executed. But his comments a few verses later indicate that he expected to be released and to visit the church at Philippi in person (2:24). It may have been that Timothy was assisting with some crucial matter in the church at Rome. Although the apostle was free to have visitors and to preach and teach without hindrance, he could not leave his rented quarters, where he was under constant guard (Acts 28:16, 23, 30–31). It may have been that Timothy was assisting Paul with the situation referred to in 1:15–17.

The only specific reason Paul mentioned for sending Timothy was **so that** he might **be encouraged when** he learned **of** the Philippians' **condition.** Despite his hope to visit Philippi soon, Paul expected Timothy to have time to reach them and report back his assessment of their **condition** before the apostle was freed. His confidence that he would **be encouraged** by that report reveals that he expected it to be positive. It was typical of Paul to be so concerned. In the case of the Corinthian church, his concerns were so deep that he had no heart for ministry until he heard of their condition (2 Cor. 7:5–9).

Because he wanted the Philippians to accept Timothy without hesitation, Paul gave them a brief profile of that dedicated servant of

Jesus Christ (vv. 20–24). The apostle highlighted seven personal characteristics for the Philippians to emulate: Timothy was similar, sympathetic,
single-minded, seasoned, submissive, sacrificial, and serviceable.

First, Timothy's spiritual character was similar to that of the apostle's. In many ways Timothy was a true **kindred spirit** with Paul. Epaphroditus (2:25–30) and a few other preachers and teachers in Rome
were faithful servants of the Lord, and Paul loved and appreciated them
(cf. 1:14–17). The apostle was in no way belittling those men, but there
was **no one else of** Timothy's stature. He had been instructed in the
Scriptures from childhood by his mother and grandmother (2 Tim. 1:5;
3:15) and was highly regarded by those who knew him (Acts 16:2). Yet
Timothy's greatest spiritual growth began when he started traveling and
ministering with Paul. Except for the Lord Jesus Christ, there has never
been a spiritual mentor on a par with Paul. Timothy had the unique and
enviable privilege of being the apostle's protégé.

Used only here in the New Testament, *isopsuchos* is a compound
adjective, composed of *isos* (equal) and *psuchē* (soul). It literally means
"equal-souled" or "one-souled," referring to persons who are like-minded,
of kindred spirit. The Septuagint (the Greek translation of the Old Testament) used the word in Psalm 55:13, where David speaks of "a man my
equal, my companion and my familiar friend," who had grievously betrayed him.

The goal of true discipleship is reproduction; when a person is
fully discipled, Jesus said, he will be like his teacher (Matt. 10:25). Over
the course of time, Timothy came to think like Paul, relate to believers
and unbelievers like Paul, evaluate ideas and situations like Paul, trust in
the Lord like Paul, and pray like Paul. Those two men of God had similar
qualities of soul, similar passions, similar objectives, and similar zeal. In
effect, Paul was saying to the believers in Philippi what he had said to
those in Corinth a few years earlier: "I exhort you, be imitators of me. For
this reason I have sent to you Timothy, who is my beloved and faithful
child in the Lord, and he will remind you of my ways which are in Christ,
just as I teach everywhere in every church" (1 Cor. 4:16–17). So here, as at
Corinth, until Paul was able to visit Philippi again, Timothy was by far his
best substitute. He was the ultimate fulfillment of the apostle's desire that
other believers be faithful imitators of him, as he was of Jesus Christ
(1 Cor. 11:1). No wonder Timothy was so beloved and dear to Paul.

Timothy also had the virtue of being sympathetic. With the utmost
confidence, Paul could assure the Philippians that Timothy **will genuinely
be concerned for** their **welfare.** The verb *merimnaō* (**concerned for**)
expresses a strong feeling for something or someone, often to the point
of being burdened. Jesus used the verb to speak of needless anxiety and
worry (cf. Matt. 6:25–28; 10:19; Luke 10:41), and later in the present letter

it is rendered "anxious" (4:6). But Paul here uses it in a positive sense to describe Timothy's great concern for the **welfare** of the Philippian church. Like his Lord, Paul had constant "concern for all the churches" (2 Cor. 11:28) and was confident that Timothy shared that concern. They were true shepherds, whose foremost concern was for the **welfare** of their sheep.

A third virtue that characterized Timothy was his single-mindedness, stated here indirectly by contrast with the leaders of the church in Rome. Paul laments the self-centered, loveless attitude of those leaders. **Seek after** translates the present tense of the verb *zēteō* and could be rendered "continually seek after." It must have deeply grieved Paul to have to say of them that **they all seek after their own interests, not those of Christ Jesus.**

Although the gospel was being proclaimed by a number of men in Rome, it was sometimes preached out of "envy and strife ... [and] selfish ambition rather than from pure motives" (1:15, 17). Paul nevertheless rejoiced "that in every way, whether in pretense or in truth, Christ is proclaimed" (v. 18). It seems that those who preached out of good will and love (vv. 15–16) either were gone or were silent. Despite Paul's presence, many preachers had become worldly and self-centered. They were not apostate or heretical but obviously had left their first love for Christ and become self-centered (cf. Rev. 2:4). Their primary **interests** now were no longer **those of Christ Jesus** but **their own.** Unlike Timothy, they were no longer single-minded but had become double minded and therefore spiritually unstable (James 1:8). They were exemplified by Demas, a dependable coworker of Paul's in Rome (Col. 4:14; Philem. 24), who would eventually desert him (2 Tim. 4:10, 16). The few faithful men with Paul in Rome, such as Luke and Aristarchus (Col. 4:10; Philem. 24), were evidently not available to travel to Philippi. The apostle was down to his last reliable coworker; faithful Timothy was the lone single-minded exception in Rome. This was again Paul's plight in his final imprisonment in Rome. In his last letter to Timothy, he said, "All who are in Asia turned away from me" (2 Tim. 1:15) and called for Timothy to remain loyal (2 Tim. 1:13). Like Paul, his dominant **interests** when Paul wrote this letter were still **those of Christ Jesus.**

Fourth, Timothy was seasoned. Paul did not have to convince the church at Philippi of that because they knew **of his proven worth. Proven worth** translates *dokimēn*, which has the basic meaning of proof after testing. Used of a person, it described proven character or tested value. Paul used the verb form numerous times in his admonitions for believers to "prove what the will of God is, that which is good and acceptable and perfect" (Rom. 12:2), and to "examine [themselves]" (1 Cor. 11:28; cf. 2 Cor. 13:5; Gal. 6:4). Believers are to "examine everything carefully; hold fast to that which is good" (1 Thess. 5:21) and "test the spirits to see whether they are from God" (1 John 4:1). Paul also used the term in regard to the Lord's testing of believers, noting that "just as we have been approved by God to be entrusted with the gospel, so we speak, not as pleasing men, but God who examines our hearts" (1 Thess. 2:4; cf. 1 Cor. 3:13; 1 Peter 1:7). Paul spoke highly of an unnamed brother "whom we have often tested and found diligent in many things" (2 Cor. 8:22), and instructed that deacons "must also first be tested [to see] if they are beyond reproach" (1 Tim. 3:10).

Timothy had been tested many times in his service to the Lord. When agitators from Thessalonica forced Paul to leave Berea, Timothy and Silas were entrusted to remain there and carry on the work (Acts 17:14). Similarly, "after he had passed through Macedonia and Achaia, ... [he] sent into Macedonia two of those who ministered to him, Timothy and Erastus" (Acts 19:21–22). A short while later, Timothy accompanied the apostle and others when they returned to Macedonia (20:3–4), of which Philippi was a key city. Paul may have written 2 Corinthians from Philippi (cf. 2 Cor. 11:9; Phil. 4:15) and in the introduction to that letter sent greetings from "Timothy our brother" (2 Cor. 1:1). The church at Philippi was well acquainted with Timothy and had benefited from his faithful service for many years.

Timothy's fifth virtue mentioned here was his submissiveness. Like Paul, whom Timothy **served with,** the young man was submissive to the Lord. *Douleuō* (**served**) was used of many types of service, including service of money (Matt. 6:24), a human master (1 Tim. 6:2), a human father (Luke 15:29), a conquering nation (Acts 7:7; cf. John 8:33), and service of believers to each other (Gal. 5:13). But it was also one of the most common verbs used in the New Testament for service to the Lord (cf. Acts 20:19; Rom. 12:11; 14:18; Col. 3:24), often in contrast to serving other people and things, such as the letter of the Mosaic Law (Rom. 7:6), the law of sin (Rom. 7:25), and sinful desires (Rom. 16:18; Titus 3:3). As the next phrase ("in the furtherance of the gospel") makes clear, **served** here refers to serving the Lord.

It is important to note that Paul is not speaking of Timothy's personal service to him, although that was considerable. Timothy was completely submissive to Paul, as an apostle, a spiritual father, and an incomparable model of godliness. But Paul makes it clear that this particular service was not to him, but **with** him. They served the Lord together in a loving and noncompetitive partnership. Paul was clearly the senior and Timothy the respectful junior. Yet the two men were both "bond-servants of Christ Jesus" (Phil 1:1), "doing the Lord's work" together (1 Cor. 16:10). Timothy not only was Paul's coworker, but also "God's fellow worker in the gospel of Christ" (1 Thess. 3:2).

Timothy's sixth virtue was his willingness to be sacrificial, as implied by his ministering with Paul **in the furtherance of the gospel like a child serving his father.** From the time the apostle chose him to serve alongside him, Timothy surrendered any personal plans he may have had for his life. He began a non-stop adventure that would bring him great fruitfulness and spiritual satisfaction, but that would also involve suffering and sacrifice.

Like Paul, Timothy considered himself under obligation to preach Christ to everyone, knowing that the gospel "is the power of God for salvation to everyone who believes, to the Jew first and also to the Greek" (Rom. 1:14–16). He, too, was "determined to know nothing . . . except Jesus Christ, and Him crucified" (1 Cor. 2:2), was willing to "become a spectacle to the world, both to angels and to men," being considered a fool "for Christ's sake," and was willing to be hungry and thirsty, poorly clothed, roughly treated, homeless, reviled, persecuted, and slandered "as the scum of the world, the dregs of all things, even until now" (1 Cor. 4:9–13). He could say sincerely with Paul that "we do not preach ourselves but Christ Jesus as Lord, and ourselves as your bond-servants for Jesus' sake," and that he was "afflicted in every way, but not crushed; perplexed, but not despairing; persecuted, but not forsaken; struck down, but not destroyed; always carrying about in the body the dying of Jesus, so that the life of Jesus also may be manifested in our body" (2 Cor. 4:5, 8–10). The Lord had also given him "the ministry of reconciliation" as an ambassador for Christ (2 Cor. 5:18, 20). And like Paul, he was eventually imprisoned for his faith (Heb. 13:23). For the sake of his Lord, he left his home and his godly mother and grandmother. There is no evidence in Scripture that he ever married, had children, and experienced the joys of family life. He could truthfully declare as Paul did to the Ephesian elders: "I do not consider my life of any account as dear to myself, so that I may finish my course and the ministry which I received from the Lord Jesus, to testify solemnly of the gospel of the grace of God" (Acts 20:24).

Timothy's seventh virtue was that he was available, a characteristic implied in the others. Because he was so eminently qualified for service, Paul could affirm without hesitation, **Therefore I hope to send him immediately.** Qualifying **immediately,** the apostle explained that he first wanted to **see how things go with me.** As noted in the discussion of verse 21, he still needed Timothy's help a while longer.

The context makes it clear that Timothy was willing to do what Paul asked of him. He had no agenda of his own. For him, being available to the Lord essentially meant being serviceable to the Lord's apostle. His staying or leaving was entirely Paul's decision, not his own. It must have been challenging for this intelligent, energetic, talented, and gifted young man to be constantly severing relationships with family, friends, and fellow workers. For most people, especially those with his capabilities, it would be all but unthinkable to be at someone else's beck and call. But Timothy was just that sort of willing, dependable, and joyful servant of Paul in their mutual service of Jesus Christ. He was ready to spend and be spent as seemed best to his beloved friend and apostle.

Paul then added, **and I trust in the Lord that I myself also will be coming shortly.** He did not minimize the value he could be to the church at Philippi by ministering to them in person. Whether or not he did, however, it is clear that he had the utmost confidence in Timothy.

Timothy had human frailties. Despite his divine calling and spiritual gifts (1 Tim. 4:14), he apparently lacked self-confidence because of his youthfulness (1 Tim. 4:12). He was tempted by youthful passions. In his second letter to him, the apostle warns: "If anyone cleanses himself from these things, he will be a vessel for honor, sanctified, useful to the Master, prepared for every good work. Now flee from youthful lusts and pursue righteousness, faith, love and peace, with those who call on the Lord from a pure heart" (2 Tim. 2:21–22). Apparently, Timothy was then at a low point in his personal life and ministry. He had victories and defeats, satisfaction and disappointment, happiness and sadness. But he heeded Paul's counsel: "Continue in the things you have learned and become convinced of, knowing from whom you have learned them. . . . Preach the word; be ready in season and out of season; reprove, rebuke, exhort, with great patience and instruction. . . . Be sober in all things, endure hardship, do the work of an evangelist, fulfill your ministry" (2 Tim. 3:14; 4:2,5).

EPAPHRODITUS: THE LOVING GAMBLER

But I thought it necessary to send to you Epaphroditus, my brother and fellow worker and fellow soldier, who is also your messenger and minister to my need; because he was longing for you all and was distressed because you had heard that he was sick. For indeed he was sick to the point of death, but God had mercy on him, and not on him only but also on me, so that I would not have sorrow upon sorrow. Therefore I have sent him all the more eagerly so that when you see him again you may rejoice and I may be less concerned about you. Receive him then in the Lord with all joy, and hold men like him in high regard; because he came close to death for the work of Christ, risking his life to complete what was deficient in your service to me. (2:25–30)

The third model spiritual servant described in 2:17–30 is **Epaphroditus,** another protégé and coworker of Paul's. He was not an apostle and spiritual statesman such as Paul or, as far as is known, even an elder, like Timothy. There is no record of any outstanding work that he accomplished. Nothing is known of his family, his personal background, his conversion, how long he had been a believer, or his specific functions in the churches at Philippi, Rome, or elsewhere.

The name **Epaphroditus** means "belonging to," or "favored by Aphrodite," the Greek goddess of love (whom the Romans called Venus), indicating that, like Timothy, he was probably born and educated in Greek culture. The name was common and later came to mean "loving," or "lovely." Although **Epaphroditus** was often abbreviated to Epaphras, there is no evidence he was the man by that name mentioned in Colossians 1:7 and 4:12. His level of sacrificial service to the Lord is especially instructive and encouraging for the believer, for whom the examples of great preachers and pastors such as Paul and Timothy may seem beyond reach. He exemplifies the spirit of sacrifice for the sake of Christ that involves no public acclaim, no prominence, no high office, no great talents or gifts. He was not a noted preacher, teacher, or leader; therefore his example seems to be more relevant and attainable.

Because they chose **Epaphroditus** to bring their gift to Paul and to minister to him (Phil. 2:25; 4:18), the Philippians obviously held him in the highest regard and trusted him implicitly. Although he may not have held an official position in their church, they knew that he met the apostle's high moral and spiritual standards. He had the soul of a servant, going willingly to Rome to help Paul in any way he could for as long as he was needed.

That he was willing to go to Rome while Paul was still imprisoned also shows great courage (cf. 2 Tim. 1:16–17). Although the apostle was allowed to live in his own rented quarters and had unlimited freedom to receive visitors (Acts 28:30–31), **Epaphroditus** understood that this situation could change overnight. If Caesar decided that Paul was indeed a threat to him as had been charged, he would not hesitate to order his immediate execution. That would put Paul's associates in danger of arrest, imprisonment, and perhaps execution. **Epaphroditus** knew that the risk he was taking was real.

After stating his intent to send **Epaphroditus** back to Philippi, Paul first gives five titles that reveal this man's character (v. 25) and then mentions several reasons for sending him back (vv. 26–30).

HIS TITLES

But I thought it necessary to send to you Epaphroditus, my brother and fellow worker and fellow soldier, who is also your messenger and minister to my need; (2:25)

The first three titles (introduced by **my**) pertain to Epaphroditus's relationship to the apostle himself—**brother, fellow worker, fellow soldier.** The latter two (introduced by **your**) pertain to his relationship to the church at Philippi—**messenger, minister.**

In using the possessive pronoun **my,** Paul manifested a deep and loving relationship with this remarkable man. The apostle was the most respected and beloved leader in the early church. Yet he deigned to call an ordinary and virtually unknown believer not only his **brother,** but also his **fellow worker** and **fellow soldier** in the service of the Lord.

Above all else, **Epaphroditus,** like all other believers, was Paul's spiritual **brother,** a fellow child of God. But the two men had also become brothers in the sense of having a profound personal affection for each other. They had developed an abiding friendship and camaraderie as they served the Lord together.

Second, **Epaphroditus** was Paul's **fellow worker,** emphasizing their common spiritual effort in addition to their common spiritual life. *Sunergos* (**fellow worker**) is a distinctly Pauline term. Of the thirteen times it is used in the New Testament all but one (3 John 8) are by Paul. In each instance it has the idea of an affectionate partnership, not merely that of an impersonal, official relationship (cf. Rom. 16:9, 21; Col. 4:11; 1 Thess. 3:2; Philem. 24). Paul twice specifically includes godly women among his fellow workers—Prisca (or Priscilla, Rom. 16:3) and Euodia and Syntyche, two godly but quarreling members of the church at Philippi who had shared Paul's "struggle in the cause of the gospel" (Phil. 4:2–3). In 1 Corinthians, he calls all believers "God's fellow workers" (1 Cor. 3:9).

Third, **Epaphroditus** was Paul's **fellow soldier,** suggesting their joint struggles against common spiritual enemies. **Fellow soldier** translates the compound Greek noun *sustratiōtēs* (used only twice in the New Testament; cf. Philem. 2), which is formed from *sun* ("with") and *stratiōtēs,* the common word for soldier (cf. Matt. 8:9; 28:12; John 19:2, 23; Acts 10:7; 12:6). Paul was chained to a *stratiōtēs* in Rome when he wrote Philippians (Acts 28:16). Using the word metaphorically, Paul admonished Timothy to suffer hardship with him "as a good soldier of Christ Jesus" (2 Tim. 2:3). The apostle looked on **Epaphroditus** not as a subordinate but, in humility, as a spiritual warrior in the service of the Lord Jesus Christ.

In the second set of titles, **Epaphroditus** is called **your messenger and minister to my need.** As mentioned above, the word **your** indicates his relationship to the church at Philippi and views his work from their perspective. Paul now **thought it necessary to send** back to Philippi the beloved brother, fellow worker, and fellow soldier they had so lovingly sent to him.

Apostolos can refer to an ordinary **messenger,** as it clearly does here. The term is used for the office of apostle, held by the Twelve (including Matthias; Acts 1:21–26) and Paul (cf. Rom. 1:1; Gal. 1:1, 19; Eph. 1:1). They were men who had seen the risen Lord and who were directly chosen by Him. In a completely unique way, Jesus is "the Apostle [*apostolon*] and High Priest of our confession" (Heb. 3:1). *Apostolos* can also refer to special messengers who were chosen and sent by the churches (cf. Acts 14:14; 2 Cor. 8:23). Clearly **Epaphroditus** was such a **messenger,** dispatched to Rome by the church at Philippi.

Epaphroditus was also a **minister** sent from Philippi to meet Paul's **need.** *Leitourgos* is one of several Greek words sometimes translated **minister** in the New Testament. Again, it is the term from which *liturgy* is derived; but it has a broad range of meanings and applications. It was used by ancient Greeks of a public official who was so passionately dedicated to his duties that he discharged them at his own expense. The word often described doing a service that had an aura of special importance, and a *leitourgos* was therefore highly respected and honored by his fellow citizens. Paul refers to human rulers in general as "servants [*leitourgoi*] of God" (Rom. 13:6), who are to be respected and obeyed (vv. 1–5, 7).

In the New Testament, *leitourgos* was most commonly used of service to the Lord. Paul spoke of himself as "a minister of Christ Jesus to the Gentiles, ministering as a priest the gospel of God" (Rom 15:16). The writer of Hebrews calls God's holy angels "His ministers" (Heb. 1:7) and even refers to Jesus Christ as "a minister in the sanctuary and in the true tabernacle" (8:2). For Paul to call **Epaphroditus** a **minister** was high praise indeed. **Epaphroditus** was himself the most valuable gift that came to Paul from Philippi—a self-giving, tireless, sacrificial, and humble servant of the highest caliber.

For that reason it must have been extremely difficult for Paul to send back to them this dear **brother, fellow worker,** and **fellow soldier.** And because the church had sent **Epaphroditus** to stay with the apostle indefinitely and serve his needs, Paul felt obligated to explain why he was sending him back. He articulates those reasons in verses 26–30.

PAUL'S REASONS FOR SENDING EPAPHRODITUS BACK

because he was longing for you all and was distressed because you had heard that he was sick. For indeed he was sick to the point of death, but God had mercy on him, and not on him only but also on me, so that I would not have sorrow upon sorrow. Therefore I have sent him all the more eagerly so that when you see him again you may rejoice and I may be less concerned about you. Receive him then in the Lord with all joy, and hold men like him in high regard; because he came close to death for the work

of Christ, risking his life to complete what was deficient in your service to me. (2:26–30)

It was not that Epaphroditus was tired of serving Paul. He was not merely homesick or restless for a change of work or scenery. Nor was he afraid of the harm that might befall him if he stayed longer. The titles Paul gave him show that he was a faithful worker who would never leave a job uncompleted and a loyal soldier who would never leave his post in the face of danger.

But Epaphroditus **was longing for** his fellow believers in Philippi, **and was distressed because** they **had heard that he was sick.** He was not at all **distressed** about his own condition or welfare but solely about the Philippians. **Distressed** translates a participial form of the verb *adēmoneō,* which refers to deep anguish, anxiety, or emotional turmoil. Both Matthew and Mark used it to describe Jesus' anguish as He prayed in the Garden of Gethsemane. He became so "grieved and distressed [*adēmonein*]" that He cried out to Peter, James, and John, "My soul is deeply grieved, to the point of death" (Matt. 26:37–38; cf. Mark 14:33–34). He prayed with such intense agony that "His sweat became like drops of blood, falling down upon the ground" (Luke 22:44).

Epaphroditus's distress was not that extreme, but it was nevertheless very real and deep. He may unintentionally have become distracted to the point of being less useful to Paul. His heart ached because he had learned that the believers in Philippi **had heard that he was sick** and were worried about him. He was not apprehensive about his life-threatening illness, but rather was **distressed** over their distress! *Astheneō* (**was sick**) translates a compound verb composed of the negative *a* and *sthenos* ("strength") and literally means "without strength." It was used to describe weaknesses of numerous kinds and varying degrees. Related nouns were used of general physical weakness (2 Cor. 12:10) as well as of spiritual weakness (Matt. 26:41). Paul even used *astheneō* to describe the weakness, because of the sinfulness of the flesh (Rom. 8:3), of the Mosaic Law to produce righteousness.

But *astheneō* was most commonly used of physical illness. It was used in the New Testament to describe sicknesses miraculously cured by Jesus (cf. Mark 6:56; Luke 4:40; John 5:3; 11:2–3), the disciples (Matt. 10:8), and the apostles after Pentecost (cf. Acts 9:37; 19:12).

The Philippians had good reason to be worried about Epaphroditus's health, because he had been **sick to the point of death.** Had **God** not **had mercy on him,** he would have died. It is interesting that, although he once had exercised the gift of healing (cf. Acts 28:8), Paul evidently did not use it to heal Epaphroditus—perhaps because the era of miraculous apostolic signs was nearly over (cf. 2 Tim. 4:20).

When God spares a person from death it is always a reflection of His **mercy,** because "the wages of sin is death" (Rom. 6:23) and every human being is a sinner (Rom. 3:23). The two blind men who begged Jesus to restore their sight realized that their only hope was through His mercy. Their initial cry, in fact, was for mercy, not healing (Matt. 9:27). Similarly, the ten lepers first cry to the Lord was, "Jesus, Master, have mercy on us, " (Luke 17:12–13). In the same way, the Canaanite woman (Matt. 15:22), the man with the deranged son (Matt. 17:15), and the blind beggar Bartimaeus (Mark 10:47; Luke 18:39) all came to Jesus asking first for mercy.

God's healing of Epaphroditus not only was of obvious benefit to him but also to Paul, who notes that **God had mercy . . . not on him only but also on me.** Along with the Philippians, he would have experienced **sorrow upon sorrow** had Epaphroditus died. Paul would not have grieved as do unbelievers, "who have no hope" (1 Thess. 4:13), but his grief over Epaphroditus's death would nonetheless have been real, deep, and long lasting.

Despite the personal loss he would experience by sending him back, Paul gladly wrote, **Therefore I have sent him all the more eagerly so that when you see him again you may rejoice and I may be less concerned about you.** The Philippians had not asked that Epaphroditus be sent back to them. His return was Paul's idea and was carried out solely on his initiative. He knew that his loss would be their gain. But their happiness in having Ephaphroditus back in their fellowship would bring Paul relief. Such is the remarkable power and reward of selfless love. Paul, Epaphroditus, and the believers in Philippi were indeed "of the same mind, maintaining the same love, united in spirit, intent on one purpose," doing "nothing from selfishness or empty conceit, but with humility of mind" regarding "one another as more important" than themselves, and "not merely look[ing] out for [their] own personal interests, but also for the interests of others" (Phil. 2:2–4). Paul selflessly exhorted the Philippians, **Receive him then in the Lord with all joy.**

Prosdechomai (**receive**) refers to favorable and glad acceptance. The Pharisees and scribes used it derogatorily of Jesus' receiving and eating with those they considered vile sinners (Luke 15:2). The root (*dechomai*) has the same connotation. Jesus used it to describe the way that humble, childlike believers (Matt. 18:5), faithful preachers of the gospel (Matt. 10:14), and the gospel itself (Luke 8:13; cf. Acts 8:14; 17:11) should be received. *Prosdechomai* describes how Phoebe, Paul's sister in the Lord and "a helper of many," was to be received by the church in Rome (Rom. 16:1–2) and how the church at Philippi was now to **receive** the honorable Epaphroditus—**in the Lord with all joy.** More than that, the Philippians were to **hold men like him in high regard; because**

he came close to death for the work of Christ, risking his life, as he sacrificially sought **to complete what was deficient,** that is, still uncompleted, in the Philippian church's **service to** Paul.

Risking translates a participial form of *paraboleuomai,* which literally means "to throw aside." It speaks of voluntarily hazarding one's welfare and thereby exposing oneself to danger. It was sometimes used of gambling, and it is for that reason that the title of this section refers to Epaphroditus as "the loving gambler." With total disregard for his own welfare, he continually put his life on the line **for the work of Christ.**

Soon after New Testament times, a group of Christians banded together in an association they called Parabolani, which means "The Gamblers." Taking Epaphroditus as their model, they visited prisoners and ministered to the sick, especially those with dangerous communicable diseases whom no one else would help. They boldly proclaimed the gospel of Jesus Christ wherever they went (William Barclay, *The Letters to the Philippians, Colossians, and Thessalonians* [rev. ed., Louisville, Ky.: Westminster, 1975], 50).

When the city of Carthage, on the Mediterranean coast of North Africa, suffered a severe plague in A.D. 252, the pagan inhabitants were so frightened of contagion that they refused to touch the dead bodies even to bury them. Cyprian, bishop of the church there, led the Christians in the arduous and dangerous task of ministering to the sick and dying and of burying the thousands of corpses. The spiritual influence of that silent but powerful testimony on their unbelieving and formerly hostile neighbors doubtless was immeasurable (Barclay, 50).

Perhaps Paul was here playing on the name Epaphroditus, which, as noted above, means "favored of Aphrodite." Because she was the goddess of gambling as well as of love, men would often cry out "Epaphroditus" as they cast the dice, hoping to be favored by her. In stark contrast to those men, Paul's beloved brother, fellow workman, and fellow soldier was **risking his life** for something immeasurably more valuable than money. His life entailed much risk; but it was no gamble. Without reservation, he could sincerely testify with Paul that "whatever things were gain to me, those things I have counted as loss for the sake of Christ. More than that, I count all things to be loss in view of the surpassing value of knowing Christ Jesus my Lord, for whom I have suffered the loss of all things, and count them but rubbish so that I may gain Christ" (Phil. 3:7–8).

Paul, Timothy, and Epaphroditus were three very different individuals: Paul the bold, fearless leader; Timothy his quiet, devoted assistant; Epaphroditus a diligent, behind-the-scenes worker. Yet all three manifested the most important characteristic of a godly leader—a life worth imitating.

The Distinguishing Qualities of True Believers (Philippians 3:1–3)

14

Finally, my brethren, rejoice in the Lord. To write the same things again is no trouble to me, and it is a safeguard for you. Beware of the dogs, beware of the evil workers, beware of the false circumcision; for we are the true circumcision, who worship in the Spirit of God and glory in Christ Jesus and put no confidence in the flesh, (3:1–3)

The good news of forgiveness and eternal life is the heart of the New Testament. Matthew, Mark, Luke, and John record the ministry of Christ, who came "to seek and to save that which was lost" (Luke 19:10). Acts records the spread of the gospel throughout the Roman world. The epistles unfold the gospel's rich theological content. They also exhort believers to the practical holiness that the gospel demands. Revelation records the ultimate triumph of the gospel in the consummation of human history.

But along with the presentation of the gospel is a closely related theme of critical concern. Having clearly set forth the truth of the gospel, the New Testament writers are concerned that people not be deceived about the genuineness of their salvation. Thus, the New Testament constantly challenges professing believers to examine themselves and make certain that their faith is genuine.

Concern for the genuineness of salvation was first addressed in the New Testament by the forerunner of the Messiah, John the Baptist. In a move that seems shocking in our day of "user-friendly" approaches to presenting the gospel, John boldly confronted the false believers of his day: "When he saw many of the Pharisees and Sadducees coming for baptism, he said to them, 'You brood of vipers, who warned you to flee from the wrath to come? Therefore bear fruit in keeping with repentance'" (Matt. 3:7–8).

In one of the most sobering passages in the Bible, Jesus warned,

"Not everyone who says to Me, 'Lord, Lord,' will enter the kingdom of heaven, but he who does the will of My Father who is in heaven will enter. Many will say to Me on that day, 'Lord, Lord, did we not prophesy in Your name, and in Your name cast out demons, and in Your name perform many miracles?' And then I will declare to them, 'I never knew you; depart from Me, you who practice lawlessness.'" (Matt. 7:21–23)

Later, Jesus reiterated that warning in a parable:

"Behold, the sower went out to sow; and as he sowed, some seeds fell beside the road, and the birds came and ate them up. Others fell on the rocky places, where they did not have much soil; and immediately they sprang up, because they had no depth of soil. But when the sun had risen, they were scorched; and because they had no root, they withered away. Others fell among the thorns, and the thorns came up and choked them out. And others fell on the good soil and yielded a crop, some a hundredfold, some sixty, and some thirty. He who has ears, let him hear." (Matt. 13:3–9)

As He explained the parable in private to His disciples, its point became unmistakably clear—not all who respond to the gospel are truly saved:

"Hear then the parable of the sower. When anyone hears the word of the kingdom and does not understand it, the evil one comes and snatches away what has been sown in his heart. This is the one on whom seed was sown beside the road. The one on whom seed was sown on the rocky places, this is the man who hears the word and immediately receives it with joy; yet he has no firm root in himself, but is only temporary, and when affliction or persecution arises because of the word, immediately he falls away. And the one on whom seed was sown among the thorns, this is the man who hears the word, and the worry of the world and the deceitfulness of wealth choke the word, and it becomes unfruitful. And the one on whom seed was sown on the good soil, this is the man who hears the word and understands it; who indeed bears fruit and brings forth, some a hundredfold, some sixty, and some thirty." (Matt. 13:18–23)

Simon Magus is a classic example of a false believer. He heard Philip's proclamation of the gospel and seemed to believe:

> Now there was a man named Simon, who formerly was practicing magic in the city and astonishing the people of Samaria, claiming to be someone great; and they all, from smallest to greatest, were giving attention to him, saying, "This man is what is called the Great Power of God." And they were giving him attention because he had for a long time astonished them with his magic arts. But when they believed Philip preaching the good news about the kingdom of God and the name of Jesus Christ, they were being baptized, men and women alike. Even Simon himself believed; and after being baptized, he continued on with Philip, and as he observed signs and great miracles taking place, he was constantly amazed. (Acts 8:9–13)

By all outward indications Simon's conversion was real. He made a profession of faith, publicly identified with Jesus Christ in baptism, and even "continued on with Philip" (Acts 8:13). Yet all was not as it seemed, as Simon's later encounter with Peter and John reveals:

> Now when the apostles in Jerusalem heard that Samaria had received the word of God, they sent them Peter and John, who came down and prayed for them that they might receive the Holy Spirit. For He had not yet fallen upon any of them; they had simply been baptized in the name of the Lord Jesus. Then they began laying their hands on them, and they were receiving the Holy Spirit. Now when Simon saw that the Spirit was bestowed through the laying on of the apostles' hands, he offered them money, saying, "Give this authority to me as well, so that everyone on whom I lay my hands may receive the Holy Spirit." But Peter said to him, "May your silver perish with you, because you thought you could obtain the gift of God with money! You have no part or portion in this matter, for your heart is not right before God. Therefore repent of this wickedness of yours, and pray the Lord that, if possible, the intention of your heart may be forgiven you. For I see that you are in the gall of bitterness and in the bondage of iniquity." But Simon answered and said, "Pray to the Lord for me yourselves, so that nothing of what you have said may come upon me." (Acts 8:14–24)

Tragically, even Simon's request that Peter pray for him does not reveal a repentant heart. He was not seeking forgiveness (or he would have prayed for it himself), but merely relief from the temporal consequences of his sin. Early church tradition names Simon as the founder of what later became Gnosticism, and reports his blasphemous claim to deity (Harold O. J. Brown, *Heresies* [Garden City, N.Y.: Doubleday, 1984], 50).

The writers of the epistles also warned people not to be deceived about the reality of their salvation. Paul exhorted the Corinthians, "Test yourselves to see if you are in the faith; examine yourselves! Or do you not recognize this about yourselves, that Jesus Christ is in you— unless indeed you fail the test?" (2 Cor. 13:5; cf. 1 Cor. 11:28). He cautioned his beloved son in the faith Timothy about those "holding to a form of godliness, although they have denied its power" (2 Tim. 3:5). Writing to another young pastor, Titus, Paul warned of people who "profess to know God, but by their deeds they deny Him, being detestable and disobedient and worthless for any good deed" (Titus 1:16). Jude wrote of "ungodly persons [in the church] who turn the grace of our God into licentiousness and deny our only Master and Lord, Jesus Christ" (Jude 4). The Lord Jesus Christ warned the apostate church at Laodicea, "Because you are lukewarm, and neither hot nor cold, I will spit you out of My mouth" (Rev. 3:16). Both James (cf. 1:2–12, 13–18, 19–27; 2:1–13, 14–26; 3:1–12, 13–18; 4:1–12, 13–17; 5:1–11, 13–18) and 1 John (cf. 1:6; 2:3–4, 9–11, 15–17; 3:3–10, 13–15, 18, 19, 23–24; 4:7–8; 5:2) list marks of genuine saving faith.

Unfortunately, despite the clear warnings of Scripture, many are deceived about their true spiritual condition. Though they think they are on the narrow road leading to heaven, they are actually on the broad road leading to hell. They base their false assurance of salvation on a number of proofs that in reality prove nothing. (For an extensive discussion of false proofs of salvation, see Matthew Mead, *The Almost Christian Discovered* [Reprint; Beaver Falls, Pa.: Soli Deo Gloria, n.d.]; Gardiner Spring, *The Distinguishing Traits of Christian Character* [Reprint; Phillipsburg, N.J.: Presbyterian and Reformed, n.d.]; John MacArthur, *The Gospel According to Jesus* [rev. ed., Grand Rapids: Zondervan, 1994]; John MacArthur, *Faith Works: The Gospel According to the Apostles* [Dallas: Word, 1993].)

Many people rest their hope of salvation on a past event. They may have prayed to receive Christ as a child, gone forward in response to an altar call, signed a card, or made a commitment at a retreat. Sometimes well-meaning people encourage such false hopes by offering what may be termed "syllogistic assurance." They present the following seemingly plausible syllogism to those who pray to receive Christ: "John 1:12 says that 'as many as received Him, to them He gave the right to become children of God, even to those who believe in His name'; you just received Christ; therefore you have become a child of God." Unfortunately, that syllogism is only true if the minor premise ("you just received Christ") is true. And that is the very point in question. As noted earlier, Jesus taught in the parable of the soils that a fruitless profession of faith proves nothing. Genuine faith will inevitably produce transformation in a person's life; false or dead faith will not (cf. James 2:14–26). Scripture nowhere points people back to a conversion experience to validate their salvation; the issue is a changed life. Simon Magus not only made a profession of faith, but also was baptized and continued with Philip for a time. Yet as his further conduct indicates, he was never saved (Acts 8:21–23).

A second non-proof of saving faith is a superficially moral life. It is certainly true that the new nature breaks the pattern of constant sin (cf. 1 John 3:9), and that all Christians should live lives of increasing moral purity (cf. Matt. 5:48; 1 Peter 1:14–16). The reverse is *not* true, however; all who live outwardly moral lives are not redeemed. Many unbelievers are honest, kind, generous, and seek to live according to high ethical standards. Such behavior is commendable, but says nothing about their spiritual state. It may impress "man" who "looks at the outward appearance," but will not deceive "the Lord" who "looks at the heart" (1 Sam. 16:7; cf. Prov. 21:2). Jesus scathingly denounced the most outwardly moral religious leaders of His day: "Woe to you, scribes and Pharisees, hypocrites! For you are like whitewashed tombs which on the outside appear beautiful, but inside they are full of dead men's bones and all uncleanness. So you, too, outwardly appear righteous to men, but inwardly you are full of hypocrisy and lawlessness" (Matt. 23:27–28).

Unsaved people may behave according to moral standards for many reasons. Some do so because they are afraid of God. Others feel peer pressure to conform to the standards and expectations of their peer group. Children often lead moral lives to please their parents and avoid punishment. And most tragically of all, many people believe that living a moral life will get them into heaven. Whatever the motivation, external morality saves no one, since in God's sight "all of us have become like one who is unclean, and all our righteous deeds are like a filthy garment; and all of us wither like a leaf, and our iniquities, like the wind, take us away" (Isa. 64:6); and "by the works of the Law no flesh will be justified in His sight" (Rom. 3:20; cf. Gal. 2:16).

The example of the rich young ruler shows that living a moral life cannot save anyone. He claimed to have kept (at least outwardly) the Ten Commandments (Matt. 19:20). Yet his question to Jesus, "Teacher, what good thing shall I do that I may obtain eternal life?" (Matt. 19:16), reveals that he knew that he did not have eternal life. Stephen Charnock comments,

> The opinion of gaining eternal life by the outward observation of the law, will appear very unsatisfactory to an inquisitive conscience. This ruler affirmed, and certainly did confidently believe, that he had fulfilled the law (v. 20): "All this have I observed from my youth;" yet he had not any full satisfaction in his own conscience; his heart misgave,

and started upon some sentiments in him, that something else was required, and what he had done might be too weak, too short to shoot heaven's lock for him. And to that purpose he comes to Christ, to receive instructions for the piecing up whatsoever was defective. (*The Existence and Attributes of God* [Reprint; Grand Rapids: Baker, 1979], 2:212)

That fact was confirmed by his refusal to follow Jesus (Matt. 19:21–26).

Another common misconception is that a mere knowledge of the facts of the gospel is evidence of salvation. But even "the demons also believe [the truth], and shudder" (James 2:19). Many people know the truth of the gospel, but remain unforgiven and under eternal condemnation. Liberal theologians often have detailed knowledge of the truths of Scripture, but criticize them and refuse to believe them. The writer of Hebrews says of such people, "The word they heard did not profit them, because it was not united by faith in those who heard" (Heb. 4:2). No one, of course, can be saved unless he knows the facts of the gospel—that God is holy, that he is a sinner for whom Christ died a substitutionary death on the cross, and that salvation is solely by grace through faith. But mere intellectual assent to those truths does not equal saving faith, which includes trust and commitment. To know the truth but refuse to act on it only results in greater condemnation (Luke 12:47–48), not salvation.

The religious and moral scribes and Pharisees, after observing Christ's life, hearing Him speak, and seeing His miracles, concluded that Jesus "casts out demons only by Beelzebul the ruler of the demons" (Matt. 12:24). Since they had willfully refused to believe the truth, Jesus declared concerning them, "Therefore I say to you, any sin and blasphemy shall be forgiven people, but blasphemy against the Spirit shall not be forgiven. Whoever speaks a word against the Son of Man, it shall be forgiven him; but whoever speaks against the Holy Spirit, it shall not be forgiven him, either in this age or in the age to come" (Matt. 12:31–32). The scribes and Pharisees heard the truth, yet they rejected it and were eternally damned. Like the scribes and Pharisees, Judas saw Jesus' miracles and heard His preaching. But, in spite of three years in His presence, he too rejected the truth, betrayed Jesus, and is lost forever.

The writer of Hebrews also warned of apostate false believers:

For in the case of those who have once been enlightened and have tasted of the heavenly gift and have been made partakers of the Holy Spirit, and have tasted the good word of God and the powers of the age to come, and then have fallen away, it is impossible to renew them again to repentance, since they again crucify to themselves the Son of God and put Him to open shame. (Heb. 6:4–6)

Nor is religious activity proof of salvation. Many who are on the broad road leading to hell faithfully attend church, are baptized, take communion, and participate in the other rituals of their church. "Holding to a form of godliness, although they have denied its power" (2 Tim. 3:5), they are tragically deceived into thinking that their religious activity proves they are saved. They are like the apostates in Israel, of whom God declared, "This people draw near with their words and honor Me with their lip service, but they remove their hearts far from Me, and their reverence for Me consists of tradition learned by rote" (Isa. 29:13; cf. 58:1–4).

The foolish virgins in Jesus' parable represent such people. Although in appearance they were no different from the wise virgins (who represent the redeemed), they actually represent unregenerate people, who will not be ready for Christ's return (Matt. 25:1–13). Ananias and Sapphira appeared to be no different from the other members of the Jerusalem church, until their greed and hypocrisy were unmasked (Acts 5:1–11). The Lord Jesus Christ declared to the church at Sardis, "I know your deeds; you have a reputation of being alive, but you are dead" (Rev. 3:1 NIV). An external form of religion without the inward reality of salvation will result in eternal damnation.

A final non-proof of salvation is service in the name of Christ. It is a sobering reality that many who preach the gospel are not saved. Even Judas, the son of perdition (John 6:70–71; 17:12), preached the gospel (Matt. 10:4–7). "Many [such people] will say to [Jesus] on that day, 'Lord, Lord, did we not prophesy in Your name, and in Your name cast out demons, and in Your name perform many miracles?' And then [He] will declare to them, 'I never knew you; depart from Me, you who practice lawlessness'" (Matt. 7:22–23).

In Philippians 3:1–3 Paul adds to the biblical teaching on the issue of distinguishing between genuine and false faith. Both by implication and explicitly, he presents five qualities of true believers: they rejoice in the Lord, exercise discernment, worship in the Spirit, glory in Christ Jesus, and put no confidence in the flesh.

TRUE BELIEVERS REJOICE IN THE LORD

Finally, my brethren, rejoice in the Lord. (3:1*a*)

Finally (*to loipon*) is better rendered "furthermore," "so then," or "now then." It is a word of transition, not conclusion, since half of Philippians follows it. Joy is an important theme, both in Philippians (cf. 1:4, 18, 25; 2:2, 17–18, 28–29; 4:1, 4, 10) and in the rest of the New Testament, where it appears in its noun and verb forms approximately 150 times.

Here, as in 4:4, 10 (cf. Luke 1:47), Paul connects rejoicing to a relationship, commanding believers to **rejoice in the Lord.** The sphere in which their joy exists is in their relationship with the Lord Jesus Christ.

The joy of which Paul writes is not the same as happiness (a word related to the term "happenstance"), the feeling of exhilaration associated with favorable events. In fact, joy persists in the face of weakness, pain, suffering, even death (cf. James 1:2). Biblical joy produces a deep confidence in the future that is based on trust in God's purpose and power. It results in the absence of any ultimate fear, since the relationship on which it is based is eternal and unshakeable (cf. Ps. 16:11; John 16:22). Nor is it a humanly produced emotion; that Paul commands it shows that rejoicing is an act of the will in choosing to obey God. The result is a supernaturally produced emotion, the fruit of walking in the Spirit (Rom. 14:17; Gal. 5:22). Thus, rejoicing marks true believers (cf. Pss. 9:14; 13:5; 32:11; 33:1, 21; 35:9; 40:16; 51:12; 70:4; Luke 10:20; John 15:11; 17:13; Rom. 15:13; 1 Thess. 5:16).

TRUE BELIEVERS EXERCISE DISCERNMENT

To write the same things again is no trouble to me, and it is a safeguard for you. Beware of the dogs, beware of the evil workers, beware of the false circumcision; (3:1b–2)

After commanding the Philippians to rejoice, Paul turns to his next major theme in the epistle. His strong and direct warning implies another distinguishing mark of true believers: their ability to discern. No one can be saved who does not understand the fundamental truths of the gospel (Rom. 6:17; 10:14, 17). But since discernment, like faith, needs to grow and mature, pastors and elders must warn the church of false teachers (Eph. 4:11–14). Thus, for Paul **to write the same things again** was **no trouble to** him, because it was a necessary **safeguard** for the Philippians. False teachers, proclaiming salvation through ritual, ceremony, and legalism, posed a serious threat to them. **Safeguard** (*asphalēs*) literally means not to trip, stumble, or be overthrown. Paul faithfully warned the Philippians so they would not stumble (cf. Acts 20:31).

The phrase **to write the same things again** indicates that Paul is about to elaborate on something he has previously mentioned. The apostle undoubtedly has in mind his exhortation in 1:27–28:

> Conduct yourselves in a manner worthy of the gospel of Christ, so that whether I come and see you or remain absent, I will hear of you that you are standing firm in one spirit, with one mind striving together for the faith of the gospel; in no way alarmed by your opponents—which

is a sign of destruction for them, but of salvation for you, and that too, from God.

In that passage, Paul told the Philippians not to be alarmed by their opponents; in the present passage he tells them how to recognize them. He describes these false teachers who opposed the gospel using three terms, each introduced by an imperative form of the verb _blepō_ (**beware**).

Paul first describes the false teachers as **dogs.** Unlike the pet dogs (_kunarion_) described in Matthew 15:26–27, _kuōn_ (**dogs**) refers to the wild scavengers that plagued ancient cities. Those curs roamed in packs, feeding on garbage (Ex. 22:31; 1 Kings 14:11; 16:4; 21:23–24) and occasionally attacking humans. They were despised, and "dog" was frequently used as a derogatory term (cf. Deut. 23:18; 1 Sam. 17:43; 24:14; 2 Sam. 9:8; 16:9; 2 Kings 8:13; Ps. 22:16; Rev. 22:15). In fact, Jews in biblical times commonly referred contemptuously to Gentiles as **dogs.**

Amazingly Paul, a Jew, called these Jewish (see the discussion below) false teachers **dogs.** He warned the Philippians to beware of those who call others **dogs,** but in reality are **dogs** themselves. The apostle's description is fitting. Are **dogs** unclean and filthy? So are the false teachers. Are **dogs** vicious and dangerous, and to be avoided? So are the false teachers. So are all those who teach salvation by works.

Paul's words seem harsh and unloving in today's climate of tolerance and diversity. Even many in the church consider it unloving and divisive to point out doctrinal error. Yet truth and love are not mutually exclusive, and believers are called to both (Eph. 4:15), as well as to discernment (cf. John MacArthur, _Reckless Faith: When the Church Loses Its Will to Discern_ [Wheaton, Ill.: Crossway, 1994). Scripture teaches that salvation is by grace alone through faith alone (Eph. 2:8–9). Those who teach otherwise are ravenous, savage wolves (Matt. 7:15; Acts 20:29), purveyors of demon doctrines (1 Tim. 4:1), who usher people onto the broad road to hell (Matt. 7:13). Pastors and elders must warn their flocks against them. Any deviation from the true doctrine of Christ is to be avoided (2 John 9–11).

Though the false teachers prided themselves on their supposed righteousness, they were in reality **evil workers.** Typically, those involved in external, ritualistic, ceremonial religions see themselves as doing good and pleasing God. Paul himself was once proud of "advancing in Judaism beyond many of [his] contemporaries among [his] countrymen, being more extremely zealous for [his] ancestral traditions" (Gal. 1:14). After his conversion, the apostle realized that all his good works were worthless: "Whatever things were gain to me, those things I have counted as loss for the sake of Christ. More than that, I count all things to be loss in view of the surpassing value of knowing Christ Jesus my Lord, for whom I have suffered the loss of all things, and count them but rubbish so that I may gain Christ" (Phil. 3:7–8). Instead of seeing himself as doing good in God's sight, Paul, at the end of his ministry, felt that he was in fact the foremost of sinners (1 Tim. 1:15–16).

Only believers controlled by the Holy Spirit can do genuine good works (Eph. 2:10; Col. 1:10; 2 Tim. 2:21; 3:17; Titus 2:14). Unbelievers can do bad things for bad reasons. They can also do good things, but only out of selfish pride, not for God's glory. Only the redeemed can do good deeds motivated by a desire to glorify God. The false teachers plaguing the Philippians saw themselves as pleasing God, earning His favor (and their salvation) through their zeal for the Law. But Paul exposed them for the prideful **evil workers** that they were.

By describing them as **the false circumcision,** Paul clearly identified these false teachers as his perennial opponents, the Judaizers. Those Jewish legalists denied the gospel of grace, teaching that circumcision and keeping the Law of Moses were necessary for salvation (Acts 15:1). The Jerusalem Council condemned their heretical teachings (Acts 15:1–29), as did Paul (e.g., Gal. 1:6–9; 2:16–21; 3:2–14, 22–25; 5:1–4, 11–14). Salvation is by grace alone through faith alone.

Circumcision has always been essential to the Jewish people, since it is the distinguishing mark of God's covenant with their forefather, Abraham (Gen. 17:11; Acts 7:8). So closely did they identify with **circumcision** that they referred to fellow Jews as the **circumcision** or the circumcised (Acts 10:45; 11:2; Rom. 15:8; Gal. 2:7; Eph. 2:11; Col. 3:11; 4:11; Titus 1:10), and to Gentiles as the uncircumcision or the uncircumcised (Judg. 14:3; 15:18; 1 Sam. 14:6; 17:26; 31:4; 2 Sam. 1:20; Acts 11:3; Gal. 2:7–9; Eph. 2:11; Col. 3:11). In obedience to God's command, every Jewish boy was (and is) circumcised on the eighth day after his birth (Gen. 17:12; Lev. 12:3). **Circumcision** was so significant that uncircumcised Jewish males were to be cut off from the covenant community (Gen. 17:14). Although **circumcision** has through the centuries provided protection from some diseases, that was not God's primary purpose in ordaining it. **Circumcision** graphically illustrated man's depravity, which is nowhere more manifest than in the procreative act, because it is then that the sin nature is passed on to a new generation (Ps. 51:5; 58:3). **Circumcision** was a symbol, picturing man's need to be cleansed from sin at the deepest root of his being. The bloodshed involved in the physical act of **circumcision** could symbolize the need for a sacrifice to accomplish that cleansing.

Like baptism in the New Covenant, **circumcision** was to reflect an inward reality. God commanded the Israelites, "Circumcise yourselves to the Lord and remove the foreskins of your heart" (Jer. 4:4; cf. 9:26; Lev. 26:41;

Deut. 10:16; 30:6; Ezek. 44:7, 9). Sadly, by Paul's day **circumcision** had become a mere outward ritual, bereft of its intended spiritual significance:

> For indeed circumcision is of value if you practice the Law; but if you are a transgressor of the Law, your circumcision has become uncircumcision. So if the uncircumcised man keeps the requirements of the Law, will not his uncircumcision be regarded as circumcision? And he who is physically uncircumcised, if he keeps the Law, will he not judge you who though having the letter of the Law and circumcision are a transgressor of the Law? For he is not a Jew who is one outwardly, nor is circumcision that which is outward in the flesh. But he is a Jew who is one inwardly; and circumcision is that which is of the heart, by the Spirit, not by the letter; and his praise is not from men, but from God. (Rom. 2:25–29)

The Jewish people zealously observed outward religious ceremonies, but their hearts had become so detached from God that their "circumcision [had] become uncircumcision." In other words, the symbol isolated from the reality is meaningless. Then Paul added, "He who is physically uncircumcised, if he keeps the Law, will he not judge you who though having the letter of the Law and circumcision are a transgressor of the Law?" God, the apostle declared, prefers uncircumcised but obedient Gentiles to circumcised but disobedient Jews. True "circumcision is that which is of the heart, by the Spirit." No ritual—not **circumcision,** baptism, communion, or any other—can transform the heart. And only those with transformed hearts can please God.

The Judaizers viewed themselves as set apart to God, and their **circumcision** as emblematic of that reality. But theirs was a **false circumcision.** *Katatomē* (**false circumcision**) literally means "mutilation"; the Septuagint (the Greek translation of the Old Testament) used the related verb *katatemnō* to describe pagan religious mutilation in Leviticus 21:5 and 1 Kings 18:28. The apostle's indictment of the Judaizers is shocking. Because it did not reflect a cleansed heart, their circumcision was as meaningless as the ritual mutilation in pagan religions.

In Galatians 5:12 Paul expressed that very truth even more forcefully: "I wish that those who are troubling you would even mutilate themselves." *Apokoptō* ("mutilate") is an even stronger term than *katatomē.* In its other New Testament uses it is translated "cut off" or "cut away" (Mark 9:43, 45; John 18:10, 26; Acts 27:32). But in extra-biblical Greek literature, *apokoptō* was also used of castration (Walter Bauer, William F. Arndt, and F. Wilbur Gingrich, *A Greek-English Lexicon of the New Testament and Other Early Christian Literature* [Chicago: Univ. of Chicago, 1979], 93), and that is the sense in which Paul used it in Galatians. The apostle's point is that if the Judaizers believed that the mere outward ritual of **circumci-**

sion pleases God, why did they not take that devotion to its ultimate extreme and castrate themselves?

Circumcision (or any external ritual or ceremony) is meaningless if it does not reflect a transformed heart. Those who teach otherwise are not praiseworthy religious people doing their best to please God. They are purveyors of demon doctrines (1 Tim. 4:1), who hold "to a form of godliness, although they have denied its power" (2 Tim. 3:5). Believers are to "avoid such men as these" (2 Tim. 3:5).

Unlike the Judaizers, the *katatomē,* **the false circumcision,** believers are the *peritomē,* **the true circumcision.** They have an inward spiritual cleansing, not a meaningless outward mark. Three explicit qualities in verse 3 identify believers as **the true circumcision.**

TRUE BELIEVERS WORSHIP IN THE SPIRIT

who worship in the Spirit of God (3:3*a*)

The first quality of a genuine believer is a heart that overflows with worship. The origin of that **worship** is supernatural, since **the Spirit of God** generates it. It involves adoration and praise to God, and transcends outward rituals or ceremonies. Humans are inveterate worshipers. But worship prompted by culture, tradition, guilt, fear, desire for acceptance and popularity, or to gain blessings is unacceptable to God. The indwelling Holy Spirit prompts true and acceptable worship out of love for the Lord. Since He only indwells Christians (Rom. 8:9), only they can truly worship their Savior.

Speaking to a Samaritan woman (John 4:1–26), Jesus clearly defined true and acceptable worship. Shocked by His omniscient exposure of her dissolute life (vv. 16–18), she tried to change the subject: "Sir, I perceive that You are a prophet. Our fathers worshiped in this mountain, and you people say that in Jerusalem is the place where men ought to worship" (vv. 19–20). In response Jesus declared, "Woman, believe Me, an hour is coming when neither in this mountain nor in Jerusalem will you worship the Father" (v. 21). True worship takes place in the heart, not at a sacred location.

The Lord then revealed a second truth about true worship: "You worship what you do not know; we worship what we know, for salvation is from the Jews" (v. 22). Acceptable worship is based on the truths of salvation revealed in the Scriptures, which were given to the Jewish people (Rom. 3:2). It is not to be performed according to the whims of the worshipers. Then Jesus gave the clearest definition of worship in all of Scripture: "But an hour is coming, and now is, when the true worshipers will worship the Father in spirit and truth; for such people the Father seeks to be His worshipers. God is spirit, and those who worship Him must worship in spirit and truth" (vv. 23–24). The twice-repeated phrase "in spirit and truth" defines the essence of true worship.

God saved believers to worship Him. It is those "true worshipers [who] worship the Father in spirit and truth" that "the Father seeks to be His worshipers." True Christians are those who worship God from the heart in obedience to His Word. In Psalm 29:2 David exhorts, "Ascribe to the Lord the glory due to His name; worship the Lord in holy array." Psalm 95:6 adds, "Come, let us worship and bow down, let us kneel before the Lord our Maker." Worship is mankind's highest duty; in the words of the Westminster Shorter Catechism, "Man's chief end is to glorify God and to enjoy Him forever."

Latreuō (**worship**) might best be translated "to render respectful spiritual service." True worship goes beyond praising God, singing hymns, or participating in a worship service. The essence of worship is living a life of obedient service to God. "Do not neglect doing good and sharing," exhorts the writer of Hebrews, "for with such sacrifices God is pleased" (Heb. 13:16). True worship involves every aspect of life.

Several characteristics mark true worshipers. First, they love God. That is in stark contrast to unbelievers, who hate Him. Jesus declared in John 7:7, "The world cannot hate you, but it hates Me because I testify of it, that its deeds are evil." In Romans 1:30 Paul describes unbelievers as "haters of God" (cf. Num. 10:35; Deut. 7:10; 2 Chron. 19:2; Ps. 81:15; John 15:23–24), while in Romans 8:7 the apostle points out that "the mind set on the flesh is hostile toward God." Christians' love for God will never be perfect in this world, but it will always be there.

Because true worshipers love God, they find in Him their source of joy and delight. They acknowledge that "the joy of the Lord is [their] strength" (Neh. 8:10). They "sing for joy in the Lord" (Ps. 33:1; cf. Pss. 84:2; 92:4; 95:1; 98:4), because they are filled "with the joy of the Holy Spirit" (1 Thess. 1:6; cf. Rom. 14:17). Like the psalmist, they find in "God [their] exceeding joy" (Ps. 43:4). True worshipers "delight to revere [His] name" (Neh. 1:11), and heed David's exhortation, "Delight yourself in the Lord" (Ps. 37:4). The contemplation of God's glory and majesty, and what He has done in their lives, is their supreme joy and delight.

True worshipers also have a confident trust in God that produces peace. That peace is based not on their circumstances, but on their relationship with God. They can exclaim with the psalmists, "As the deer pants for the water brooks, so my soul pants for You, O God" (Ps. 42:1); and "Whom have I in heaven but You? And besides You, I desire nothing on earth" (Ps. 73:25). This "peace of God, which surpasses all comprehension" (Phil. 4:7) comes only to those who "seek first His kingdom and His righteousness" (Matt. 6:33).

True worship is **in** the power of **the Spirit of God,** because only He can produce the love, joy, and peace that characterize true worshipers (cf. Gal. 5:22). Those who worship in the flesh "draw near with their words and honor [God] with their lip service, but they remove their hearts far from [Him], and their reverence for [Him] consists of tradition learned by rote" (Isa. 29:13).

True worshipers are devoted to God; He has no rival for their affection. They "worship the Lord [their] God, and serve Him only" (Matt. 4:10), knowing that He "will not give [His] glory to another" (Isa. 42:8; 48:11). They affirm Jesus' declaration that "he who loves father or mother more than Me is not worthy of Me; and he who loves son or daughter more than Me is not worthy of Me" (Matt. 10:37). Holding nothing back, they "present [their] bodies a living and holy sacrifice, acceptable to God, which is [their] spiritual service of worship" (Rom. 12:1).

True Christians are not simply marked by attending church or performing religious duties, but by a worshiping heart.

TRUE WORSHIPERS GLORY IN CHRIST JESUS

and glory in Christ Jesus (3:3b)

Kauchaomai (**glory**) describes boasting with exultant joy about what a person is most proud of. It is a favorite term of Paul's; thirty-five of its thirty-seven appearances in the New Testament are in his epistles. It can be used in a negative sense to describe proud, inappropriate boasting (e.g., Rom. 2:17, 23; Gal. 6:13). *Kauchaomai* is also used, however, to describe believers' joyful exulting in Christ (e.g., Rom. 5:2, 11; 1 Cor. 1:31; Gal. 6:14), as it is here. True Christians give the credit for all that they are and have to the Lord Jesus Christ. With Paul they declare, "By the grace of God I am what I am" (1 Cor. 15:10; cf. Phil. 3:8–9) and "Therefore in Christ Jesus I have found reason for boasting in things pertaining to God" (Rom. 15:17). They obey the biblical injunction "Let him who boasts, boast in the Lord" (1 Cor. 1:31; 2 Cor. 10:17; cf. Pss. 20:7; 34:2; Jer. 9:23–24; Gal. 6:14).

In contrast, false believers "boast according to the flesh" (2 Cor. 11:18), believing that their good works and religious activities earn them favor with God. But salvation is "by grace . . . through faith; . . . it is the gift of God"; it is "not . . . a result of works, so that no one may boast" (Eph. 2:8–9; cf. Rom. 3:27). It was the biblical truth that sinful men can do nothing to merit salvation that led the Reformers to teach that salvation is *sola fide* (by faith alone) and *sola gratia* (by grace alone). Those who think they can earn God's grace by their own works give evidence that they lack saving faith.

TRUE WORSHIPERS PUT NO CONFIDENCE IN THE FLESH

and put no confidence in the flesh, (3:3c)

The **flesh** represents man's fallen, unredeemed humanness; it pictures human ability apart from God. Unlike the "many [who] boast according to the flesh" (2 Cor. 11:18), true Christians **put no confidence in** it. They understand that "it is the Spirit who gives life; the flesh profits nothing" (John 6:63), and agree with Paul's declaration, "For I know that nothing good dwells in me, that is, in my flesh" (Rom. 7:18). Because it is fallen and unredeemed, the flesh cannot do anything to please God; it serves only the law of sin (v. 25). Therefore, it is a distinguishing characteristic of the redeemed that they "do not walk according to the flesh but according to the Spirit" (8:4), because "the mind set on the flesh is death" (v. 6; cf. v. 13) and "those who are in the flesh cannot please God" (v. 8).

Because of the pervasive influence of the sinful flesh (what theologians call total depravity), no one can in any way merit salvation. It is only those who turn from sinful self-efforts and embrace the truth of salvation by grace alone through faith alone who are saved. That marks the genuine repentance that is a necessary element of saving faith (cf. Mark 1:15; Luke 5:32; 13:3, 5; 15:7, 10; 24:47; Acts 3:19; 5:31; 11:18; 17:30; 20:21; 26:20; Rom. 2:4; 2 Cor. 7:10; 2 Tim. 2:25; 2 Peter 3:9). True repentance involves sorrow over the evil of sinful deeds; false repentance involves only sorrow over their harmful consequences. False repentance concerns itself with conduct; true repentance with man's inner condition. False repentance deals with the symptoms; true repentance with the disease. Only true repentance, which puts **no confidence in the flesh,** leads to salvation.

Giving Up to Gain (Philippians 3:4–11)

15

although I myself might have confidence even in the flesh. If anyone else has a mind to put confidence in the flesh, I far more: circumcised the eighth day, of the nation of Israel, of the tribe of Benjamin, a Hebrew of Hebrews; as to the Law, a Pharisee; as to zeal, a persecutor of the church; as to the righteousness which is in the Law, found blameless. But whatever things were gain to me, those things I have counted as loss for the sake of Christ. More than that, I count all things to be loss in view of the surpassing value of knowing Christ Jesus my Lord, for whom I have suffered the loss of all things, and count them but rubbish so that I may gain Christ, and may be found in Him, not having a righteousness of my own derived from the Law, but that which is through faith in Christ, the righteousness which comes from God on the basis of faith, that I may know Him and the power of His resurrection and the fellowship of His sufferings, being conformed to His death; in order that I may attain to the resurrection from the dead. (3:4–11)

This autobiographical passage introduces the most dramatic and compelling salvation testimony in the New Testament, that of the apostle Paul. It is also one of the most significant statements of the doctrine of salvation in Scripture, revealing the internal work of God in a truly repentant and believing sinner. The apostle relates what was going on in his mind when he met the risen Christ on the Damascus Road. Acts 9:1–9 provides the historical record of Paul's dramatic conversion:

> Now Saul, still breathing threats and murder against the disciples of the Lord, went to the high priest, and asked for letters from him to the synagogues at Damascus, so that if he found any belonging to the Way, both men and women, he might bring them bound to Jerusalem. As he was traveling, it happened that he was approaching Damascus, and suddenly a light from heaven flashed around him; and he fell to the ground and heard a voice saying to him, "Saul, Saul, why are you persecuting Me?" And he said, "Who are You, Lord?" And He said, "I am Jesus whom you are persecuting, but get up and enter the city, and it will be told you what you must do." The men who traveled with him stood speechless, hearing the voice but seeing no one. Saul got up from the ground, and though his eyes were open, he could see nothing; and leading him by the hand, they brought him into Damascus. And he was three days without sight, and neither ate nor drank.

But since Luke's account of that amazing incident does not reveal the transformation in Paul's thinking, in Philippians 3:4–11 the apostle himself provides those details of the Spirit's work in his heart. Salvation is a sovereign act of God in which He invades sinners' darkness with the glorious light of His truth, and redeems them. Paul describes the miracle from the inside that transformed him from the arch-persecutor of Christians into their most beloved leader. That day on the Damascus Road the living Christ broke through the spiritual blindness of the proud, self-righteous Pharisee, Saul of Tarsus. As a result, his trust in his religious accomplishments was shattered, and the root of his self-confidence was forever uprooted as conviction and truth flooded his darkened soul.

In this passage Paul speaks of salvation as a transaction or an exchange. He even uses business and accounting terminology in verses 7 and 8, which form the heart of the passage. *Kerdos* ("gain") describes what is in the profit column; *zēmia* ("loss") what is in the loss column; *hēgeomai* means "to count," or "to reckon." Paul spent his life accumulating what he imagined was personally earned righteousness that would achieve salvation. But when he met Christ, the apostle realized that all those things were actually in the loss column. He exchanged them all for the righteousness that comes from God on the basis of faith. That exchange is the theme of this passage.

Jesus described salvation as an exchange or transaction; in fact, an exchange of all that the sinner is for all that Christ is. In Matthew

16:25–26 He said, "For whoever wishes to save his life will lose it; but whoever loses his life for My sake will find it. For what will it profit a man if he gains the whole world and forfeits his soul? Or what will a man give in exchange for his soul?" In Matthew 13, Jesus told two parables that illustrate the exchange involved in salvation:

> The kingdom of heaven is like a treasure hidden in the field, which a man found and hid again; and from joy over it he goes and sells all that he has and buys that field. (v. 44)

> Again, the kingdom of heaven is like a merchant seeking fine pearls, and upon finding one pearl of great value, he went and sold all that he had and bought it. (vv. 45–46)

Both parables picture people who have accumulated earthly wealth. But they find in the kingdom of heaven (the sphere of salvation where God rules) a treasure far more valuable. They then gladly sell all they have to get that treasure. So must sinners abandon everything for Christ.

Paul interjects his testimony here to reinforce the point he made in verse 3, that believers "are the true circumcision, who worship in the Spirit of God and glory in Christ Jesus and put no confidence in the flesh." They do not trust in their self-righteousness to earn salvation. But as noted in the previous chapter of this volume, the Philippians were being assaulted by the heretical group known as the Judaizers. They were Jewish legalistic false teachers who taught that circumcision and obedience to the Law of Moses were necessary for salvation. Paul warned the Philippians against the Judaizers in no uncertain terms, bluntly denouncing them as "dogs," "evil workers," and the "false circumcision" or mutilation (3:2).

Having unmasked the Judaizers in verse 2 and defined Christians as the "true circumcision" in verse 3, Paul anticipates the Judaizers' response. They would undoubtedly argue that the Philippians, being Gentiles, did not understand the rich heritage of Judaism. But the same could not be said of the apostle Paul. His Jewish credentials were impeccable, easily equaling or surpassing those of the Judaizers. He knew firsthand all that Judaism had to offer. Describing his life before his conversion, Paul wrote, "I was advancing in Judaism beyond many of my contemporaries among my countrymen, being more extremely zealous for my ancestral traditions" (Gal. 1:14). In today's jargon, he had "been there … done that."

If anyone could have achieved salvation by self-effort, it would have been Paul. His impressive credentials enabled him to declare emphatically **I myself might have confidence even in the flesh. If**

anyone else has a mind to put confidence in the flesh, I far more.
Paul did not make that seemingly prideful statement to boost his ego, or
to claim spiritual superiority over others. He understood the foolishness
of boasting, and did so only for the sake of argument. As he did in the situation in Corinth (cf. 2 Cor. 11:16–12:1), Paul sets forth his own credentials to counter his opponents' foolish arguments.

Paul's testimony may be divided into two parts, based on the
accounting terminology in verses 7 and 8 noted earlier. The apostle first
lists those things that he once imagined to be in the spiritual profit column, purchasing eternal life for him, but which in reality were in the loss
column, damning him. That column might be titled "religious credits that
do not impress God." The true spiritual profit column might be headed
"the surpassing benefits of knowing Christ."

RELIGIOUS CREDITS THAT DO NOT IMPRESS GOD

**circumcised the eighth day, of the nation of Israel, of the tribe of
Benjamin, a Hebrew of Hebrews; as to the Law, a Pharisee; as to
zeal, a persecutor of the church; as to the righteousness which is
in the Law, found blameless.** (3:5–6)

Paul lists seven items that he once put in his spiritual profit column, but now places in his loss column. When he understood the gospel
of Christ, the apostle realized that all of these credentials, achievements,
privileges, and rights were worthless. Paul is not saying that they are of no
social, cultural, educational, or historical value. Instead, he is saying that
they are of no value salvifically; they could not save him or anyone else.

SALVATION IS NOT BY RITUAL

circumcised the eighth day, (3:5*a*)

Paul begins with circumcision because that was the major issue
for the Judaizers (cf. Acts 15:1; Gal. 6:12–13). The apostle went through
the defining rite of Judaism (Gen. 17:10–12; Lev. 12:3) when he was **circumcised the eighth day** after his birth. The Greek text literally reads,
"with respect to circumcision an eighth-dayer." Unlike some of the Judaizers,
Paul was not a Gentile proselyte to Judaism. He was a Jew by birth and
followed the Jewish rituals from the beginning. At the proper time, he
had gone through the ceremony that initiated him into the covenant
people. He, like most Jews, had long forgotten that circumcision was to

depict in a dramatic way how sinful and in need of cleansing people are, and had made that surgery a badge of righteousness.

Yet Paul includes circumcision, the most essential rite in Judaism, in his spiritual loss column. Salvation does not come by any ritual or ceremony, whether Jewish circumcision, the Roman Catholic mass, infant or adult baptism, or the Protestant observance of the Lord's Supper.

SALVATION IS NOT BY RACE

of the nation of Israel, (3:5*b*)

Paul's declaration that he was **of the nation of Israel** supports the idea that some of the Judaizers were Gentile converts to Judaism. But Paul was by birth a member of God's chosen people, of whom God declared, "You only have I chosen among all the families of the earth" (Amos 3:2; cf. Ex. 19:5–6; Ps. 147:19–20). He inherited all the blessings of being part of the covenant nation. Writing to the Romans, the apostle delineated some of those blessings:

> Then what advantage has the Jew? Or what is the benefit of circumcision? Great in every respect. First of all, that they were entrusted with the oracles of God. (Rom. 3:1–2)

> For I could wish that I myself were accursed, separated from Christ for the sake of my brethren, my kinsmen according to the flesh, who are Israelites, to whom belongs the adoption as sons, and the glory and the covenants and the giving of the Law and the temple service and the promises, whose are the fathers, and from whom is the Christ according to the flesh, who is over all, God blessed forever. Amen. (Rom. 9:3–5)

Paul was a physical descendant of Abraham, Isaac, and Jacob—a heritage that the Jewish people relied on, along with circumcision, for salvation. But racial heritage, like circumcision, is unable to save anyone; no standing with God is gained by birth.

SALVATION IS NOT BY RANK

of the tribe of Benjamin, (3:5*c*)

Another of Paul's seemingly impressive credentials was that he was a member **of the tribe of Benjamin,** one of the most prominent tribes in Israel. Benjamin was the younger of the two sons born to Jacob's favorite wife, Rachel. He was also the last of Jacob's sons to be born and the only one born in the Promised Land. Saul, Israel's first king, was a member of the tribe of Benjamin (1 Sam. 9:21; 10:21; Acts 13:21). When the Promised Land was divided among the twelve tribes, the holy city of Jerusalem was included in Benjamin's territory (Judg. 1:21). When the kingdom split after Solomon's death, only Benjamin and Judah remained loyal to the Davidic dynasty. The great leader Mordecai, used by God along with Esther to save the Jews from genocide, was also from the tribe of Benjamin (Est. 2:5). Thus, the tribe of Benjamin was one of the most noble in Israel.

By Paul's day, many Jews no longer knew what tribe they belonged to. Intermarriage during the years of exile had blurred the tribal lines. But Paul's family had remained pure Benjamites. That again elevated him above some of the Judaizers, who probably did not know their tribal descent. But Paul's privileged status as a Benjamite did not impress God. Family status has nothing to do with salvation.

SALVATION IS NOT BY TRADITION

a Hebrew of Hebrews; (3:5d)

Paul did not personally contribute anything to earn the first three privileges on his list, but inherited them from his parents. The last four are things that he himself achieved. The apostle's claim to be **a Hebrew of Hebrews** is best understood as a declaration that as he grew to manhood Paul strictly maintained his family's traditional Jewish heritage. He was born in Tarsus, a city in Asia Minor, not in Israel. But unlike many Jews in the Diaspora (dispersion), Paul remained firmly committed to the language (Acts 21:40), orthodox traditions, and customs of his ancestors. He did not become a Hellenized Jew (cf. Acts 6:1; 9:29), one who had been assimilated into the Greco-Roman culture. Instead, he left Tarsus for Jerusalem to study under the famous rabbi Gamaliel (Acts 22:3; 26:4). So tightly did Paul cling to his Jewish heritage that he could confidently declare, "So then, all Jews know my manner of life from my youth up, which from the beginning was spent among my own nation and at Jerusalem" (Acts 26:4). Paul's zealous devotion to his Jewish heritage was widely known. Yet after he saw the glory of Christ, it became merely one more item transferred from the gain to the loss column.

SALVATION IS NOT BY RELIGION

as to the Law, a Pharisee; (3:5e)

Paul pursued his Jewish heritage to the extreme. He was so zealous for **the Law** that he became a **Pharisee.** To the Sanhedrin Paul declared, "Brethren, I am a Pharisee, a son of Pharisees" (Acts 23:6). At his hearing before Agrippa, Paul testified, "I lived as a Pharisee according to the strictest sect of our religion" (Acts 26:5). To become a **Pharisee** was to reach the highest level in devout, legalistic Judaism. The Pharisees were supremely devoted to **the Law,** including the Old Testament and all the traditions that had been added to it. In fact, the word **Pharisee** probably derives from a Hebrew verb meaning "to separate," signifying that they were set apart to **the Law.** The term **Law** is not limited to the Pentateuch or the Old Testament, but includes the whole rabbinic system of prescriptions. Jesus said they had actually substituted those traditions for **the Law** of God (Matt. 15:1–9).

The origin of the Pharisees is not known for certain, but the sect probably arose formally during the intertestamental period. It had been developing since Ezra's time when the concern for God's law was revived (Neh. 8:1–8). Although relatively few in number (the first-century Jewish writer Josephus estimated their number at 6,000), they had the greatest religious influence on the common people. To be a **Pharisee** was to be a member of an elite, influential, and highly respected group of men who fastidiously lived to know, interpret, guard, and obey **the Law.**

Paul's cherished status as a Pharisee was but one more item in his spiritual loss column. No priest, monk, theological scholar, or member of a devout sect can achieve salvation by such involvement.

SALVATION IS NOT BY SINCERITY

as to zeal, a persecutor of the church; (3:6a)

As further evidence of his **zeal** for his Jewish heritage, Paul confessed that he had been **a persecutor of the church.** The Jews viewed **zeal** as the supreme religious virtue. It is a two-sided coin; one side is love, the other hate. To be zealous is to love God and hate what offends Him. Paul's zealous but misguided love for God caused him to hate and persecute Christianity.

The intensity of his zeal can be seen in the degree to which he persecuted the church. After Stephen's martyrdom, Paul "began ravaging the church, entering house after house, and dragging off men and women, he would put them in prison" (Acts 8:3). So devastatingly effective was his persecution that the Jerusalem church was scattered: "Therefore, those who had been scattered went about preaching the word" (Acts 8:4). Later, "Saul [Paul], still breathing threats and murder against the disciples of the Lord, went to the high priest, and asked for letters from him to the synagogues at Damascus, so that if he found any belonging to the Way, both men and women, he might bring them bound to Jerusalem" (Acts 9:1–2). His persecution was so violent that after Paul's conversion "all those hearing him continued to be amazed, and were saying, 'Is this not he who in Jerusalem destroyed those who called on this name, and who had come here for the purpose of bringing them bound before the chief priests?'" (Acts 9:21). He reminded the angry mob in Jerusalem, "I persecuted this Way to the death, binding and putting both men and women into prisons, as also the high priest and all the Council of the elders can testify. From them I also received letters to the brethren, and started off for Damascus in order to bring even those who were there to Jerusalem as prisoners to be punished" (Acts 22:4–5). Describing his persecution of Christians in his defense before Agrippa, Paul declared,

> So then, I thought to myself that I had to do many things hostile to the name of Jesus of Nazareth. And this is just what I did in Jerusalem; not only did I lock up many of the saints in prisons, having received authority from the chief priests, but also when they were being put to death I cast my vote against them. And as I punished them often in all the synagogues, I tried to force them to blaspheme; and being furiously enraged at them, I kept pursuing them even to foreign cities. (Acts 26:9–11)

The shame of what he had done stayed with Paul for the rest of his life. In 1 Corinthians 15:9 he said, "For I am the least of the apostles, and not fit to be called an apostle, because I persecuted the church of God." To the Galatians he wrote, "For you have heard of my former manner of life in Judaism, how I used to persecute the church of God beyond measure and tried to destroy it" (Gal. 1:13). Late in his life he confessed to Timothy, "I was formerly a blasphemer and a persecutor and a violent aggressor. Yet I was shown mercy because I acted ignorantly in unbelief" (1 Tim. 1:13).

In terms of zeal, Paul went the Judaizers one better. They only proselytized the church; he had persecuted it. His zeal for God led him to relentlessly, unsparingly, and mercilessly try to stamp out Christianity. Paul was sincere, but wrong. The world is full of people who, like him, are sincere in their religious beliefs. They will make any effort, pay any price, and sacrifice anything in their attempts to please God. They may be devout, orthodox Jews, loyal Roman Catholics who attend Mass regularly, or even Protestants who are involved in church services and ceremonies. They may pray, fast, or live in poverty, and seek to do human good. But religious zeal guarantees nothing. Those people can be absolutely wrong. When Paul faced the reality of Jesus Christ, the zealous persecutor of the church realized that his misguided zeal was a spiritual killer and belonged in the spiritual loss column.

SALVATION IS NOT BY LEGALISTIC RIGHTEOUSNESS

as to the righteousness which is in the Law, found blameless. (3:6*b*)

Before his conversion Paul outwardly conformed **to the righteousness which is in the Law.** Again, Paul uses **Law** in the broad sense of the Jewish tradition, not just the Old Testament. Those who observed his life would have **found** his behavior **blameless.** He was not, of course, denying that he sinned. That would contradict both Jewish theology and his testimony in Romans 7:7–11:

> What shall we say then? Is the Law sin? May it never be! On the contrary, I would not have come to know sin except through the Law; for I would not have known about coveting if the Law had not said, "You shall not covet." But sin, taking opportunity through the commandment, produced in me coveting of every kind; for apart from the Law sin is dead. I was once alive apart from the Law; but when the commandment came, sin became alive and I died; and this commandment, which was to result in life, proved to result in death for me; for sin, taking an opportunity through the commandment, deceived me and through it killed me.

But by all outward appearances, Paul was to the people who knew him a model Jew who lived by Jewish law. He was not, however, like Zacharias and Elizabeth, who "were both righteous in the sight of God, walking blamelessly in all the commandments and requirements of the Lord" (Luke 1:6).

Paul seemingly had it all. He had undergone the proper rituals, he was a member of God's chosen people, he was from a favored tribe in Israel, he had scrupulously maintained his orthodox heritage, he was one of the most devout legalists in Judaism, he was zealous to the point that he persecuted Christians, and he rigidly conformed to the outward requirements of Judaism. Yet he saw that as useless for salvation, and the reality of salvation by grace through faith in Jesus Christ was revealed to him. The apostle did not come to believe that those things were good, but Christ was better; instead, he viewed all of them as bad. They were deadly, because they deceived him into thinking that he was right with God. False religion deceives the mind and consequently damns the soul.

THE SURPASSING BENEFITS OF KNOWING CHRIST

But whatever things were gain to me, those things I have counted as loss for the sake of Christ. More than that, I count all things to be loss in view of the surpassing value of knowing Christ Jesus my Lord, for whom I have suffered the loss of all things, and count them but rubbish so that I may gain Christ, and may be found in Him, not having a righteousness of my own derived from the Law, but that which is through faith in Christ, the righteousness which comes from God on the basis of faith, that I may know Him and the power of His resurrection and the fellowship of His sufferings, being conformed to His death; in order that I may attain to the resurrection from the dead. (3:7–11)

The statement **but whatever things were gain to me, those things I have counted as loss for the sake of Christ** sums up the dramatic change that took place in Paul's perspective when he met Christ. All of the cherished treasures in his **gain** column suddenly became deficits. But by God's marvelous grace, those **things** that he wrongly imagined would give him eternal life were replaced by five matchless benefits that were his in Christ.

KNOWLEDGE

More than that, I count all things to be loss in view of the surpassing value of knowing Christ Jesus my Lord, for whom I have suffered the loss of all things, and count them but rubbish so that I may gain Christ, and may be found in Him, (3:8–9a)

The forceful phrase **more than that** is an untranslatable string of five Greek particles (lit. "but indeed therefore at least even"). It strongly emphasizes the contrast between the religious credits that do not impress God and the incalculable benefits of knowing Christ. In verse 7, Paul counted the religious credits in verses 5 and 6 as loss; here he expands that conviction and declares **all things to be loss in view of the surpassing value of knowing Christ Jesus.** The verb translated "I have counted" in verse 7 is in the perfect tense; the same verb translated here **I count** is in the present tense. That indicates that all the meritorious works that Paul had counted on to earn God's favor, and any that he might do in the present or future, are but **loss.**

Paul abandoned his past religious achievements **in view of the surpassing value of knowing Christ Jesus.** The participle *huperchon* (**the surpassing value**) refers to something of incomparable worth. The word **knowing** in the Greek text is not a verb, but a form of the noun *gnōsis*, from the verb *ginōskō*, which means to know experimentally or experientially by personal involvement. The **surpassing** knowledge of Christ that Paul describes here is far more than mere intellectual knowledge of the facts about Him.

The New Testament frequently describes Christians as those who know Christ. In John 10:14 Jesus said, "I am the good shepherd, and I know My own and My own know Me." In John 17:3 He defined eternal life as knowing Him: "This is eternal life, that they may know You, the only true God, and Jesus Christ whom You have sent." To the Corinthians Paul wrote, "For God, who said, 'Light shall shine out of darkness,' is the One who has shone in our hearts to give the Light of the knowledge of the glory of God in the face of Christ" (2 Cor. 4:6), while in Ephesians 1:17 he prayed "that the God of our Lord Jesus Christ, the Father of glory, may give to you a spirit of wisdom and of revelation in the knowledge of Him." In his first epistle John declared, "And we know that the Son of God has come, and has given us understanding so that we may know Him who is true; and we are in Him who is true, in His Son Jesus Christ. This is the true God and eternal life" (1 John 5:20). Salvation involves a personal, relational knowledge of the Lord Jesus Christ.

To the Greeks, *gnōsis* could describe secret, cultic, mystical communion with a deity. Those who were initiated into the mystery claimed to have ascended beyond the mundane knowledge possessed by the masses. They imagined that they alone enjoyed some personal experience of their deity. The Greeks often sought such an elevated state through drunken revelry. In the second century, the dangerous heresy of Gnosticism attempted to syncretize the Greek concept of *gnōsis* and Christian truth. Like their pagan counterparts, the Gnostics claimed a higher, truer knowledge of God than the average Christian experienced. But Paul uses *gnōsis* here to describe the transcendent communion with Christ that all true believers experience.

There is also an Old Testament context for *gnōsis*. The verb form was used in the Septuagint (the Greek translation of the Old Testament) to translate the Hebrew word *yada*. *Yada* often denoted an intimate knowledge, even a union or bond of love. It was sometimes used in Scripture as a euphemism for sexual intercourse (e.g., Gen. 4:1, 17, 25; 19:8; 24:16; Num. 31:17–18, 35; Judg. 21:11–12; 1 Sam. 1:19). It also described God's intimate love bond with Israel: "You only have I known of all the families of the earth" (Amos 3:2 NKJV). Thus, the word can have the connotation both of a transcendent knowledge and an intimate love bond.

Adding personal warmth to the rich theological concept of **knowing Christ Jesus,** Paul describes Him as **my Lord.** That threefold description encompasses Christ's three offices of prophet, priest, and king. **Christ** views Him as the Messiah, the messenger or prophet of God. **Jesus** views Him as Savior, emphasizing His role as believers' great High Priest. **Lord** views Him as sovereign King over all creation.

Salvation comes only through the deep knowledge of and intimate love bond with Jesus Christ that God gives by grace through faith. Commenting on the believer's knowledge of Christ, F. B. Meyer wrote,

> We may know Him personally intimately face to face. Christ does not live back in the centuries, nor amid the clouds of heaven: He is near us, with us, compassing our path in our lying down, and acquainted with all our ways. But we cannot know Him in this mortal life except through the illumination and teaching of the Holy Spirit. . . . And we must surely know Christ, not as a stranger who turns in to visit for the night, or as the exalted king of men—there must be the inner knowledge as of those whom He counts His own familiar friends, whom He trusts with His secrets, who eat with Him of His own bread.
>
> To know Christ in the storm of battle; to know Him in the valley of shadow; to know Him when the solar light irradiates our faces, or when they are darkened with disappointment and sorrow; to know the sweetness of His dealing with bruised reeds and smoking flax; to know the tenderness of His sympathy and the strength of His right hand—all this involves many varieties of experience on our part, but each of them like the facets of a diamond will reflect the prismatic beauty of His glory from a new angle. (*The Epistle to the Philippians* [Grand Rapids: Baker, 1952], 162–63)

For the inestimable privilege of knowing Jesus Christ, Paul gladly **suffered the loss of all things** by which he might have sought to earn salvation apart from Christ. The apostle went so far as to **count them but rubbish so that** he might **gain** (personally appropriate) **Christ.** All efforts to obtain salvation through human achievement are as much **rubbish** as the worst vice. *Skubalon* (**rubbish**) is a very strong word that could also be rendered "waste," "dung," "manure," or even "excrement." Paul expresses in the strongest possible language his utter disdain for all the religious credits with which he had sought to impress man and God. In view of the surpassing value of knowing Christ, they are worthless. Paul would have heartily endorsed Isaiah's declaration that "all of us have become like one who is unclean, and all our righteous deeds are like a filthy garment; and all of us wither like a leaf, and our iniquities, like the wind, take us away" (Isa. 64:6).

The phrase **in Him** expresses the familiar Pauline truth that believers are in Christ, a concept found more than seventy-five times in his epistles. Believers are inextricably intertwined with Christ in an intimate life and love bond. "I have been crucified with Christ," wrote Paul to the Galatians; "and it is no longer I who live, but Christ lives in me; and the life which I now live in the flesh I live by faith in the Son of God, who loved me and gave Himself up for me" (Gal. 2:20).

RIGHTEOUSNESS

not having a righteousness of my own derived from the Law, but that which is through faith in Christ, the righteousness which comes from God on the basis of faith, (3:9*b*)

Paul had spent his adult life futilely trying to obtain **a righteousness of** his **own derived from** keeping **the Law.** That **righteousness** —one of self-effort, external morality, religious ritual, and moral works, all produced by the flesh—had been a crushing, unbearable burden (cf. Matt. 23:4; Luke 11:46; Acts 15:10). Although Paul did his best, he fell far short of God's standard (cf. Rom. 3:23), which no one can meet: "Now we know that whatever the Law says, it speaks to those who are under the Law, so that every mouth may be closed and all the world may become accountable to God; because by the works of the Law no flesh will be justified in His sight; for through the Law comes the knowledge of sin" (Rom. 3:19–20; cf. Acts 13:39; Gal. 2:16; 3:10–13; 5:4; Eph. 2:8–9). He was like the rest of his countrymen who, "not knowing about God's righteousness and seeking to establish their own, they did not subject themselves to the righteousness of God" (Rom. 10:3).

In Romans 7:9–13, Paul expands on the awakening in his heart:

> I was once alive apart from the Law; but when the commandment came, sin became alive and I died; and this commandment, which was to result in life, proved to result in death for me; for sin, taking an opportunity through the commandment, deceived me and through it killed me. So then, the Law is holy, and the commandment is holy and righteous and good. Therefore did that which is good become a cause of death for me? May it never be! Rather it was sin, in order that it might be shown to be sin by effecting my death through that which is good, so that through the commandment sin would become utterly sinful.

Once, though devoted to the law of Judaism, he was living and thinking apart from the law of God. When he faced the true divine law, he saw himself as a sinner dead in sin and headed for eternal death. The law of Judaism gave him life, he thought. The law of God killed him. When he saw himself as utterly sinful, he renounced works of righteousness of his own doing and accepted the free gift of God's righteousness by grace.

Paul gladly exchanged the burden of legalistic self-righteousness for the righteousness **which is through faith in Christ, the righteousness which comes from God on the basis of faith.** Faith is the confident, continuous confession of total dependence on and trust in Jesus Christ for the necessary requirements to enter God's kingdom. It involves more than mere intellectual assent to the truth of the gospel; saving faith includes trust in the Lord Jesus Christ and surrender to His lordship. It is **on the basis of faith** alone that **righteousness . . . comes from God** to repentant sinners.

Righteousness is right standing with God and acceptance by Him. That repentant sinners have their sin imputed to Christ and His righteousness imputed to them is the heart of the gospel. In 2 Corinthians 5:21, Paul declared that God "made Him [Christ] who knew no sin to be sin on our behalf, so that we might become the righteousness of God in Him." Paul gladly shed the threadbare robe of his own righteousness and stretched out his empty hands to receive the glorious royal robe of God's righteousness in Christ. This doctrine is at the core of the gospel. On the cross, God judged Jesus as if He had personally committed every sin ever committed by every person who ever truly believed. When a sinner embraces Jesus as Lord and trusts only in His sacrifice for sin, God treats that sinner as if he lived Christ's sinless life (cf. Isa. 53; 2 Cor. 5:21; 1 Peter 2:24).

POWER

that I may know Him and the power of His resurrection (3:10a)

Paul had already mentioned the deep, experiential knowledge of Jesus Christ that comes at salvation (v. 8). But still the cry of his heart was **that I may know Him.** That initial saving knowledge of Christ became the basis of Paul's lifelong pursuit of an ever deeper knowledge of His Savior. Specifically, Paul longed to experience **the power of His resurrection.** He knew there was no power in the Law. He also knew there was no power in his flesh to overcome sin or serve God (cf. Rom. 7:18). But because he knew Christ and had His righteousness imputed to him, Paul had been given the Holy Spirit and the same spiritual power that raised Jesus from the dead.

His resurrection was the greatest display of Christ's power. Rising from the dead (cf. John 2:19–21; 10:17–18) revealed His absolute power over both the physical and spiritual realms (cf. Col. 2:14–15; 1 Peter 3:18–20). Paul experienced Christ's resurrection power in two ways. First, it was that power that saved him, a truth he affirmed in

Romans 6:4–5: "Therefore we have been buried with Him through baptism into death, so that as Christ was raised from the dead through the glory of the Father, so we too might walk in newness of life. For if we have become united with Him in the likeness of His death, certainly we shall also be in the likeness of His resurrection." In salvation, believers are identified with Christ in His death and resurrection. But more than that, it is Christ's resurrection power that sanctified him (and all believers) to defeat temptation and trials, lead a holy life, and boldly and fruitfully proclaim the gospel. Paul gladly exchanged his impotence for Christ's resurrection power, and desired to experience its fullness.

FELLOWSHIP

and the fellowship of His sufferings, being conformed to His death; (3:10*b*)

A fourth benediction salvation brought Paul was **fellowship** with Jesus Christ. The apostle speaks specifically here of the **fellowship of His sufferings.** As he has just noted, Paul was **conformed to His death** at salvation (cf. Rom. 6:4–5). But he has something more in mind here, a deep partnership and communion with Christ in suffering. When he met Christ, Paul gained a companion to be with him in his suffering—One who endured far more intense persecution and suffering than anyone else who ever lived, all of it undeserved.

The deepest moments of spiritual fellowship with the living Christ are at times of intense suffering; suffering drives believers to Him. They find in Him a merciful High Priest, a faithful friend who feels their pain, and a sympathetic companion who faced all the trials and temptations that they face (Heb. 4:15). He is thus uniquely qualified to help them in their weaknesses and infirmities (Heb. 2:17). That blessed, comforting truth led Paul to exclaim, "Therefore I am well content with weaknesses, with insults, with distresses, with persecutions, with difficulties, for Christ's sake; for when I am weak, then I am strong" (2 Cor. 12:10).

GLORY

in order that I may attain to the resurrection from the dead. (3:11)

A final and consummate benefit Paul obtained when he met Christ was the guarantee of his future resurrection, when he would share

Christ's glory. The Greek phrase the NASB translates **in order that** actually reads "if somehow." However, that does not express doubt on Paul's part, but rather humility. Paul's sense of unworthiness never left him. In 1 Corinthians 15:9 he wrote, "For I am the least of the apostles, and not fit to be called an apostle, because I persecuted the church of God." In Ephesians 3:8 he described himself as "the very least of all saints." Paul was confident **that** he would **attain to the resurrection from the dead** and share Christ's glory.

The phrase **the resurrection from the dead** is unique in Scripture. It literally reads "the out resurrection from among the corpses." Believers will **attain to** that **resurrection** at the Rapture, when "we will not all sleep, but we will all be changed, in a moment, in the twinkling of an eye, at the last trumpet; for the trumpet will sound, and the dead will be raised imperishable, and we will be changed. For this perishable must put on the imperishable, and this mortal must put on immortality" (1 Cor. 15:51–53). Believers will be taken out from among the rest of the **dead** corpses, who will not be raised until the end of the millennial kingdom, and transformed into the image of Christ.

Paul hated the weakness of his flesh and longed to be rid of it. Because he saw himself as wretched (Rom. 7:24), he wrote to the Romans, "We ourselves, having the first fruits of the Spirit, even we ourselves groan within ourselves, waiting eagerly for our adoption as sons, the redemption of our body" (Rom. 8:23). The redemption of the body at the resurrection is another of the surpassing benefits of knowing Christ.

What do believers gain by their union with Christ? The knowledge of Christ in their identification with Him; the righteousness of Christ imputed to them in justification; the power of Christ for their sanctification; participation in the sufferings of Christ; and sharing Christ's glory in their glorification. No wonder Paul gladly exchanged the religious credits in his loss column for the surpassing benefits of knowing Christ.

Matthew 19 records the story of another man who came to the same crossroads as Paul. In reply to his question about how to obtain eternal life, Jesus told him to obey the Law. In response, "the young man said to Him, 'All these things I have kept; what am I still lacking?'" (Matt. 19:20). He, too, had his spiritual profit column filled with self-effort, religious ritual, and works righteousness. But unlike Paul, he counted those things gain and rejected Christ. Paul counted them loss and gained Christ.

Everyone stands at the same crossroads. People can cling to their religious credits and follow the rich young ruler onto the broad path that leads to eternal destruction. Or they can forsake them in favor of the surpassing benefits of knowing Christ and follow Paul onto the narrow path that leads to eternal life.

Reaching for the Prize—Part 1: The Prerequisites (Philippians 3:12–16)

16

Not that I have already obtained it or have already become perfect, but I press on so that I may lay hold of that for which also I was laid hold of by Christ Jesus. Brethren, I do not regard myself as having laid hold of it yet; but one thing I do: forgetting what lies behind and reaching forward to what lies ahead, I press on toward the goal for the prize of the upward call of God in Christ Jesus. Let us therefore, as many as are perfect, have this attitude; and if in anything you have a different attitude, God will reveal that also to you; however, let us keep living by that same standard to which we have attained. (3:12–16)

Judging from the frequent use of athletic metaphors in his writings, the apostle Paul must have been a sports fan. Speaking of his desire to be effective in his Christian life, Paul wrote, "I box in such a way, as not beating the air" (1 Cor. 9:26b). He described the Christian life to the Ephesians as a "struggle [*palē;* a wrestling match or fight] . . . not against flesh and blood, but against the rulers, against the powers, against the world forces of this darkness, against the spiritual forces of wickedness in the heavenly places" (Eph. 6:12). In what might be considered his epitaph, Paul declared triumphantly, "I have fought the good fight" (2 Tim. 4:7; cf.

1 Tim. 6:12). In an allusion to the Isthmian Games (held in Corinth and second in importance only to the Olympic Games), he reminded the Corinthians, "Everyone who competes in the games exercises self-control in all things. They then do it to receive a perishable wreath, but we an imperishable" (1 Cor. 9:25).

But Paul's favorite athletic metaphor is that of a footrace. He declared to the Ephesian elders, "But I do not consider my life of any account as dear to myself, so that I may finish my course and the ministry which I received from the Lord Jesus, to testify solemnly of the gospel of the grace of God" (Acts 20:24). To the Romans he wrote, "So then it does not depend on the man who wills or the man who runs, but on God who has mercy" (Rom. 9:16). Reminding the Corinthians of the dedicated athletes who competed in the Isthmian Games the apostle wrote, "Do you not know that those who run in a race all run, but only one receives the prize? Run in such a way that you may win. . . . Therefore I run in such a way, as not without aim" (1 Cor. 9:24, 26). In Galatians 2:2 Paul expressed his "fear that [he] might be running, or had run, in vain," while in Galatians 5:7 he lamented to the Galatians, "You were running well; who hindered you from obeying the truth?" At the close of his life, Paul could declare, "I have finished the course, I have kept the faith" (2 Tim. 4:7). It is that metaphor of the Christian life as a race, expressed in the familiar fourteenth verse ("I press on toward the goal for the prize of the upward call of God in Christ Jesus"), that is the theme of Philippians 3:12–21. The passage reveals Paul's passionate concern for spiritual growth.

The previous passage (3:4–11) described Paul's transformation when he encountered the risen Christ on the Damascus Road and understood the gospel. In that powerful and moving passage, the apostle recited his impressive religious credentials. Then, dramatically, he declared that compared to the surpassing value of knowing Jesus Christ, those achievements were mere rubbish. Paul exchanged his useless human achievements for the knowledge, righteousness, power, fellowship, and glory of the Lord Jesus Christ.

Some in Philippi might have mistakenly assumed that, having gained those marvelous benefits, Paul had reached spiritual perfection. The Judaizers may also have taught the Philippians that spiritual perfection was attainable through being circumcised and keeping the Law. There were also heretics (forerunners of the second-century Gnostics) who taught that spiritual perfection awaited those who attained a certain level of knowledge. To counter such false ideas, Paul quickly added this passage, which is a forceful disclaimer of spiritual perfection. Though he was a new creature (2 Cor. 5:17), with a new heart (Ezek. 36:26), a new disposition that strongly desired holiness (Rom. 7:22; 2 Cor. 4:16; Eph. 3:16), was united with Christ (Gal. 2:20), possessed a renewed mind (Rom. 12:2; Eph. 4:23), had the mind of Christ (1 Cor. 2:16), had right standing before God (Rom. 8:1), had been justified (Rom. 5:1), had been forgiven (Eph. 1:7), had Christ's righteousness imputed to him (2 Cor. 5:21), and was indwelt by the Holy Spirit (Rom. 8:9, 11; 1 Cor. 3:16; 2 Tim. 1:14), Paul was not perfect. He was still subject to temptation, still possessed his unredeemed flesh, and was still a sinner (cf. Rom. 7:14–25; 1 Tim. 1:15). Far from having obtained perfection, he was pursuing it with all his might. Like Peter, Paul understood that the Christian life is a life-long process of "grow[ing] in the grace and knowledge of our Lord and Savior Jesus Christ" (2 Peter 3:18; cf. 1 Peter 2:1–2).

This passage deals a devastating blow to the false doctrine of perfectionism that still prevails in some denominations and churches. Perfectionism is the teaching that believers can reach a place of spiritual and moral perfection in this life. Perfectionists teach that in a second work of grace, believers may instantaneously be made sinless. Some even go so far as to teach the eradication of the sin nature. But the apostle Paul, undoubtedly the most committed, dedicated, spiritually mature Christian who ever lived, confessed gladly that he had failed to reach spiritual perfection thirty years after his conversion. And that confession was clear evidence of his true and mature spirituality. Who, then, could make a legitimate claim to have done so? To maintain the fiction that they have achieved sinless perfection, perfectionists are forced to make an unbiblical distinction between willful sin and "mistakes." But Scripture teaches that any violation of God's law—whatever the intent—is sin. No Christian will ever become perfect in this life; that awaits the redemption of the body (Rom. 8:23). Perfection in this life will always be a goal, never an achievement. If we say we do not sin, we make God a liar, because He says we do (1 John 1:7–9).

Some may question why they should bother to pursue spiritual growth. After all, believers are promised "an inheritance which is imperishable and undefiled and will not fade away, reserved in heaven for [them]" (1 Peter 1:4). But that question is a moot point. Spiritual children, like physical children, cannot help but grow (cf. 1 Peter 2:1–2); they have a built-in desire and drive for growth.

Apart from that, there are several compelling reasons that Christians must grow spiritually. First, it glorifies God. Second, it provides evidence that their salvation is genuine. Third, it adorns and makes visible the truth of God to others (cf. Titus 2:10). Fourth, it brings assurance of salvation. Fifth, it preserves believers from the sorrow and suffering associated with spiritual immaturity. Sixth, it protects the cause of Christ from reproach. Seventh, it produces joy in believers' lives. Eighth, it equips them for ministry to others in the body of Christ. Finally, it enhances their witness to the lost world.

In the next passage (3:17–21), Paul gives specific instructions on how to pursue the prize of spiritual perfection, which is Christlikeness. Later in this epistle, Paul reminded the Philippians that "our citizenship is in heaven, from which also we eagerly wait for a Savior, the Lord Jesus Christ; who will transform the body of our humble state into conformity with the body of His glory, by the exertion of the power that He has even to subject all things to Himself" (Phil. 3:20–21). The apostle John echoed that thought: "Beloved, now we are children of God, and it has not appeared as yet what we will be. We know that when He appears, we will be like Him, because we will see Him just as He is" (1 John 3:2). Christlikeness is the prize that must be pursued, though that prize will not be attained this side of heaven. But before Paul writes of the pursuit, he first sets forth six necessary prerequisites for effectively striving for the prize of Christlikeness. The effort requires from the believer a proper awareness, a maximum effort, a focused concentration, a proper motivation, a proper recognition, and a proper conformity.

PURSUING THE PRIZE REQUIRES A PROPER AWARENESS

Not that I have already obtained it or have already become perfect, (3:12a)

All that believers are now in Christ and will enjoy forever in heaven is eternally fixed by God's gracious purpose (cf. 1 Peter 1:4). That spiritual reality and promise cannot be improved upon, but believers' virtue in this present life can and must be. Knowing that we are not now what we should be, and what we someday will be in glory, must not produce apathy and indolence, but a zeal for moving in the direction of the prize. That is the Spirit's work in us (2 Cor. 3:18) and the longing of the regenerated soul. The awareness of the need to improve one's spiritual condition is a necessary prerequisite to pursuing the prize of spiritual perfection.

Paul had that awareness, and expressed it in the two words that begin verse 12, **not that.** He had not yet **obtained** (from *lambanō;* "to receive," "acquire," or "attain") the prize he pursued; he had not yet **become perfect** (from *teleioō;* "to attain perfection," "reach a goal," or "accomplish"). The twice-repeated word **already** indicates that Paul was still imperfect when he wrote this epistle.

Despite the rich blessings that were his in Christ, the apostle knew that he was not perfect. His knowledge of Christ was still incomplete (1 Cor. 13:12). Christ's righteousness had been imputed to him (2 Cor. 5:21), yet he still needed to "cleanse [himself] from all defilement of flesh and spirit, perfecting holiness in the fear of God" (2 Cor. 7:1). Paul had Christ's power at work in him (1 Cor. 15:10; Col. 1:29), but that power still worked through his weakness (2 Cor. 12:9). The rich fellowship with Christ that he experienced was also imperfect; he still did not know how to pray as he should, and depended on the Holy Spirit to intercede for him (Rom. 8:26–27). While his body was a temple of the glorious Holy Spirit who indwelt him (1 Cor. 6:19), Paul longed for the day when Christ "will transform the body of [his] humble state into conformity with the body of His glory" (Phil. 3:21).

Obviously, pursuing the prize of spiritual perfection begins with dissatisfaction with one's present spiritual condition. Those who think they have reached spiritual perfection will not see the need to pursue a better condition; why should they chase something they believe they already have? Such complacent, contented people are in grave danger of becoming insensitive to their sin and blind to their weaknesses. It is only those who are aware of their desperate spiritual need who come to Christ for salvation (Matt. 5:6). And it is only those who continue to recognize the need to eliminate sin and cultivate holiness who will make progress in the Christian life. This pursuit by the power of the sanctifying Spirit produces a decreasing frequency of sin and increasing love for holiness, which makes less sin feel like more. The truly mature and godly have the most sensitive awareness of their sins, and are the humblest before God because of it.

PURSUING THE PRIZE REQUIRES A MAXIMUM EFFORT

but I press on so that I may lay hold of that for which also I was laid hold of by Christ Jesus. (3:12b)

True believers will not pursue the prize of spiritual perfection until they recognize the need to improve their condition, but awareness of the need is not enough; there must also be a diligent pursuit. **I press on** means "to run" or "follow after." It speaks of an aggressive, energetic endeavor. Paul pursued the spiritual prize with all his might, straining every spiritual muscle as he ran to win (1 Cor. 9:24).

The "let go and let God" mentality was foreign to Paul. He was totally dependent on God's power working in his life (2 Cor. 12:9; Col. 1:29). Yet he also described the Christian life as "labor and striving" (Col. 1:29), and "the good fight of faith" (1 Tim. 6:12; cf. 2 Tim. 4:7). He taught that "through many tribulations we must enter the kingdom of God" (Acts 14:22), and repeatedly stressed the inevitability of suffering in the Christian life (e.g., Rom. 8:17; 1 Thess. 3:4; 2 Tim. 1:8; 3:12).

The somewhat enigmatic phrase **so that I may lay hold of that for which also I was laid hold of by Christ Jesus** states the goal of Paul's strenuous efforts. The verb translated **I may lay hold of; I was laid hold of** could be translated "to overtake," "seize," or "catch." Paul was running spiritually to catch the very thing for which **Christ Jesus** had come after him. In other words, Paul's goal in life was consistent with Christ's goal in saving him.

What was Christ's goal in saving Paul? The apostle stated it in Romans 8:29: "For those whom He foreknew, He also predestined to become conformed to the image of His Son, so that He would be the firstborn among many brethren." God chose Paul, as He did all believers, to make him like Jesus Christ. That purpose for which God saved us is also the purpose for which we live. "It was for this He called you through our gospel," wrote Paul to the Thessalonians, "that you may gain the glory of our Lord Jesus Christ" (2 Thess. 2:14). The Christian life is a life-long pursuit of Christlikeness. That was the Lord's goal in saving Paul and was his goal in response.

PURSUING THE PRIZE REQUIRES A FOCUSED CONCENTRATION

Brethren, I do not regard myself as having laid hold of it yet; but one thing I do: forgetting what lies behind and reaching forward to what lies ahead, (3:13)

A maximum effort without focused concentration is useless. Every athlete knows that runners in a race must fix their eyes ahead of them; those who watch the crowd or their own feet are likely to trip and fall. To make a maximum effort in any athletic endeavor requires the participants to concentrate on a point straight ahead.

Paul addresses the Philippians with the gentle, intimate, affectionate term **brethren** to move their hearts away from the Judaizers and toward him. For the third time in this passage, Paul adds the disclaimer **I do not regard myself as having laid hold of it yet.** The apostle's intent is polemical. He is directing his argument at those who were teaching error, and he wants to make the truth abundantly clear. Despite the false teachers' claims to the contrary, spiritual perfection is not attainable in this life.

Though Paul had not achieved spiritual perfection, he had that blessed discontent that motivated him to pursue it. In fact, it had become the one pursuit of his life, expressed in the phrase **but one thing I do. I do** is not in the Greek text, but was added by the translators because it is implied. In the Greek text Paul communicates his single-mindedness in a staccato, brief, impassioned, almost abrupt manner. The apostle's focus on his goal was total, his level of concentration acute.

It is such singularly focused people who succeed in athletics and in other pursuits of life. Many people dabble in much, but succeed at nothing. Despite all the energy they expend, they accomplish little. Their lives are full of sound and fury, signifying nothing. James called them "double-minded . . . unstable in all [their] ways" (James 1:8). To avoid such lack of focus the psalmist prayed, "Unite my heart to fear Your name" (Ps. 86:11), and Solomon counseled, "Let your eyes look directly ahead and let your gaze be fixed straight in front of you. Watch the path of your feet and all your ways will be established. Do not turn to the right nor to the left" (Prov. 4:25–27). When believers have one driving compulsion, to be like Christ, they will move toward spiritual perfection.

Such concentration possesses both a negative and a positive aspect. Negatively, Paul maintained his focus by **forgetting what lies behind.** A runner who looks back risks being passed. Nor does a runner's performance in past races guarantee success or failure in present or future races. The past is not relevant; what matters is making the maximum effort in the present so as to sustain momentum in the future. Perfectionists and legalists look to their past achievements to validate their supposed spiritual status. The Judaizers sought to ensnare the Galatians in the past, prompting Paul to write, "But now that you have come to know God, or rather to be known by God, how is it that you turn back again to the weak and worthless elemental things, to which you desire to be enslaved all over again?" (Gal. 4:9).

Paul made a break with everything in his past, both good and bad. Religious achievements, virtuous deeds, great successes in ministry, as well as sins, missed opportunities, and disasters must all be forgotten. They do not control the present or the future. Believers cannot live on past victories, nor should they be debilitated by the guilt of past sins.

Churches are full of spiritual cripples, paralyzed by the grudges, bitterness, sins, and tragedies of the past. Others try to survive in the present by reliving past successes. They must break with that past if they are to pursue the spiritual prize. God is interested in what believers do now and in the future. "No one," declared Jesus, "after putting his hand to the plow and looking back, is fit for the kingdom of God" (Luke 9:62). The clearest vision belongs to those who forget the past.

Positively, Paul maintained his focus by **reaching forward to what lies ahead. Reaching forward** translates a participial form of the verb *epekteinō,* a compound verb made up of two prepositions added to the verb *teinō* ("to stretch"). It describes stretching a muscle to its limit, and pictures a runner straining every muscle to reach the finish line.

As already noted, the goal on which believers must focus is being like Jesus Christ. It was also the goal of Paul's ministry to "present every man complete in Christ" (Col. 1:28). He also expressed that goal to the Ephesians:

> And He gave some as apostles, and some as prophets, and some as evangelists, and some as pastors and teachers, for the equipping of the saints for the work of service, to the building up of the body of Christ; until we all attain to the unity of the faith, and of the knowledge of the Son of God, to a mature man, to the measure of the stature which belongs to the fullness of Christ. As a result, we are no longer to be children, tossed here and there by waves and carried about by every wind of doctrine, by the trickery of men, by craftiness in deceitful scheming. (Eph. 4:11–14)

To the Galatians Paul wrote that he was "in labor until Christ is formed in you" (Gal. 4:19). He exhorted the Corinthians to "be made complete" (2 Cor. 13:11), and his coworker Epaphras prayed that the Colossians would "stand perfect and fully assured in all the will of God" (Col. 4:12). Pursuing Christlikeness here and now, until we are made like Him in glory, defines the progress of the Christian life and the target of ministry.

PURSUING THE PRIZE REQUIRES A PROPER MOTIVATION

I press on toward the goal for the prize of the upward call of God in Christ Jesus. (3:14)

As noted earlier, this verse is the heart of the passage. The present tense verb translated **I press on** denotes Paul's continuous effort to pursue the "impossible dream" and defeat "the unbeatable foe." The root meaning of the preposition *kata* (**toward**) is "down." Paul again expressed his single-minded focus, saying, "I continually bear down on the **goal** (*skopos;* "a mark on which to fix one's eyes")."

That **prize** was what motivated him to run to win (1 Cor. 9:24). Believers will not receive the **prize** (Christlikeness, with all its eternal benefits) until **the upward** (lit. "above," denoting both the source of the call and to where it leads) **call of God in Christ Jesus** ushers them into God's glorious presence in heaven. As noted above, perfection is not attainable in this life. The finish line is the threshold of heaven, where the rewards will be handed out (cf. Matt. 5:12; Luke 6:23; 1 Cor. 3:12–15). It is not until Christ "appears, [that] we will be like Him, because we will see Him just as He is" (1 John 3:2).

Like a runner triumphantly pumping his fist in the air as he approaches the finish line, Paul declared at the end of his life, "I have fought the good fight, I have finished the course, I have kept the faith; in the future there is laid up for me the crown of righteousness, which the Lord, the righteous Judge, will award to me on that day" (2 Tim. 4:7–8). Only "in the future" in heaven would Paul receive "the crown of righteousness" (Christ's righteousness perfected in him); only then would he receive the **prize** which he so diligently pursued.

PURSUING THE PRIZE REQUIRES A PROPER RECOGNITION

Let us therefore, as many as are perfect, have this attitude; and if in anything you have a different attitude, God will reveal that also to you; (3:15)

Paul was not in the spiritual race alone; it includes all Christians, described here by the phrase **as many as are perfect** (cf. Heb. 10:14). The apostle is not speaking of practical perfection; that would contradict what he said earlier in the passage. Practical perfection does not come until believers are glorified. Rather, in a play on words, he describes believers as those who are positionally **perfect** in Christ. Since this is a polemic passage directed against those who taught that perfection is attainable in this life, Paul's use of **perfect** may be a bit double-edged, with a tinge of sarcasm. Those false teachers were not perfect in practice, and also were not perfect in position.

Every true Christian must **have this** same **attitude** that Paul had. *Phroneō* (**have this attitude**) literally means "to think this way," "to be intent on this," or "to set one's mind on this." It might be translated "continually think like this." Like Paul, believers must be totally focused on making the maximum effort to pursue the prize of Christlikeness. We know how Christ thinks because the Scripture gives us His mind (1 Cor. 2:16). When we think biblical, divine thoughts, viewing all of life from the Lord's perspective, those thoughts will move our behavior to become like His (cf. Col. 3:16).

But Paul was an experienced pastor and knew that not all believers would share the strength and relentlessness of his focus on pursuing the prize. To them Paul says, **if in anything you have a different attitude, God will reveal that also to you.** Those who refuse to heed Paul's message will hear that same message from God. He will correct them through His Word, His Spirit, or through chastening. God will do whatever it takes to make believers recognize their need to pursue the prize of Christlikeness. He will also provide the resources they need to do that (2 Peter 1:3).

Pursuing the Prize Requires a Proper Conformity

however, let us keep living by that same standard to which we have attained. (3:16)

Plēn (**however**) could also be translated "one more thing." It is often used to express one final thought. This last prerequisite for pursuing the prize might also be described as consistency. Having developed a proper awareness, effort, focus, motivation, and recognition, believers must consistently **keep living by that same standard to which** they **have attained.** *Stoicheō* (**keep living**) means "to line up," or "to follow in line." Believers must keep to the spiritual path that they have been following. To use the metaphor of a race, they must keep running in their lane.

Four divinely provided resources help believers to consistently pursue the prize of Christlikeness. First is the Word of God. Peter wrote, "Like newborn babies, long for the pure milk of the word, so that by it you may grow in respect to salvation" (1 Peter 2:2). Second is prayer. Paul prayed that the Corinthians would "be made complete" (2 Cor. 13:9). Third is following a godly example. Paul exhorted the Corinthians, "Be imitators of me" (1 Cor. 4:16; cf. 11:1; Phil. 3:17; 1 Thess. 1:6; 2 Thess. 3:7, 9; 1 Tim. 4:12; Heb. 13:7; 1 Peter 5:3). Finally, God uses trials to mold believers into the image of Jesus Christ: "After you have suffered for a little while, the God of all grace, who called you to His eternal glory in Christ, will Himself perfect, confirm, strengthen and establish you" (1 Peter 5:10; cf. James 1:2–4).

At the foot of one of the Swiss Alps is a marker honoring a man who fell to his death attempting the ascent. The marker gives his name and this brief epitaph: "He died climbing." The epitaph of every Christian should be that they died climbing the upward path toward the prize of Christlikeness.

Reaching for the Prize—Part 2: The Procedure (Philippians 3:17–21)

17

Brethren, join in following my example, and observe those who walk according to the pattern you have in us. For many walk, of whom I often told you, and now tell you even weeping, that they are enemies of the cross of Christ, whose end is destruction, whose god is their appetite, and whose glory is in their shame, who set their minds on earthly things. For our citizenship is in heaven, from which also we eagerly wait for a Savior, the Lord Jesus Christ; who will transform the body of our humble state into conformity with the body of His glory, by the exertion of the power that He has even to subject all things to Himself. (3:17–21)

People who make an impact in the world invariably have a single-minded commitment to reaching their goals. Whether those goals are to conquer the world, succeed in business, or win a championship, they are willing to make whatever sacrifices are necessary to achieve them. On the other hand, those who are consumed with their own needs and comfort rarely accomplish much.

The same is true in the Christian life. There are no hidden secrets, gimmicks, or shortcuts to a life that makes an impact on the world for the truth of Jesus Christ. Such lives are the direct result of a maximum effort to reach the spiritual goals of Christlikeness in life and ministry. Many noble servants of God have suffered much to reach those goals. Many even paid with their lives. All had one thing in common—their own comfort was less important to them than being like the Lord Jesus Christ in this world. They left their mark on the church through their undying devotion to Him and their untiring efforts for His gospel.

Unfortunately, few in the church today have that level of commitment to the cause of Christ. There are many reasons for that, not the least of which is the devastating impact humanistic psychology has made on the church. One of the basic assumptions of modern psychology is that people exist for their own satisfaction. The primary goal of life, then, is for people to have all of their perceived needs and desires met. Only then will they be happy, content, and fulfilled.

Contemporary presentations of the gospel often reflect that humanistic philosophy. God has become a sort of utilitarian genie, who exists to grant people whatever it takes to make them happy and fulfilled. Scripture presents Jesus Christ as sovereign Lord and Savior, before whom every knee must bow in absolute submission and obedience (Phil. 2:10). But contemporary gospel presentations offer Him as the quick cure for all of life's problems—despite His own warning, "In the world you have tribulation" (John 16:33; cf. Acts 14:22; 1 Thess. 3:4; 2 Tim. 3:12). The most glaring example of the current man-centered approach is the prosperity gospel, with its unabashed pursuit of the things of the world. Those attitudes of selfish satisfaction are the opposite of the attitude of true spirituality, which is humble, self-effacing awareness of sin and deep gratitude for the least expression of God's grace.

The narcissism that pervades contemporary Christianity has also corrupted the doctrine of sanctification. Jesus taught, "If anyone wishes to come after Me, he must deny himself, and take up his cross daily and follow Me" (Luke 9:23). In stark contrast, the emphasis today is on meeting people's needs and fulfilling their desires. Only then, it is argued, can they be effective Christians. That is the focus of much preaching, teaching, and writing.

Commenting on this new paradigm for the Christian life, Tony Walter writes,

> It is fashionable to follow the view of some psychologists that the self is a bundle of needs and that personal growth is the business of progressively meeting these needs. Many Christians go along with such beliefs....
>
> One mark of the almost total success of this new morality is that the Christian Church, traditionally keen on mortifying the desires of the flesh, on crucifying needs of the self in pursuit of [Christlikeness], has eagerly adopted the language of needs for itself. . . . We now hear that

"Jesus will meet your every need," as though He were some kind of divine psychiatrist or divine detergent, as though God were there simply to service us. (*Need: The New Religion* [Downers Grove, Ill.: Inter-Varsity, 1985], Preface, 5)

The church's adoption of the need mentality of humanistic psychology leads to a man-centered theology, a man-centered quasi-salvation, and a man-centered substitute for sanctification. For many, the goal of Christian living is getting their needs met, being fulfilled, being happy, having a good self-image, and eliminating all of life's problems. The focus is on people, not Christ.

But the sub-Christian "need theology" is diametrically opposed to what the Bible teaches. The satisfaction of human need is not the goal of either salvation or sanctification. The goal of salvation is for believers to be conformed to the image of God's Son (Rom. 8:29). Hence, Christian sanctification looks outward to Christ, not inward to believers' felt needs. The goal of Christian living is not believers' satisfaction, but God's. In fact, believers flourish when they are overwhelmed with weakness (2 Cor. 12:9–10).

That Christians are to be like Jesus Christ is the simple truth that tends to be obscured by the plethora of theologies, seminars, books, formulas, and tapes that purport to unlock the secret of spiritual growth. Some of those offerings may be helpful, but only to the degree that they equip believers to become more like Jesus Christ.

The repeated command of the Lord Jesus Christ, "Follow Me" (cf. Matt. 4:19; 8:22; 9:9; 16:24; 19:21), has not been replaced or improved upon. It is the most basic obligation of a believer. Paul expressed that same truth to the Galatians: "My children, with whom I am again in labor until Christ is formed in you" (Gal. 4:19) and to the Corinthians, "Be imitators of me, just as I also am of Christ" (1 Cor. 11:1). The apostle John taught that "the one who says he abides in Him ought himself to walk in the same manner as He walked" (1 John 2:6).

When Paul told the Philippians, "One thing I do" (3:13), he reduced the Christian life to that one objective. For example, Christians are to glorify God, but can only do so to the degree that they are like Jesus Christ. When they evangelize the lost, they are imitating the Lord, who came "to seek and to save that which was lost" (Luke 19:10). As believers mature spiritually they "grow in the grace and knowledge of [their] Lord and Savior Jesus Christ" (2 Peter 3:18). When they "die to sin and live to righteousness" (1 Peter 2:24) they become more and more like Jesus, "who knew no sin" (2 Cor. 5:21; cf. Heb. 7:26; 1 Peter 2:22; 1 John 3:5).

There is both an objective and a subjective resource for pursuing the prize of Christlikeness. The objective resource is the Word of God. The

Bible is the revelation of Christ, "in whom are hidden all the treasures of wisdom and knowledge" (Col. 2:3). When Paul wrote that believers have "the mind of Christ" (1 Cor. 2:16), he was referring to the revelation of Scripture given by the apostles and those New Testament writers associated with them.

The subjective power for becoming more like Jesus Christ is the work of the Holy Spirit. He uses the knowledge of Christ gleaned from Scripture to progressively change believers into Christ's image (2 Cor. 3:18). The New Testament is clear that Christian growth results from study of the Scripture and submission to the Holy Spirit.

In this passage, Paul gives three practical elements of pursuing Christlikeness: following after examples, fleeing from enemies, and focusing on expectations.

FOLLOWING AFTER EXAMPLES

Brethren, join in following my example, and observe those who walk according to the pattern you have in us. (3:17)

For the third time in this chapter Paul affectionately addresses the Philippians as **brethren** (cf. vv. 1, 13). The phrase **join in following my example** literally reads in the Greek text "be fellow imitators with me." Paul urged the Philippians to imitate the way he lived. He was not putting himself on a pedestal of spiritual perfection (cf. the discussion of vv. 12–16 in the previous chapter of this volume). Instead, he was encouraging the Philippians to follow him, an imperfect sinner, as he pursued the goal of Christlikeness.

The New Testament records Paul's failures as well as his triumphs. Outraged at his abusive treatment at the hands of the high priest, he cried out, "God is going to strike you, you whitewashed wall! Do you sit to try me according to the Law, and in violation of the Law order me to be struck?" (Acts 23:3)—an outburst for which he promptly apologized (Acts 23:5). Because of his struggle with pride, the Lord gave Paul a thorn in the flesh (2 Cor. 12:7). Three decades after his conversion, he still thought of himself as the foremost of sinners (1 Tim. 1:15).

Had he been perfect, Paul would not have been an example believers could follow. We need to follow someone who is not perfect so we can see how to overcome our imperfections; someone who can show us how to handle the struggles of life, its disappointments, and its trials; someone who can show us how to handle pride, resist temptation, and put sin to death. Christ is the perfect standard, model, and pattern for believers to emulate. But Christ never pursued perfection; He has always been perfect. Paul was a fellow traveler on the path toward the unattainable spiritual perfection, and thus a model for believers to follow. He modeled virtue, morality, overcoming the flesh, victory over temptation, worship, service to God, patient endurance of suffering, handling possessions, and handling relationships.

Moving beyond himself, Paul commanded the Philippians also to **observe those who walk according to the pattern you have in us.** *Skopeō* (**observe**) is the verb form of the noun translated "goal" in verse 14, and could be translated "fix your gaze on." Paul is in effect saying, "Focus on **those** whose **walk** (daily conduct) is **according to the** correct **pattern**—the one **you have in us.**" That would include Timothy and Epaphroditus, whom the Philippians knew, as well as the overseers and deacons at Philippi (cf. 1:1). The word **us,** however, is most likely a literary plural, a humble way for Paul to refer to himself.

Paul's example was available to the Philippians in print, as it is to believers today. But they had also observed his life firsthand during his stay in Philippi. Believers have always needed examples of godly living as patterns. Those examples are the pastors and elders of the church, who are to "show [themselves examples] of those who believe" (1 Tim. 4:12) by modeling humility, unselfish service, willingness to suffer, devotion to Christ, courage, and dedication to spiritual growth.

Those who teach and preach the Word must handle it accurately. That is especially important today, when the correct interpretation of Scripture has been hopelessly blurred and seemingly any view is tolerated. Paul exhorted Timothy, "Be diligent to present yourself approved to God as a workman who does not need to be ashamed, accurately handling the word of truth" (2 Tim. 2:15). But accurate teaching of the truth must be backed up by a godly life.

FLEEING FROM ENEMIES

For many walk, of whom I often told you, and now tell you even weeping, that they are enemies of the cross of Christ, whose end is destruction, whose god is their appetite, and whose glory is in their shame, who set their minds on earthly things. (3:18–19)

The apostle warned that in pursuing the spiritual prize of Christlikeness it must be recognized that there are **many** examples to be avoided. The **enemies** of which Paul warned do not appear to have been openly hostile to the Christian faith. Like their evil master, Satan, they were deceptive, disguising themselves as messengers of Christ, angels of light, and servants of righteousness (2 Cor. 11:13–15). They

became part of the church, possibly even in leadership roles. Their subtlety made them exceptionally dangerous.

The New Testament constantly warns of the danger posed by
false teachers. In the Sermon on the Mount, Jesus warned, "Beware of the
false prophets, who come to you in sheep's clothing, but inwardly are ravenous wolves" (Matt. 7:15). In the Olivet Discourse He added, "See to it
that no one misleads you. For many will come in My name, saying, 'I am
the Christ,' and will mislead many" (Matt. 24:4–5). Acts records the false
teachers Simon Magus (Acts 8:9–24) and Elymas (Acts 13:8–11), while
Paul dealt with Hymenaeus and Alexander at Ephesus (1 Tim. 1:20). The
apostle warned both Timothy (1 Tim. 1:4) and Titus (Titus 3:9) to avoid
false teachers who dabbled in myths and genealogies. Both Peter (2 Peter)
and Jude wrote of the danger of false teachers. John also warned his
readers to beware of false teachers:

> Beloved, do not believe every spirit, but test the spirits to see whether
> they are from God, because many false prophets have gone out into
> the world. By this you know the Spirit of God: every spirit that confess-
> es that Jesus Christ has come in the flesh is from God; and every spirit
> that does not confess Jesus is not from God; this is the spirit of the
> antichrist, of which you have heard that it is coming, and now it is
> already in the world. (1 John 4:1–3)

In his second epistle he added, "Many deceivers have gone out into the
world, those who do not acknowledge Jesus Christ as coming in the
flesh. This is the deceiver and the antichrist" (2 John 7).

Sadly, because of apathy toward the truth and shallow biblical
knowledge, the church today lacks discernment. It is astonishing and dis-
turbing to see the things Christians believe and the people they follow. A
lack of consistent and long-term precise biblical exposition from the pul-
pit has led to a lack of precise biblical thinking and discernment. The
tragic result is the widespread victimization of the church by enemies of
the Cross of Christ. (For a further discussion of the lack of discernment in
the church, see John MacArthur, *Reckless Faith: When the Church Loses
Its Will to Discern* [Wheaton, Ill.: Crossway, 1994].)

Unlike the godly examples of verse 17, the **walk** (daily conduct)
of the false teachers is not to be imitated. Some see the phrase **of whom
I often told you** as a reference to 1:28. More likely, however, it refers to
warnings Paul gave the Philippian church when he was with them in person. He gave a similar warning to the elders from the Ephesian church:

> Be on guard for yourselves and for all the flock, among which the Holy
> Spirit has made you overseers, to shepherd the church of God which
> He purchased with His own blood. I know that after my departure sav-
> age wolves will come in among you, not sparing the flock; and from

among your own selves men will arise, speaking perverse things, to draw away the disciples after them. Therefore be on the alert, remembering that night and day for a period of three years I did not cease to admonish each one with tears. (Acts 20:28–31)

Paul warned the Philippians that false teachers **are enemies of the cross of Christ.** But he did so not with gladness, but with **weeping.** This is the only place in the New Testament that Paul speaks of himself as crying in the present tense. He was a sensitive, passionate man, and the plight of lost sinners or the threat to his beloved congregations often brought him to tears (cf. Acts 20:19, 31; Rom. 9:2; 2 Cor. 2:4). Paul was heartbroken as he recognized the havoc the false teachers could cause in the Philippian church. He no doubt also wept over the false teachers' fate (cf. Rom. 9:2). The damnation of the enemies of the Cross, their destructive impact on the church, and the reproach they brought on the cause of Christ caused Paul grief.

Paul described the false teachers as **enemies of the cross of Christ.** The term **cross** is not limited to the actual wooden instrument of death (1 Cor. 1:17–18, 23; 2:2; Gal. 3:1; 6:14; Eph. 2:16; Col. 1:20; 2:14; 1 Peter 2:24), but signifies Christ's atoning death in all its aspects. The false teachers were against salvation!

Paul did not label the specific **enemies of the cross of Christ** who were troubling the Philippians. There are, however, only two options: they were either Jews or Gentiles, or both. The Jewish false teachers who identified with the church were known as the Judaizers (cf. Acts 15). They argued that the gospel alone was insufficient to save; circumcision and keeping the Law were also necessary. Paul forcefully denounced them in 3:2 as "dogs, . . . evil workers," and "the false circumcision." Though they thought of themselves as the sheep of God's pasture, the Judaizers were actually mangy, scroungy mongrels. Their spiritual descendants—those who add works to salvation—plague the church to this day.

Since Paul did not specifically identify these **enemies of the cross** as Judaizers, they may have been Gentiles. Some Gentile false teachers held to the dualistic philosophy prevalent in contemporary Greek thought. Those heretics, forerunners of the dangerous second-century heresy known as Gnosticism, taught that spirit was good and matter was evil. Since the body is made of matter, it is intrinsically evil. Salvation ultimately involves not the redemption of the body, but deliverance from it. Thus, since the body is incurably evil, it does not matter what one does with it. Its desires can be satiated; a person can be a glutton, a drunkard, a homosexual, or an adulterer. All those things, the heretics taught, were inconsequential, since they affected only the body, not the spirit. The Judaizers added to the gospel; the Gentile false teachers subtracted from it.

That same spirit of antinomian libertinism lives on today. There are those in the contemporary church who teach that saving faith need not result in a life of holiness. Since Jesus' death paid for believers' sins, they argue, it does not matter how they live. Some even teach that all who profess faith in Christ are saved—even if they later become atheists.

Paul gave four marks of the **enemies of the cross** in verse 19.

THE DOOM THEY FACE

whose end is destruction, (3:19a)

Having rejected the one and only truth of salvation—the cross of Christ—all false teachers face the same fate. Their **end** (the Greek word *telos* refers here to their ultimate destiny) will be eternal **destruction** (torment, punishment) in hell (Matt. 25:46; 2 Thess. 1:9). The Judaizers deserved this fate because they added human works to the cross of Christ. To believe the truth about Him but also to believe that human works are necessary for salvation is to be damned forever. The Gentile heretics deserved their fate because they stripped the cross of Christ of its power to transform lives. The result is a dead faith, unable to save (James 2:14–26).

THE DEITY THEY SERVE

whose god is their appetite, (3:19b)

Appetite translates *koilia,* which refers anatomically to the abdomen, particularly the stomach. Here it is used metaphorically to refer to all unrestrained sensual, fleshly, bodily desires (cf. 1 Cor. 6:13). The false teachers were condemned because they did not worship God but bowed down to their sensual impulses. It could be a reference to the Judaizers' emphasis on keeping the Jewish dietary laws. Or if the false teachers in view were Gentiles, it could refer to their unrestrained pursuit of sensual pleasures. Jude described such people as "ungodly persons who turn the grace of our God into licentiousness and deny our only Master and Lord, Jesus Christ" (Jude 4).

THE DISGRACE THEY BEAR

whose glory is in their shame, (3:19c)

Shockingly, the false teachers boasted in the very things that brought them **shame.** This is the most extreme form of wickedness—when the sinner's most wretched conduct before God is his highest point of self-exaltation. The Judaizers boasted in their "rubbish" (3:8)—as Paul himself had done before he learned to count all that "as loss for the sake of Christ" (3:7). The Gentile libertines also boasted—of their supposed freedom to pursue sensual desires. They were most proud of their worst perversions (cf. 1 Cor. 5:1–2).

THE DISPOSITION THEY DISPLAY

who set their minds on earthly things. ($3:19d$)

Their **earthly** focus offers evidence that the false teachers were not saved. James asked, "Do you not know that friendship with the world is hostility toward God? Therefore whoever wishes to be a friend of the world makes himself an enemy of God" (James 4:4). "If anyone loves the world, the love of the Father is not in him" (1 John 2:15). The Judaizers focused on ceremonies, festivals, feasts, sacrifices, new moons—"things which are a mere shadow of what is to come; but the substance belongs to Christ" (Col. 2:17). The libertines focused on the passing sensual pleasures of the world.

The enemies of the Cross, whether they add to the gospel or take away from it, are to be avoided, never imitated.

FOCUSING ON EXPECTATIONS

For our citizenship is in heaven, from which also we eagerly wait for a Savior, the Lord Jesus Christ; who will transform the body of our humble state into conformity with the body of His glory, by the exertion of the power that He has even to subject all things to Himself. (3:20–21)

The underlying motivation for pursuing Christlikeness is the hope of the return of Jesus Christ. Since Christ is in heaven, those who love Him must be preoccupied with heaven, longing for Christ to return and take them to be with Him (1 Thess. 4:17).

Paul had little interest in the comforts and pleasures of this world, as the following passages indicate:

> We are afflicted in every way, but not crushed; perplexed, but not despairing; persecuted, but not forsaken; struck down, but not

destroyed; always carrying about in the body the dying of Jesus, so that the life of Jesus also may be manifested in our body. (2 Cor. 4:8–10)

In everything commending ourselves as servants of God, in much endurance, in afflictions, in hardships, in distresses, in beatings, in imprisonments, in tumults, in labors, in sleeplessness, in hunger, in purity, in knowledge, in patience, in kindness, in the Holy Spirit, in genuine love, in the word of truth, in the power of God; by the weapons of righteousness for the right hand and the left, by glory and dishonor, by evil report and good report; regarded as deceivers and yet true; as unknown yet well-known, as dying yet behold, we live; as punished yet not put to death, as sorrowful yet always rejoicing, as poor yet making many rich, as having nothing yet possessing all things. (2 Cor. 6:4–10)

Are they servants of Christ?—I speak as if insane—I more so; in far more labors, in far more imprisonments, beaten times without number, often in danger of death. Five times I received from the Jews thirty-nine lashes. Three times I was beaten with rods, once I was stoned, three times I was shipwrecked, a night and a day I have spent in the deep. I have been on frequent journeys, in dangers from rivers, dangers from robbers, dangers from my countrymen, dangers from the Gentiles, dangers in the city, dangers in the wilderness, dangers on the sea, dangers among false brethren; I have been in labor and hardship, through many sleepless nights, in hunger and thirst, often without food, in cold and exposure. Apart from such external things, there is the daily pressure on me of concern for all the churches. Who is weak without my being weak? Who is led into sin without my intense concern? (2 Cor. 11:23–29)

This view led him to the conviction that made him write, "I am hard-pressed from both directions, having the desire to depart and be with Christ, for that is very much better" (1:23).

It is consistent for believers to have a heavenly focus, because **our citizenship is in heaven.** *Politeuma* (**citizenship**) appears only here in the New Testament, though Paul used the related verb in 1:27. It refers to the place where one has official status, the commonwealth where one's name is recorded on the register of citizens. Though believers live in this world, they are citizens of heaven. They are members of Christ's kingdom, which is not of this world (John 18:36). Their names are recorded in heaven (Luke 10:20; cf. Phil. 4:3; Heb. 12:23; Rev. 13:8; 21:27); their Savior is there (Acts 1:11; 1 Thess. 4:16); their fellow saints are there (Heb. 12:23); their inheritance is there (1 Peter 1:4); their reward is there (Matt. 5:12); and their treasure is there (Matt. 6:20).

Though they do not yet live in heaven, believers live in the heavenly realm (Eph. 2:6); they experience to some degree the heavenly life here on earth. They have the life of God within them, are under the rule of heaven's King, and live for heaven's cause.

Paul's reference to **citizenship** may have been especially meaningful to the Philippians, since Philippi was a Roman colony. The Philippians were Roman citizens, though obviously living outside of Rome, just as believers are citizens of heaven living on earth.

It is from heaven that **we eagerly wait for a Savior, the Lord Jesus Christ.** To the disciples who watched as Christ ascended into heaven the angels said, "Men of Galilee, why do you stand looking into the sky? This Jesus, who has been taken up from you into heaven, will come in just the same way as you have watched Him go into heaven" (Acts 1:11). In John 14:2–3 Jesus Himself promised, "In My Father's house are many dwelling places; if it were not so, I would have told you; for I go to prepare a place for you. If I go and prepare a place for you, I will come again and receive you to Myself, that where I am, there you may be also." Because of those promises, believers are to be "awaiting eagerly the revelation of our Lord Jesus Christ" (1 Cor. 1:7), and "to wait for His Son from heaven, whom He raised from the dead, that is Jesus, who rescues us from the wrath to come" (1 Thess. 1:10). Until He returns, believers "groan within [themselves], waiting eagerly for [their] adoption as sons, the redemption of [the] body" (Rom. 8:23).

The hope of Christ's return provides believers with motivation, accountability, and security. In this promise there is positive motivation to be found faithful when He returns to reward believers; to be accountable to God for living lives that produce gold, silver, and precious stones instead of wood, hay, and straw (1 Cor. 3:12). There is a corresponding negative reality, as John wrote: "Watch yourselves, that you do not lose what we have accomplished, but that you may receive a full reward" (2 John 8). Finally, the promise of Christ's return provides security, since Jesus promised, "This is the will of Him who sent Me, that of all that He has given Me I lose nothing, but raise it up on the last day. For this is the will of My Father, that everyone who beholds the Son and believes in Him will have eternal life, and I Myself will raise him up on the last day" (John 6:39–40).

Believers are not to wait for Christ's return with attitudes of passive resignation or bored disinterest. Instead, they are to **eagerly wait for a Savior,** the Lord Jesus Christ. Believers are not waiting for an event but a Person. *Apekdechomai* (**eagerly wait**) is often used to speak of waiting for Christ's second coming (e.g., Rom. 8:19, 23, 25; 1 Cor. 1:7; Gal. 5:5; Heb. 9:28). It describes not only eagerness, but also patience.

As noted above, Christ's return marks the end of believers' struggling pursuit of the elusive prize of holy perfection, for it is then that He **will transform the body of our humble state into conformity with the body of His glory.** It is then that the eagerly awaited redemption of the body will take place (Rom. 8:23). It is "when He appears [that] we will be like Him, because we will see Him just as He is" (1 John 3:2). Until then, the new creature (2 Cor. 5:17) is incarcerated in the unredeemed humanness ("the body of this death"; Rom. 7:24) from which it longs to be liberated.

For believers who die before Christ's return, death means the temporary separation of the spirit from the body. The body goes into the grave, while the spirit goes immediately into the presence of God (1:21, 23; 2 Cor. 5:6, 8). Heaven is currently occupied by "the spirits of the righteous made perfect" (Heb. 12:23). Those believers who live from Pentecost to the Rapture will have their spirits joined to their resurrection bodies at the Rapture (1 Thess. 4:15–17). The Old Testament believers and those saved during the Tribulation will receive their resurrection bodies at Christ's second coming (Dan. 12:2; Rev. 20:4).

Christ will totally **transform** the bodies of all believers, each group at its appointed time (cf. 1 Cor. 15:22–23), to make them fit for heaven. Believers' bodies will have a new schematic; they will be refashioned and redesigned. Christ will change the present **body of our humble state into conformity with the body of His glory.** Like Christ's resurrection body, believers' resurrected bodies will be recognizable. They will be able to eat, talk, and walk, but will not have the physical restrictions of our present bodies. After His resurrection Christ appeared and disappeared at will, even entering a room whose doors were locked (John 20:19). Paul gives the most detailed description of believers' resurrection bodies in 1 Corinthians 15:35–49:

> But someone will say, "How are the dead raised? And with what kind of body do they come?" You fool! That which you sow does not come to life unless it dies; and that which you sow, you do not sow the body which is to be, but a bare grain, perhaps of wheat or of something else. But God gives it a body just as He wished, and to each of the seeds a body of its own. All flesh is not the same flesh, but there is one flesh of men, and another flesh of beasts, and another flesh of birds, and another of fish. There are also heavenly bodies and earthly bodies, but the glory of the heavenly is one, and the glory of the earthly is another. There is one glory of the sun, and another glory of the moon, and another glory of the stars; for star differs from star in glory. So also is the resurrection of the dead. It is sown a perishable body, it is raised an imperishable body; it is sown in dishonor, it is raised in glory; it is sown in weakness, it is raised in power; it is sown a natural body, it is raised a spiritual body. If there is a natural body, there is also a spiritual body. So also it is written, 'The first man, Adam, became a living soul.' The last Adam became a life-giving spirit. However, the spiritual is not first, but the natural; then the spiritual. The first man is from the earth, earthy; the second man is from heaven. As is the earthy, so also are those who are

earthy; and as is the heavenly, so also are those who are heavenly. Just as we have borne the image of the earthy, we will also bear the image of the heavenly.

The combination of a redeemed spirit and a glorified body will enable all believers to perfectly manifest the glory of God. Sin, weakness, sorrow, disappointment, pain, suffering, doubt, fear, temptation, hate, and failure will give way to perfect joy (Matt. 25:21), pleasure (Ps. 16:11), knowledge (1 Cor. 13:12), comfort (Luke 16:25), and love (1 Cor. 13:13).

Salvation involves far more than mere deliverance from hell. God's ultimate goal in redeeming believers is to transform their bodies **into conformity with the body of His glory.** They will "become conformed [*summorphos*; the same word translated **conformity** in v. 21] to the image of His Son" (Rom. 8:29; cf. 1 John 3:2). "Just as we have borne the image of the earthy, we will also bear the image of the heavenly" (1 Cor. 15:49).

Their transformed bodies will permit believers finally to be the perfect creation God intends for them to be for the joy of perfect fellowship with Him forever. Describing heaven, John wrote, "I heard a loud voice from the throne, saying, 'Behold, the tabernacle of God is among men, and He will dwell among them, and they shall be His people, and God Himself will be among them'" (Rev. 21:3; cf. John 14:1–3; 1 Thess. 4:17). Those bodies will also allow believers to see God. In the Beatitudes Jesus said, "Blessed are the pure in heart, for they shall see God" (Matt. 5:8), while John wrote that in heaven "there will no longer be any curse; and the throne of God and of the Lamb will be in it, and His bond-servants will serve Him; they will see His face, and His name will be on their foreheads" (Rev. 22:3–4). Believers' resurrection bodies will also be perfectly suited for the eternal service they will render to God (cf. Rev. 7:15).

Lest any doubt Christ's power to transform believers' bodies, Paul notes that He will accomplish it **by the exertion of the power that He has even to subject all things to Himself.** *Hupotassō* (**subject**) means "to arrange in order of rank" or "to manage." Christ will have the power to rule the millennial kingdom (Rev. 12:5, 19:15; cf. Isa. 9:6; 32:1; Zech. 14:9). By His power Christ will also transform the earth's topography (Zech. 14:4–8) and the natural kingdom (Isa. 11:6–9). Paul's point is that if Christ can subject the entire universe to His sovereign control (cf. 1 Cor. 15:24–27), He has the power to transform believers' bodies into His image.

As they run the spiritual race (Heb. 12:1), believers must look to godly examples for inspiration and instruction. They must also look out for those enemies of the truth who would lead them astray. Finally, they must focus on the glorious hope that is theirs at the return of Christ—the transformation of their bodies into conformity with His. Then, regenerated fully in soul and body, they will be suited to eternal, holy glory and joy.

Spiritual Stability— Part 1: Harmony, Joy, Contentment, Faith (Philippians 4:1–6*a*)

18

Therefore, my beloved brethren whom I long to see, my joy and crown, in this way stand firm in the Lord, my beloved. I urge Euodia and I urge Syntyche to live in harmony in the Lord. Indeed, true companion, I ask you also to help these women who have shared my struggle in the cause of the gospel, together with Clement also and the rest of my fellow workers, whose names are in the book of life. Rejoice in the Lord always; again I will say, rejoice! Let your gentle spirit be known to all men. The Lord is near. Be anxious for nothing, (4:1–6*a*)

The church of Jesus Christ is under attack, just as Jesus predicted it would be. In John 16:33 He warned, "In the world you have tribulation, but take courage; I have overcome the world." Paul echoed the Lord's warning when he said, "Through many tribulations we must enter the kingdom of God" (Acts 14:22), and wrote to Timothy, "Indeed, all who desire to live godly in Christ Jesus will be persecuted" (2 Tim. 3:12). Not surprisingly, the church has faced persecution from its inception (cf. Acts 4:1–31; 5:17–41).

The assault on the church comes from three sources. The world with all its allurements endeavors to entice believers. It also persecutes the church, both openly and subtly. The church dares not compromise with the world, because "whoever wishes to be a friend of the world makes himself an enemy of God" (James 4:4), and "if anyone loves the world, the love of the Father is not in him" (1 John 2:15). The flesh (believers' fallen, unredeemed humanness) is another source of attack. Jesus exhorted, "Keep watching and praying that you may not enter into temptation; the spirit is willing, but the flesh is weak" (Matt. 26:41). Even after his salvation Paul could still cry out, "Wretched man that I am! Who will set me free from the body of this death?" (Rom. 7:24). Energizing both the world and the flesh is the devil, who "prowls around like a roaring lion, seeking someone to devour" (1 Peter 5:8).

The world is tempting, the flesh is vulnerable, and the devil is lionlike in his aggression. As a result, church life involves a great amount of instability. Thus, the issue of spiritual stability is very much on Paul's heart in 4:1–9. It is true that the Philippian church had a special love bond with Paul. They alone supported him when he left Macedonia (4:15). Nor did Paul have to sharply rebuke them for wavering doctrinally (as he did the Galatians), or tolerating sin (as he did the Corinthians). But that does not mean that the church in Philippi was all that it should have been, or that there was no instability there. There are hints throughout the epistle of the destabilizing threats facing the Philippian congregation. They were experiencing persecution (1:28–30). There was a lack of unity, thus Paul urged them, "Make my joy complete by being of the same mind, maintaining the same love, united in spirit, intent on one purpose" (2:2), and, "Do all things without grumbling or disputing" (2:14). False teachers also posed a threat (3:18–19). But perhaps the most serious threat facing the Philippians was the dispute between two prominent women in the congregation (4:2–3). That dispute threatened to split the church into rival factions. The situation was compounded by the failure of the elders and deacons to deal with it (cf. the discussion of 4:3 below). As a result of those destabilizing factors, some of the Philippians had failed to trust God and had given way to anxiety (4:6).

A concern for believers' spiritual stability permeates the New Testament. After a Gentile church was founded at Antioch, the Jerusalem church sent Barnabas to them, who, "when he arrived and witnessed the grace of God, . . . rejoiced and began to encourage them all with resolute heart to remain true to the Lord" (Acts 11:23). Thus, the first apostolic message to the fledgling Gentile church was to be spiritually stable. As part of their ministry, Paul and Barnabas were "strengthening the souls of the disciples, encouraging them to continue in the faith, and saying, 'Through many tribulations we must enter the kingdom of God'" (Acts 14:22). To the Corinthians Paul wrote, "Therefore, my beloved brethren, be steadfast, immovable, always abounding in the work of the Lord, knowing that your toil is not in vain in the Lord" (1 Cor. 15:58), and "Be on the alert, stand firm in the faith, act like men, be strong" (1 Cor. 16:13). He exhorted the Galatians, "It was for freedom that Christ set us free; therefore keep standing firm and do not be subject again to a yoke of slavery" (Gal. 5:1). In a passage dealing with spiritual warfare, Paul three times commanded believers to stand firm (Eph. 6:11, 13, 14). Earlier in this epistle, Paul expressed his desire to the Philippians that they remain stable: "Only conduct yourselves in a manner worthy of the gospel of Christ, so that whether I come and see you or remain absent, I will hear of you that you are standing firm in one spirit, with one mind striving together for the faith of the gospel" (1:27). To the Colossians he wrote, "For even though I am absent in body, nevertheless I am with you in spirit, rejoicing to see your good discipline and the stability of your faith in Christ" (Col. 2:5).

Paul was so concerned about the spiritual stability of the churches under his care that he wrote to the Thessalonians, "Now we really live, if you stand firm in the Lord" (1 Thess. 3:8), and "So then, brethren, stand firm and hold to the traditions which you were taught, whether by word of mouth or by letter from us" (2 Thess. 2:15). James described the person lacking spiritual stability as "a double-minded man, unstable in all his ways" (James 1:8). As he closed out his first epistle, Peter pleaded, "I have written to you briefly, exhorting and testifying that this is the true grace of God. Stand firm in it!" (1 Peter 5:12). In his second epistle he warned of false teachers who were "enticing unstable souls" (2 Peter 2:14). He also cautioned believers to beware of "the untaught and unstable" false teachers, who "distort [Paul's inspired epistles], as they do also the rest of the Scriptures, to their own destruction. You therefore, beloved, knowing this beforehand, be on your guard so that you are not carried away by the error of unprincipled men and fall from your own steadfastness" (2 Peter 3:16–17). Jude reminded believers that God wants to make them "stand in the presence of His glory blameless with great joy" (Jude 24).

Spiritual instability leads to disappointment, doubt, discouragement, and ineffective witness. Unstable people are likely to be crushed by their trials. They are also susceptible to temptation. An Old Testament example of an unstable person who fell into sin is Reuben, Jacob's firstborn son. In his patriarchal blessing of his sons, Jacob said of Reuben, "Unstable as water, you shall not excel, because you went up to your father's bed; then you defiled it—he went up to my couch" (Gen. 49:4 NKJV). Reuben's instability led him to commit fornication with one of Jacob's concubines (Gen. 35:22). As a result, he lost the birthright that should have been his as Jacob's firstborn son (1 Chron. 5:1).

In this passage, Paul addresses the vital question of how believers can be spiritually stable. *Stēkō* (**stand firm**) is the main verb of verses

1–9. It is an imperative, a command with almost a military ring to it. Like soldiers in the front line, believers are commanded to hold their position while under attack (cf. Eph. 6:11, 13, 14). They are not to collapse under persecution and compromise, to fail under testing and complain, or to yield to temptation and sin.

The passage opens with the transitional word **therefore,** which indicates that what Paul is about to write builds on what he has just written. The preceding passage (3:12–21) described the believer's pursuit of Christlikeness, which is both the goal in this life and the prize in the next life.

The Lord Jesus Christ provides the perfect example of firmness for us who await our perfection. He faced persecution, but never compromised; He "endured . . . hostility by sinners against Himself" without wavering (Heb. 12:3). He was "tempted in all things as we are, yet without sin" (4:15). Facing a more severe trial than any believer will ever undergo, "Jesus . . . for the joy set before Him endured the cross, despising the shame, and has sat down at the right hand of the throne of God" (Heb. 12:2). Jesus Christ is the perfect model of standing firm that believers are to follow.

The phrase **my beloved brethren whom I long to see, my joy and crown . . . my beloved** expressed Paul's gracious, loving, pastoral heart. He was about to give the Philippians a strong exhortation, so he prefaced it by affirming his love and care for them. Paul's statement was not contrived, manipulative, dishonest flattery; it was the expression of his heart. **Beloved** is the adjectival form of the richest, deepest, and strongest Greek word for love.

Paul had a special and unique love for the Philippians. In 1:3–9 he declared,

> I thank my God in all my remembrance of you, always offering prayer with joy in my every prayer for you all, in view of your participation in the gospel from the first day until now. For I am confident of this very thing, that He who began a good work in you will perfect it until the day of Christ Jesus. For it is only right for me to feel this way about you all, because I have you in my heart, since both in my imprisonment and in the defense and confirmation of the gospel, you all are partakers of grace with me. For God is my witness, how I long for you all with the affection of Christ Jesus. And this I pray, that your love may abound still more and more in real knowledge and all discernment.

Paul's loving concern for the Philippians' firmness caused him to send his beloved coworkers Timothy and Epaphroditus to Philippi (2:19–30). The love bond between Paul and the Philippians was intensified by their faithful financial support of him (4:15).

Further expressing his love for them, Paul added the phrase **whom I long to see,** which translates another adjective. Thus, the entire phrase could be translated "my beloved and longed-for brethren" (NKJV).

Not only did Paul love the Philippians, but they also were his **joy** (cf. 1:4; 2:2, 17; 4:10). Paul's joy did not arise from circumstances; when he wrote Philippians he was under house arrest in Rome, chained to a Roman soldier (1:12–13; Acts 28:16, 20, 30). Further, some preachers, motivated by jealousy for Paul, were "proclaim[ing] Christ out of selfish ambition rather than from pure motives, thinking to cause [him] distress in [his] imprisonment" (Phil. 1:17). Instead, Paul found his joy in the people whom he loved. To the Thessalonians Paul wrote, "For who is our hope or joy or crown of exultation? Is it not even you, in the presence of our Lord Jesus at His coming? For you are our glory and joy" (1 Thess. 2:19–20). Later in that same epistle he added, "For what thanks can we render to God for you in return for all the joy with which we rejoice before our God on your account" (1 Thess. 3:9). The joy of seeing his beloved Philippians grow more like Jesus Christ motivated Paul's exhortation to stand firm.

The Philippians were also Paul's **crown.** *Stephanos* (**crown**) does not refer to a royal crown, but to the laurel wreath given to victors in athletic events (1 Cor. 9:25), or given to those honored by their peers, much as trophies and plaques are today. Such an honoree would be given a feast, where he would receive his wreath. The Philippians were Paul's trophy or wreath of honor; they were the proof of his effective service (cf. 1 Cor. 9:2; 1 Thess. 2:19).

The question naturally arises as to how Paul's command to stand firm is to be implemented. Paul's answer, introduced by the phrase **in this way,** unfolds in verses 2–9. He lists seven basic, practical principles that lead to spiritual stability: cultivating harmony in the church fellowship, maintaining a spirit of joy, learning to be content, resting on a confident faith in the Lord, reacting to problems with thankful prayer, thinking on godly virtues, and obeying God's standard.

CULTIVATING HARMONY IN THE CHURCH FELLOWSHIP

I urge Euodia and I urge Syntyche to live in harmony in the Lord. Indeed, true companion, I ask you also to help these women who have shared my struggle in the cause of the gospel, together with Clement also and the rest of my fellow workers, whose names are in the book of life. (4:2–3)

The fellowship and support of the body of Christ is an important factor in developing and maintaining spiritual stability. The general strength of the fellowship becomes the strength of each individual. The more isolated a believer is from other Christians, the more spiritually unstable he or she is likely to be. The church should be a place where people support each other, hold each other accountable, and care for each other. It should be a communion of life in which believers restore those who have fallen into sin (Gal. 6:1) and bear each other's burdens (v. 2). The church is to "admonish the unruly, encourage the fainthearted, help the weak, be patient with everyone" (1 Thess. 5:14).

But Paul knew that such edifying ministry could take place only in an atmosphere of harmony. Therefore any threats to the church's unity must be confronted. Paul dealt with a serious threat to the Philippian church's unity in verses 2 and 3. He identified the problem in specific terms, naming the two women who were involved, and exhorting a third person to help resolve the crisis.

Since conflict between influential people in a church will generate instability throughout the congregation, the two quarreling women at Philippi posed a danger to the entire church's stability. There was a real possibility that the Philippians would become critical, bitter, vengeful, hostile, unforgiving, and proud. Paul knew that unless decisive action was taken quickly, the Philippian church could dissolve into divisive, hostile factions. It was imperative that the Philippians be "diligent to preserve the unity of the Spirit in the bond of peace" (Eph. 4:3; cf. Col. 3:14).

The twice repeated phrase **I urge . . . I urge** shows Paul to be in a pleading, begging, encouraging mode as he addressed the issue of the divisive women. The apostle's mention of such a seemingly mundane matter after the lofty doctrinal material of chapter 2 and the warnings against dangerous false teachers in chapter 3 may seem surprising. But Paul understood that discord and divisiveness pose an equally crippling threat to the church. Even if its doctrine is sound, disunity robs a church of its power and destroys its testimony. And a church facing hostile external enemies cannot afford to have its members fighting among themselves. Such infighting frequently gives the enemies of the Cross an avenue of attack. The resulting discord, disunity, and conflict could have devastated the integrity of the Philippian church's testimony.

There are hints earlier in this epistle of Paul's concern for the Philippian church's unity. In 1:27 he urged them, "Only conduct yourselves in a manner worthy of the gospel of Christ, so that whether I come and see you or remain absent, I will hear of you that you are standing firm in one spirit, with one mind striving together for the faith of the gospel." He pled with them in 2:2 to "make my joy complete by being of the same mind, maintaining the same love, united in spirit, intent on one purpose." That Paul's joy was not complete implies that there was some discord in the Philippian congregation. A further hint of discord among the Philippians was the apostle's exhortation to "do all things without grumbling or disputing" (2:14).

What he had earlier hinted at, Paul now addressed directly. Little is known about **Euodia** and **Syntyche,** but several facts about the situation are evident. First, they were church members, not troublemakers from outside the congregation. Second, their dispute was evidently not over a doctrinal issue. If it had been, Paul would have resolved it by siding with the one who was correct and rebuking the one who was in error. Third, they were prominent women, well respected by the Philippian congregation. They may even have heard Paul preach on the banks of the Gangites River when he first came to Philippi (Acts 16:13). Already the dispute between these women was causing significant dissension in the Philippian fellowship.

Paul's solution to the quarrel was simple and direct: he commanded the two women involved **to live in harmony in the Lord.** There is a time when conflict is acceptable, namely when truth is at stake. Paul even confronted Peter when the latter was in error: "When Cephas [Peter] came to Antioch, I opposed him to his face, because he stood condemned" (Gal. 2:11). The apostle John also did not shrink from conflict for the sake of truth:

> I wrote something to the church; but Diotrephes, who loves to be first among them, does not accept what we say. For this reason, if I come, I will call attention to his deeds which he does, unjustly accusing us with wicked words; and not satisfied with this, he himself does not receive the brethren, either, and he forbids those who desire to do so and puts them out of the church. (3 John 9–10)

But mere personal conflicts must be resolved and harmony restored, so Paul commanded Euodia and Syntyche to **live in harmony.** The Greek text literally reads, "to be of the same mind"—an essential prerequisite if Christians are **to live in harmony.** To the quarreling, faction-ridden Corinthian church Paul wrote, "Now I exhort you, brethren, by the name of our Lord Jesus Christ, that you all agree and that there be no divisions among you, but that you be made complete in the same mind and in the same judgment" (1 Cor. 1:10). Peter also urged his readers, "All of you be harmonious, sympathetic, brotherly, kindhearted, and humble in spirit" (1 Peter 3:8). Agreement between Euodia and Syntyche was essential, and the sphere in which they had to find their harmony was **in the Lord.** Paul knew that if they both got right with the Lord, they would be right with each other.

Because of the seriousness of their disagreement, Paul realized that Euodia and Syntyche needed the church's help to resolve their animosity. The Greek particle translated **indeed** expresses strong affirmation

and could be translated "yes," or "certainly." Then Paul addressed someone whom the NASB 1995 identifies as **true companion.** *Suzugos* (**true
companion**) means "yokefellow," and refers to someone who shares a
common burden. The picture is one of two oxen pulling the same load.

Several possible explanations for the identity of this individual
have been offered. Some believe he was an individual Paul knew, but
chose not to name. But since in the immediate context Paul named Euodia, Syntyche, and Clement, why would he not have named this individual? The Philippians surely knew who he was, whether or not Paul
named him. Others argue that Paul used the singular term *suzugos* in a
collective sense to refer to the Philippian church as a whole.

The best explanation is to leave *suzugos* untranslated and take it
as a proper name. That Paul calls him **true** or genuine Suzugos is a play
on words, indicating that Suzugos was a genuine yokefellow and thus
lived up to his name. Paul made a similar play on words in Philemon
10–11, "I appeal to you for my child Onesimus, whom I have begotten in
my imprisonment, who formerly was useless to you, but now is useful
[Onesimus means "useful"] both to you and to me." Similarly Barnabas
lived up to his name, which means "Son of Encouragement" (Acts 4:36).
Suzugos was a genuine yokefellow, just as Onesimus was genuinely useful and Barnabas was a true son of encouragement.

Suzugos was probably one of the overseers (elders) mentioned
in 1:1. The elders obviously had not resolved the dispute between Euodia and Syntyche, since it was still going on. So Paul reminded Suzugos
of his duty by writing, **I ask you also to help these women.**

Paul also had a personal reason for wanting Euodia and Syntyche to be reconciled: they had **shared** his **struggle in the cause of the
gospel.** *Sunathleō* (**shared my struggle**) means "to fight alongside of"
or "labor together with." As noted above, Euodia and Syntyche may have
been two of the women who heard Paul preach when he first came to
Philippi (Acts 16:13). If so, they witnessed the turbulent events that
marked the founding of the Philippian church. After Lydia's conversion
(16:14), the apostle and his ministry team stayed with her at her home
(16:15). After being harassed for several days by a fortune-telling,
demon-possessed girl (16:16–17), Paul finally cast the demon out of her
(16:18). Her masters, infuriated by the loss of her moneymaking potential, hauled Paul and Silas before the authorities (16:19–21). As a result,
the two preachers were beaten and thrown into jail (16:22–24). But God
sent an earthquake and released them from prison, which led to the jailer's conversion (16:25–34). After discovering to their horror that they
had beaten and wrongfully imprisoned Roman citizens, the frightened
authorities begged Paul and Silas to leave Philippi (16:35–39). They did
so after a last visit to the believers gathered in Lydia's house (16:40).

The tragic conflict between Euodia and Syntyche reveals that even the most mature, faithful, and committed people can become so selfish as to be embroiled in controversy if they are not diligent to maintain unity.

There were others in the Philippian congregation whom the apostle wished to acknowledge. Nothing is known of **Clement,** so there is no way to identify him with the Clement who was bishop of Rome at the close of the first century, as some have. The name was a common one. To make sure he did not leave anyone out, Paul mentioned **the rest of** his **fellow workers.** It does not matter that their names are not in the book of Philippians; what matters is that their **names are in the book of life.** The **book of life** is the register where God keeps the names of the redeemed (Ex. 32:32; Ps. 69:28; Dan. 12:1; Mal. 3:16–17; Luke 10:20; Rev. 3:5; 13:8; 20:12, 15; 21:27). Their names were written there in eternity past (Matt. 25:34; Eph. 1:4; 2 Tim. 1:9).

Loving unity in the fellowship of believers creates an environment of stability. But discord leaves the church collectively and its members individually vulnerable and unstable. Spiritual stability requires peace and harmony in the church. Blessed indeed are the peacemakers (Matt. 5:9).

MAINTAINING A SPIRIT OF JOY

Rejoice in the Lord always; again I will say, rejoice! (4:4)

This verse expresses the theme of the book of Philippians, that believers are to **rejoice in the Lord always** (cf. 3:1). Joy is such a vitally important factor in believers' spiritual stability that Paul repeats his command for emphasis: **again I will say, rejoice!** This repetition presupposes the reality that it was not easy to be joyful. The Philippians needed to rise above their circumstances.

Some, wrongly identifying joy as a purely human emotion, find Paul's twice-repeated command to **rejoice** puzzling. How, they ask, can people be commanded to produce an emotion? But joy is not a feeling; it is the deep-down confidence that God is in control of everything for the believer's good and His own glory, and thus all is well no matter what the circumstances. *Chairete* (**rejoice**) is a present imperative, calling believers to the continual, habitual practice of rejoicing. Neither Paul's imprisonment nor the Philippians' trials should eclipse their joy.

It is true that believers often cannot find reason to **rejoice** in their specific circumstances. Certainly the general wickedness, sorrow, misery, and death in the world evoke no joy. Nor are people a reliable source of joy, since they can change, hurt, and disappoint. The only sure, reliable, unwavering, unchanging source of joy is God. That is why Paul commands believers to **rejoice in the Lord**. The phrase **in the Lord** introduces an important principle: Spiritual stability is directly related to how a person thinks about God. No one has stated that truth more clearly than A. W. Tozer. In his classic book on the attributes of God, *The Knowledge of the Holy,* Tozer wrote,

> What comes into our minds when we think about God is the most important thing about us.
> The history of mankind will probably show that no people has ever risen above its religion, and man's spiritual history will positively demonstrate that no religion has ever been greater than its idea of God. Worship is pure or base as the worshiper entertains high or low thoughts of God.
> For this reason the gravest question before the Church is always God Himself, and the most portentous fact about any man is not what he at a given time may say or do, but what he in his deep heart conceives God to be like. We tend by a secret law of the soul to move toward our mental image of God. This is true not only of the individual Christian, but of the company of Christians that composes the Church. Always the most revealing thing about the Church is her idea of God, just as her most significant message is what she says about Him or leaves unsaid, for her silence is often more eloquent than her speech. She can never escape the self-disclosure of her witness concerning God.
> Were we able to extract from any man a complete answer to the question, "What comes into your mind when you think about God?" we might predict with certainty the spiritual future of that man. (Reprint; New York: Harper & Row, 1975, 9)

Knowledge of God is the key to rejoicing. Those who know the great truths about God find it easy to rejoice; those with little knowledge of Him find it difficult to rejoice. God gave the Psalms to Israel in poetic form so they could be easily memorized and set to music. The first three verses of the book of Psalms promise blessings to those who meditate on Scripture:

> How blessed is the man who does not walk in the counsel of the wicked, nor stand in the path of sinners, nor sit in the seat of scoffers! But his delight is in the law of the Lord, and in His law he meditates day and night. He will be like a tree firmly planted by streams of water, which yields its fruit in its season and its leaf does not wither; and in whatever he does, he prospers. (Ps. 1:1–3)

It is from that knowledge of God and repeated recitation and singing of His nature and attributes that believers' joy flows. So deep was the apostles' knowledge of God's character and purposes that even suffering for Jesus Christ was a cause of joy: "So they went on their way from the presence of the Council, rejoicing that they had been considered worthy to suffer shame for His name" (Acts 5:41).

Moses' father-in-law Jethro "rejoiced over all the goodness which the Lord had done to Israel, in delivering them from the hand of the Egyptians" (Ex. 18:9; cf. Deut. 26:11). After the dedication of the temple, Solomon "sent the people to their tents, rejoicing and happy of heart because of the goodness that the Lord had shown to David and to Solomon and to His people Israel" (2 Chron. 7:10).

Believers rejoice in the contemplation of God's redemption. In 1 Samuel 2:1, "Hannah prayed and said, 'My heart exults in the Lord; my horn is exalted in the Lord, my mouth speaks boldly against my enemies, because I rejoice in Your salvation.'" In Psalm 13:5 David confidently asserted, "I have trusted in Your lovingkindness; my heart shall rejoice in Your salvation" (cf. Pss. 21:1; 35:9; 40:16; Isa. 61:10; Hab. 3:18). In Psalm 71:23 the psalmist exulted, "My lips will shout for joy when I sing praises to You; and my soul, which You have redeemed."

Another reason for believers to rejoice is that God has promised to supply all their needs. Paul reminded the Philippians, "God will supply all your needs according to His riches in glory in Christ Jesus" (Phil. 4:19). In the Old Testament counterpart to that promise, the psalmist wrote, "For the Lord God is a sun and shield; the Lord gives grace and glory; no good thing does He withhold from those who walk uprightly" (Ps. 84:11). In the Sermon on the Mount, the Lord Jesus Christ made God's promise to provide for believers' needs unmistakably clear:

> Why are you worried about clothing? Observe how the lilies of the field grow; they do not toil nor do they spin, yet I say to you that not even Solomon in all his glory clothed himself like one of these. But if God so clothes the grass of the field, which is alive today and tomorrow is thrown into the furnace, will He not much more clothe you? You of little faith! Do not worry then, saying, "What will we eat?" or "What will we drink?" or "What will we wear for clothing?" For the Gentiles eagerly seek all these things; for your heavenly Father knows that you need all these things. But seek first His kingdom and His righteousness, and all these things will be added to you. (Matt. 6:28–33)

Paul rejoiced because of the privilege of serving God. To Timothy he wrote, "I thank Christ Jesus our Lord, who has strengthened me, because He considered me faithful, putting me into service" (1 Tim. 1:12). He also rejoiced when God's truth was proclaimed (Phil. 1:18).

Paul's declaration to the Philippians earlier in this epistle, "For to me, to live is Christ and to die is gain" (1:21), reveals that even the prospect of death could not quench his joy. The confidence "that neither death, nor life, nor angels, nor principalities, nor things present, nor things to come, nor powers, nor height, nor depth, nor any other created thing, will be able to separate us from the love of God, which is in Christ Jesus our Lord" (Rom. 8:38–39) produces both deep-seated joy and spiritual stability.

LEARNING TO BE CONTENT

Let your gentle spirit be known to all men. (4:5a)

Epieikēs (**gentle spirit**) has a richer meaning than any single English word can convey. Hence, commentators and Bible versions vary widely in how they render it. Sweet reasonableness, generosity, goodwill, friendliness, magnanimity, charity toward the faults of others, mercy toward the failures of others, indulgence of the failures of others, leniency, bigheartedness, moderation, forbearance, and gentleness are some of the attempts to capture the rich meaning of *epieikēs*. Perhaps the best corresponding English word is *graciousness*—the graciousness of humility; the humble graciousness that produces the patience to endure injustice, disgrace, and mistreatment without retaliation, bitterness, or vengeance. It is contentment.

Gracious humility runs counter to the cult of self-love that was rampant in ancient society, and is rampant in modern society as well. But focusing on self-love, self-esteem, and self-fulfillment leads only to greater and greater instability and anxiety. On the other hand, those whose focus is not on themselves cannot be knocked off balance by inequity, injustice, unfair treatment, lies, or humiliation. They can say with Paul, "I have learned to be content in whatever circumstances I am" (4:11). Spiritual stability belongs to the graciously humble.

RESTING ON A CONFIDENT FAITH IN THE LORD

The Lord is near. Be anxious for nothing, (4:5b–6a)

There is no greater source of spiritual stability than the confidence that **the Lord is near.** *Engus* (**near**) can mean near in space or near in time. Some take *engus* in a chronological sense, either as a reference to Christ's return (3:20–21; James 5:8), or to believers' death, which ushers them into the Lord's presence (1:23; 2 Cor. 5:8). While those are comforting truths, it seems that Paul's emphasis here is on the Lord's nearness in the sense of His presence. He is near both to hear the cry of the believer's heart, and to help and strengthen them. In Psalm 73:28 the psalmist declared, "The nearness of God is my good" (cf. Pss. 34:18; 75:1; 119:151; 145:18). Because of God's nearness, believers should not be fearful, anxious, or wavering. They should not collapse, but be strong and stable (Josh. 1:6–9; Pss. 27:14; 125:1).

Unfortunately, when they face trials, believers often seem to forget what they know about God. They lose their confident trust in Him, lose their self-control and spiritual stability, and are defeated. Even strong believers are not immune to an occasional lapse, as an incident from the life of David reveals. Seeking refuge from Saul's relentless pursuit, David sought asylum in the Philistine city of Gath. Some of the Philistines recognized him and said to Achish, the king of Gath, "Is this not David the king of the land? Did they not sing of this one as they danced, saying, 'Saul has slain his thousands, and David his ten thousands'?" (1 Sam. 21:11). Realizing that his true identity had become known, "David . . . greatly feared Achish king of Gath" (v. 12). Instead of trusting God to deliver him, David panicked and "disguised his sanity before [the Philistines], and acted insanely in their hands, and scribbled on the doors of the gate, and let his saliva run down into his beard" (v. 13). His act produced the desired results: "Then Achish said to his servants, 'Behold, you see the man behaving as a madman. Why do you bring him to me? Do I lack madmen, that you have brought this one to act the madman in my presence? Shall this one come into my house?'" (vv. 14–15). As a result, "David departed from there and escaped to the cave of Adullam" (1 Sam. 22:1). There, with the crisis past, David had time to reflect on how he should have handled the situation in Gath. In Psalm 57, written at that time, he reaffirmed the truths about God that he had temporarily forgotten:

> Be gracious to me, O God, be gracious to me, for my soul takes refuge in You; and in the shadow of Your wings I will take refuge until destruction passes by. I will cry to God Most High, to God who accomplishes all things for me. He will send from heaven and save me; He reproaches him who tramples upon me. Selah. God will send forth His lovingkindness and His truth. (Ps. 57:1–3)

Remembering the character of God restored David's spiritual stability and his joy, enabling him to declare, "My heart is steadfast, O God, my heart is steadfast; I will sing, yes, I will sing praises!" (Ps. 57:7).

Like David, the prophet Habakkuk faced a crisis. But unlike David, he maintained his spiritual stability. In Habakkuk 1:2–4 the prophet cried out to God about His apparent indifference to Judah's apostasy:

> How long, O Lord, will I call for help, and You will not hear? I cry out to You, "Violence!" Yet You do not save. Why do You make me see iniquity, and cause me to look on wickedness? Yes, destruction and violence are before me; strife exists and contention arises. Therefore the law is ignored and justice is never upheld. For the wicked surround the righteous; therefore justice comes out perverted.

To Habakkuk's dismay, God answered that things were going to get even worse:

> Look among the nations! Observe! Be astonished! Wonder! Because I am doing something in your days—you would not believe if you were told. For behold, I am raising up the Chaldeans, that fierce and impetuous people who march throughout the earth to seize dwelling places which are not theirs. They are dreaded and feared; their justice and authority originate with themselves. Their horses are swifter than leopards and keener than wolves in the evening. Their horsemen come galloping, their horsemen come from afar; they fly like an eagle swooping down to devour. All of them come for violence. Their horde of faces moves forward. They collect captives like sand. They mock at kings and rulers are a laughing matter to them. They laugh at every fortress and heap up rubble to capture it. Then they will sweep through like the wind and pass on. But they will be held guilty, they whose strength is their god. (Hab. 1:5–11)

Instead of answering Habakkuk's original question, God's reply raised a second even more vexing question: How could He use a godless, pagan nation to chasten His people?

Faced with Judah's apostasy, the impending Chaldean invasion, and his own unanswered questions, Habakkuk reminded himself of what he knew to be true about God: "Are You not from everlasting, O Lord, my God, my Holy One? We will not die. You, O Lord, have appointed them to judge; and You, O Rock, have established them to correct. Your eyes are too pure to approve evil, and You can not look on wickedness with favor" (Hab. 1:12–13). Habakkuk reminded himself of God's eternity, faithfulness, justice, sovereignty, and holiness.

Despite the trials, doubts, and questions he faced, Habakkuk's faith and trust in God stood firm. He affirmed the importance of living a life of faith in Habakkuk 2:4: "The righteous will live by his faith." Both initially in justification, and continually in sanctification, the Christian life is a life of faith in God. As he reminded himself of the greatness of his God,

Habakkuk's faith grew stronger. By the end of his prophecy he was able to sing triumphantly of God's glorious nature and power,

> Though the fig tree should not blossom and there be no fruit on the vines, though the yield of the olive should fail and the fields produce no food, though the flock should be cut off from the fold and there be no cattle in the stalls, yet I will exult in the Lord, I will rejoice in the God of my salvation. The Lord God is my strength, and He has made my feet like hinds' feet, and makes me walk on my high places. (Hab. 3:17–19)

Habakkuk's faith in God made him a spiritually stable man—so much so that even if the normal, dependable things in life suddenly collapsed, he would still rejoice in God.

The **Lord** who is **near** is the almighty, true, and living God revealed in Scripture. Those who delight themselves in His holy power, love, and wisdom and cultivate a deep knowledge of Him by studying and meditating on His Word will live by the foundation of that truth and be spiritually stable. Because of the presence of God, believers are to **be anxious for nothing.** Nothing is outside of His sovereign control or too difficult for Him to handle. A low view of God leads to a myriad of problems in the church:

> The Church has surrendered her once lofty concept of God and has substituted for it one so low, so ignoble, as to be utterly unworthy of thinking, worshiping men. This she has done not deliberately, but little by little and without her knowledge; and her very unawareness only makes her situation all the more tragic.
>
> The low view of God entertained almost universally among Christians is the cause of a hundred lesser evils everywhere among us. A whole new philosophy of the Christian life has resulted from this one basic error in our religious thinking. (Tozer, *The Knowledge of the Holy,* 6)

Weak, struggling, unstable Christians need to build their strength on the foundation of what the Bible says about God. The result of the church's failure to equip believers with the knowledge of God's character and works is a lack of understanding of His nature and purposes, and a subsequent lack of confidence in Him. The shifting sands of shallow or faulty theology provide no stable footing for the believer.

Anxious, fretful, worried, harried believers are inherently unstable and vulnerable to trials and temptations. Anxiety is both a violation of Scripture and totally unnecessary. In a magnificent passage in the Sermon on the Mount, Jesus pointed out the sinful folly of anxiety:

For this reason I say to you, do not be worried about your life, as to what you will eat or what you will drink; nor for your body, as to what you will put on. Is not life more than food, and the body more than clothing? Look at the birds of the air, that they do not sow, nor reap nor gather into barns, and yet your heavenly Father feeds them. Are you not worth much more than they? And who of you by being worried can add a single hour to his life? And why are you worried about clothing? Observe how the lilies of the field grow; they do not toil nor do they spin, yet I say to you that not even Solomon in all his glory clothed himself like one of these. But if God so clothes the grass of the field, which is alive today and tomorrow is thrown into the furnace, will He not much more clothe you? You of little faith! Do not worry then, saying, "What will we eat?" or "What will we drink?" or "What will we wear for clothing?" For the Gentiles eagerly seek all these things; for your heavenly Father knows that you need all these things. But seek first His kingdom and His righteousness, and all these things will be added to you. So do not worry about tomorrow; for tomorrow will care for itself. Each day has enough trouble of its own. (Matt. 6:25–34)

Harmony in the fellowship, joy in the Lord, contentment in circumstances, and confident trust in God are the first steps on the path to spiritual stability.

Spiritual Stability— Part 2: Gratitude, Godly Thinking, Obedience (Philippians 4:6b–9)

19

but in everything by prayer and supplication with thanksgiving let your requests be made known to God. And the peace of God, which surpasses all comprehension, will guard your hearts and your minds in Christ Jesus. Finally, brethren, whatever is true, whatever is honorable, whatever is right, whatever is pure, whatever is lovely, whatever is of good repute, if there is any excellence and if anything worthy of praise, dwell on these things. The things you have learned and received and heard and seen in me, practice these things, and the God of peace will be with you. (4:6b–9)

Our society admires people who stand firm, hold to their convictions, are courageous and bold, and cannot be bought, intimidated, or defeated. Rudyard Kipling described such people in his famous poem "If," a tribute to the noblest humanism:

> If you can keep your head when all about you
>   Are losing theirs and blaming it on you;
> If you can trust yourself when all men doubt you,
>   But make allowance for their doubting too;
> If you can wait and not be tired by waiting,

Or, being lied about, don't deal in lies,
Or, being hated, don't give way to hating,
And yet don't look too good, nor talk too wise;

If you can dream—and not make dreams your master;
If you can think—and not make thoughts your aim;
If you can meet with triumph and disaster
And treat those two imposters just the same;
If you can bear to hear the truth you've spoken
Twisted by knaves to make a trap for fools,
Or watch the things you gave your life to broken,
And stoop and build 'em up with worn-out tools;

If you can make one heap of all your winnings
And risk it on one turn of pitch-and-toss,
And lose, and start again at your beginnings
And never breathe a word about your loss;
If you can force your heart and nerve and sinew
To serve your turn long after they are gone,
And so hold on when there is nothing in you
Except the Will which says to them:"Hold on!"

If you can talk with crowds and keep your virtue,
Or walk with kings—nor lose the common touch;
If neither foes nor loving friends can hurt you;
If all men count with you, but none too much;
If you can fill the unforgiving minute
With sixty seconds' worth of distance run—
Yours is the Earth and everything that's in it,
And—which is more—you'll be a Man, my son!

If courage of conviction, integrity, credibility, and an uncompromising devotion to virtue are admirable qualities for people of the world, how much more essential are they for Christians? The very name "Christian" identifies believers with Jesus Christ—the most perfect model of uncompromising, courageous integrity who ever lived. The New Testament repeatedly commands believers to follow Him by standing firm in submission to God (cf. 1:27; 1 Cor. 16:13; 2 Cor. 1:24; Gal. 5:1; Eph. 6:11, 13, 14; 1 Thess. 3:8; 2 Thess. 2:15; Heb. 3:6, 14; 1 Peter 5:9, 12).

Paul was concerned that his beloved Philippian congregation be unwavering in the faith. From 4:2–9 seven basic principles for developing and maintaining spiritual stability emerge. The previous chapter in this volume considered the first four: cultivating harmony in the church fellowship, maintaining a spirit of joy, learning to be content, and resting on a confident faith in the Lord. This chapter will consider the last three:

reacting to problems with thankful prayer, thinking on godly virtues, and obeying God's standard.

REACTING TO PROBLEMS WITH THANKFUL PRAYER

but in everything by prayer and supplication with thanksgiving let your requests be made known to God. And the peace of God, which surpasses all comprehension, will guard your hearts and your minds in Christ Jesus. (4:6*b–7*)

Spiritually stable people react to trials with thankful prayer. Such prayer is the antidote to worry and the cure for anxiety. The theology of prayer is not in view here, but rather its priority and the attitude the believer brings to it. The three synonyms used here, **prayer, supplication,** and **requests,** all refer to specific, direct offerings of petition to God. The assumption of the text is that believers will cry out to God when they have a need or a problem, not with doubting, questioning, or even blaming God, but **with thanksgiving** (cf. Col. 4:2). Instead of having a spirit of rebellion against what God allows, believers are to trustingly cast "all [their] anxiety on Him, because He cares for [them]" (1 Peter 5:7).

God's promises support the wisdom of gratitude. He has promised that no trial believers face will be too difficult for them to handle (1 Cor. 10:13). He has also promised to use everything that happens in believers' lives for their ultimate good (Rom. 8:28). Even suffering leads to their being perfected, confirmed, strengthened, and established (1 Peter 5:10). Believers should also be thankful for God's power (Ps. 62:11; 1 Peter 1:5; Rev. 4:11), for His promises (Deut. 1:11; 2 Cor. 1:20), for the hope of relief from suffering (2 Cor. 4:17; 1 Peter 5:10), for the hope of glory (Rom. 5:2; Col. 1:27), for His mercy (Rom. 15:9), and for His perfecting work in them (Phil. 1:6).

People become worried, anxious, and fearful because they do not trust in God's wisdom, power, or goodness. They fear that God is not wise enough, strong enough, or good enough to prevent disaster. It may be that this sinful doubt is because their knowledge of Him is faulty, or that sin in their lives has crippled their faith. Thankful prayer brings release from fear and worry, because it affirms God's sovereign control over every circumstance, and that His purpose is the believer's good (Rom. 8:28).

Once the sinner has made "peace with God" (Rom. 5:1), that is, in salvation having ceased to be God's enemy and become His child, he can enjoy the **peace of God,** the inward tranquility of soul granted by God. It is a confident trust in His flawless wisdom and infinite power that provides calm amid the storms of life. Isaiah wrote of this supernatural peace:"The steadfast of mind You will keep in perfect peace, because he trusts in You" (Isa. 26:3). Paul prayed for the Romans that "the God of hope [would] fill [them] with all joy and peace in believing" (Rom. 15:13). In his high priestly blessing on Israel Aaron said,"The Lord lift up His countenance on you, and give you peace" (Num. 6:26). In Psalm 29:11 David wrote,"The Lord will bless His people with peace." Shortly before His death Jesus promised,"Peace I leave with you; My peace I give to you; not as the world gives do I give to you. Do not let your heart be troubled, nor let it be fearful" (John 14:27). God's peace is not for everyone, however; "'There is no peace for the wicked,' says the Lord" (Isa. 48:22), neither *with* God, nor *from* God.

Paul further defines this supernatural peace as that **which surpasses all comprehension.** It transcends human intellectual powers, human analysis, human insights, and human understanding. It is superior to human scheming, human devices, and human solutions, since its source is the God whose judgments are unsearchable and whose ways are unfathomable (Rom. 11:33). It is experienced in a transcendent calm that lifts the believer above the most debilitating trial. Since it is a supernatural work, it resists any human **comprehension.** The real challenge of the Christian life is not to eliminate every unpleasant circumstance; it is to trust in the good purpose of our infinite, holy, sovereign, powerful God in every difficulty. Those who honor Him by trusting Him will experience the blessings of His perfect peace.

When realized in believers' lives, God's peace **will guard** them from anxiety, doubt, and worry. *Phroureō* (**will guard**) is a military term used of soldiers on guard duty. The picture would have been familiar to the Philippians, since the Romans stationed troops in Philippi to protect their interests in that part of the world. Just as soldiers guard and protect a city, so God's peace guards and protects believers who confidently trust in Him. Paul's use of the phrase **hearts** and **minds** was not intended to imply a distinction between the two; he was merely making a comprehensive reference to the believer's inner person. Once again, Paul reminds his readers that true peace is not available through any human source, but only **in Christ Jesus.**

THINKING ON GODLY VIRTUES

Finally, brethren, whatever is true, whatever is honorable, whatever is right, whatever is pure, whatever is lovely, whatever is of good repute, if there is any excellence and if anything worthy of praise, dwell on these things. (4:8)

The word **finally** indicates that Paul has arrived at the climax of his teaching on spiritual stability. The principle that he is about to relate is both the summation of all the others and the key to implementing them. The phrase **dwell on these things** introduces an important truth: spiritual stability is a result of how a person thinks. The imperative form of *logizomai* (**dwell on**) makes it a command; proper thinking is not optional in the Christian life. *Logizomai* means more than just entertaining thoughts; it means "to evaluate," "to consider," or "to calculate." Believers are to consider the qualities Paul lists in this verse and meditate on their implications. The verb form calls for habitual discipline of the mind to set all thoughts on these spiritual virtues.

The Bible leaves no doubt that people's lives are the product of their thoughts. Proverbs 23:7 declares, "For as he thinks within himself, so he is." The modern counterpart to that proverb is the computer acronym GIGO (Garbage In, Garbage Out). Just as a computer's output is dependent on the information that is input, so people's actions are the result of their thinking. Jesus expressed that truth in Mark 7:20–23: "That which proceeds out of the man, that is what defiles the man. For from within, out of the heart of men, proceed the evil thoughts, fornications, thefts, murders, adulteries, deeds of coveting and wickedness, as well as deceit, sensuality, envy, slander, pride and foolishness. All these evil things proceed from within and defile the man."

Paul's call for biblical thinking is especially relevant in our culture. The focus today is on emotion and pragmatism, and the importance of serious thinking about biblical truth is downplayed. People no longer ask "Is it true?" but "Does it work?" and "How will it make me feel?" Those latter two questions serve as a working definition of truth in our society that rejects the concept of absolute divine truth. Truth is whatever works and produces positive emotions. Sadly, such pragmatism and emotionalism has crept even into theology. The church is often more concerned about whether something will be divisive or offensive than whether it is biblically true.

Such a perspective is far different from the noble Bereans, who searched the Scriptures to see if what Paul said was true, not whether it was divisive or practical (Acts 17:11). Too many people go to church not to think or reason about the truths of Scripture, but to get their weekly spiritual high; to feel that God is still with them. Such people are spiritually unstable because they base their lives on feeling rather than on thinking. Bill Hull writes,

> What scares me is the anti-intellectual, anti-critical-thinking philosophy that has spilled over into the Church. This philosophy tends to romanticize the faith, making the local church into an experience center. . . .
> Their concept of "church" is that they are spiritual consumers and that

the church's job is to meet their felt needs. (*Right Thinking* [Colorado Springs, Colo: NavPress, 1985], 66)

John Stott also warned of the danger of Christians living by their feelings: "Indeed, sin has more dangerous effects on our faculty of feeling than on our faculty of thinking, because our opinions are more easily checked and regulated by revealed truth than our experiences" (*Your Mind Matters* [Downers Grove, Ill: InterVarsity, 1972], 16).

God commands people to think. He said to rebellious Israel, "Come now, and let us reason together" (Isa. 1:18). Jesus chided the unbelieving Pharisees and Sadducees for demanding a miraculous sign from Him. Instead, He challenged them to think and draw inferences from the evidence they had, just as they did to predict the weather (Matt. 16:1–3). In Luke 12:57 He said to the crowds, "And why do you not even on your own initiative judge what is right?" God gave His revelation in a book, the Bible, and expects people to use their minds to understand its truths.

Careful thinking is the distinctive mark of the Christian faith. James Orr expressed that reality clearly:

> If there is a religion in the world which exalts the office of teaching, it is safe to say that it is the religion of Jesus Christ. It has been frequently remarked that in pagan religions the doctrinal element is at a minimum—the chief thing there is the performance of a ritual. But this is precisely where Christianity distinguishes itself from other religions—it does contain doctrine. It comes to men with definite, positive teaching; it claims to be the truth; it bases religion on knowledge, though a knowledge which is only attainable under moral conditions. I do not see how any one can deal fairly with the facts as they lie before us in the Gospels and Epistles, without coming to the conclusion that the New Testament is full of doctrine. . . . A religion divorced from earnest and lofty thought has always, down the whole history of the Church, tended to become weak, jejune, and unwholesome; while the intellect, deprived of its rights within religion, has sought its satisfaction without, and developed into godless rationalism. (*The Christian View of God and the World* [New York: Scribner, 1897], 20–21)

Scripture describes the unsaved mind as depraved (Rom. 1:28; 1 Tim. 6:5; 2 Tim. 3:8), focused on the flesh (Rom. 8:5), which leads to spiritual death (Rom. 8:6), hostile to God (Rom. 8:7; Col. 1:21), foolish (1 Cor. 2:14), hardened to spiritual truth (2 Cor. 3:14), blinded by Satan (2 Cor. 4:4), futile (Eph. 4:17), ignorant (Eph. 4:18), and defiled (Titus 1:15).

Because of that, the first element in salvation is a proper mental understanding of the truth of the gospel. Jesus said in Matthew 13:19,

"When anyone hears the word of the kingdom and does not understand it, the evil one comes and snatches away what has been sown in his heart." Romans 10:17 could be translated, "Faith comes from hearing a speech about Christ," emphasizing again that faith involves thinking (cf. Isa. 1:18). That is why Peter commands believers to always be "ready to make a defense to everyone who asks you to give an account for the hope that is in you" (1 Peter 3:15). J. Gresham Machen observed, "What the Holy Spirit does in the new birth is not to make a man a Christian regardless of the evidence, but on the contrary to clear away the mists from his eyes and enable him to attend to the evidence" (*The Christian Faith in the Modern World* [Grand Rapids: Eerdmans, 1965], 63).

God saves people to be worshipers, and "those who worship Him must worship in spirit and truth" (John 4:24). It is therefore impossible to worship God apart from truth. When Paul visited Athens, the cultural capital of the ancient world, "his spirit was being provoked within him as he was observing the city full of idols" (Acts 17:16). But what disturbed him as much as the blatant idolatry was that he "found an altar with this inscription, 'TO AN UNKNOWN GOD'" (Acts 17:23). Natural minds can see the world and conclude that there is a God. But by human reason it can only be known that He exists, not who He is. To the natural reason He is the "unknown" and the unknowable God. He can only be truly known by supernatural theology, the revelation of Scripture. God will not accept worship based on ignorance. Paul therefore proceeded to explain to the Athenian philosophers who God has revealed Himself to be (Acts 17:24–31).

In sharp contrast to the contemporary definition of faith, biblical faith is not an irrational "leap in the dark." It is not a mystical encounter with the "wholly other" or the "ground of being." Nor is it optimism, psychological self-hypnosis, or wishful thinking. True faith is a reasoned response to revealed truth in the Bible, and salvation results from an intelligent response, prompted by the Holy Spirit, to that truth.

In Matthew 6:25–34, Jesus rebuked the disciples for the sin of worry. In a remarkable section of his classic work *Studies in the Sermon on the Mount,* D. Martyn Lloyd-Jones points out that the disciples' problem was that they failed to think. Instead, they allowed themselves to be controlled by their circumstances.

> Faith, according to our Lord's teaching in this paragraph, is primarily thinking; and the whole trouble with a man of little faith is that he does not think. He allows circumstances to bludgeon him. That is the real difficulty in life. Life comes to us with a club in its hand and strikes us upon the head, and we become incapable of thought, helpless and defeated. The way to avoid that, according to our Lord, is to think. We must spend more time in studying our Lord's lessons in observation

and deduction. The Bible is full of logic, and we must never think of faith as something purely mystical. We do not just sit down in an armchair and expect marvelous things to happen to us. That is not Christian faith. Christian faith is essentially thinking. Look at the birds, think about them, and draw your deductions. Look at the grass, look at the lilies of the field, consider them.

The trouble with most people, however, is that they will not think. Instead of doing this, they sit down and ask, What is going to happen to me? What can I do? That is the absence of thought; it is surrender, it is defeat. Our Lord, here, is urging us to think, and to think in a Christian manner. That is the very essence of faith. Faith, if you like, can be defined like this: It is a man insisting upon thinking when everything seems determined to bludgeon and knock him down in an intellectual sense. The trouble with the person of little faith is that, instead of controlling his own thought, his thought is being controlled by something else, and, as we put it, he goes round and round in circles. That is the essence of worry.... That is not thought; that is the absence of thought, a failure to think. (Grand Rapids: Eerdmans, 1971, 2:129–30)

Thinking is essential to saving faith, as well as to sanctifying faith.

Salvation involves the transformation of the mind. In Romans 8:5 Paul writes, "Those who are according to the flesh set their minds on the things of the flesh." Unsaved, fleshly people have an unsaved, fleshly mind-set. They think as fallen, unredeemed people. On the other hand, "those who are according to the Spirit [set their minds on] the things of the Spirit." Their renewed minds are focused on spiritual truth. Consequently, "the mind set on the flesh is death, but the mind set on the Spirit is life and peace" (Rom. 8:6). The Holy Spirit now controls the mind that before salvation was depraved, ignorant, and blinded by Satan (2 Cor. 4:4). The redeemed mind no longer thinks on the fleshly level, but on the spiritual level.

In 1 Corinthians 1:30 Paul described one of the most amazing realities of salvation: "Christ Jesus . . . became to us wisdom from God." Believers' renewed minds can plunge into the deep thoughts of the eternal God (cf. Ps. 92:5) and never reach the bottom. In 1 Corinthians 2:11–16 Paul expanded on that thought:

For who among men knows the thoughts of a man except the spirit of the man which is in him? Even so the thoughts of God no one knows except the Spirit of God. Now we have received, not the spirit of the world, but the Spirit who is from God, so that we may know the things freely given to us by God, which things we also speak, not in words taught by human wisdom, but in those taught by the Spirit, combining spiritual thoughts with spiritual words. But a natural man does not accept the things of the Spirit of God, for they are foolishness to him;

and he cannot understand them, because they are spiritually appraised. But he who is spiritual appraises all things, yet he himself is appraised by no one. For who has known the mind of the Lord, that he will instruct Him? But we have the mind of Christ.

In contrast to the "natural man [who] does not accept the things of the Spirit of God," the Holy Spirit grants to believers the ability to "know the things freely given to us by God." In fact, "we have the mind of Christ"; through the Spirit, believers have knowledge of God that they would otherwise never have had.

Just as the believers' initial act of saving faith leads to a life of faith, so also the transforming of the mind at salvation initiates a lifelong process of renewing the mind. In Romans 12:2 Paul wrote, "Do not be conformed to this world, but be transformed by the renewing of your mind."To the Ephesians he wrote, "Be renewed in the spirit of your mind" (Eph. 4:23). Jesus, answering the question as to which was the greatest commandment of the Law, said, "You shall love the Lord your God with all your heart, and with all your soul, and with all your mind" (Matt. 22:37). Peter also spoke of renewing the mind when he commanded, "Prepare your minds for action" (1 Peter 1:13). Paul called for believers to "set [their] mind[s] on the things above, not on the things that are on earth" (Col. 3:2). More than a dozen times in his epistles Paul asked his readers, "Do you not know?" The apostle expected believers to think and evaluate. Nor is that an exclusively New Testament perspective. In Proverbs 2:1–6 Solomon counseled,

> My son, if you will receive my words and treasure my commandments within you, make your ear attentive to wisdom, incline your heart to understanding; for if you cry for discernment, lift your voice for understanding; if you seek her as silver and search for her as for hidden treasures; then you will discern the fear of the Lord and discover the knowledge of God. For the Lord gives wisdom; from His mouth come knowledge and understanding.

The psalmist cried out, "Give me understanding, that I may observe Your law and keep it with all my heart" (Ps. 119:34).

Believers must discipline their spiritually sensitive minds to think about right spiritual realities. In this brief list, Paul catalogues eight godly virtues to concentrate on.

The Word of God is the repository of what is **true.** In His High Priestly Prayer Jesus said to the Father, "Your word is truth" (John 17:17). In Psalm 19:9 David wrote, "The judgments of the Lord are true," while Psalm 119:151 adds, "All Your commandments are truth." The Bible is true because the "God of truth" (Ps. 31:5; Isa. 65:16; cf. Eph. 4:21) inspired it. Thinking on **whatever is true** means reading, analyzing, and meditating on the Word of God. The remaining seven virtuous categories of thought are all based on the truth of God's Word. All of them are ways to view the truths of Scripture.

Second, believers are to think on **whatever is honorable,** whatever is noble, dignified, and worthy of respect. *Semnos* (**honorable**) comes from a word meaning "to revere," or "to worship." In its other New Testament uses, it describes the dignified lifestyle required of deacons (1 Tim. 3:8), deaconesses (1 Tim. 3:11), and older men (Titus 2:2). Believers must not think on what is trivial, temporal, mundane, common, and earthly, but rather on what is heavenly, and so worthy of awe, adoration, and praise. All that is true in God's Word is **honorable.**

Third, believers are to think on **whatever is right.** *Dikaios* (**right**) is an adjective, and should be translated "righteous." It describes whatever is in perfect harmony with God's eternal, unchanging standards, again as revealed in Scripture. Believers are to think on matters that are consistent with the law of God.

Fourth, believers are to think on **whatever is pure.** *Hagnos* (**pure**) describes what God in Scripture defines as holy, morally clean, and undefiled. In 1 Timothy 5:22 it is translated "free from sin." Believers are to purify themselves because Jesus Christ is pure (1 John 3:3).

Fifth, believers are to think on **whatever is lovely.** *Prosphilēs* (**lovely**) appears only here in the New Testament. It could be translated "sweet," "gracious," "generous," or "patient." Believers must focus their thoughts on what the Bible says is pleasing, attractive, and amiable before God.

Sixth, believers are to think on **whatever is of good repute.** *Euphēmos* also appears only here in the New Testament. It describes what is highly regarded or well thought of. Believers' thoughts are elevated by Scripture to fix on the loftiest themes.

In summary, Paul exhorts, **if there is any excellence and if anything worthy of praise, dwell on these things.** The key to godly living is godly thinking, as Solomon wisely observed: "Watch over your heart with all diligence, for from it flow the springs of life" (Prov. 4:23).

OBEYING GOD'S STANDARD

The things you have learned and received and heard and seen in me, practice these things, and the God of peace will be with you. (4:9)

This verse introduces a final element that is essential for spiritual stability. The preceding seven attitudes must not be viewed as mere abstract principles; godly thinking cannot be divorced from behavior. When all is said and done, spiritual stability comes down to living a disciplined life of obedience to God's standards. People in whom the Word of God richly dwells (Col. 3:16), and who therefore live obediently, stand firm when the winds of difficulty, temptation, and compromise blow around them.

Prassō (**practice**) refers to repetition or continuous action. The English word can have the same connotation. We speak of a lawyer or a doctor as having a practice, because their profession maintains a normal routine. Christians are to make it their practice to lead godly, obedient lives.

Holy living can take place only when right attitudes and right thoughts police the flesh. That is why Paul confronted the priority of thoughts (4:2–8) before exhorting the church to righteous behavior (4:9). Understanding and embracing God's law comes first, followed by the conduct habitually controlled by that devotion to the truth. By so doing, we "overcome evil with good" (Rom. 12:21).

Before the completion of the New Testament Scriptures, the apostles themselves were the source of divine truth. After the church's birth on the Day of Pentecost, the believers "were continually devoting themselves to the apostles' teaching" (Acts 2:42). In Ephesians 4:11–13 Paul wrote of the foundational nature of the apostles' ministry:

> He gave some as apostles, and some as prophets, and some as evangelists, and some as pastors and teachers, for the equipping of the saints for the work of service, to the building up of the body of Christ; until we all attain to the unity of the faith, and of the knowledge of the Son of God, to a mature man, to the measure of the stature which belongs to the fullness of Christ.

The apostles were more than the source of doctrinal knowledge; they also modeled the standards of Christian behavior. For that reason Paul exhorted the Philippians earlier in this letter, "Brethren, join in following my example, and observe those who walk according to the pattern you have in us" (3:17; cf. 1 Cor. 4:16; 11:1; 1 Thess. 1:6; 1 Peter 5:3). Paul repeats that exhortation here, urging the Philippians to put into practice **the things** they had **learned and received and heard and seen in** him. His life exemplified the spiritual duties to which he called them. The terms **learned, received, heard, and seen** each focus on an important aspect of Paul's ministry to the Philippians.

Learned translates a form of the verb *manthanō*, which is related to the noun *mathētēs* (disciple). *Manthanō* refers to teaching, learning, instructing, and discipling. Paul is referring here to his personal instruction and discipling of the Philippians. His practice wherever he ministered was not only to teach "publicly," but also "from house to house" (Acts 20:20). Paul wrote to his son in the faith, Timothy, "You followed my teaching, conduct, purpose, faith, patience, love, perseverance" (2 Tim. 3:10). Before the completion of the New Testament, such teaching was vital.

Paralambanō (**received**) is sometimes used in the New Testament as a technical term for God's revelation (e.g., 1 Cor. 11:23; 15:1, 3; Gal. 1:9, 12; 1 Thess. 4:1–2; 1 Tim. 6:20). To the Thessalonians Paul wrote, "For this reason we also constantly thank God that when you received the word of God which you heard from us, you accepted it not as the word of men, but for what it really is, the word of God, which also performs its work in you who believe" (1 Thess. 2:13). Paul called upon the Philippians to practice in their lives the truths of God's Word that he had delivered to them. They were not only to receive those truths, but also to pass them on. As Paul wrote to Timothy, "The things which you have heard from me in the presence of many witnesses, entrust these to faithful men who will be able to teach others also" (2 Tim. 2:2).

The word **heard** adds another dimension to Paul's discussion. He has already covered what he taught the Philippians as God revealed it to him. Here Paul alluded to what the Philippians had heard about him from other people. His reputation was impeccable, and they had certainly heard from others about Paul's character, lifestyle, and preaching. They were also to imitate the godly virtue that the apostle had become known for.

By reminding the Philippians of what they had **seen** in him, Paul appealed to their firsthand experience with him. They had observed his character during the apostle's stay in Philippi, and they knew there was no credibility gap between the message he preached and the life he lived. Because he modeled the standards he preached, Paul could exhort the Philippians to pattern their lives after his.

The promise attached to such obedience is that **the God of peace will be with you.** The God whose character is peace is the giver of peace. The title **God of peace** is one of Paul's favorites (cf. Rom. 15:33; 16:20; 2 Cor. 13:11; 1 Thess. 5:23). It is a reminder that those who have godly attitudes, thoughts, and deeds will be guarded both by the peace of God and by the **God of peace.** His presence is essential for the strength, tranquility, and contentment necessary for spiritual stability.

But that will not happen apart from self-discipline. D. Martyn Lloyd-Jones wrote,

> I defy you to read the life of any saint that has ever adorned the life of the Church without seeing at once that the greatest characteristic in the life of that saint was discipline and order. Invariably it is the universal

characteristic of all the outstanding men and women of God. Read about Henry Martyn, David Brainerd, Jonathan Edwards, the brothers Wesley, and Whitfield—read their journals. It does not matter what branch of the Church they belonged to, they have all disciplined their lives and have insisted upon the need for this; and obviously it is something that is thoroughly scriptural and absolutely essential. (*Spiritual Depression: Its Causes and Cure* [Grand Rapids: Eerdmans, 1965])

Believers must be disciplined to add to their faith the proper attitudes, thoughts, and actions described in this passage. Only then will they develop spiritual stability in their lives.

The Secret of Contentment (Philippians 4:10–19)

20

But I rejoiced in the Lord greatly, that now at last you have revived your concern for me; indeed, you were concerned before, but you lacked opportunity. Not that I speak from want, for I have learned to be content in whatever circumstances I am. I know how to get along with humble means, and I also know how to live in prosperity; in any and every circumstance I have learned the secret of being filled and going hungry, both of having abundance and suffering need. I can do all things through Him who strengthens me. Nevertheless, you have done well to share with me in my affliction. You yourselves also know, Philippians, that at the first preaching of the gospel, after I left Macedonia, no church shared with me in the matter of giving and receiving but you alone; for even in Thessalonica you sent a gift more than once for my needs. Not that I seek the gift itself, but I seek for the profit which increases to your account. But I have received everything in full and have an abundance; I am amply supplied, having received from Epaphroditus what you have sent, a fragrant aroma, an acceptable sacrifice, well-pleasing to God. And my God will supply all your needs according to His riches in glory in Christ Jesus. (4:10–19)

Contentment is a highly prized, but elusive virtue. Though it comes only from being rightly related to God and trusting His sovereign, loving, purposeful providence, people nevertheless seek it where it cannot be found—in money, possessions, power, prestige, relationships, jobs, or freedom from difficulties. But by that definition, contentment is unattainable, for it is impossible in this fallen world to be completely free from problems. In sharp contrast to the world's understanding of contentment is this simple definition of spiritual contentment penned by the Puritan Jeremiah Burroughs: "Christian contentment is that sweet, inward, quiet, gracious frame of spirit, which freely submits to and delights in God's wise and fatherly disposal in every condition" (*The Rare Jewel of Christian Contentment* [Reprint; Edinburgh: Banner of Truth, 1964], 19).

The Bible has much to say about contentment. For example, John the Baptist said to some soldiers who asked him how to manifest genuine repentance, "Be content with your wages" (Luke 3:14). To Timothy Paul wrote, "If we have food and covering, with these we shall be content" (1 Tim. 6:8), a thought echoed by the writer of Hebrews: "Make sure that your character is free from the love of money, being content with what you have" (Heb. 13:5). Paul was even "well content with weaknesses, with insults, with distresses, with persecutions, with difficulties, for Christ's sake" (2 Cor. 12:10), because he knew that the "godliness" produced by those trials "actually is a means of great gain when accompanied by contentment" (1 Tim. 6:6). The Bible not only identifies contentment as a virtue, but also prescribes it as a command.

Before concluding this letter to his beloved Philippian congregation, Paul wanted to express his deeply felt gratitude to them. He had had a special relationship with them since the founding of the church at Philippi. At one point in Paul's ministry many years earlier, they were the only church that had supported him financially (4:15–16). Now they had again sent him a gift, and 4:10–19 is Paul's thank-you note to them for it.

The Philippians' generosity was especially meaningful to Paul because it reached him during a very trying time in his life. He was a prisoner in Rome, confined to a small apartment (Acts 28:30) and guarded around the clock by a Roman soldier (Acts 28:16). He could no longer minister with the freedom he had once enjoyed. Being unable to work to support himself, he was in a dependent condition, probably existing on a bare subsistence level on help from generous friends. The only contact he had with the churches that were his constant concern (2 Cor. 11:28) was through letters or the occasional visitor who sought him out. Constantly looming over him was the anticipation of his trial before the emperor—the infamous Nero (cf. Acts 25:11–12, 21; 26:32; 27:24; 28:19). Commenting on this period in Paul's life, F. B. Meyer wrote that he was "deprived of every comfort, and cast as a lonely man on the shores of the great strange metropolis, with every movement of his hand clanking a fetter, and nothing before him but the lion's mouth or the sword" (*The Epistle to the Philippians* [Grand Rapids: Baker, 1952], 242).

Beneath the surface of Paul's expression of thanks to the Philippians is the picture of a man utterly content in spite of such severe circumstances. In the direct statement of 4:9, Paul offered himself as an example of spiritual stability. In verses 10–19, as he thanked the Philippians for their gift, he indirectly offered himself as an example of contentment. Paul knew how to rejoice in every circumstance and be free from anxiety and worry, because his heart was guarded by the peace of God and the God of peace. His example is especially relevant to our utterly discontented culture.

Five principles of contentment flow from this seemingly mundane conclusion to Paul's letter. A contented person is confident in God's providence, satisfied with little, independent from circumstances, strengthened by divine power, and preoccupied with the well-being of others.

A Contented Person Is Confident in God's Providence

But I rejoiced in the Lord greatly, that now at last you have revived your concern for me; indeed, you were concerned before, but you lacked opportunity. (4:10)

Ten years had passed since Paul's ministry in Philippi had resulted in the founding of the church in that city. The Philippians had generously supported him when he left Philippi to minister in the Macedonian cities of Thessalonica and Berea (Acts 17:1–13). When Paul moved south into Achaia, the Philippians continued their support as he ministered in Athens and Corinth (Acts 17:14–18:18). As the years passed they had consistently been **concerned** about Paul, but **lacked** any **opportunity** to provide support for him. The reason for that lack is not given. Perhaps it was due to their preoccupation with their crushing poverty (cf. 2 Cor. 8:1–2). Or they may have been unaware of the apostle's needs, or unable to locate him.

But recently opportunity arose when Epaphroditus arrived in Rome, bringing with him a generous gift from the Philippians (4:18) for which Paul **rejoiced in the Lord greatly.** He did so not primarily because the gift met his need, but because it gave evidence of their love for him. His joy overflowed **that now at last,** after ten years, they had **revived** their **concern for** him. The Greek verb translated **revived** is a horticultural term describing a plant flowering again. The Philippians' generous affection for Paul, after lying dormant for nearly ten years, had once again bloomed. The apostle's statement indeed, **you were concerned before, but you lacked opportunity** was intended to allay any misunderstanding on the Philippians' part. Paul knew they **were concerned before** this, but he understood that they had **lacked** the **opportunity** to support him (cf. 2 Cor. 8:12).

Paul's gracious attitude reflects his patient confidence in God's sovereign providence. He was certain that God in due time would arrange his circumstances to meet his needs. There was no panic on his part, no attempt to manipulate people, no taking matters into his own hands. Paul was content because he knew that the times, seasons, and opportunities of life are controlled by the sovereign God "who works all things after the counsel of His will" (Eph. 1:11), thereby causing "all things to work together for good to those who love God, to those who are called according to His purpose" (Rom. 8:28). Those who seek to control their own lives will inevitably be frustrated. A confident trust in God's providence is foundational to contentment.

Providence and miracle are the two ways God acts in the world. A miracle is God's direct, sovereign intervention into the natural world. It is an event so contrary to the normal course of events that there is no scientific or naturalistic explanation for it other than the power of God. There is no natural insight to explain the parting of the Red Sea, restoring the sight of those blind from birth, or raising people from the dead.

On the other hand, God's providence is not miraculous in the sense that it interrupts the natural order. Rather, it allows for all the contingencies, events, words, acts, decisions, and elements of normal life. God supernaturally weaves them all together to fit His purpose exactly. This is as supernatural as a miracle. Solomon acknowledged God's providential control over events when he wrote, "The mind of man plans his way, but the Lord directs his steps" (Prov. 16:9; cf. 19:21; Jer. 10:23; Acts 4:27–28; Phil. 2:13). God providentially arranged for Joseph to rise to a high position in Egypt to preserve His people. As he explained to his brothers, "As for you, you meant evil against me, but God meant it for good in order to bring about this present result, to preserve many people alive" (Gen. 50:20). God also providentially arranged for Esther to be in a position to save Israel, as Mordecai reminded her: "For if you remain silent at this time, relief and deliverance will arise for the Jews from another place and you and your father's house will perish. And who knows whether you have not attained royalty for such a time as this?" (Est. 4:14).

An understanding of God's sovereign, providential control of events is critical to contentment.

A Contented Person Is Satisfied with Little

Not that I speak from want, for I have learned to be content in whatever circumstances I am. (4:11)

Lest the Philippians misunderstand his statement in verse 10, Paul quickly added a disclaimer. He did **not** mean to imply that he spoke **from want** when he thanked them for their gift. In fact, he had **learned to be content in whatever circumstances** he found himself. Though his situation was extremely difficult, Paul was not discontent. It did not matter that he was a prisoner, living in a small apartment, chained to a Roman soldier, subsisting on a sparse diet. None of that affected his contentment, because he was satisfied with what little he had. His contentment was not affected by his physical deprivations.

The Greek word translated **content** in verse 11 appears only here in the New Testament. In extra-biblical Greek it was used to speak of being self-sufficient, having enough, or not being dependent on others. One ancient writer used the word in reference to a country that supplied itself and had no need of imports. True contentment comes only from God, and enables believers to be satisfied and at ease in the midst of any problem.

The contented attitude of someone like Paul or the Shunammite woman, who when asked what she needed replied simply, "I live among my own people" (2 Kings 4:13), is incomprehensible to today's society. People are not content with either little or much. In fact, it seems that those who are the wealthiest are often the most miserable and discontented. Instead, people are obsessed with delineating their needs and loudly demanding that they be met. Need has become the number one value in our culture. Starting from the humanistic premise that God does not exist and man is therefore ultimate, the goal of life for people becomes getting their needs met.

Adding to the discontent is the blurring of the distinction between needs and wants. In actual practice, virtually everything has become a "need." Thus, men "need" better jobs, fancier cars, and bigger homes; women "need" careers outside the home, and, paradoxically, "need" children; young people "need" unending sexual encounters to liberate their repressed egos; children "need" the freedom to express themselves outside the "bondage" of parental control. Like a hamster running around and around on a wheel and going nowhere, people desperately chase the contentment that is always tantalizingly just out of reach. Even the church has begun to build its ministry around people's "felt needs."

But Paul knew that the chief end of man is not to have his needs met, but to glorify God and enjoy Him forever. Because of that, he was satisfied with whatever God graciously granted him. As he wrote to Timothy, "If we have food and covering, with these we shall be content" (1 Tim. 6:8). Although he wrote to the Corinthians, "The Lord directed those who proclaim the gospel to get their living from the gospel" (1 Cor. 9:14), Paul often chose not to exercise that right (cf. Acts 20:34; 1 Cor. 9:12, 15; 1 Thess. 2:9; 2 Thess. 3:8). He worked hard, and was content to let God control the results. When difficult times came, Paul remained content because he was satisfied with little.

A CONTENTED PERSON IS INDEPENDENT FROM CIRCUMSTANCES

I know how to get along with humble means, and I also know how to live in prosperity; in any and every circumstance I have learned the secret of being filled and going hungry, both of having abundance and suffering need. (4:12)

Paul expands on what he alluded to in the previous verse. The twice-repeated phrase **I know how . . . I also know how** reveals that he had **learned** by experience and spiritual maturity to live above his circumstances and not to let them affect his contentment. That is an important lesson for believers to learn, for it is the difficult circumstances in life that most frequently steal our contentment.

Paul's statement **I know how to get along with humble means,** to be **hungry,** and to **suffer need** indicates that he had had his share of poverty. He knew what it was to get by with meager material things. He also knew how to **live in prosperity,** to be **filled,** and to **have** an **abundance** when God graciously granted him more than he needed. All six of those terms refer to the material, earthly needs of this life, not to spiritual needs.

Paul was no ivory tower theologian; he had lived and ministered in the trenches. His life was not exactly a testimonial for the prosperity gospel. The apostle's trials began at Damascus shortly after his conversion. Enraged that Paul

> kept increasing in strength and confounding the Jews who lived at Damascus by proving that this Jesus is the Christ, . . . the Jews plotted together to do away with him, but their plot became known to [Paul]. They were also watching the gates day and night so that they might put him to death; but his disciples took him by night and let him down through an opening in the wall, lowering him in a large basket. (Acts 9:22–25)

At Lystra on his first missionary journey, hostile "Jews came from Antioch and Iconium, and having won over the crowds, they stoned Paul and dragged him out of the city, supposing him to be dead" (Acts 14:19). Many of the Philippian believers no doubt remembered what happened to Paul and his fellow preacher Silas in Philippi:

> The crowd rose up together against them, and the chief magistrates tore their robes off them and proceeded to order them to be beaten with rods. When they had struck them with many blows, they threw them into prison, commanding the jailer to guard them securely; and he, having received such a command, threw them into the inner prison and fastened their feet in the stocks. (Acts 16:22–24)

Things did not get much better for the apostle in Thessalonica, where

> the Jews, becoming jealous and taking along some wicked men from the market place, formed a mob and set the city in an uproar; and attacking the house of Jason, they were seeking to bring them out to the people. When they did not find them, they began dragging Jason and some brethren before the city authorities, shouting, "These men who have upset the world have come here also; and Jason has welcomed them, and they all act contrary to the decrees of Caesar, saying that there is another king, Jesus." They stirred up the crowd and the city authorities who heard these things. And when they had received a pledge from Jason and the others, they released them. The brethren immediately sent Paul and Silas away by night to Berea. (Acts 17:5–10)

Trouble, in the form of hostile, unbelieving Jews, followed Paul from Thessalonica to Berea: "But when the Jews of Thessalonica found out that the word of God had been proclaimed by Paul in Berea also, they came there as well, agitating and stirring up the crowds" (Acts 17:13). Forced to flee Berea, Paul went to Athens, where he was mocked and ridiculed by the skeptical Greek philosophers gathered on Mars Hill (Acts 17:18–34). From Athens the apostle went to Corinth where, "while Gallio was proconsul of Achaia, the Jews with one accord rose up against Paul and brought him before the judgment seat" (Acts 18:12). After ministering for three months in Greece, "a plot [to kill Paul] was formed against him by the Jews as he was about to set sail for Syria" (Acts 20:3). When he got to Jerusalem, Paul was attacked and savagely beaten after Jews from Asia Minor recognized him in the temple (Acts 21:26–30). Rescued from certain death by the quick action of a Roman officer (Acts 21:31–35), Paul began his long stay in Roman custody. Two years later, after hearings before the Sanhedrin and the Roman governor failed to resolve the situation, Paul exercised his right as a Roman citizen to appeal to Caesar.

After a harrowing sea voyage, which included a terrifying, two-week-long storm that ended in a shipwreck (Acts 27), Paul finally arrived in Rome (Acts 28). As he penned this letter to the Philippians, Paul was again a prisoner in Rome.

Summing up his arduous, difficult, painful life Paul wrote,

> Are they servants of Christ?—I speak as if insane—I more so; in far more labors, in far more imprisonments, beaten times without number, often in danger of death. Five times I received from the Jews thirty-nine lashes. Three times I was beaten with rods, once I was stoned, three times I was shipwrecked, a night and a day I have spent in the deep. I have been on frequent journeys, in dangers from rivers, dangers from robbers, dangers from my countrymen, dangers from the Gentiles, dangers in the city, dangers in the wilderness, dangers on the sea, dangers among false brethren; I have been in labor and hardship, through many sleepless nights, in hunger and thirst, often without food, in cold and exposure. Apart from such external things, there is the daily pressure on me of concern for all the churches. Who is weak without my being weak? Who is led into sin without my intense concern? If I have to boast, I will boast of what pertains to my weakness. The God and Father of the Lord Jesus, He who is blessed forever, knows that I am not lying. In Damascus the ethnarch under Aretas the king was guarding the city of the Damascenes in order to seize me, and I was let down in a basket through a window in the wall, and so escaped his hands. (2 Cor. 11:23–33)

In all Paul's unique and constant sufferings, he had **learned the secret** of rising above them. In the midst of all his trials, he kept his focus on heavenly realities (cf. Col. 3:1–2). In 2 Corinthians 4:17, the apostle wrote, "For momentary, light affliction is producing for us an eternal weight of glory far beyond all comparison." With that perspective, is it any wonder that no amount of pain, suffering, or disappointment could affect his contentment?

A CONTENTED PERSON IS STRENGTHENED BY DIVINE POWER

I can do all things through Him who strengthens me. (4:13)

No matter how difficult his struggles may have been, Paul had a spiritual undergirding, an invisible means of support. His adequacy and sufficiency came from his union with the adequate and sufficient Christ: "I have been crucified with Christ; and it is no longer I who live, but Christ lives in me; and the life which I now live in the flesh I live by faith in the Son of God, who loved me and gave Himself up for me" (Gal. 2:20).

When Paul wrote **I can do all things** he had in mind physical, not spiritual **things.** *Ischuō* (**I can do**) means "to be strong," "to have power," or "to have resources." It is variously translated "overpowered" (Acts 19:16), "prevailing" (Acts 19:20), and "effective" (James 5:16). The Greek text emphasizes the word translated **all things** (a reference to physical needs; cf. vv. 11–12) by placing it first in the sentence. Paul was strong enough to endure anything **through Him who strengthen[ed]** him (cf. 1 Tim. 1:12; 2 Tim. 4:17). The apostle does not, of course, mean that he could physically survive indefinitely without food, water, sleep, or shelter. What he is saying is that when he reached the limit of his resources and strength, even to the point of death, he was infused with the strength of Christ. He could overcome the most dire physical difficulties because of the inner, spiritual strength God had given him. In the words of Isaiah,

> He gives strength to the weary, and to him who lacks might He increases power. Though youths grow weary and tired, and vigorous young men stumble badly, yet those who wait for the Lord will gain new strength; they will mount up with wings like eagles, they will run and not get tired, they will walk and not become weary. (Isa. 40:29–31)

Perhaps the clearest illustration of this truth in Paul's life comes from 2 Corinthians 12:7–10:

> Because of the surpassing greatness of the revelations, for this reason, to keep me from exalting myself, there was given me a thorn in the flesh, a messenger of Satan to torment me—to keep me from exalting myself! Concerning this I implored the Lord three times that it might leave me. And He has said to me, "My grace is sufficient for you, for power is perfected in weakness." Most gladly, therefore, I will rather boast about my weaknesses, so that the power of Christ may dwell in me. Therefore I am well content with weaknesses, with insults, with distresses, with persecutions, with difficulties, for Christ's sake; for when I am weak, then I am strong.

Paul was tormented by a "thorn in the flesh," most likely a demon who was behind the false teachers tearing up his beloved church in Corinth. This was the worst of all trials for him, because of his "concern for all the churches" (2 Cor. 11:28). He repeatedly begged the Lord to deliver him from the torment of that demonic attack on the church. But instead of delivering him, the Lord pointed Paul to the sufficiency of His grace. Contentment comes to believers who rely on the sustaining grace of Christ infused into believers when they have no strength of their own. In that sense, contentment is a by-product of distress.

Lest any doubt the sufficiency of Christ's strengthening power, it is the same power Paul described in his prayer in Ephesians 3:

> For this reason I bow my knees before the Father, from whom every family in heaven and on earth derives its name, that He would grant you, according to the riches of His glory, to be strengthened with power through His Spirit in the inner man. . . . Now to Him who is able to do far more abundantly beyond all that we ask or think, according to the power that works within us. (Eph. 3:14–16, 20)

God's power that indwells believers is far more than sufficient to strengthen and sustain them in any trial. Contentment belongs to those who confidently trust in that power rather than in their own resources. Jeremiah Burroughs observes,

> A Christian finds satisfaction in every circumstance by getting strength from another, by going out of himself to Jesus Christ, by his faith acting upon Christ, and bringing the strength of Jesus Christ into his own soul, he is thereby enabled to bear whatever God lays on him, by the strength that he finds from Jesus Christ. . . . There is strength in Christ not only to sanctify and save us, but strength to support us under all our burdens and afflictions, and Christ expects that when we are under any burden, we should act our faith upon him to draw virtue and strength from him. (*The Rare Jewel of Christian Contentment,* 63)

It is important to note that only those who live lives of obedience to God's will can count on His power to sustain them. Those whose continued sin has led them into the pit of despair cannot expect God to bring them contentment from their circumstances. In fact, He may even add to their difficulties to chasten them and bring them to repentance.

D. Martyn Lloyd-Jones compares the flow of God's power into the believer's life to the issue of physical health:

> Now I suggest that that is analogous to this whole subject of power in one's life as a Christian. Health is something that results from right living. Health cannot be obtained directly or immediately or in and of itself. There is a sense in which I am prepared to say that a man should not think of his health as such at all. Health is the result of right living, and I say exactly the same thing about this question of power in our Christian lives.
>
> Or let me use another illustration. Take this question of preaching. No subject is discussed more often than power in preaching. "Oh, that I might have power in preaching," says the preacher and he goes on his knees and prays for power. I think that that may be quite wrong. It certainly is if it is the only thing that the preacher does. The way to have

power is to prepare your message carefully. Study the Word of God, think it out, analyse it, put it in order, do your utmost. That is that message God is most likely to bless—the indirect approach rather than the direct. It is exactly the same in this matter of power and ability to live the Christian life. In addition to our prayer for power and ability we must obey certain primary rules and laws.

I can therefore summarise the teaching like this. The secret of power is to discover and to learn from the New Testament what is possible for us in Christ. What I have to do is to go to Christ. I must spend my time with Him. I must meditate upon Him, I must get to know Him. That was Paul's ambition—"that I might know Him." I must maintain my contact and communion with Christ and I must concentrate on knowing Him.

What else? I must do exactly what He tells me. I must avoid things that would hamper. If in the midst of persecution we want to feel as Paul felt, we must live as Paul lived. I must do what He tells me, both to do and not to do. I must read the Bible, I must exercise, I must practise the Christian life, I must live the Christian life in all its fullness. (*Spiritual Depression: Its Causes and Cure* [Grand Rapids: Eerdmans, 1965], 298–99)

God's power will bring contentment to those who have no strength of their own, but only if they have been living righteously. There is no quick fix, no shortcut to contentment. It comes only to those strengthened by divine power, and that divine power does not come from counselors, therapy, or self-help formulas, but only from consistent godly living.

A CONTENTED PERSON IS
PREOCCUPIED WITH THE WELL-BEING OF OTHERS

Nevertheless, you have done well to share with me in my affliction. You yourselves also know, Philippians, that at the first preaching of the gospel, after I left Macedonia, no church shared with me in the matter of giving and receiving but you alone; for even in Thessalonica you sent a gift more than once for my needs. Not that I seek the gift itself, but I seek for the profit which increases to your account. But I have received everything in full and have an abundance; I am amply supplied, having received from Epaphroditus what you have sent, a fragrant aroma, an acceptable sacrifice, well-pleasing to God. And my God will supply all your needs according to His riches in glory in Christ Jesus. (4:14–19)

A final strand in the tapestry of contentment woven by Paul is concern for others. Those who live only for themselves will never be content, because contentment for them can come only when their circumstances are exactly as they want them to be. And that will never happen. Only those who unselfishly put others' well-being above their own will find contentment. Paul prayed that the Philippians' "love may abound still more and more" (1:9); one of the qualities of true biblical love is unselfishness (1 Cor. 13:5). He also exhorted them, "Do nothing from selfishness or empty conceit, but with humility of mind regard one another as more important than yourselves; do not merely look out for your own personal interests, but also for the interests of others" (2:3–4). That is the attitude "which was also in Christ Jesus" (2:5); if He had looked out only for His own interests, he would never have left heaven to sacrifice Himself for sinful, fallen people.

Nevertheless introduces an important transition in Paul's thought. What he had written in verses 10–13 could easily have sent the wrong message to the Philippians. Despite their poverty (cf. 2 Cor. 8:1–2), they had sent a sacrificial gift to Paul through Epaphroditus (4:18). After staying in Rome for a while and ministering to the apostle, Epaphroditus had returned to Philippi, bringing this letter from Paul with him. In it the church would read, "Not that I speak from want, for I have learned to be content in whatever circumstances I am"; "I have learned the secret of being filled and going hungry, both of having abundance and suffering need"; and "I can do all things through Him who strengthens me" (4:11–13). If the letter had ended at that point, the Philippians would have concluded that Paul neither needed nor appreciated their sacrificial gift to him.

To make certain that the Philippians did not misunderstand him, Paul hastened to reassure them that they had **done well** (*kalōs;* something noble or beautiful in character) **to share with** him **in** his **affliction.** But he then needed to explain to them how their gift could have been a noble act if he did not need it.

Paul began by taking his readers back ten years to his **first preaching of the gospel** in Philippi. During that time, and even **after** he **left Macedonia** for the Achaian cities of Athens and Corinth, **no** other **church shared with** him **in the matter of giving and receiving.** That phrase reflects business terminology. The word translated **matter** is sometimes translated "accounts" (Matt. 18:23; 25:19) or "accounting" (Luke 16:2) and the terms **giving** and **receiving** can mean "credit" and "debit." Evidently Paul was a careful steward of his resources and kept an account of his receipts and expenditures. Even before he **left Macedonia** the Philippians supported him; during his ministry **in Thessalonica** they **sent a gift more than once for** his **needs.** Their generosity, along with Paul's own hard work, allowed him to minister free of charge in Thessalonica (1 Thess. 2:9; 2 Thess. 3:8) and Corinth (Acts 18:5; 2 Cor. 11:8).

Paul could rejoice over their gift yet still be content in God's sovereign provision for him because he was selfless. That selflessness led him to write, **Not that I seek the gift itself, but I seek for the profit which increases to your account** (cf. Matt. 6:19–20; 1 Tim. 6:17–19). Their gift brought Paul joy not because of its personal material benefit to him, but because of its spiritual benefit to them. The principle that those who give generously will be blessed is taught repeatedly in Scripture. Solomon wrote, "There is one who scatters, and yet increases all the more, and there is one who withholds what is justly due, and yet it results only in want. The generous man will be prosperous, and he who waters will himself be watered" (Prov. 11:24–25). Later in Proverbs he added, "One who is gracious to a poor man lends to the Lord, and He will repay him for his good deed" (Prov. 19:17), "He who is generous will be blessed" (Prov. 22:9), and "He who gives to the poor will never want" (Prov. 28:27). In Luke 6:38 Jesus said, "Give, and it will be given to you. They will pour into your lap a good measure—pressed down, shaken together, and running over. For by your standard of measure it will be measured to you in return." To the Corinthians Paul wrote, "Now this I say, he who sows sparingly will also reap sparingly, and he who sows bountifully will also reap bountifully" (2 Cor. 9:6). Paul himself was an example of one who generously gave to the poor, as he reminded the Ephesian elders: "In everything I showed you that by working hard in this manner you must help the weak and remember the words of the Lord Jesus, that He Himself said, 'It is more blessed to give than to receive'" (Acts 20:35).

Three statements summarize Paul's joy and gratitude. The Greek verb in the phrase **I have received everything in full** was commonly used in a commercial sense in extra-biblical Greek to denote payment in full. This statement is in effect Paul's receipt to the Philippians for their gift. **Have an abundance** translates a Greek verb that means "to overflow," "to have an excess," or "to have more than enough." The Greek verb in Paul's final statement **I am amply supplied** speaks of being filled up completely. Taken together those three phrases show that Paul, **having received from Epaphroditus what** they had **sent** to him, was overwhelmed by the Philippians' generosity.

Using sacrificial language from the Old Testament, Paul described the Philippians' gift as **a fragrant aroma** (cf. Gen. 8:20–21; Ex. 29:18; Lev. 1:9, 13, 17; Num. 15:3), **an acceptable sacrifice** (cf. Lev. 19:5; 22:29; Isa. 56:7), **well-pleasing to God** (cf. Ps. 51:19). Paul saw the Philippians' gift as a sacrificial act of worship to God. Such spiritual sacrifices are required of New Covenant believers instead of the animal sacrifices of the Old Covenant. In Romans 12:1 Paul commands believers, "Present your bodies a living and holy sacrifice, acceptable to God, which is your spiritual service of worship." The writer of Hebrews exhorts, "Through

Him then, let us continually offer up a sacrifice of praise to God, that is, the fruit of lips that give thanks to His name. And do not neglect doing good and sharing, for with such sacrifices God is pleased" (Heb. 13:15–16). Peter reminds believers that they are "a holy priesthood, to offer up spiritual sacrifices acceptable to God through Jesus Christ" (1 Peter 2:5). Paul's joy that the Philippians would make such an acceptable sacrifice to God far surpassed his joy at receiving their gift.

Paul knew that the Philippians would not only receive spiritual blessings in heaven for their generosity, but also that **God** would **supply all** their physical **needs** in this life. The Philippians had sacrificially (cf. 2 Cor. 8:1–3) given of their earthly possessions to support God's servant, Paul. In return, God would amply supply their needs; He would not be in their debt. Having sown bountifully, they would reap bountifully (2 Cor. 9:6); having "honor[ed] the Lord from [their] wealth and from the first of all [their] produce ... [their] barns will be filled with plenty and [their] vats will overflow with new wine" (Prov. 3:9–10). They would discover that it is impossible to outgive God.

The phrase **according to His riches in glory in Christ Jesus** reveals the extent to which God would supply the Philippians' needs. He would do so **according to His riches,** not out of them; His giving to them would be relative to the immensity of His eternal wealth, that is, as generously as is consistent with **His riches in glory in Christ Jesus.** The New Testament repeatedly presents **Christ Jesus** as the source of all of God's riches. In Him "are hidden all the treasures of wisdom and knowledge" (Col. 2:3); to the Colossians Paul wrote, "For it was the Father's good pleasure for all the fullness to dwell in Him. ... For in Him all the fullness of Deity dwells in bodily form" (Col. 1:19; 2:9). "The God and Father of our Lord Jesus Christ ... has blessed us with every spiritual blessing in the heavenly places in Christ" (Eph. 1:3). In Ephesians 1:23 the apostle described Jesus as "Him who fills all in all," and he reminded the Corinthians of "the grace of God which was given [them] in Christ Jesus, that in everything [they] were enriched in Him" (1 Cor. 1:4–5). Echoing that thought, Peter wrote, "His divine power has granted to us everything pertaining to life and godliness, through the true knowledge of Him who called us by His own glory and excellence" (2 Peter 1:3).

The crucial lessons in contentment illustrated here in the life of Paul may be summarized in five words: faith, humility, submission, dependence, and unselfishness. Those virtues characterize all who have learned to be content.

The Saints of God
(Philippians 4:20–23)

21

Now to our God and Father be the glory forever and ever. Amen. Greet every saint in Christ Jesus. The brethren who are with me greet you. All the saints greet you, especially those of Caesar's household. The grace of the Lord Jesus Christ be with your spirit. (4:20–23)

The theme of the concluding passage of the book of Philippians is found in the familiar but often misunderstood word **saint.** The word has drifted far from its New Testament meaning, and has been loaded down with all sorts of cultural and religious baggage. To some it has an insulting, "holier than thou" connotation. They would not call themselves saints for fear of sounding egotistical, boastful, and proud. Others believe saints are those who do remarkable good for humanity. To others the term *saint* conjures up the image of a gaunt, ethereal figure etched in the stained glass window of a cathedral.

Much of the confusion about saints stems from the teachings of the Roman Catholic Church. A saint in Roman Catholic theology is someone who, because of his or her exemplary virtue, merit, devotion, and religious achievement, is already exalted in heaven (as opposed to the majority of faithful Catholics, who can expect to enter heaven only after a prolonged stay in purgatory). Such a person is elevated to saint-hood by an official decree of the pope known as canonization, and is considered a model whose life is to be emulated.

But canonization by the Catholic Church means far more than just setting forth the saint as an example to be followed; canonized saints are also publicly venerated. Churches are often dedicated in their mem-ory, a festival day honoring them is observed, and masses are celebrated in their honor. The Catholic Church also encourages its members to appeal to the saints to intercede with God on their behalf. Thus, prayers are offered to them, and their statues and relics are venerated. According to Roman Catholic theology, the saints can intercede not only for the liv-ing, but also for those in purgatory (in Catholic theology, a place of after-death punishment to make one fit for heaven). Living Catholics can therefore appeal to the saints to intercede with God on behalf of their loved ones suffering in purgatory.

But according to the New Testament, a saint is not an ecclesiasti-cal relic crystallized in a stained glass window, immortalized in a statue, or canonized by Rome. A saint is anyone who has come to saving faith in the Lord Jesus Christ. In fact, "saint" is the apostle Paul's favorite term for Christians, appearing forty times in his epistles. He addressed all the believers in Philippi as saints in the opening verse of this epistle (cf. Rom. 1:7; 1 Cor. 14:33; 2 Cor. 1:1; Eph. 1:1; Col. 1:2; Heb. 13:24). Paul even addressed the members of the Corinthian church, the most troubled, sin-plagued church in the New Testament, as "those who have been sancti-fied in Christ Jesus, saints by calling" (1 Cor. 1:2). A saint is not a superhero of the faith; a saint is anyone who has eternal life in Christ (Rom. 6:23) and from whom the light of Christ shines (Phil. 2:15).

In this concluding portion of his letter to the Philippians, likely written with his own hand (cf. 1 Cor. 16:21; Gal. 6:11; Col. 4:18; 2 Thess. 3:17), Paul reminds them of their identification as saints. He describes the character of saints, the worship of saints, the fellowship of saints, the joy of saints, and the resource of saints.

THE CHARACTER OF SAINTS

saint ... saints (4:21, 22)

Inherent in the definition of *hagios* (**saint**) or *hagioi* (**saints**) is the character or nature of saints. The term can be translated "set apart ones," "separated ones," "sanctified ones," or, perhaps best, "holy ones." It is also used in the New Testament of the elect angels (Mark 8:38; Luke 9:26; Acts 10:22; Rev. 14:10) and, supremely, of God (Mark 1:24; Luke 1:49; 4:34;

John 6:69; 17:11; Acts 2:27; 3:14; 4:27, 30; 13:35; 1 Peter 1:15, 16; 1 John 2:20; Rev. 3:7; 4:8; 6:10; 15:4; 16:5). God's holiness is His utter and complete separation from sin. A **saint,** therefore, is someone who has been separated from sin to God for holy purposes.

"In Christ Jesus" (v. 21) is the spiritual sphere in which sainthood is the reality; the saints are those who are in Jesus Christ. That reality is unique to Christianity. The adherents of other world religions do not see themselves as being united with their religion's founder; they merely follow his teachings. But Christians do not just believe that Christ lived, died, rose from the dead, and is coming again; they are also in Him in a union of life (cf. 1:21; 4:1; Rom. 8:1; 16:11–13; 1 Cor. 1:30; 3:1; 7:22; 2 Cor. 1:21; 5:17; Eph. 5:8; 6:10; Col. 1:2, 28; 4:7). Because of that they can say with Paul, "I have been crucified with Christ; and it is no longer I who live, but Christ lives in me; and the life which I now live in the flesh I live by faith in the Son of God, who loved me and gave Himself up for me" (Gal. 2:20).

Through His sacrificial death on the cross, Jesus Christ sets believers apart to God and makes them holy. The writer of Hebrews notes, "We have been sanctified [set apart to God] through the offering of the body of Jesus Christ once for all" (Heb. 10:10). To the Corinthians Paul wrote, "Therefore if anyone is in Christ, he is a new creature; the old things passed away; behold, new things have come. . . . He made Him who knew no sin to be sin on our behalf, so that we might become the righteousness of God in Him" (2 Cor. 5:17, 21). Baptism pictures the believer's union with Christ in His death, burial, and resurrection (Rom. 6:3–4). Thus, every believer is a saint, because every believer is separated from sin to God through faith in Jesus Christ. By calling the Philippians saints, Paul reminded them that they must live as those separated from sin to righteousness.

THE WORSHIP OF SAINTS

Now to our God and Father be the glory forever and ever. Amen. (4:20)

This paean of praise is a sample of the saints' worship. Saints are not people to be worshiped; they are people who worship. Worship defines the redeemed, and Paul began the concluding portion of Philippians with a doxology. The English word "doxology" comes from two Greek words, *doxa* ("glory") and *logos* ("word"). Thus, a doxology is a word about **glory;** it is an outburst of praise and adoration that honors and ascribes **glory** to God.

Doxologies in Scripture are fitting responses to doctrinal truth.

This one flowed from Paul's exuberant joy over the magnificent truths he had been inspired by God to expound in this letter. True worship flows from divine truth.

In the doxology of Romans 11:33–36, Paul rejoiced and praised God for the monumental truths revealed in Romans chapters 1 to 11—the most magnificent doctrinal treatise in all of Scripture. He wrote,

> Oh, the depth of the riches both of the wisdom and knowledge of God! How unsearchable are His judgments and unfathomable His ways! For who has known the mind of the Lord, or who became His counselor? Or who has first given to Him that it might be paid back to him again? For from Him and through Him and to Him are all things. To Him be the glory forever. Amen.

As he concluded the epistle five chapters later, Paul's heart was still overflowing with praise for the marvelous truths it contained:

> Now to Him who is able to establish you according to my gospel and the preaching of Jesus Christ, according to the revelation of the mystery which has been kept secret for long ages past, but now is manifested, and by the Scriptures of the prophets, according to the commandment of the eternal God, has been made known to all the nations, leading to obedience of faith; to the only wise God, through Jesus Christ, be the glory forever. Amen. (Rom. 16:25–27)

In Ephesians, after three chapters of rich doctrinal truth, Paul again burst out in a doxology of praise and worship: "Now to Him who is able to do far more abundantly beyond all that we ask or think, according to the power that works within us, to Him be the glory in the church and in Christ Jesus to all generations forever and ever. Amen" (Eph. 3:20–21). In Galatians 1:5 Paul penned this brief doxology in anticipation of the truths he would soon share with the Galatians: "To [God] be the glory forevermore. Amen."

A doxology is also an appropriate response to all that God has done for believers. In gratitude for the wonder of his salvation, Paul wrote: "Now to the King eternal, immortal, invisible, the only God, be honor and glory forever and ever. Amen" (1 Tim. 1:17). Facing martyrdom, he could nevertheless confidently exult, "The Lord will rescue me from every evil deed, and will bring me safely to His heavenly kingdom; to Him be the glory forever and ever. Amen" (2 Tim. 4:18). Jude penned a doxology of praise for believers' eternal security: "Now to Him who is able to keep you from stumbling, and to make you stand in the presence of His glory blameless with great joy, to the only God our Savior, through

Jesus Christ our Lord, be glory, majesty, dominion and authority, before all time and now and forever. Amen" (Jude 24–25).

Paul identified the object of his doxology first as **our God,** the **God** whom Christians worship, the only true and living God. John 5:44 describes Him as "the one and only God"; John 17:3 as "the only true God"; Romans 16:27 as "the only wise God"; 1 Timothy 1:17 and Jude 25 as "the only God." The pronoun **our** emphasizes believers' personal relationship with Him; they are to worship the true God in personal, intimate fellowship. As previously noted, the habitual act of worshiping God defines believers; they "are the true circumcision, who worship in the Spirit of God and glory in Christ Jesus and put no confidence in the flesh" (Phil. 3:3). The object of redemption was to make people worshipers. Jesus declared to the Samaritan woman at the well in Sychar, "But an hour is coming, and now is, when the true worshipers will worship the Father in spirit and truth; for such people the Father seeks to be His worshipers" (John 4:23; cf. Rev. 5:9; 7:9–10).

Worshiping the true God cannot be done in ignorance. It is impossible to worship Him unless one knows who He is. Nor does God want ignorant worship. In Hosea 6:6 God declared, "I delight in loyalty rather than sacrifice, and in the knowledge of God rather than burnt offerings," while Jesus said in John 4:24, "God is spirit, and those who worship Him must worship in spirit and truth." Ignorant worship is unacceptable because it is a form of idolatry. Idolatry is not only worshiping false gods, but also entertaining thoughts about the true God that are untrue and unworthy of Him. A. W. Tozer writes,

> Among the sins to which the human heart is prone, hardly any other is more hateful to God than idolatry, for idolatry is at bottom a libel on His character. The idolatrous heart assumes that God is other than He is—in itself a monstrous sin—and substitutes for the true God one made after its own likeness. Always this God will conform to the image of the one who created it and will be base or pure, cruel or kind, according to the moral state of the mind from which it emerges.
>
> A god begotten in the shadows of a fallen heart will quite naturally be no true likeness of the true God. "Thou thoughtest," said the Lord to the wicked man in the psalm, "that I was altogether such an one as thyself." Surely this must be a serious affront to the Most High God before whom cherubim and seraphim continually do cry, "Holy, holy, holy, Lord God of Sabaoth."
>
> Let us beware lest we in our pride accept the erroneous notion that idolatry consists only in kneeling before visible objects of adoration, and that civilized peoples are therefore free from it. The essence of idolatry is the entertainment of thoughts about God that are unworthy of Him. (*The Knowledge of the Holy* [New York: Harper & Row, 1975], 11)

The only cure for such idolatry is for the church as well as individual believers to make knowing God their primary pursuit. Those with a man-centered theology cannot be obedient worshipers.

A second truth about God that flows out of Paul's doxology is that He is believers' **Father.** In the New Testament, God is first and foremost the **Father** of the Lord Jesus Christ (cf. Rom. 15:6; 2 Cor. 1:3; 11:31; Eph. 1:3; 1 Peter 1:3; Rev. 1:6)—a fact Jesus attested to by referring to or addressing Him as "My Father" nearly forty times in the Gospels. That fact is a proof of Christ's deity; He and the Father share the same common life, the same deity, the same essence. The implication of Jesus' calling God His Father was not lost on the unbelieving Jews, as John 5:18 records: "For this reason therefore the Jews were seeking all the more to kill Him, because He not only was breaking the Sabbath, but also was calling God His own Father, making Himself equal with God."

But Paul has in mind here the truth that God is also the **Father** of believers (1:2; cf. Matt. 5:16, 45, 48; 6:1; 10:29; Rom. 8:15; 1 Cor. 1:3; 2 Cor. 1:2; Gal. 1:3; Eph. 1:2; Col. 1:2; 2 Thess. 1:1; 2:16; Philem. 3), whom He has adopted as His children (Rom. 8:15, 23; Gal. 4:5; Eph. 1:5). Unlike pagans, who fearfully approach threatening, aloof, uncaring deities (cf. 1 Kings 18:25–29), believers worship the God who loves them as His children. That causes them to "cry out, 'Abba! Father!'" (Rom. 8:15; Gal. 4:6). Believers might be afraid to approach the infinitely wondrous, majestic, and awe-inspiring God. But the intimate term **Father** bridges the gap between sinful, finite believers and their infinite, holy God.

The phrase **forever and ever** indicates the duration of believers' worship of God. The Greek text literally reads "to the ages of the ages," and describes "a very long and indefinite period—the image taken from the cycles or calendars of time, to represent an immeasurable eternity" (John Eadie, *A Commentary on the Greek Text of the Epistle of Paul to the Philippians* [Reprint; Grand Rapids: Baker, 1979], 286). The worship of the saints will not be limited to this life, but will extend throughout all eternity in heaven. To that glorious truth Paul can only add the confessional affirmation **Amen**—"so let it be."

THE FELLOWSHIP OF SAINTS

Greet every saint in Christ Jesus. The brethren who are with me greet you. All the saints greet you, (4:21–22a)

Paul's threefold repetition of the word **greet** implies a strong bond of fellowship. As he closed his letter to them, Paul expressed his love for the members of the Philippian congregation and his concern for their spiritual well-being. His injunction was specifically for the leaders of the Philippian congregation (1:1), who would receive the letter from Epaphroditus. The apostle charged them to greet the individual members of the congregation on his behalf, and assure them of his love and concern for their spiritual well-being.

The apostle's use of the individualistic term **every** instead of the collective term "all" reveals that every saint was worthy of his care and affection. Paul reinforced the point he made in 2:2, where he urged the Philippians to "make [his] joy complete by being of the same mind, maintaining the same love, united in spirit, intent on one purpose." There must be no favoritism in the church, because "there is no partiality with God" (Rom. 2:11; cf. Deut. 10:17; 2 Chron. 19:7; Job 34:19; Acts 10:34; Gal. 2:6; Eph. 6:9). All believers are saints, and any stratification in the body of Christ is contrary to the intention of the Spirit of God. All those accepted in God's Beloved Son (Eph. 1:6) must be accepted by God's beloved children in the church. All believers are what they are in God's sight solely by His grace (1 Cor. 15:10).

Paul's concern for individuals reflected that of the Lord Jesus Christ. Even when surrounded by large crowds, He was aware of individuals and their needs, as the following story reveals:

> A woman who had had a hemorrhage for twelve years, and had endured much at the hands of many physicians, and had spent all that she had and was not helped at all, but rather had grown worse—after hearing about Jesus, she came up in the crowd behind Him and touched His cloak. For she thought, "If I just touch His garments, I will get well." Immediately the flow of her blood was dried up; and she felt in her body that she was healed of her affliction. Immediately Jesus, perceiving in Himself that the power proceeding from Him had gone forth, turned around in the crowd and said, "Who touched My garments?" And His disciples said to Him, "You see the crowd pressing in on You, and You say, 'Who touched Me?'" And He looked around to see the woman who had done this. (Mark 5:25–32)

Paul further illustrated the point of equal affection for all believers by noting that **the brethren who are with me greet you.** Those **brethren,** Paul's close coworkers whom he distinguished from the rest of the believers at Rome (v. 22), included some of the most illustrious names in the early church. Timothy, Paul's protégé and beloved son in the faith, was one of them (1:1; 2:19); Epaphroditus (2:25; 4:18) was also with the apostle at the time he wrote this letter. Tychicus, bearer of the letters of Ephesians (Eph. 6:21), Colossians (Col. 4:7), and Philemon (vv. 4–9), may also have been with Paul at that time. Aristarchus, another long-time companion of the apostle (Acts 19:29; 20:4; 27:2), could have also been among the **brethren** Paul mentioned (Col. 4:10; Philem. 24). The group may have also included Onesimus, the runaway slave who was the subject of Paul's letter to Philemon (Col. 4:9; Philem. 10), and two of the gospel writers, Mark and Luke (Philem. 24). As prominent as they were, though, all those luminaries were simply described as the **brethren.**

The fellowship of the saints is a common bond of love without strata. None of Paul's more prominent coworkers wore backward collars, or appropriated ecclesiastical titles for themselves. That they were uniquely gifted and used by God did not make them spiritually superior; Paul identified himself as "the least of the apostles" (1 Cor. 15:9), and as the foremost of sinners (1 Tim. 1:15–16). They understood well the teaching of Jesus on the equality of believers:

> Do not be called Rabbi; for One is your Teacher, and you are all brothers. Do not call anyone on earth your father; for One is your Father, He who is in heaven. Do not be called leaders; for One is your Leader, that is, Christ. But the greatest among you shall be your servant. Whoever exalts himself shall be humbled; and whoever humbles himself shall be exalted. (Matt. 23:8–12)

The wider circle of believers at Rome's church also sent their greetings, as Paul noted in the phrase **All the saints greet you.** Though differently gifted, and at different levels of faithfulness and spiritual maturity, they were spiritually equal to their more prominent brethren. Using the metaphor of the human body, Paul stressed that point to the Corinthians:

> But now there are many members, but one body. And the eye cannot say to the hand, "I have no need of you"; or again the head to the feet, "I have no need of you." On the contrary, it is much truer that the members of the body which seem to be weaker are necessary; and those members of the body which we deem less honorable, on these we bestow more abundant honor, and our less presentable members become much more presentable, whereas our more presentable members have no need of it. But God has so composed the body, giving more abundant honor to that member which lacked, so that there may be no division in the body, but that the members may have the same care for one another. And if one member suffers, all the members suffer with it; if one member is honored, all the members rejoice with it. Now you are Christ's body, and individually members of it. (1 Cor. 12:20–27)

The sharing of a common, non-discriminating love bond and a mutual desire for each other's spiritual well-being is an essential characteristic of saints.

THE JOY OF SAINTS

especially those of Caesar's household. (4:22*b*)

The greatest joy of saints is to see sinners come to faith in Christ. In Luke 15, Jesus told two parables that illustrated salvation. The first told of a man who rejoiced at finding his lost sheep (Luke 15:5–6); the second told of a woman who rejoiced at finding her lost coin (Luke 15:9). Both express the joy believers have at the salvation of lost sinners. Similarly when Paul and Barnabas described "in detail the conversion of the Gentiles [they brought] great joy to all the brethren" (Acts 15:3).

Paul's reference to **those of Caesar's household** was especially meaningful to the Philippians. Philippi was a Roman colony (Acts 16:12) and its citizens were Roman citizens (Acts 16:21). Because of their close ties with Rome, it is possible that the Philippians knew some of the members of **Caesar's household. Caesar's household** included more than just the members of his family; it included all those in his direct employ, both lowly slaves and high-ranking freemen. In today's terminology, they were government workers. During his imprisonment at Rome, Paul would have come into contact with many of them.

Some of the members of the imperial household, such as those of the praetorian guard the apostle refers to in 1:13, were led to faith in Christ by Paul. Others, however, were already Christians before Paul came to Rome. The nineteenth-century New Testament scholar J. B. Lightfoot found some striking parallels between the names Paul lists in Romans 16:8–15 and the names of members of Caesar's household on lists dating from Paul's time (cf. *St. Paul's Epistle to the Philippians* [Reprint; Grand Rapids: Zondervan, 1953], 171–78). He concludes, "As a result of this investigation, we seem to have established a fair presumption, that among the salutations in the Epistle to the Romans some members at least of the imperial household are included" (*Philippians,* 177).

Paul includes both groups, those saved through his ministry and those already believers, in his greetings from **Caesar's household.** Both he and the Philippians were no doubt thrilled that the **household** of the pagan emperor had yielded up many souls to the kingdom of Christ. The joy of saints is to see others rescued from the dark depths of sin and brought to salvation in Christ.

THE RESOURCE OF SAINTS

The grace of the Lord Jesus Christ be with your spirit. (4:23)

Paul has now come full circle. He began this letter by wishing the Philippians grace (1:2), and he concludes it the same way. The apostle ended all his letters by wishing God's grace for their recipients (cf. Rom. 16:24; 1 Cor. 16:23; 2 Cor. 13:14; Gal. 6:18; Eph. 6:24; Col. 4:18; 1 Thess. 5:28; 2 Thess. 3:18; 1 Tim. 6:21; 2 Tim. 4:22; Titus 3:15; Philem. 25).

The resource all believers need most is **the grace** that comes from **the Lord Jesus Christ.** Grace is the unmerited favor or undeserved, beneficent love of God in Christ that brought about believers' redemption (Eph. 2:5, 8; Rom. 3:24; 2 Tim. 1:9). God's work of grace in believers' lives will continue until their glorification. Paul expressed that truth in Romans 5:2: "Through [Christ] also we have obtained our introduction by faith into this grace in which we stand; and we exult in hope of the glory of God." Believers are not only saved by grace, but also sustained by grace. They are governed by grace, guided by grace, kept by grace, strengthened by grace, sanctified by grace, and enabled by grace. They are constantly dependent on the forgiveness, comfort, peace, joy, boldness, and instruction that come through God's grace.

God's sustaining grace comes to believers through **the Lord Jesus Christ.** He is the theme of this epistle, being mentioned almost forty times in its four chapters. Paul described himself as a servant of Christ (1:1); he addressed the Philippians as saints in Christ (1:1); his imprisonment was for the cause of Christ (1:13); for him to live was Christ (1:21) and death ushered him into Christ's presence (1:23); he exhorted the Philippians to conduct themselves in a manner worthy of Christ (1:26) by having the attitude of Christ (2:5); he called for them to glory in Christ (3:3); he counted everything in his past as garbage in view of the riches he found in Christ (3:8); he was saved by faith in Christ (3:9); he eagerly awaited Christ's return (3:20); and his sufficiency was in Christ (4:19).

The character, worship, fellowship, joy, and resources of saints are all bound up in Jesus Christ. Paul aptly summed up the Christian life when he wrote, "For to me, to live is Christ and to die is gain" (1:21).

Bibliography

Carson, D. A., Douglas J. Moo, and Leon Morris. *An Introduction to the New Testament.* Grand Rapids: Zondervan, 1992.

Eadie, John. *A Commentary on the Greek Text of the Epistle of Paul to the Philippians.* Reprint. Grand Rapids: Baker, 1979.

Gromacki, Robert G. *Stand United in Joy: An Exposition of Philippians.* Grand Rapids: Baker, 1980.

Guthrie, Donald. *New Testament Introduction.* Rev. ed. Downers Grove, Ill: InterVarsity, 1990.

Harrison, Everett F. *Introduction to the New Testament.* Grand Rapids: Eerdmans, 1964.

Hendriksen, William. *New Testament Commentary: Philippians, Colossians, and Philemon.* Grand Rapids: Baker, 1979.

Hiebert, D. Edmond. *An Introduction to the New Testament: The Pauline Epistles.* Rev. ed. Chicago: Moody, 1977.

Lenski, R. C. H. *The Interpretation of St. Paul's Epistles to the Galatians, to the Ephesians, and to the Philippians.* Minneapolis: Augsburg, 1961.

Lightfoot, J. B. *St. Paul's Epistle to the Philippians.* Reprint. Grand Rapids: Zondervan, 1953.

Martin, Ralph P. *The Epistle of Paul to the Philippians.* The Tyndale New Testament Commentaries. Grand Rapids: Eerdmans, 1975.

Meyer, F. B. *The Epistle to the Philippians.* Reprint. Grand Rapids: Baker, 1952.

Muller, Jac. J. *The Epistles of Paul to the Philippians and to Philemon.* The New International Commentary on the New Testament. Grand Rapids: Eerdmans, 1955.

O' Brien, Peter T. *The Epistle to the Philippians.* The New International Greek Testament Commentary. Grand Rapids: Eerdmans, 1991.

Silva, Moises. *Philippians.* The Wycliffe Exegetical Commentary. Chicago: Moody, 1988.

Vincent, Marvin R. *The Epistles to the Philippians and to Philemon.* The International Critical Commentary. Edinburgh: T & T Clark, 1979.

Indexes

Index of Greek Words

Index of Hebrew Words

Index of Scripture

Isaiah		Lamentations		Matthew	
1:18	286, 287	1:20	32	1:20–21	130
6:1	171	2:11	32	3:7–8	210
6:5	171	3:39	179	3:17	128, 130, 150
9:6	263			4:1–11	130
11:6–9	263	Ezekiel		4:3–4	125
13:6–22	28	36:26	242	4:10	222
14:12–17	109	44:7	219	4:19	253
16:11	32	44:9	219	5:3	112, 124
26:3	284			5:5	112
29:13	215, 222	Daniel		5:6	245
29:16	178	12:1	273	5:8	31, 263
32:1	263	12:2	262	5:9	273
40:29–31	303	12:3	185	5:10–12	180
42:3	105			5:12	248, 260
42:6	185	Hosea		5:14	185
42:8	222	6:6	313	5:16	166, 185,
45:9	178	9:4	192		186, 314
45:22–23	145	11:8–9	173	5:43–46	42
45:23	146			5:45	166, 314
48:11	222	Joel		5:48	47, 166,
48:22	284	1:15	28		213, 314
49:6	185	2:11	28	6:1	166, 314
52:5	185			6:9	166
53	238	Amos		6:13	161
53:3	131	3:2	229, 235	6:14–15	35
53:6	129	6:12	53	6:16–17	114
55:6–7	173			6:19–20	307
55:11	68	Jonah		6:20	260
56:7	307	4:1–9	68	6:24	14, 199
58:1–4	215			6:25–28	197
61:10	275	Habakkuk		6:25–34	33, 280,
63:15	32	1:2–4	33, 277		287
63:16	166	1:5–11	278	6:28–33	275
64:6	213, 236	1:12–13	278	6:33	221
64:8	166	2:4	278	7:5	50
65:16	290	3:17–18	33	7:12	43
		3:17–19	279	7:13	217
Jeremiah		3:18	275	7:15	92, 217, 256
4:4	218			7:21–23	144, 148,
7:18	192	Zechariah			210
9:23–24	222	9:9	112	7:22–23	215
9:26	218	14:4–8	263	7:22–27	148
10:23	298	14:9	263	8:9	203
15:16	10			8:20	124
18:6	178	Malachi		8:22	253
29:13	31	3:16–17	167, 273	9:2	131
31:20	32			9:6	131

Index of Subjects

Titles in the
MacArthur New Testament Commentary Series

MOODY
PUBLISHERS

THE NAME YOU CAN TRUST.

1-800-678-6928 www.MoodyPublishers.org